Recent Studies
in Early Christianity

A Collection of Scholarly Essays

Series Editor

Everett Ferguson

A GARLAND SERIES

Series Contents

?

Forms of Devotion
Conversion, Worship, Spirituality, and Asceticism

Edited with an introduction by
Everett Ferguson

GARLAND PUBLISHING, INC.
A MEMBER OF THE TAYLOR & FRANCIS GROUP
New York & London
1999

Library of Congress Cataloging-in-Publication Data

Forms of devotion : conversion, worship, spirituality, and asceticism /
    edited, with introductions by Everett Ferguson.
        p.   cm. — (Recent studies in early Christianity ; 5)
    Includes bibliographical references.
    ISBN 0-8153-3072-3 (alk. paper)
    1. Christian life—History—Early church, ca. 30–600.
I. Ferguson, Everett, 1933– . II. Series.
BR195.C5F67 1999
270.1—dc21   99-26290
                                         CIP

Printed on acid-free, 250-year-life paper
Manufactured in the United States of America

Contents

Series Introduction

Garland published in 1993 *Studies in Early Christianity: A Collection of Scholarly Essays*, an eighteen-volume set of classic articles on the early history of Christianity. The present set of six volumes, *Recent Studies in Early Christianity*, continues that first series by selecting articles written during the last decade. The chronological scope is the same, the first six centuries of the common era. The arrangement once more is topical but with a conflation and realignment of topics to fit the smaller number of volumes. The present series of essays will serve as an important supplement for those who possess the first series. For those without the first series, it will introduce key areas of research and debate on the early history of Christianity.

The growing academic interest in Christianity during its early centuries, as noted in the series introduction to *Studies in Early Christianity*, has greatly accelerated. There has been a proliferation of studies during the last decade on the subject of Christianity in late antiquity. The very popularity of the designation "late antiquity" says something about the current intellectual climate in which these studies arise: a shift from a primary emphasis on Christianity itself to the larger cultural setting of which it was a part, a shift from doctrinal studies to the church as a social institution, and a shift from concern for orthodoxy to the popular religious attitudes and expressions.

The increased study of this period finds expression in more doctoral students, record membership in professional organizations, like the North American Patristics Society and the Association internationale d'études patristiques, and large attendance at the International Conferences on Patristic Studies in Oxford (August 16-21, 1999, marks the thirteenth of these meetings that occur every four years), in addition to participation in specialized conferences on Origen, Gregory of Nyssa, Augustine, and others. Expanded literary productivity is evidenced by new journals (*The Journal of Early Christian Studies*, edited by Elizabeth Clark and Everett Ferguson, a continuation of *The Second Century*; *Zeitschrift für Antikes Christentum/Journal of Ancient Christianity*, edited by H.C. Brennecke and C. Markschies), new reference works (*The Encyclopedia of Early Christianity* [New York: Garland], edited by Everett Ferguson, first edition in 1990, second and greatly expanded edition in 1997, paperback edition 1998; *The Encyclopedia of the Early Church* [New York: Oxford University Press, 1992], English translation of *Dizionario Patristico e di Antichità Cristiane*, edited by Angelo Di Berardino), and substantial scholarly monographs in the field.

In some ways the selection of articles for six volumes on a decade of scholarship is more difficult than eighteen volumes on a century: We do not have the perspective of time to judge what is of enduring worth. Although some of these pieces will no doubt become classics, the guiding principle in selection has been to point to areas that are drawing the greatest attention. Some subjects have become virtually independent subdisciplines in the study of religion in late antiquity. This is notably true of Gnosticism, although the very term is under attack as a proper category.

The six volumes of this collection of scholarly essays take up the following broad topics: (1) the social setting of the early church, with attention to such matters as women, family, friendship, funerary practices, education, and slavery; (2) the political, cultural, and religious setting of early Christianity in relation to Romans, Greeks, and Jews; (3) the internal development of the church as it recognized its canon of scriptures, interpreted those scriptures, defined its confession of faith, and articulated standards of conduct; (4) the diversity — geographical, doctrinal, disciplinary — that counterbalanced the efforts to achieve a unified orthodoxy; (5) the many expressions of devotion and spirituality that both nourished and manifested faith; and (6) the varied ways in which early Christians wrestled with the limitations of historical existence and human language yet voiced their hopes for another and better world.

These topics represent the emphases in the modern study of early Christianity: social history and the application of the social sciences to the understanding of the historical texts, women's concerns and gender issues, Christians' relations with their Jewish and pagan neighbors, variety in early Christianity (especially fueled by the Nag Hammadi texts but not exclusively so), types of asceticism, literary forms and criticism, and Christianity's relationship to late antiquity and the transition to the medieval world. Some themes long present in the study of early Christianity continue to gain attention: the creedal definition of the faith, the causes and effects of persecution, different approaches to the interpretation of the Bible, forms of worship and spirituality, Christian morality, and the Christian hope.

One person's judgment and one small set of essays cannot do full justice to the rich flowering of studies in the field of early Christianity. We can only point to the areas of emphasis and call attention to some significant studies. These studies will lead teachers and students into the larger field and, we hope, spark their interest in pursuing some of these questions and related matters more extensively, thereby enlarging the number of researchers in a field not only intellectually challenging but also spiritually significant.

Volume Introduction

In the early centuries Christians "were made not born,"[1] so conversion from a former manner of life was the principal expression of Christian devotion. The apocryphal acts of the apostles, in this respect similar to the canonical Acts, have many conversion stories, and in spite of their apocryphal setting, these acts do seem to give realistic depictions of some of the factors in and obstacles to the spread of the Christian message and especially of the means and the effects of conversion (Gallagher). It is argued, on the other hand, that the most famous conversion scene from the ancient church, that of Augustine, is his own apocryphal creation and did not happen,[2] a view that has not won many converts.

The instruction given to new converts (catechesis) was based on the norms of faith and life — studied in Volume III of this set. Catechesis and apologetics had much in common, both being designed to win over inquirers to the Christian faith. Christian intellectuals at Alexandria developed the most ambitious program of catechetical instruction and with it the most ambitious defense and exposition of Christian faith. In doing so, they built on Jewish precedents, and this school tradition, despite claims that it was purely a private enterprise, probably did indeed in the early period have church connections (van den Hoek).[3]

Justification by faith was an important theme for the apostle Paul, reappropriated in a new context with a new meaning in the Reformation. In the intervening period Origen and Augustine shaped eastern and western Christian theology respectively on this subject, as in many other ways. C.P. Bammel's comparison opens up wide-ranging theological comparisons.

The most famous convert in the early church was Constantine (cf. Vol. II), and with him the language of the pagan mysteries found a greater acceptance in Christian descriptions of their sacred ceremonies.[4] The baptism of Constantine at the end of his life initiated a common practice of death-bed baptism in the early church, a practice that church leaders sought to discourage.[5] The practice raises the question of the ordinary age of baptism. We know infant baptism was practiced and accepted, but the striking fact remains that those church leaders whose age of baptism is known were all baptized when grown.[6] It might be argued that the fact of baptism at the attainment of manhood was remembered because it was exceptional, but the evidence suggests that although infant baptism was accepted (especialy in cases of a health emergency), it was much later in becoming the norm than was previously thought. Martyrdom (also Vol. II) was interpreted as a baptism, and baptism was interpreted as a martyrdom (Jeannes). Doctrinal considerations were important in the connection of baptism with the creed[7] and entered into debate over the practice of single or triple immersion.[8] The social setting was significant in the controversy over the rebaptism of converts from heretical and schismatic bodies (J. P. Burns). Conversion could be to one doctrinal form of the Christian faith, as in the case of the famous missionary to the Goths, Ulfilas (Sivan).

The catechetical process introduced the convert not only into the doctrinal beliefs of the church[9] but also into its liturgical life.[10] Worship and devotion took several forms, of which only a small representation can be studied here. Already in one of the first pagan notices of the Christian meetings, Pliny had shown interest in the distinctive character of Christian gatherings.[11] One feature of Christian meetings, shared with the Jewish synagogue, was the presence of preaching.[12] Prayer was central to the devotional experience; Sebastian Brock studies the "prayer of the heart." There was also daily prayer,[13] and congregational prayer, the high point of which was the anaphora or eucharistic prayer.[14]

"Psalms, hymns, and songs," terms that were used as essentially synonymous,[15] had their place in the liturgy, in daily life, and in monastic devotions.[16] John Chrysostom's spirituality found expression in his commentary on the Psalms (Robert C. Hill[17]) and his thoughts on music and psalmody have drawn several studies.[18] The Psalms made their impression on the theology and spirituality of other significant thinkers as well, like Evagrius[19] and Augustine (Paul Burns). Nowhere did the Psalter shape spirituality more than in monasticism.[20] Syriac Christianity (Vol. IV) produced significant liturgical poetry that influenced Byzantine hymnography.[21]

Martyrdom was considered (studied in Vol. II) as part of the church's relationship with the Roman state. As an individual act, it was the ultimate expression of devotion. The cult of the martyrs developed quite early (McGuckin).[22] Its popularity merged with other factors so that devotion was extended from holy persons to holy places (Markus).[23]

The early centuries were formative in shaping Christian spirituality and mysticism, often expressed as the "vision of God." Among those important for spirituality were the eastern thinkers Origen,[24] Gregory of Nazianzus,[25] Gregory of Nyssa, and Maximus the Confessor,[26] and the western pope Gregory the Great (Zinn).[27] The most intense forms of devotion occurred in the desert fathers, whose spirituality was brought west by John Cassian, who also typifies the way Christian spirituality was closely related to the understanding of the Bible (Stewart).[28]

Asceticism and monasticism have received much study in the last decade, and these studies are showing that the withdrawal to the desert bulked larger in the literary portrayal than in practice; most ascetics and monks lived closer to centers of population than has been generally recognized, often in villages and towns. James Goehring in his studies reprinted here, and in other studies, has led the way in this new understanding.[29] Elizabeth Clark is among those at the forefront of recent studies on early Christian asceticism and relating the phenomenon to other currents in church history. Martin Parmentier makes available in English translation an important treatise from a later philosophical theorist of asceticism, Evagrius of Pontus.

There were often tensions between the episcopally organized church and the withdrawal represented by the monks, but some bishops worked to keep the monastic impulse within the orthodox church.[30]

Notes

[1] Tertullian, *Apology* 18; *Testimony of the Soul* 1; in both contexts, from another viewpoint, Tertullian can claim the "testimony of the soul by nature Christian" (*Apol.* 17) to the truths of Christianity. The statement is repeated by Jerome, *Ep.* 107.1.

[2] Leo C. Ferrari, "St. Augustine's Conversion Scene," *Studia Patristica* 22 (1989):235–50.

[3] Cf. also her "Techniques of Quotation in Clement of Alexandria: A View of Ancient Literary Working Methods," *Vigiliae Christianae* 50 (1996):223–43.

[4] E.J. Yarnold, "The Baptism of Constantine," *Studia Patristica* 26 (1993):95–101.

[5] Everett Ferguson, "Exhortations to Baptism in the Cappadocians," *Studia Paristica* 32 (1997):121–29.

[6] David F. Wright, "At What Ages Were People Baptized in the Early Centuries?" *Studia Patristica* 30 (1997):389–94.

[7] David F. Wright, "The Meaning and Reference of 'One Baptism for the Remission of Sins' in the Nicaeno-Contantinopolitan Creed," *Studia Patristica* 19 (1989):281–85.

[8] Maurice F. Wiles, "Triple and Single Immersion: Baptism in the Arian Controversy," *Studia Patristica* 30 (1997):337–49.

[9] Thomas M. Finn, "Quodvultdeus: The Preacher and his Audience: Homilies on the Creed," *Studia Patristica* 31 (1997):42–58.

[10] M.A. Kappes, "The Voice of Many Waters: The Baptismal Homilies of Narsai of Nisibis," *Studia Patristica* 33 (1997):534–47.

[11] J.C. Salzmann, "Pliny (ep. 10,96) and Christian Liturgy — a Reconsideration," *Studia Patristica* 20 (1989):389–95.

[12] Sermons at a festival to which modern scholars have given little attention, the Ascension, are studied by Hendrik F. Stander, "Fourth- and Fifth-Century Homilists on the Ascension of Christ," in Abraham J. Malherbe, Frederick W. Norris and James W. Thompson, eds., *The Early Church in Its Context: Essays in Honor of Everett Ferguson* (Leiden: E. J. Brill, 1998), pp. 268–86.

[13] Graham Woolfenden, "Daily Prayer: Its Origin and Its Function," *Studia Patristica* 30 (1997):364–88.

[14] C.G. Cuming, "The Shape of the Anaphora," *Studia Patristica* 20 (1989):333–45.

[15] A.A.R. Bastiaensen, "Psalmi, hymni, and cantica in Early Jewish Christian Tradition," *Studia Patristica* 21 (1989):15–26.

[16] Everett Ferguson, "Toward a Patristic Theology of Music," *Studia Patristica* 24 (1993):266–83 shows how the church fathers gave a Christian understanding to Pythagorean ideas of music.

[17] His translation of *St. John Chrysostom: Commentary of the Psalms* is now published, 2 vols. (Brookline: Holy Cross Orthodox Press, 1998).

[18] E.g., J.C.B. Petropoulos, "The Church Father as Social Informant: Chrysostom on Folk Songs," *Studia Patristica* 22 (1989):199–64; Barry Wylie, "Musical Aesthetics and Biblical Interpretation in John Chrysostom," *Studia Patristica* 32 (1997):386–92.

[19] Luke Dysinger, "The Significance of Psalmody in the Mystical Theology of Evagrius of Pontus," *Studia Patristica* 30 (1997):176–82.

[20] Graham W. Woolfenden, "The Use of the Psalter by Early Monastic Communities," *Studia Patristica* 26 (1993):88–94.

[21] Sebastian Brock, "From Ephrem to Romanos," *Studia Patristica* 20 (1989):139–51.

[22] See also David Frankfurter, "The Cult of the Martyrs in Egypt Before Constantine: The Evidence of the Coptic *Apocalypse of Elijah*," *Vigiliae Christianae* 48 (1994):25–47.

[23] Also Peter W. L. Walker, "Eusebius, Cyril, and the Holy Places," *Studia Patristica* 20 (1989):306–14.

[24] John Anthony McGuckin, "Origen on the Glory of God," *Studia Patristica* 21 (1989):316–24.

[25] John Anthony McGuckin, "The Vision of God in St. Gregory of Nazianzus," *Studia Patristica* 32 (1997):145–52.

[26] Paul Blowers, "Maximus the Confessor, Gregory of Nyssa, and the Concept of 'Perpetual Progress,'" *Vigiliae Christianae* 46 (1992):151–71.

[27] See also Bernard McGinn, "Contemplation in Gregory," in John Cavadini, ed., *Gregory the Great: A Symposium* (Notre Dame: University of Notre Dame Press, 1995), pp. 146–67.

[28] Douglas Burton-Christie, "Scripture, Self-Knowledge, and Contemplation in Cassian's *Conferences*,"

and Columba Stewart, "Scripture and Contemplation in the Monastic Spiritual Theology of John Cassian," *Studia Patristica* 25 (1993):339–45 and 457–61.

[29] James Goehring, "The Encroaching Desert: Literary Production and Ascetic Space in Early Christian Egypt," *Journal of Early Christian Studies* 1 (1993):281–96.

[30] Henry Chadwick, "Bishops and Monks," *Studia Patristica* 24 (1993):45–61.

Conversion and Salvation in the Apocryphal Acts of the Apostles

EUGENE V. GALLAGHER

Whatever other factors were involved, the rise of Christianity in the Roman world was fueled by the decisions of individuals, whole households, and even large crowds to join that new religious movement. Tertullian's remark that "Christians are made, not born" (*Apology* 18.4) attests to the prominent role of such conversions. But despite Gustave Bardy's claim that "the only interesting conversions are those which are resolute and deliberate, and which have their origins in personal reflection,"[1] there is little detailed evidence from the period before Constantine about what provoked such decisions and how they unfolded in individual lives.[2]

In order to avoid relying on a small literary elite, Ramsey MacMullen has recently focused on reports about large groups of people joining the Christian church.[3] Arguing that "what pagans saw *in* Christianity . . . depended greatly on what they saw *of* it," he finds that the texts indicate time and again that the performance, or even a report, of miracles produced converts.[4]

EUGENE V. GALLAGHER is Professor of Religious Studies, Connecticut College, New London, CT 06320.

[1]Gustave Bardy, *La Conversion au Christianisme durant les premiers siècles* (Paris: Aubier, 1949) 161; cf. 250.

[2]That is especially the case if the few extant conversion autobiographies are acknowledged as the products of literary artifice. Cf., for example, Adolf Harnack, *The Mission and Expansion of Christianity*, James Moffatt, ed. & trans. (Gloucester, MA: Peter Smith, 1972 rpr.) 393; on the proportions of history and fiction in Justin's conversion story in his *Dialogue with Trypho* see J. C. M. Van Winden, *An Early Christian Philosopher: Justin Martyr's Dialogue With Trypho Chapters One to Nine* (Leiden: Brill, 1971) 108–110.

[3]Cf. Ramsey MacMullen, *Christianizing the Roman Empire* (New Haven: Yale, 1984) 1, 23f., 57f., 108, 115.

[4]Ramsey MacMullen, "Two types of Conversion to Early Christianity," *Vigiliae Christianae* 37 (1983): 174, cf. idem., *Paganism in the Roman Empire* (New Haven: Yale University Press) 95–98.

MacMullen's concentration on both crowds of anonymous converts and on the role of miracles departs from previous work. Bardy, for example, had identified "the longing for truth, the longing for deliverance and for salvation, the longing for holiness"[5] as the great motives for conversion to Christianity. Similarly, Arthur Darby Nock concluded that

> the success of Christianity is the success of an institution which united the sacramentalism and the philosophy of the time. It satisfied the inquiring turn of mind, the desire for escape from Fate, the desire for security in the hereafter; like Stoicism, it gave a way of life and made man at home in the universe, but unlike Stoicism it did this for the ignorant as well as the lettered. It satisfied also social needs and it secured men against loneliness.[6]

For both Nock and Bardy, miracles played a lesser role.

Thus, one of the effects of MacMullen's work is to raise questions about how to study conversion to Christianity in the Roman world. What kinds of data are most important, what motives were most significant, what types of activity were most effective?

In what follows I will focus on the Apocryphal Acts of the Apostles (AAA) from the second and third centuries; that is, the *Acts of John* (AJ), the *Acts of Peter* (APt), the *Acts of Paul* (AP), the *Acts of Andrew* (AAn), and the *Acts of Thomas* (AT).[7] Those texts depict at some length the successful missionary activity of their apostle-heroes, often directly due to their miracle-working ability.

---

[5]Bardy, *La Conversion*, p. 157. Bardy also argues (158f.) that miracles did not play an important role in primitive Christian apologetic, citing Paul (1 Cor. 1:22–25), and that by the third century the apologists recognized that the great epoch of Christian miracles lay in the past and that their own age had not produced many miracles.

[6]Arthur Darby Nock, *Conversion* (Oxford: Oxford University Press, 1933) 210f.

[7]For texts and English translations of the Apocryphal Acts, I follow R. A. Lipsius & M. Bonnet, *Acta Apostolorum Apocrypha* (Darmstadt: Wissenschaftliche Buchgesellschaft, 1959, rpr.), 3 vols., and Edgar Hennecke & Wilhelm Schneemelcher, eds., *New Testament Apocrypha*, vol. II, R. McL. Wilson, trans. (Philadelphia: Westminster, 1964). For AJ see now the text and French translation in *Acta Iohannis*, Eric Junod & Jean-Daniel Kaestli, eds., and trans. (Turnhout: Brepols, 1983), 2 vols., in the Corpus Christianorum Series Apocryphorum. I will not treat the various Acts as a unified corpus, but certain similarities and interrelationships justify treating them together. Cf. A. F. J. Klijn, "The Apocryphal Acts of the Apostles," *Vigiliae Christianae* 37 (1983): 193–199. For an overview of scholarship on the AAA see Eric Junod, et al., *Les Actes Apocryphes des Apôtres* (Geneva: Labor et Fides, 1981) and Eckhard Plumacher, "Apokryphe Apostelakten" in *Pauly-Wissowa, Supplementband XV* (Munich: Druckenmuller, 1978) col. 11–70. See also Stevan L. Davies, *The Revolt of the Widows: The Social World of the Apocryphal Acts* (Carbondale: Southern Illinois, 1980) for arguments about the social context and authorship of the AAA. The introductory essays in Hennecke-Schneemelcher, *NTA*, date the Acts of John, Peter, Paul, Andrew, and Thomas to the late second or third centuries. Davies, *Widows*, p. 4 would add the *Acts of Xanthippe*.

2

The information about conversion in those texts, as in any narrative texts, comes in three different forms. Conversion *stories* have at least a minimal plot line; they present dialogue and sustained interaction between the missionary and the convert(s) and often describe the indirect effects of that interaction on a crowd of onlookers. The outcome, of course, is conversion, broadly construed as any distinct change of allegiance, which would include return from apostasy (a prominent feature in the *Acts of Peter*) as well as initial entry into a new faith and community.[8] Conversion *reports* simply represent the narrator's summary of events; they generally contain no dialogue and only a minimal description of interaction. They typically recount the conversion of anonymous crowds. For example: "But Peter stayed in Rome and rejoiced with the brethren in the Lord and gave thanks night and day for the mass of people who were daily added to the holy name by the grace of the Lord" (APt 33). Occasionally, the reports focus on specific individuals, but few other details are added: "While Paul was spending some time in Rome and strengthening many in the faith, it happened that a woman by name Candida, the wife of Quartus, a prison officer, heard Paul speak and paid attention to his words and believed. And when she had instructed her husband also and he believed, Quartus gave leave to Paul to leave the city (and go) where he wished" (APt 1). The third category, *references*, would include all other information that can be drawn from the texts. Like reports, they are often the tip of the iceberg. In the *Acts of Paul,* for example, a crowd shouts, "Away with the sorcerer! For he has corrupted all our wives" (AP 15), which could suggest widespread effectiveness of Paul's mission, especially among women, the emphasis on celibacy in his message, and perhaps even miracle-working; but it is difficult to reconstruct the underlying situation with any confidence. Though they might overlap, the three categories of information can be distinguished from each other by degrees of specificity. While reports and references furnish very little detail, they establish the identity of the apostle as an effective missionary and wonder worker. The conversion stories then provide vivid examples of the general activity.

By my reckoning, the AAA include some twenty-nine conversion sto-

---

[8] See the definitions of conversion in Paul Aubin, *La Problème de la "Conversion"* (Paris: Beauchesne, 1963) 106, Nock, *Conversion* 7–8, and in two studies of new religious movements, James T. Richardson, ed., *Conversion Careers* (Beverly Hills: Sage, 1978) and James A. Beckford, *Cult Controversies* (New York: Tavistock, 1985) 102–103, 174–175; for bibliography see Lewis Rambo, "Current Research on Religious Conversion," *Religious Studies Review* 8 (1982):146–159. For a careful treatment of prominent conversion texts in the New Testament, see Beverly Roberts Gaventa, *From Darkness to Light: Aspects of Conversion in the New Testament* (Philadelphia: Fortress, 1986).

ries.[9] There are six interrelated and well-developed stories in the *Acts of John,* along with another brief story; the *Acts of Peter* contains five stories which focus on the return to the true faith of apostates who had been lured away by Simon Magus; the *Acts of Paul* presents seven shorter narratives, though they seem not to occupy the most prominent place; the *Acts of Thomas,* by far the longest text preserved, presents ten conversion stories. Only the fragmentary *Acts of Andrew* lacks any clear examples of the type, though it does contain an interesting allegorical interpretation of the significance of conversion. In addition, allusions in the text make it clear that two further stories are missing from the present text of AJ.[10] Though women and the well-to-do are relatively more prominent than men and the less wealthy, the texts feature a large cast of characters, including passionate youths, a ship's captain, a priest of Artemis, various people of high station and their retainers, and the ever-present crowd of credulous onlookers.

MacMullen's point about the prominence of miracles gains added support from a simple calculation. Of the twenty-nine conversion stories, twenty-two recount how the performance of a miracle elicited the conversion of individuals, households, or crowds. Of the seven remaining stories at least two others are tinged with the miraculous as well. Moreover, an even dozen of the stories recount the "raising up" of a definitely, apparently, or nearly dead person. *More than anything else, in the AAA the miracle of resurrection is portrayed as eliciting conversion.*

MacMullen uses such stories to support his contention that "credence in miracles" was the primary motive for conversion in the ancient world.[11] Without directly challenging that specific conclusion, I want to show that the conversion stories in the AAA also reveal consistent, well-developed understandings of conversion. The references, reports, and stories, as they describe the process of conversion in retrospect, are shaped by their authors' beliefs about the significance of conversion and their participation in a community of the converted; both the details and the "messages" of conversion stories express communal beliefs about the event in question and about the process of conversion in general. Those beliefs would then be reinforced by social approbation whenever the stories are told and heard.[12]

---

[9]If the *Acts of Xanthippe* were included, the tally would rise to some 34 conversion stories, 25 of which include the occurrence of some sort of miracle.

[10]Cf. Hennecke-Schneemelcher, *NTA,* 2.211; Junod & Kaestli, *Acta Iohannis,* pp. 87, 99. Conversion stories might have occupied the present lacunae of other texts as well.

[11]Cf. MacMullen, *Christianizing,* p. 108.

[12]Conversion stories report on the "facts," insofar as those facts themselves are determined by a particular view of the world. My treatment of conversion stories follows the lead of several social scientists, including James A. Beckford, "Accounting for Conver-

Thus, the preponderance of healings, and especially of "raisings up," in the AAA provides information not only about events, but about the array of convictions, beliefs, and assumptions that made those events, whatever they were, intelligible.

To be sure, no single understanding or ideology of conversion predominates in the AAA. The simplest view of conversion is that reflected by the reports; the apostles speak or act and many join the faith. There is very little interpretive overlay in such notices. They reinforce a belief in the charismatic power of the apostles' words and deeds and depict the inexorable success of the Christian mission. The references are far too sketchy to reveal any specific understandings of conversion. But the stories often give evidence of being carefully composed in order to express how conversion should be understood, how it actually happens, how it is motivated, and what its proper results are.[13] That concern to purvey certain images of conversion is most evident in the stories about the apostles raising up the definitely, apparently, or nearly dead.

The Acts of John

The most interesting cluster of such stories occurs in the *Acts of John*. Five separate and closely interwoven stories punctuate John's first stay in Ephesus and span chapters 19 through 54. Two other stories, not preserved in the manuscripts, apparently belong with them. Another long story is set during John's second stay in Ephesus, while a briefer episode takes place in Smyrna. The first five display a variety of links to each other. Initially, John prays that his activity will convert a multitude (22), but the crowd, though "stirred" by his first miracle, does not profess conversion until the climactic third story, which recounts the destruction of the Ephesian temple of Artemis.[14] Similarly, the priest of Artemis, in the background of the third story, becomes the main character of the fourth. Junod and Kaestli have also noted the alteration between private (homes, tombs) and public (theatre, temple) settings and several other aspects of narrative construction which reinforce the unity of the cycle

sion," *British Journal of Sociology* 29 (1978):249–262; Bryan Taylor, "Conversion and Cognition," *Social Compass* 23 (1976): 5–22; Benetta Jules-Rosette, *African Apostles: Ritual and Conversion in the Church of John Maranke* (Ithaca: Cornell, 1975) 61ff. For a general treatment of conversion from the perspective of the sociology of knowledge, see Peter L. Berger & Thomas Luckmann, *The Social Construction of Reality* (New York: Doubleday, 1966) 147–163.

[13]I will restrict my analysis to the final forms of the texts as they have been transmitted, without broaching questions of sources and their subsequent redaction(s). For an interesting argument about the oral sources of the *Acts of Paul*, see Dennis Ronald MacDonald, *The Legend and the Apostle: The Battle for Paul in Story and Canon* (Philadelphia: Westminster, 1983).

[14]Cf. Junod & Kaestli, *Acta Iohannis*, p. 433.

5

of stories.[15] All of the stories focus on the superior power of John's God, which is nowhere more clearly demonstrated than in the destruction of the temple of Artemis. John states his case directly to the Ephesians:

> For now is the time! Either you must be converted by my God, or I myself will die at the hands of your goddess; for I will pray in your presence and entreat my god that you may find mercy. (40)

When, in response to John's prayer, the altar of Artemis is split into pieces and collapses to the floor, the assembled onlookers exclaim:

> (There is but) one God, (the God) of John! (There is but) one God who has mercy upon us; for thou alone art God! We are converted, now that we have seen thy marvellous works! Have mercy on us, O God, according to thy will, and save us from our great error. (42)

In that context, what does the Ephensians' acclamation mean? Clearly, they have identified John's God as being more powerful than Artemis; moreover, they are willing to pledge their allegiance to that greater power, to whom they attribute the capability to save them from their error and even to preserve their lives. Indeed, the whole incident is portrayed as a matter of life and death (cf. 39), and the Ephesians explicitly recognize John's ability to carry out his threats when they beg, "Do not destroy us like that, we implore you, John; we know that you can do it!" (40). Various other indications suggest that the text views the conversion of the Ephesians as a passage from imminent and certain death to a new life. After their initial profession of belief John commands the Ephesians to "Rise up from the ground, . . . and pray to my God" (43). Later, in chapter 45, when they receive instruction in the basics of their new allegiance, they are depicted as children who are not yet ready to be weaned. The passage from death to life is a leitmotiv of the Acts of John and the clearest expression of its understanding of conversion.[16] It is more vividly expressed in several other miracles performed by John.

All four of the conversion stories surrounding the climactic destruction of the temple of Artemis focus on John's ability to raise up the dead.[17] The stories present a unified repertoire of motifs including resurrection of the dead or sick person, individual and group conversion, confidence in salvation gained, and the entrance into a new life. The regular pattern of motifs suggests that whatever events lie behind the narratives have been absorbed into a definite interpretive scheme. The texts consistently understand conversion by the metaphor of death and resurrection; the converts die to their old lives which were dominated by error (cf. 33, 35,

[15]Cf. ibid., pp. 426–428.

[16]Cf. ibid., p. 513.

[17]Cf. ibid., p. 442.

42), shameful desires (cf. 33, 35), an attraction to the things of this world (cf. 34, 35, 36), unbelief (cf. 39), and idols (cf. 40, 41); and they rise into a new life which is immediately marked by celibacy, purity, and abstinence (cf. 53) and which offers a foretaste of eternal life (cf. 47). John's address to the resurrected priest of Artemis brings several of those themes to the fore:

> Now that you have risen, you are not really living, nor are you a partner and heir to the true life; will you belong to him by whose name and power you were raised up? So now, believe, and you shall live for all eternity. (47)

Not the miracle of resurrection, but the conscious decision of the priest himself effects the conversion. The simple regaining of bodily functions counts for nothing; it is "not really living." "True life" is a matter of giving allegiance to that deity whose superior power has just been demonstrated. A new life, even life "for all eternity" can then be gained. There is an indirect critique of the performance of miracles in that passage; in themselves, they are insufficient; they are merely attention-getters.[18] What matters is the priest's response to the question "Will you belong to him by whose name and power you were raised up?" A similar emphasis turns up in the fifth story. When John raises up an old man who had been beaten to death by his intemperate son, he says "[If] you are arising to this same [life], you should rather be dead; but rouse yourself to a better (one)!" (52). The specifics of that better life are spelled out in the speeches attributed to John, such as the one in chapters 34–36 which inveighs against the pleasures of this world and promises that all sorts of evil-doing will be punished.[19]

It seems that the conception of conversion as a death and resurrection, an entrance into a new life, also shaped the description of miracles which do not strictly involve resurrection. In the second story John hears in a vision that he should "Send for the old women who are sick, and be with them in the theatre and through me heal them; for some of them who come to see this sight I will convert through these healings" (30). John's action again is described as "raising up" (33), just as it was in the case of the priest of Artemis and the old man killed by his son. In the first story also, the lines between death and sickness blur, and John raises up not only the paralyzed Cleopatra (23, cf. 19), who is also described as dead (21), but also her husband Lycomedes, who apparently had fainted (21) but who also is described as being dead (23, 24). Were the text not so consistent in describing miracles of healing as resurrections, those instances might be dismissed. But the consistency suggests that a powerful

---

[18]Cf. ibid., pp. 443, 498, 510, 513.

[19]On the fairly standard nature of John's moral instruction, see ibid., pp. 462f.

7

conception of conversion dominates the text and that its typical metaphors and images have influenced the presentation of John's miracles. It is almost as if the text in its present form is designed to get across that conception of conversion; the specific miracle stories are grist for that mill, and can be adapted to its purpose. Indeed, all of the conversion stories in AJ recount the performance of miracles; four of them clearly employ the language of resurrection and new life, while two others make some use of it. Only in the brief account of John's exorcism in Smyrna, which uses the somewhat paler imagery of sickness and health, is it missing.[20]

The story of Drusiana and Callimachus, which is sparked by the familiar romantic conflict between lust and chastity, plays out the familiar themes at considerable length. The chaste, married Drusiana dies rather than yield to the advances of Callimachus. Undeterred, he pursues her literally to her grave, but a serpent intervenes, strikes his helper dead, and fells him with a single bite. Again, the text wavers between describing Callimachus as dead (74, 75) or merely temporarily out of commission (71). Whatever their states, Drusiana, Callimachus, and the servant who had aided him are all to be "raised up." The links between that miraculous activity, conversion, and salvation are made explicit in Callimachus' report of the vision he had after being struck down by the serpent. Twice he heard someone say to him: "You must die in order to live" (76). And, as Callimachus tells John:

> That voice has indeed accomplished its effect; for that man is dead, that faithless, lawless, godless man; and I have been raised at your hands, and will be faithful and Godfearing, knowning the *truth, which* I beg you may be shown me by you. (76)

Again, the miracle of "raising up" and the depiction of conversion as the entrance into a new life and the beginning of salvation are closely linked. But, like the other stories in AJ, the narrative about Drusiana and Callimachus makes it clear that the miracle of raising up in itself is insufficient. That is dramatized in the results of the three separate resurrections. Drusiana, already a Christian, dies rather than be defiled; when she is raised up she remains firm in her faith. Callimachus undergoes the most profound transformation, from lusty youth and would-be necrophiliac to a new, Christian man. But Fortunatus, the servant who had accompanied Callimachus to the tomb, fails to understand that he is "not really living" and that he must "die in order to live" and thus rejects the possibility of a new life:

> O, what end is there to the powers of these terrible men! I did not want to be resurrected, but would rather be dead, so as not to see them. (83)

---

[20]Cf. ibid. pp. 92–96, 524–527.

The cases of Callimachus and Fortunatus, whose death quickly follows his abortive resurrection, both demonstrate the text's attempt to define and interpret the significance of the miracles. In neither case does the miracle, in itself, lead directly to a new life. For Fortunatus it never comes, and his death results from his refusal to complete his resurrection by changing his own life. Callimachus, like the reformed parricide who had overzealously emasculated himself for the sake of purity and like Lycomedes who thought that he could capture the significance of the apostle in a portrait, needs further instruction on the implications of his own conversion.[21]

The conversion stories in AJ, then, present a coherent picture. Though they undeniably focus on the power of God which the apostle unleashes through his miracles, they adopt a rather conservative stance toward the miracles themselves. In six of seven cases the stories are colored and shaped by an ideology of conversion whose dominant metaphor is death and resurrection, whose central imperative is "you must die in order to live," whose new man or woman is defined by a rejection of the various pleasures of the world, specifically sex, error, unbelief, and the worship of idols. Salvation depends more on commitment and action than on passive acceptance of the miraculous; Fortunatus is the prime case in point. The consistency and prominence of that ideology of conversion suggests that the miracle stories themselves should be treated with some suspicion. They might be viewed more as vividly imagined exemplars for the text's dominant understanding of conversion than as historical events whose embellishments can be peeled away to reveal the core of the physically possible and historically probable.[22] Given the character of the AAA as relatively popular entertainments, that seems at least plausible.[23]

---

[21]For an interesting modern account of how conversion stories are shaped by the convert's participation in the new community, see Jules-Rosette, *African Apostles*, p. 61: "Part of the dramatic impact of the conversion experience emerged through examining and constructing it in retrospect," and p. 72: "Before baptism, a dream was simply that, perhaps frightening or pleasurable but certainly not a prophetic sign or warning. After conversion, every dream and imagining became a potential message integrated into a new order of reality. Both present and past dreams influenced daily experiences as focial parts of a spiritual world. Church prophets encouraged me to recast past events in terms of images predicting them."

[22]MacMullen (*Christianizing*, pp. 23f., 132, note 22) is more confident about easily reaching that historical core than I am.

[23]Cf. Junod & Kaestli, *Acta Iohannis*, pp. 426, 684; Jean-Daniel Kaestli, "Les principales orientations de la recherche sur les acts apocryphes des apôtres" in Junod *et al.*, *Les Actes Apocryphes des Apôtres*, pp. 49–67; Plumacher, "Apokryphe Apostelakten," col. 61–65; Rosa Söder, *Die apokryphen Apostelgeschichten und die romanhafte Literatur de: Antike* (Stuttgart: Kohlhammer, 1932) 186–187.

The Acts of Peter

Traces of the ideology of conversion that dominates AJ can be found in the other AAA as well. In the *Acts of Peter,* for example, the climactic showdown between Peter and Simon Magus centers on their attempts to raise up a dead youth. Before Peter succeeds in raising the youth, he claims, "Now that God and my Lord Jesus Christ is tested among you, he is doing such signs and wonders through me for the conversion of his sinners" (26). When the youth gets up, the crowd echoes the acclamation from AJ: "There is but one God, the one God of Peter" (26). Peter goes on to perform two more resurrections. The first evokes a similar acclamation: "Thou art God the Saviour, thou, the God of Peter, the invisible God, the Saviour!" (27). The third case gives Simon a final chance to demonstrate his power, but when he fails again and Peter succeeds, Peter makes this plea.

> Men of Rome, this is how the dead are restored to life, this is how they speak, this is how they walk when they are raised up, and live for so long as God wills. Now therefore, you people who have gathered to (see) the show, if you turn now from these wicked ways of yours and from all your man-made gods and from every kind of uncleanness and lust, you shall receive the fellowship with Christ through faith, so that you may come to everlasting life. (28)

Peter's emphasis on *how* the dead are raised again indicates that, for the author of APt, it is not the performance of an apparent miracle in itself that elicits conversion. The young man had made an explicit profession of faith immediately upon rising: "I beg you, sir, let us go to our Lord Jesus Christ whom I saw talking with you; who said to you, as he showed me to you, 'Bring him here to me, for he is mine'" (28). The same repertoire of ideas that expressed the ideology of conversion in AJ is operative in those passages as well. The resurrection leads to the youth's conversion and garners the crowd's attention, but they are also exhorted to make a decision to turn away from their idols and attachments to pleasure. They stand to gain fellowship and everlasting life, both immediate and ultimate transformation. Given the prior mass defection of Roman Christians to the side of Simon (cf. APt 4, 5, 6), the story also makes a point about the characteristics of true conversion in contrast to mass delusion.

Admittedly, other ideas about the causes and processes of conversion are present in the text. For example, the captain of a ship on which Peter sails has a vision, receives instruction from Peter, and gradually comes to believe (5; this text is noteworthy as an isolated depiction of conversion through gradual instruction in AAA); Peter makes a smoked fish swim and many onlookers believe (13; the basic form of several conversion reports); and Peter's speeches are successful in persuading many (cf. 32–

34). But the contest with Simon, and within it the three resurrections, are the central actions of the text.

The Acts of Paul

Though they are not developed as fully as those in some of the other texts and they do not dominate the narrative as they do in AJ or even APt, five of the seven conversion stories in the *Acts of Paul* involve miracles, and three of those involve resurrection. Early in the martydom section of the text, Paul raises Nero's cup-bearer, Patroclus, from the dead, but Patroclus' profession of his newly-gained faith before the emperor only gets him thrown in jail. Other accounts, of the raising of one Hermocrates and possibly his son Dion, and of an anonymous dead boy, seem also to provoke conversions, but the stories are too sketchy to support much further analysis. It appears, at least, that the familiar repertoire of motifs is present, though it is not exploited at any length.

The Acts of Thomas

The material in the *Acts of Thomas* is much richer. Of the ten full conversion stories, six highlight the performance of miracles and four of those focus on resurrections. The others depict the success of Thomas' preaching. The resurrection of a passionate youth who had been killed by a jealous serpent recalls a scene from AJ. Compelled by the apostle, the serpent withdraws his venom from the youth, and then dies himself. During his brief death, the young man, literally, saw the light.

> I found him whose works are light and his deeds truth, of which if a man does them he does not repent. I have been freed from him whose lie is persistent, before whom darkness goes as a veil and behind whom follows shame, shameless darkness in inactivity; but I found him who revealed to me beautiful things, that I might take hold of them, the Son of Truth, who is kinsman of concord, who driving away the mist enlightens his own creation, and healing its wound overthrows its enemies. (34)

Though the imagery is peculiar to AT, the renunciation of error and passion and the attainment of clarity, truth, and concord sketch a familiar scene. Also familiar, especially from the stories of Callimachus and the young parricide in AJ, is Thomas' warning that the youth should not take lightly the miracle of his resurrection "and turn again to [his] former doings" (35). The language of raising up takes a gnostic turn when Thomas addresses the crowd.

> Ye men who have come to the assembly of Christ and wish to believe in Jesus, take an example (a lesson) from this and see that unless you are lifted up you cannot see me who am small and though I am like you you cannot observe me. If then you cannot see me, who am like you, unless you raise yourselves a little from the earth, how can you see him who dwells in the height and now is found in the depth, unless you first raise yourselves out of your former condition and your unprofitable

deeds, and the desires that do not abide, and the wealth which is left here, and the possession which [comes] of the earth [and] grows old, and the clothing which deteriorates, and the beauty which grows old and vanishes, and indeed the whole body in which all these are stored and which growing old becomes dust, returning to its own nature? (37)

The initial instructions about the importance of being raised up in order to attain a mystic vision are blended with a familiar polemic against the ephemeral lures of the pleasures of this world. Although the new life envisioned by AT may well differ from that seen in the other AAA, the central metaphor of resurrection serves AT equally well.

A more familiar scenario emerges from the story in which Thomas raises from the dead a woman who had been killed by her former lover because she did not share his rather extreme enthusiasm for chastity. On rising, she recounts her tour of hell, and the apostle borrows her fire and brimstone to exhort the ever-present crowd: "Each one of you, therefore, put off the old man and put on the new, and abandon your first way of life and conduct" (58). The resurrection, the apostle's speech, and his subsequent healings spark a chain reaction of group conversions. Again, in that text, the plea for conversion is couched in language which evokes the early Christian understanding of baptism and links the conversion story to the frequent descriptions of a ceremony of initiation in AT.[24]

Conclusions

The AAA, in different degrees and with different emphases, consistently express the convictions that more than anything else miracles initiate the process of conversion and that resurrections are the most effective miracles. Furthermore, the accounts of conversions sparked by miracles in AAA are permeated with an ideology that uses the metaphor of resurrection to express an understanding of the powerful changes wrought by conversion. The prevalence of that ideology raises questions about MacMullen's interpretation of the role of miracles in conversion. For example, when MacMullen argues that "some real happening at the base of an account may be reconstructed by shrinking the account down to the physically possible,"[25] he slights the very ideological element which animates the texts. Moreover, the status of the stories themselves as reconstructions of past events designed to serve current purposes makes such "shrinking" a risky proposition.[26] It is difficult to establish whether the

[24]Cf. Gunther Bornkamm in Hennecke-Schneemelcher, *NTA*, 2. 437–440.

[25]MacMullen, *Christianizing*, p. 23.

[26]Cf. Taylor, "Conversion and Cognition," p. 18: "Thus, data from converted individuals concerning sociocultural circumstance prior to conversion is *not* data relating to pre-conversion identity, but *is* data relating to post-conversion identity." See also Beckford,

"real happening at the base" of a conversion story in the AAA is a "miracle" more palatable to a modern historian, some other event, or an act of the author's imagination designed to convey a particular message. In the texts as they stand we have more evidence about how the authors thought about conversion and used conversion stories as vehicles for their own ideas. For example, the texts stress that miracles, in themselves, only lead people *toward* conversion. As the stories about Lycomedes, the parricide, Callimachus, and Fortunatus in AJ suggest, those who benefit from the miracle (and by implication the crowd of onlookers) must respond to the demonstration of God's power with the proper resolve for the process of conversion to continue.

The use of the metaphor of death and resurrection to describe elements of the process of conversion is hardly unique in early Christianity. But while the New Testament contains both a nexus of theological ideas and a few stories with formal similarities, at no point does it provide a coherent model for both the narrative form and the ideology of the conversion stories in the AAA. A sample of some other early Christian texts provides similar negative conclusions.

For example, the conception of entrance into Christian communities as rebirth occurs prominently in the Pauline literature. Paul observes in his letter to the Romans that

> We were buried therefore with him by baptism into death, so that as Christ was raised from the dead by the glory of the Father, we too might walk in newness of life. For if we have been united with him in a death like his, we shall certainly be united with him in a resurrection like his. (Rom. 6:4–5)

Similarly, the letter to the Ephesians (2:1–2, 4–8; 4:22–24) links death to the pleasures of the world, resurrection into a new life, and salvation, and the same images recur in the letter to the Colossians (cf. 2:11–15; 3:1–17).[27] Each of those texts draws on the repertoire of images that also occurs in the AAA, but none of them employs the images in a narrative about an apostle's miraculous raising up of a sick or dead person. Although they establish the antecedent existence of a trove of ideas in the

"Accounting for Conversion," p. 260: "Accounts of conversion are constructions (or reconstructions) of experiences which draw upon resources available *at the time of construction* to lend them sense. They are not fixed, once-for-all descriptions of phenomena as they occurred in the past. Rather, their meaning emerges in the very process of construction, and this takes place at different times in different contexts."

[27]On Pauline baptismal imagery see Wayne A. Meeks, *The First Urban Christians* (New Haven: Yale University Press, 1983) 154–157. For the later interpretation of such imagery, see Hugh M. Riley, *Christian Initiation* (Washington, DC: The Catholic University of America Press, 1974) 211ff.

Christian tradition, the Pauline texts can hardly be taken as the models for the conversion *stories* in the AAA.[28]

The canonical Acts of the Apostles adds little to the possible background of the dominant conception of conversion in the AAA. None of the conversion stories in that text brings together the familiar repertoire of images; the similarities that do appear are too general to be of any help. In the specifics of their conversion stories, at least, the AAA owe very little to the canonical Acts.[29]

The closest parallel in the New Testament occurs in the Gospel according to John, where Jesus' resurrection of Lazarus is explicitly described as provoking the conversion of many of the onlookers (cf. John 11:45; 12:11). But although that story offers a few formal similarities to the conversion stories in the AAA, it lacks the vivid exchange between healer and healed that often conveys the theological point in the AAA. In John 11, the conversation between Jesus and Lazarus' sisters makes the point, and that point has more to do with the identity of Jesus than with the process of conversion. The formal parallels between the Lazarus story and some of the conversion stories in the AAA do lend further support to Junod and Kaestli's idea that the AAA tend to play down the role of Jesus and to replace him with the apostle,[30] but they do not establish any direct links between John 11 and the conversion stories in the AAA.

That conclusion holds also for several early Christian texts outside the New Testament. For example, in his *Dialogue with Trypho* Justin both describes his own conversion and seeks the conversion of his interlocutors (and, perhaps, his non-Christian readers). A prolonged search for philosophical truth and an encounter with the scriptures, rather than any type of miracle, are the spurs to action in Justin's view (cf. *Dial.* 8). In his *Second Apology* (*2 Apol.* 12) Justin also links his conversion to the

---

[28]The close association of the Pauline texts with the ritual of baptism does lead further, particularly in the case of AJ. Junod and Kaestli (*Acta Iohannis*, p. 685) have suggested that AJ's silence on the subject of baptism might stem from its intention to arouse the spiritual interest of non-Christian readers without going too far into the details. Nonetheless, the author has still managed to suffuse the conversion stories with imagery which evokes the Christian understanding of baptism.

[29]On the relative absence of influence of the canonical Acts on the AAA, see F. Bovon, "La vie des apôtres: traditions bibliques et narrations apocryphes" in Bovon, *et al., Les Actes Apocryphes*, pp. 141–158; and Plumacher, "Apokryphe Apostelakten," col. 13, 54.

[30]Cf. Junod & Kaestli, *Acta Iohannis*, p. 681; Francois Bovon, "La vie des apôtres," p. 152; however, Junod, "Les vies de philosophes et les Actes apocryphes: un dessein similaire?" in Bovon, et al. *Les Actes Apocryphes*, pp. 209–219 would describe the prominence as secondary to his function as God's missionary.

impression which the Christian martyrs made on him.[31] Elsewhere, Justin does describe baptism as a rebirth and entrance to new life (cf. *1 Apol.* 61) but he doesn't explicitly link that idea to conversion, just as he had not used the metaphor of death and resurrection to describe his own conversion. Similarly, Tatian's account of his own conversion in his *Oration to the Greeks* offers no formal or ideological parallels to the conversion stories in the AAA. Tertullian, in his *Apology* (23.18), does claim that the demonstration of the Christian's power over pagan deities in exorcism "regularly makes Christians," but that mention of the link between miracles and conversion is not developed any further. He devotes more energy to praising the superiority of Christian books and to defending them from external attack (cf. *Apology* 17.1–4; 47).[32]

Origen also acknowledges the importance of miracles in the conversion of the many uneducated people who swelled the ranks of Christianity (cf. *Contra Celsum* 1.46, 2.38, 49). But he prizes above all those who convert through the exercise of reason and the reading of the scriptures (cf. *In Jer. hom.* 4.6).[33] Those patristic discussions of conversion, like the ones in the New Testament, contain some elements in common with the AAA, but they simply express different understandings of conversion than that found in the AAA.

Similarly, the early Acts of the Christian martyrs contain reports about the martyrs' attempt to gain understanding and toleration of their faith, if not outright conversion, indications that the prosecuting authorities suspected those brought before them of actively seeking converts, and brief stories of individual and mass conversions brought about by the preaching and steadfast courage of the martyrs or even through supernatural means. But none of the reports or stories offers close formal or ideological parallels to the conversion stories in the AAA.[34]

---

[31]Cf. Oskar Skarsaune, "The Conversion of Justin Martyr," *Studia Theologica* 30 (1976): 53–73.

[32]I follow the text and translation in Loeb edition of T. R. Glover & G. H. Rendall, trans., *Tertullian, Apology; De Spectaculis; Minucius Felix, Octavius* (Cambridge: Harvard, 1966).

[33]Cf. John Clark Smith, "Conversion in Origen," *Scottish Journal of Theology* 32 (1979): 217–240, and Aubin, *La Problème de la "Conversion,"* pp. 137–159 for general, theological treatments of Origen's views on conversion.

[34]For texts and translations see Herbert Musurillo, ed. & trans., *The Acts of the Christian Martyrs* (Oxford, Clarendon, 1972); for examples of attempts to gain toleration or conversion: *The Martyrdom of St. Polycarp* 10; *The Martyrdom of Pionius the Presbyter and his Companions* 7; for suspicion of missionary activity: *The Martyrdom of Justin and Companions* 4; for reports of conversions: *The Martyrdom of Potamiaena and Basilides*; *The Martyrdom of Saints Marian and James* 9, 10.

Finally, although the Pseudo-Clementines depict Peter's activity in Tyre and Sidon as a mix of preaching, healing, and baptizing, they do not employ the metaphor of death and resurrection to describe the effects of Peter's healings. Instead, they seem more concerned to portray Peter as an effective organizer, as this summary report of his activity suggests.

> Such were the addresses that Peter gave in Sidon. There also within a few days many were converted and believed and were healed. So Peter founded a church there and enthroned as bishop one of the elders who were accompanying him.[35]

The conversion story of Clement himself, which opens the text, unites a variety of themes from early Christian literature. Like Justin, he makes the rounds of philosophical schools; like many he hears directly the message of an early Christian missionary, and the testimony witnesses to the miracles that have recently been performed. But although Clement is plagued by thoughts about his mortality, the text stops short of describing his conversion as a rebirth into a new life; it focuses instead on his desire to emulate the missionary he has heard and to "preach the kingdom and righteousness of Almightly God."[36]

The lack of strong parallels to the form and content of the conversion stories and the ideology that they express supports Junod and Kaestli's characterization of AJ, and by extension of the other AAA, as an original text whose form and content were determined much more by its author(s) than by any predecessor.[37] The various motifs which the AAA often use to describe the process of conversion and the ideology which those motifs express are, if not unique, relatively distinctive. Though the frequency with which miracles produce conversions in the AAA could support MacMullen's claim that the performance of miracles was the primary spur to conversion in early Christianity, such use of the conversion stories in the AAA should be tempered by a recognition of their present status as reconstructions of past events designed to communicate their authors' present point of view. The texts tend to view miracles as in themselves insufficient to produce conversion and to treat miracles of resurrection as metaphors for the complex process of leaving an old way of life and entering a new one.

Junod has suggested that the spectacular scenes of healing and resurrection in the AAA serve as visible images of the invisible transformations that make up the spiritual drama of the soul. He has also proposed that the apostles themselves serve implicitly as sources of inspiration for

[35]Pseudo-Clement, *Hom.* 7.8 in Hennecke-Schneemelcher, *NTA*, 2. 562.
[36]Cf. ibid., p. 541.
[37]Cf. Junod & Kaestli, *Acta Iohannis*, p. 684.

the spiritual lives of the readers of the AAA.[38] In the specific case of the conversion stories, the texts aim to inspire by urging their readers to conceive of conversion as a miraculous transformation equal in its impact to a passage from death to life. But if Junod is correct, the miracle lies less in what the apostles do and more in what the converts themselves have done and what they think about it. The conversion stories in the AAA draw on the details of communal life, perhaps particularly the rituals of initiation which had long been the focus for dramatic descriptions of personal transformation, to imbue the process of conversion with a retrospective meaning that is not peculiar to the convert but common to all. Thus the life of the community shapes its understanding of the past and its hope for the future. Conversion stories portray what conversion *already means* to those who have accomplished it and what it *can mean* to those who might consider it.[39]

[38]Cf. Junod, "Les vies des philosophes et les Actes apocryphes," pp. 211–213.

[39]In that sense conversion stories can serve both as *models of* and *models for* the process of conversion. For that notion of model see Clifford Geertz, "Religion as a Cultural System" in *The Interpretation of Cultures* (New York: Basic Books, 1973) 87–125, esp. 93.

The "Catechetical" School of Early Christian Alexandria and Its Philonic Heritage[*]

Annewies van den Hoek
Harvard University

■ Introduction

For centuries, the so-called catechetical school in Alexandria has intrigued scholars and stimulated speculation on its origins and early practices.[1] The relationship of this school to Jewish-Hellenistic antecedents has made the problem doubly fascinating. Hypotheses about the school, how-

[*]I wish to dedicate this article to André Méhat because of his insight into Clement's language and thought, and his generosity in sharing his experience. Part of this article was presented to the Philo of Alexandria Group at the Annual Meeting of the Society of Biblical Literature in New Orleans in 1996. The discussion with members of the group, in particular with the other panelists John Collins, David Runia, and Greg Sterling, helped in defining some of the issues. Many thanks go to the Curator of the Department of Classical Art at the Museum of Fine Arts, Boston, and to Stephanos Alexopoulos, Pieter van de Bunt, Sister Lois and Margaret Studier for their help. I am indebted to Everett Ferguson for his comments on the offices in the early church, to Birger Pearson for his remarks on Basilides and Valentinus, and to Miroslaw Marcovich for a frank exchange of opinions on some text-critical problems.

[1]Gustave Bardy ("Aux origines de l'école d'Alexandrie," *RevScRel* 27 [1937] 65–90; cf. idem, "L'église et l'enseignement pendant les trois premiers siècles" *RevScRel* 12 [1932] 1–28; idem, "Pour l'histoire de l'école d'Alexandrie,' *Vivre et penser* [1942] 80–109) was the first to discuss the Alexandrian school in a more critical way. In this he drew upon the then recent study on the catechumenate in Rome by Bernard Capelle, "L'introduction du catéchuménat à Rome," *Recherches de théologie ancienne et médiévale* 5 (1933) 129–54. For subsequent

HTR 90:1 (1997) 59–87

ever, have sometimes far exceeded the limits of the scanty information surviving in ancient authors, who themselves had incomplete evidence for their reconstructions. Without presenting here yet another theory on the school's early configuration, one must offer some kind of assessment before drawing Philo into the discussion, since his relation to the school obviously presents an extra complication.

David Runia's comprehensive study on Philo in early Christian literature is indispensable for the subject at hand and serves as an excellent guide for further explorations.[2] More recently Roelof van den Broek and Clemens Scholten have advanced new reconstructions of the school of Alexandria that contrast with the image of the school as Eusebius, the prime source on the subject, had presented it.[3] To varying degrees they follow an older line of scholarship that treats Eusebius's account as an unreliable reconstruction not only based on sketchy evidence but also distorted for a specific purpose.[4] Writing from a later perspective of established Christian organiza-

---

studies, see Adolf Knauber, "Katechetenschule oder Schulkatechumenat? Um die rechte Deutung des 'Unternehmens' der ersten grossen Alexandriner," *TThZ* 60 (1951) 243–66; Manfred Hornschuh, "Das Leben des Origenes und die Entstehung der alexandrinischen Schule," *ZKG* 71 (1960) 1–25, 193–214; Francesco Pericoli Ridolfini, "Le origini della scuola di Alessandria," *RSO* 37 (1962) 211–30; Pierre Nautin, *Origène: Sa vie et son oeuvre* (Paris: Beauchesne, 1977); André Tuilier, "Les évangélistes et les docteurs de la primitive église et les origines de l'école d'Alexandrie,' *StPatr* 17/2 (1982) 738–49; Ulrich Neymeyr, *Die christlichen Lehrer im zweiten Jahrhundert* (Leiden: Brill, 1989); Roelof van den Broek, "The Christian 'School' of Alexandria in the Second and Third Centuries," in Jan Willem Drijvers and Alasdair A. MacDonald, eds. *Centers of Learning: Learning and Location in Pre-Modern Europe and the Near East* (Leiden: Brill, 1995) 39–47; and Clemens Scholten, "Die alexandrinische Katechetenschule," *JAC* 38 (1995) 16–37; for a review of the scholarly discussion and further bibliography, see Robert Lewis Wilken, "Alexandria: A School for Training in Virtue," in Patrick Henry, ed., *Schools of Thought in the Christian Tradition* (Philadelphia: Fortress, 1984) 15–18; Alain Le Boulluec, "L'école d'Alexandrie: De quelques aventures d'un concept historiographique," in *ΑΛΕΞΑΝΔΡΙΝΑ (in Honor of Père Claude Mondésert)* (Paris: Cerf, 1987) 403–17; David T. Runia, *Philo in Early Christian Literature: A Survey* (Assen: Van Gorcum, 1993) 132–33 and n. 3; van den Broek, "Christian 'School' of Alexandria," 39–40; and Scholten, "Die alexandrinische Katechetenschule," 16–18.

[2]Runia, *Philo in Early Christian Literature*; see also idem, *Philo and the Church Fathers: A Collection of Papers* (Leiden: Brill, 1995).

[3]Van den Broek, "Christian 'School' of Alexandria"; and Scholten, "Die alexandrinische Katechetenschule." These two studies are very different in character. Van den Broek follows the critical approach of scholarship that started in the 1930s. In his article, as in earlier publications, he stresses both the diversity of the Alexandrian Christian communities and the link of Alexandrian Christianity with earlier Jewish traditions. Scholten, on the other hand, deals primarily with a later period of the Alexandrian school and focuses on Origen and his ambiance. Scholten's very well documented study (a real "*Fundgrube*" for other researchers) puts emphasis on the "academic" aspects of the school and brings up Clement only marginally at the end.

[4]Most prominently Bardy, "Aux Origines de l'école d'Alexandrie," and Hornschuh, "Leben

tions, Eusebius created chains of succession of bishops or prominent teachers, usually with their starting points in apostolic times, in order to give the organizations of his time an enhanced legitimacy. In the view of Eusebius's severest critics, therefore, an Alexandrian school with a continuous line of succession or a fixed tradition did not exist in the second century.[5] Only with Origen, when a monarchic episcopacy was in place, would the "official" catechetical instruction have started.[6] The so-called school of Pantenus and Clement was not an "official" but a "private" undertaking of independent philosophers, a situation comparable to Justin Martyr's in Rome.[7] These teachers, the argument goes, were not ecclesiastical officials but laymen, even charismatic leaders, who as διδάσκαλοι ("teachers") and πρεσβύτεροι ("elders") played a role analogous to that of the elders in the Jewish community.[8]

In responding to this reconstruction, Eusebius will be my primary source, but his reports will be viewed against the information—the little that survives—that one can extract from the works of early Alexandrian writers themselves. Since Pantenus left no textual evidence,[9] my main target will be Clement, and to a lesser degree, Origen.

■ Didaskaleion

On several occasions in his *Church History*, Eusebius mentions a "didaskaleion" of Alexandria. First, in connection with Pantenus, he writes,

> At that time a man most famous for his learning, whose name was
> Pantenus, headed the course of studies (διατριβή) of the faithful there

des Origenes." For Eusebius, see Timothy David Barnes, *Constantine and Eusebius* (Cambridge, MA: Harvard University Press, 1981); idem, *From Eusebius to Augustine* (Aldershot, UK: Variorum, 1994); for a bibliography of Eusebius as a historiographer, see Scholten, "Die alexandrinische Katechetenschule," 18 and n. 8; and Nautin, *Origène: Sa vie et son oeuvre*, 25–98.

[5]Van den Broek ("Christian 'School' of Alexandria," 41) writes: "Nevertheless, the whole idea of a Christian school with a διαδοχή ["succession"] of teachers handing down a fixed tradition of learning to their pupil successors is completely false, at least until the second decade of the third century."

[6]Scholten ("Die alexandrinische Katechetenschule," 37) plays down the catechetical part of the instruction: "Das Ergebnis läßt sich in wenige Sätzen fassen: Die Bezeichnung 'Katechetenschule' sollte man, weil mißverständlich, aufgeben. Die alexandrinische Einrichtung ist keine Anstalt zur Vorbereitung der Taufbewerber, sondern die theologische Hochschule der dortigen Kirche." ("The result can be summed up in a few sentences: one should give up the name 'catechetical school' since it is ambiguous. The Alexandrian institution does not prepare candidates for baptism but is the theological academy of the church there.").

[7]For the characterization in the scholarly debate of the school as "private," "free," and "independent" (and similar terms), see Neymeyr, *Die christlichen Lehrer*, 86.

[8]Van den Broek, "Christian 'School' of Alexandria," 43.

[9]See Pierre Nautin, "Pantène," in *Tome commémoratif du millénaire de la bibliothèque*

21

(i. e. Alexandria), since, from an old tradition, a school (διδασκαλεῖον) of sacred words existed among them.[10]

After many virtuous actions, he, Pantenus, was head of the school (διδασκαλεῖον) in Alexandria until his death, explaining through teaching and writing the treasures of the divine beliefs.[11]

Later, when dealing with his favorite subject, the life of Origen, Eusebius brings up the school again, which this time he qualifies as "catechetical":

He [Origen] was in his eighteenth year when he became head of the school (διδασκαλεῖον) of catechetical instruction, and there he progressed [spiritually] during the persecutions at the time of Aquila, the governor of Alexandria. . . .[12]

But when he saw that he could not spend enough time on studying the divine things at a deeper level, through close examination and interpretation of the sacred books, and, moreover, when he saw that he could not handle the instruction of those who came to him, since they did not give him space to breathe—for from dawn to dusk one batch of students after the other was running in and out of his school (διδασκαλεῖον)—he divided up the masses, selected Heraclas from his pupils—a man who was serious in divine matters and also very learned and not bereft of philosophy—and made him partner in the instruction, leaving to him the first introduction of those who were just instructed in the basics, and keeping for himself the lecture course for those who were trained.[13]

---

patriarcale d'Alexandrie (Alexandria, 1953) 145–52; André Méhat, "Pantène," in Dictionnaire de la spiritualité 12 (1983) 159–61. For a review of the sources on Pantenus, see Adolf von Harnack, Geschichte der altchristlichen Literatur (2 vols; Leipzig: Hinrichs, 1896–1904) 1. 291–96.

[10]Hist. eccl. 5.10.1: Ἡγεῖτο δὲ τηνικαῦτα τῆς τῶν πιστῶν αὐτόθι διατριβῆς ἀνὴρ κατὰ παιδείαν ἐπιδοξότατος, ὄνομα αὐτῷ Πάνταινος, ἐξ ἀρχαίου ἔθους διδασκαλείου τῶν ἱερῶν λόγων παρ' αὐτοῖς συνεστῶτος.

[11]Ibid., 5.10. 4: ὅ γε μὴν Πάνταινος ἐπὶ πολλοῖς κατορθώμασι τοῦ κατ' Ἀλεξάνδρειαν τελευτῶν ἡγεῖται διδασκαλείου, ζώσῃ φωνῇ καὶ διὰ συγγραμμάτων τοὺς τῶν θείων δογμάτων θησαυροὺς ὑπομνηματιζόμενος. The view that Pantenus could not have produced any literary works is unjustified; see note 95 below.

[12]Ibid. 6.3.3 (see also 3.1; 3.8): ἔτος δ' ἦγεν ὀκτωκαιδέκατον καθ' ὃ τοῦ τῆς κατηχήσεως προέστη διδασκαλείου· ἐν ᾧ καὶ προκόπτει ἐπὶ τῶν κατὰ Ἀκύλαν τῆς Ἀλεξανδρείας ἡγούμενον διωγμῶν. . . .

[13]Ibid. 6.15.1 (cf. 14.11; 26.1): ὃ δ' ὡς ἑαυτὸν ἑώρα μὴ ἐπαρκοῦντα τῇ τῶν θείων βαθυτέρᾳ σχολῇ τῇ τε ἐξετάσει καὶ ἑρμηνείᾳ τῶν ἱερῶν γραμμάτων καὶ προσέτι τῇ τῶν προσιόντων κατηχήσει μηδ' ἀναπνεῦσαι συγχωρούντων αὐτῷ, ἑτέρων ἐφ' ἑτέροις ἐξ ἕω καὶ μέχρις ἑσπέρας ἐπὶ τὸ παρ' αὐτῷ διδασκαλεῖον φοιτώντων, διανείμας τὰ πλήθη, τὸν Ἡρακλᾶν τῶν γνωρίμων προκρίνας, ἔν τε τοῖς θείοις σπουδαῖον καὶ ἄλλως ὄντα λογιώτατον ἄνδρα καὶ φιλοσοφίας οὐκ ἄμοιρον, κοινωνὸν καθίστη τῆς κατηχήσεως, τῷ μὲν τὴν πρώτην τῶν ἄρτι στοιχειουμένων εἰσαγωγὴν ἐπιτρέψας, αὐτῷ δὲ τὴν τῶν ἐν ἕξει φυλάξας ἀκρόασιν.

In all of these instances, διδασκαλεῖον could be translated as "school" or "place of teaching."[14] Other passages in Eusebius's works and elsewhere show that διδασκαλεῖον can bear different meanings; for example, when Origen's fame became widespread, the mother of the emperor, Julia Mamaea, sought his company:

> She was then staying in Antioch and had him sent for with a military escort. After spending some time with her and pointing out to her a great many things that were to the glory of the Lord and that had to do with the excellence of the divine teaching (διδασκαλεῖον), he hastened back to his customary studies.[15]

In this passage the "school" as "teaching-place" has become a "school of thought" and thus "teaching" or "doctrine."[16] The word διδασκαλεῖον has thereby taken on a considerable range of meanings, and its usage extends beyond the Christian realm—whether orthodox or heterodox—to non-Christian contexts.[17] From other writers such as Justin, Irenaeus, and Epiphanius, one can learn more about the usage of the word. In Justin it occurs only once as a definition of the teaching of Christ as a "school of divine virtue."[18] Irenaeus, on the other hand, connects διδασκαλεῖον (*doctrina* in Latin) primarily with the teaching of heretics such as Valentinus, Marcion, and Tatian.[19] In that respect he finds an eager follower in Epiphanius some centuries later, who also uses the word primarily in an antiheretical context.[20]

The word διδασκαλεῖον is more difficult to find in the works of Clement of Alexandria. As is well known, the related words διδάσκαλος

[14]LSJ s.v. διδασκαλεῖον, offers this as the sole definition; but compare *LPGL* s.v. διδασκαλεῖον; and Anatole Bailly, ed., *Dictionnaire Grec Français* (Paris: Hachette, 1950) s.v. διδασκαλεῖον.

[15]Eusebius *Hist. eccl.* 6.21.4: ἐπ' Ἀντιοχείας δῆτα διατρίβουσα μετὰ στρατιωτικῆς δορυφορίας αὐτὸν ἀνακαλεῖται· παρ' ἧ χρόνον διατρίψας πλεῖστά τε ὅσα εἰς τὴν τοῦ κυρίου δόξαν καὶ τῆς τοῦ θείου διδασκαλείου ἀρετῆς ἐπιδειξάμενος, ἐπὶ τὰς συνήθεις ἔσπευδεν διατριβάς.

[16]*LPGL* s.v. διδασκαλεῖον has these three meanings, in addition to a fourth ("position or office of a teacher") that is not relevant here.

[17]Eusebius *Praep. ev.* 5.34.4; 11.2.3 (Greek schools); 12.33.3 (Christian); idem, *Hist. eccl.* 5.13.4 (Marcionites).

[18]Justin 2 *Apol.* 2.13: καὶ πάλιν, τὰ καλὰ ἑαυτῷ συνεπιστάμενος διὰ τὴν ἀπὸ τοῦ Χριστοῦ διδαχήν, τὸ διδασκαλεῖον τῆς θείας ἀρετῆς ὡμολόγησεν ("and again, being aware of the noble goods that the teaching of Christ had brought to him, he confessed about the school of divine virtue").

[19]*Adv. haer.* 1.11.1 (Valentinus, cf. *Adv. haer.* 1.24.7, 2.31.1); *Adv. haer.* 1.27.1–2 (Marcion; also in Eusebius *Hist. eccl.* 4.11.2); *Adv. haer.* 1.28.1 (Tatian; also in Eusebius *Hist. eccl.* 4.29.3).

[20]Epiphanius *Panarion* 27.1.1; 28.6.4; 30.30.1; 31.32.1; 46.1.6; 46.2.4; 66.32.1; 67.7.8.

("teacher") and διδασκαλία ("teaching") occur very frequently in his works and, moreover, these terms have significant theological implications.[21] Yet Clement does not use them to characterize his own teaching. He depicts himself in more humble terms as a παιδαγωγός ("pedagogue")[22] and uses διδάσκαλος primarily to label Christ as the teacher par excellence.[23] Usage also extends to God, the law, or people closely related to Christ, the apostles and their immediate circle. While he does apply the title παιδαγωγός to Christ, Clement hardly ever calls himself a διδάσκαλος. The pedagogue-instructors were called "fathers," as Clement points out. It may well be that their title of address was πάπας rather than πατήρ, since in classical Latin "papas" was the title by which children addressed their "paedagogus."[24]

The *Thesaurus Linguae Graecae* turns up only one passage with the word διδασκαλεῖον.[25] This text occurs toward the end of the *Pedagogue*:

> It is not my task, says the pedagogue, to teach these things any longer, but we need a teacher to whom we should go for the explanation of

[21]For Clement διδασκαλία represents the teaching of Christ, the apostles, and the church. The "true" teaching is closely related to his concept of gnosis.

[22]The pedagogue was originally a slave who guided or accompanied the child from home to school and back again but could also be a private, household teacher. He became an almost legendary figure in Greek literature, as the now-beloved, now-ridiculous companion and mentor of a boy. The figure is prominent in Greek and Roman art, and his female equivalent, the old nurse, is equally popular; both also stood as emblems of dedication and lifelong commitment. The pedagogue may have been servile in origin, but the concept eventually became emancipated and could represent a dignified profession.

[23]For a discussion of διδάσκαλος, see André Méhat, *Étude sur les "Stromates" de Clément d'Alexandrie* (Paris: du Seuil, 1966) 61; Alain Le Boulluec and Pierre Voulet, *Les Stromates, Stromate V* (SC 278; 2 vols; Paris: Cerf, 1981) 2.14. For παιδαγωγός, see Henri-Irénée Marrou, *Histoire de l'education dans l'antiquité* (2d ed.; Paris: du Seuil, 1950) 61–62; Henri-Irénée Marrou and Marguerite Harl, *Le Pédagogue* (SC 70; Paris: Cerf, 1960) 7–105; and Annewies van den Hoek, "Hymn of the Holy Clement to Christ the Savior," in Mark Kiley, ed., *Critical Anthology of Hellenistic Prayer* (London/New York: Routledge, 1997) 296–303.

[24]See Juvenalis 6.633; and *Oxford Latin Dictionary* s.v. *"papas"*; also *Inscriptiones Muratorii*, 1297.11. The word *pater* seems to have been reserved for the more lofty positions of poets and philosophers, see *Oxford Latin Dictionary* s. v. *"pater"* 8, and the equivalent "πατήρ" in Greek, see *LPGL*. Clement mentions the "instructor-fathers" in *Strom*. 1.3.1; αὐτίκα πατέρας τοὺς κατηχήσαντάς φαμεν, κοινωνικὸν δὲ ἡ σοφία καὶ φιλάνθρωπον ("Further we call those who instruct us fathers; wisdom is held in common and is human loving") (also ibid., 3.98.4; 5.15.3, and the letter of Alexander in Eusebius, *Hist. eccl.* 6.14.8). From the third century onwards the Greek word πάπας becomes a title of the bishop, particularly of the bishop of Alexandria; cf. *LPGL* s. v. πάπας (παπᾶς, πάππας) and *Pass. Perp. et Fel.* 13.3. As Stephanos Alexopoulos points out (personal communication), in modern Greek this usage continues in two terms: Πάπας and Παπᾶς. The first is the title of both the pope of Rome and the patriarch of Alexandria. Other patriarchs in the Orthodox Church do not have the title Πάπας. The second term, Παπᾶς, with the accent on the last syllable, can be a title of any priest.

[25]*Thesaurus Linguae Graecae, CD ROM # D* (Regents of the University of California, 1992).

24

those holy words. So it is time for me to stop my pedagogy, and for you to listen to the Teacher. After receiving you, who have been reared with a good building of character, he will teach you the words thoroughly. The church is here for the good, and your bridegroom (is) the only teacher, good will of a good father, true wisdom, sanctuary of knowledge.[26]

The problem with this passage is that the word διδασκαλεῖον does not appear in the manuscript tradition; it is an emendation by Eduard Schwartz, who did not like the original text. MS P has εἰς καλόν, which formed the basis for διδασκαλεῖον in Stählin's edition.[27] The conjecture is unnecessary, since εἰς καλόν makes perfectly good sense and occurs a number of other times in Clement's writings, and even once in a similar context.[28] Clement, therefore, did not use διδασκαλεῖον here and apparently never employed the word at all.

The passage and its context are nevertheless important because they reveal how Clement perceived the process of education and his own role in it. In the preceding passage he had pointed out how certain texts from the scriptures served the pedagogue's moral instruction of his students.[29] He then speaks about the people's receiving precepts appropriate to their various functions as presbyters, bishops, deacons, and widows.[30] Many of these

[26]*Paed.* 3.97.3–98.1: Ἀλλ᾽ οὐκ ἐμόν, φησὶν ὁ παιδαγωγός, διδάσκειν ἔτι ταῦτα, διδασκάλου δὲ εἰς τὴν ἐξήγησιν τῶν ἁγίων ἐκείνων λόγων χρήζομεν, πρὸς ὃν ἡμῖν βαδιστέον. Καὶ δὴ ὥρα γε ἐμοὶ μὲν πεπαῦσθαι τῆς παιδαγωγίας, ὑμᾶς δὲ ἀκροᾶσθαι τοῦ διδασκάλου. Παραλαβὼν δὲ οὗτος ὑμᾶς ὑπὸ καλῇ τεθραμμένους ἀγωγῇ ἐκδιδάξεται τὰ λόγια. Εἰς καλὸν ‹Διδασκαλεῖον› δὲ ἡ ἐκκλησία ἥδε καὶ ὁ νυμφίος ὁ μόνος διδάσκαλος, ἀγαθοῦ πατρὸς ἀγαθὸν βούλημα, σοφία γνήσιος, ἁγίασμα γνώσεως. Εἰς καλόν is the text in MS P (*Paris. Graec.* 451). Eduard Schwartz emended this to διδασκαλεῖον which changes the meaning of the sentence; it then reads: "The school is the church here. . . ."

[27]Otto Stählin, *Clemens Alexandrinus erster Band: Protrepticus und Paedagogus* (GCS 12; Leipzig, 1905; 3d ed., Berlin: Ursula Treu, 1972).

[28]See *Strom.* 1.85.5; 1.158.5; 4.87.2; a similarity exists with *Strom.* 1.85.5: πάντα μὲν οὖν οἰκονομεῖται ἄνωθεν εἰς καλόν, ἵνα γνωρισθῇ διὰ τῆς ἐκκλησίας ἡ πολυποίκιλος σοφία τοῦ θεοῦ . . . "Everything is arranged from above for the good 'in order that through the church the many-colored wisdom of God may be made known' (Eph 3:10). . . ."

[29]*Paed.* 3.97.1: Ὀλίγα ταῦτα ἐκ πολλῶν δείγματος χάριν ἀπ᾽ αὐτῶν διεξελθὼν τῶν θείων γραφῶν ὁ παιδαγωγὸς τοῖς αὑτοῦ παρατίθεται παισίν, δι᾽ ὧν, ὡς ἔπος εἰπεῖν, ἄρδην ἐκκόπτεται κακία καὶ περιγράφεται ἀδικία ("These are a few of the many texts that the pedagogue sets before his children as an example as he goes through the divine scriptures, by which, so to speak, vice is fully eradicated and injustice is eliminated"). See also Clement *Strom.* 3.90.1, 6.106–7.

[30]Ibid., 3.97.2: Μυρίαι δὲ ὅσαι ὑποθῆκαι εἰς πρόσωπα ἐκλεκτὰ διατείνουσαι ἐγγεγράφαται ταῖς βίβλοις ταῖς ἁγίαις, αἳ μὲν πρεσβυτέροις, αἳ δὲ ἐπισκόποις ‹καὶ› διακόνοις, ἄλλαι χήραις, περὶ ὧν ἄλλος ἂν εἴη λέγειν καιρός ("Innumerable are the commands that touch the elect people who are inscribed in the holy books; some are for presbyters, others for bishops (and) deacons, others for widows, about whom we will speak at another time").

words, he explains, are cryptic, but they can be profitable for those who read them.[31] For their understanding, however, he refers not to himself, a mere pedagogue, but to the Didaskalos, the Logos itself. By his instruction, the pedagogue guides his pupils through the scriptures to a certain point but then bids them farewell and urges his audience to listen carefully henceforth to the Didaskalos.

Although the passage is rather complex, the basic situation seems clear; the instructor has done his work, and his beloved students have graduated to a further stage of their religious and spiritual life.[32] Clement is talking to catechumens or to the recently baptized. In this context, the church does not serve as an ideal image, since there is an explicit description of the functions in the church. Just before the hymn that concludes the *Pedagogue*, the subject is reiterated:

> Because, by appointing us in the church, the Pedagogue himself entrusted us to himself, the Logos, who teaches and watches over all. . . .[33]

It is noteworthy that Clement uses καθίστημι ("to appoint") here, a verb that is common in connection with the appointment of clergy.[34] Clement evidently sees himself in an ecclesiastical setting, appointed in the church by no less than Christ himself. The ultimate Pedagogue entrusts the human pedagogue to the Logos.

When Eusebius first introduced the school of Pantenus, he mentioned not catechetical instruction but only a long-standing tradition of biblical scholarship. The catechetical element only enters with his discussion of Origen and then reappears in a later passage tracing the succession from Pantenus through Clement to Origen. Yet it remains unclear from Eusebius's account whether Pantenus participated in the catechetical part of the operation:

> Clement, who succeeded Pantenus, was head of the catechetical instruction at Alexandria up to such a time that Origen also was one of his students.[35]

[31]Ibid., 3.97.3: Πολλὰ δὲ καὶ δι᾽ αἰνιγμάτων, πολλὰ δὲ καὶ διὰ παραβολῶν τοῖς ἐντυγχάνουσιν ἔξεστιν ὠφελεῖσθαι ("Many of these words have hidden meanings, many are expressed in parables, but they can be beneficial for those who read them closely").

[32]For "father" as a title of address, see footnote 24 above.

[33]*Paed.* 3.101.3: Ἐπεὶ δὲ εἰς τὴν ἐκκλησίαν ἡμᾶς καταστήσας ὁ παιδαγωγὸς αὐτὸς ἑαυτῷ παρακατέθετο τῷ διδασκαλικῷ καὶ πανεπισκόπῳ λόγῳ. . . .

[34]"To appoint, esp. clergy" is the first meaning in *LPGL*, which cites various examples, such as *1 Clem.* 44.2 (the appointment of bishops); Irenaeus *Adv. haer.* 3.43 (Eusebius, *Hist. eccl.* 4.14.3; Polycarp's appointment as bishop by the apostles).

[35]*Hist. eccl.* 6.6.1: Πάνταινον δὲ Κλήμης διαδεξάμενος τῆς κατ᾽ Ἀλεξάνδρειαν κατηχήσεως εἰς ἐκεῖνο τοῦ καιροῦ καθηγεῖτο ὡς καὶ τὸν Ὠριγένην τῶν φοιτητῶν γενέσθαι αὐτοῦ.

In still another passage Clement appears to be working together with Pantenus:

> At this time Clement, who was the namesake of the pupil of the apostles who long ago led the church of the Romans, became known in Alexandria for teaching the holy scriptures together [with Pantenus].[36]

The question of the succession will be addressed later, but first a closer look is necessary at what Clement's relationship with catechetical instruction may have been.

■ Catechesis

To understand the intimate connection between instruction and the Christian community that Clement served, one must take a closer look at some passages where the subject of catechesis arises. His book, the *Pedagogue*, which is a kind of handbook for catechumens and the recently baptized, provides several examples:[37]

> All our sins are washed away, and immediately afterwards we are no longer evil. That is the unique grace of illumination, that we are not the same as before the washing, since knowledge, which enlightens the mind in a flash, rises up with the illumination; and immediately we, the unlearned learners receive instruction. As to the question at what moment this learning accrued, that is hard to tell. For catechetical instruction leads to faith, and at the moment of baptism faith is instructed by the Holy Spirit.[38]

The account then turns to some important Pauline texts, in which the key word is milk.[39] After citing the well-known image in 1 Cor 3:1–2 of the

---

[36]Ibid., 5.11.1: Κατὰ τοῦτον ταῖς θείαις γραφαῖς συνασκούμενος ἐπ᾽ Ἀλεξανδρείας ἐγνωρίζετο Κλήμης, ὁμώνυμος τῷ πάλαι τῆς Ῥωμαίων ἐκκλησίας ἡγησαμένῳ φοιτητῇ τῶν ἀποστόλων·

[37]See Marrou, *Pédagogue*, 7; Adolf Knauber, "Ein frühchristliches Handbuch katechumenaler Glaubensinitiation: der Paidagogos des Klemens von Alexandrien," *MThZ* 23 (1972) 311–24.

[38]*Paed.* 1.30.1–2: Πάντα μὲν οὖν ἀπολουόμεθα τὰ ἁμαρτήματα, οὐκέτι δέ ἐσμεν παρὰ πόδας κακοί. Μία χάρις αὕτη τοῦ φωτίσματος τὸ μὴ τὸν αὐτὸν εἶναι τῷ πρὶν ἢ λούσασθαι τὸν τρόπον· ὅτι δὲ ἡ γνῶσις συναντέλλει τῷ φωτίσματι περιαστράπτουσα τὸν νοῦν· καὶ εὐθέως ἀκούομεν μαθηταὶ οἱ ἀμαθεῖς. πότερον πότε τῆς μαθήσεως ἐκείνης προσγενομένης οὐ γὰρ ἂν ἔχοις εἰπεῖν τὸν χρόνον. Ἡ μὲν γὰρ κατήχησις εἰς πίστιν περιάγει, πίστις δὲ ἅμα βαπτίσματι ἁγίῳ παιδεύεται πνεύματι. The phrase πότερον πότε may be corrupt, but Potter's conjecture ‹πρότερον› is no improvement. The interrogative adverb πότερον sometimes occurs in Clement without a second part of the question, see *Strom.* 7.29.1. One might also consider πότερον πότε a kind of dittography that survives in the text.

[39]See Annewies van den Hoek, "Milk and Honey in the Theology of Clement of Alexandria," in Hans J. Auf der Maur et al., eds., *Fides Sacramenti—Sacramentum Fidei: Studies in*

newborn, who are fed with milk and not yet with solid food, Clement notes the difficulty in interpreting it. He suggests that,

> it is possible that the word "as," which indicates a comparison, means something as follows and that the passage should be read: "I gave you milk to drink in Christ" (1 Cor 3:1); and then, after a little pause, we should continue "as little children," in order that by this pause we might understand the words in this way: "I instructed you in Christ with simple, real, and natural spiritual food. (cf. 1 Cor 10:3.)[40]

It sounds as if Clement alludes to another passage from Paul, namely 1 Cor 10:3, but that is only partly true, since κατηχέω is not part of the Pauline text.[41] It may be a word that, in Clement's view, Paul should have written but did not. The apostle only spoke of spiritual and fleshly people and of spiritual nourishment. The theme of instruction, therefore, is Clement's own addition—possibly with a slight nod to the letter to the Hebrews—and it well reflects his own interest. Playing further on the key text provided by Paul, Clement gives various other interpretations:

> It is equally possible to understand scripture as follows: "but brothers I could not speak to you as spiritual but as fleshly people, as little children in Christ," so that "fleshly" could be understood as the recent catechumens, still little ones in Christ. He calls those "spiritual" who already have come to faith through the Holy Spirit, while he calls "in the flesh" the new catechumens, who have not yet been purified; he calls them "in the flesh" obviously because they still have fleshly thoughts like the pagans.[42]

Scholarly discussions of whether Clement's accounts reflect actual situations of liturgical life often dismiss these texts as references to a meta-

---

Honour of Pieter Smulders (Assen: Van Gorcum, 1981) 27–39; Denise Kimber Buell, "Procreative Language in Clement of Alexandria" (Ph.D. diss., Harvard University, 1995); Verna E. F. Harrison, "Male and Female in Clement of Alexandria's Theology," *StPatr* (forthcoming).

[40]*Paed.* 1.35.2: Μή τι οὖν τὸ "ὡς," παραβολῆς ὂν δηλωτικόν, τοιοῦτόν τι ἐμφαίνει, καὶ δὴ ἀναγνωστέον ὡδέ πως τὸ ῥητόν· "γάλα ὑμᾶς ἐπότισα ἐν Χριστῷ" καὶ διαστήσαντες ὀλίγον ἐπαγάγωμεν "ὡς νηπίους," ἵνα κατὰ τὴν διαστολὴν τῆς ἀναγνώσεως τοιαύτην ἀποδεξώμεθα διάνοιαν· κατήχησα ὑμᾶς ἐν Χριστῷ ἁπλῇ καὶ ἀληθεῖ καὶ αὐτοφυεῖ τροφῇ τῇ πνευματικῇ·

[41]1 Cor 10:3: καὶ πάντες τὸ αὐτὸ πμευματικὸν βρῶμα ἔφαγον. . . ("and all ate the same spiritual food"). Milk and teaching are also connected in Heb 5:12–14.

[42]*Paed.* 1.36.2: Ἔξεστι δὲ καὶ οὕτως ἐκλαμβάνειν τὴν γραφήν· "κἀγὼ δέ, ἀδελφοί, οὐκ ἐδυνήθην λαλῆσαι ὑμῖν ὡς πνευματικοῖς, ἀλλ' ὡς σαρκίνοις, ὡς νηπίοις ἐν Χριστῷ", ὡς δύνασθαι σαρκίνους νοεῖσθαι τοὺς νεωστὶ κατηχουμένους καὶ νηπίους ἔτι ἐν Χριστῷ. Πνευματικοὺς μὲν γὰρ τοὺς πεπιστευκότας ἤδη τῷ ἁγίῳ πνεύματι προσεῖπεν, σαρκικοὺς δὲ τοὺς νεοκατηχήτους καὶ μηδέπω κεκαθαρμένους, οὓς "ἔτι σαρκικοὺς" εἰκότως λέγει ἐπ' ἴσης τοῖς ἐθνικοῖς τὰ σαρκὸς ἔτι φρονοῦντας.

phorical image and not to a reality.[43] Indeed, Clement's way of writing gives ample reason for such an assessment. He often speaks in ideal terms about church or baptism and also expands the notion of initial instruction to a kind of continuing education program. In the same paragraph, for example, in yet another elaboration on the Pauline text, he says:

> Therefore he (the apostle) also says, "I gave you milk to drink," which means: I poured knowledge into you, which from catechism onwards nourishes up to eternal life.[44]

Clement depicts a gradual process that in its initial phase reaches faith through catechism and baptism. From there, through a continuous training, the faithful aim at a higher spiritual and virtuous realm, namely that of knowledge. This elevated way of thinking does not, however, mean that no 'down-to-earth' practices lie behind the thought. It seems virtually certain that Clement's metaphorical language masks an actual situation and that his theological reflection develops from this reality.[45] The concrete basis becomes clear from the wording of these and other passages. The words have become technical terms of church practice. The noun κατηχήσις itself is a clear example of such a technical usage. Clement is a pioneer in using the word to mean specifically "instruction of those preparing for baptism."[46] The many instances in which he uses the word in connection with baptism make this clear.[47] He even refers to an earlier stage, that of procatechesis,[48]

---

[43]See, for example, Hornschuh, "Das Leben des Origenes," 199 n. 74, 201 n. 81.

[44]*Paed.* 1.36.4: Διὸ καὶ "γάλα ὑμᾶς ἐπότισα," φησίν, τὴν γνῶσιν ὑμῖν ἐνέχεα, λέγων, τὴν ἐκ κατηχήσεως ἀνατρέφουσαν εἰς ζωὴν ἀΐδιον (cf. 1 Pet 2:2). Hereafter Clement speaks about the eucharist.

[45]Neymeyr, *Die christlichen Lehrer*, 89 also argues (against Hornschuh, "Das Leben des Origenes") that Clement's language reflects a real situation in the church.

[46]See *LPGL* s. v. κατηχήσις 2a, which cites several examples from Clement's works. The linkage with baptism is evident in the usage of the noun but also exists in the verb. Although other texts employ the word in a more general sense, as instruction of faith, one should not disregard specifically baptismal terminology in these contexts; note also the term νεωστὶ κατηχούμενος and νεοκατήχητος for the new catechumens, in *Paed.* 1.36.3 above (νεοκατήχητος also in *Strom.* 6.130.1). For a further discussion of the terminology, see André Turck, "Catéchein et Catéchèse chez les premiers pères," *RSPhTh* 47 (1963) 361–72; Adolf Knauber, "Zur Grundbedeutung der Wortgruppe κατήχεω-catechizo," *Oberrheinisches Pastoralblatt* 68 (1967) 294; and Eugen Paul, *Geschichte der christlichen Erziehung* (Freiburg: Herder, 1993) 40–41.

[47]See *Paed.* 6.30.2, 35.3, 36.2–3; *Strom.* 1.19.4; 5.15.3; 5.66.2; and 6.89.1–2 (with a possible reference to the "inscriptio nominis"); *Ecl. proph.* 28; and André Méhat, *Étude sur les "Stromates" de Clément d'Alexandrie* (Paris: du Seuil, 1966) 62–70.

[48]*Prot.* 10.96.2: Ὑμεῖς δέ οὐ γὰρ τὰ πάτρια ὑμᾶς ἔτι τῆς ἀληθείας ἀπασχολεῖ ἔθη προκατηχημένους ἀκούοιτ᾿ ἂν ἤδη τὸ μετὰ τοῦτο ὅπως ἔχει ("You, listen finally to what the following message is—for your ancestral customs no longer divert you from the truth, since you received preliminary instruction"). Translations have connected the participle

which shows that a complex system of initiation was already in place and, thus, that preparation for baptism was becoming more formalized by this time.[49]

The content of this catechetical instruction is hard to distill from Clement's words, but only a generation later, with Origen, its contours became clearer. In a well documented study based on Origen's sermons, Auf der Maur and Waldram trace out the structure and various phases of the instruction.[50] One of the central features is moral instruction. In an important passage Origen says:

> With the nourishment of milk, holy scripture means the first moral instruction, which is given to the beginners as to small children (cf. 1 Cor 3:1–2). For not immediately at the beginning should one teach the candidates about the deep and more secret mysteries, but one should introduce to them the improvement of their lifestyle, the correction of their morality, and the first elements of religious conduct and simple faith.[51]

Origen places the same emphasis on the Pauline text and makes the same connection with the preparation for baptism as Clement, something other authors had not previously done.[52]

For Origen, the main emphasis of catechesis was moral instruction. Other important elements were antiheretical instruction and (especially) the reading of scripture, which would have taken place in the noneucharistic com-

---

προκατηχημένους with "ancestral customs," but see *LPGL* s.v. προκατηχέω in support of my interpretation, which I also share with Otto Stählin in his translation of the Protrepticus (*Des Clemens von Alexandreia Mahnrede an die Heiden* [Bibliothek der Kirchenväter 2. 7; Munich: Kösel, 1934] 172). In addition to the passage in *Prot.* 10.96.2, the word κατήχησις πρώτη is used in *Strom.* 5.48.9. See also Origen, *Cels.* 3.51, and Hans Jörg Auf der Maur and Joop Waldram, "Illuminatio Verbi Divini—Confessio Fidei—Gratia Baptismi," in Hans Jörg Auf der Maur, *Fides Sacramenti*, 41–95, esp. 47.

[49]Everett Ferguson (in a letter) finds this a significant point, since for a long time scholars have minimized the importance of the catechetical setting for early Christian literature. Recent literature, however, takes the catechetical aspects more seriously.

[50]Auf der Maur and Waldram, "Illuminatio Verbi Divini."

[51]Origen *Hom. in Jud.*, 5: "Lactis cibus esse dicitur in scripturis sanctis prima haec moralis institutio, quae incipientibus velut parvulis traditur. Non enim in initiis statim discipulis de profundis et secretioribus tradendum est sacramentis, sed morum correctio, emendatio disciplinae, religiosae conversationis et simplicis fidei prima iis elementa traduntur." It is as if Clement is speaking here. The Latin translation, however, gives the thought a stiffer and more institutional flavor than that of the Greek of either Clement or Origen.

[52]Both Irenaeus and Tertullian interpret 1 Cor 13:1–2 mostly in a "Pauline" way; see Irenaeus, *Adv. haer.* 4.38.1–2; 5.8.2–3; 5.9.2; 5.10.2; Tertullian, *Praescr. haer.* 27.4; *De monogamia* 11.6; *De corona* 3.3; *Marc.* 4.5.1; Irenaeus (*Adv. haer.* 4.38.2) and Tertullian (*De monogamia* 11.6) mentions teaching, but not in connection with baptism. Tertullian (*De corona* 3.3) describes the mixture of milk and honey in the baptismal rite.

munal services.[53] It would be interesting to compare Clement's and Origen's catechetical terminology more fully. Suffice it to say here that throughout the former's works moral instruction, biblical reading, and antiheretical discussion are equally central, and that a continuity exists in their approach to teaching.

These examples do not necessarily mean that there was no development in the time between Clement and Origen, but only that the latter's approach seems rooted in practices evident in the intellectual and spiritual milieu of the former. Church practices, after all, evolve slowly and rarely derive from a single theologian. Baptismal instruction is part of communal and liturgical life, and no individual person, not even an Origen, could have changed these customs drastically.[54]

It thus becomes clear that Clement instructed catechumens and that a system of instruction that included moral education, biblical interpretation, and a clear antiheretical element was already in place. As is well known, moreover, Clement was involved in other levels of teaching as well. His more advanced theological speculations in the *Stromateis* make this clear. He also indicated a division between the beginners and the more advanced, just as Origen did when he put the beginners in the hands of a "teaching assistant" and kept the advanced students for himself.[55] All things considered, it seems likely that these traditions of catechetical instruction, biblical training, and theological or philosophical debates were already in existence and that they passed on from Clement's Alexandria to that of Origen in a continuous line.

■ School or Church?

Scholars have long discussed whether these early Alexandrian teachers represented a school outside the church or a school with close links to the church.[56] In either case these same scholars argued that the school was essentially independent of the church. From Clement's perspective, however, a contrast between church and school is nonexistent. His instruction moved the faithful through baptism and then toward wisdom and knowledge within the context of the church:

[53]Auf der Maur and Waldram, "Illuminatio Verbi Divini," 59; see also the passage in Socrates *Hist. eccl.* 5.22, who reports that services of the word took place on Wednesday and Friday in Alexandria; cf. Hornschuh, *Das Leben des Origenes*, 194.

[54]Scholars have often pointed out that by the beginning of the third century an established system of baptismal instruction was in place in various geographical areas, such as North Africa (Tertullian) and Rome (Hippolytus); Paul, *Geschichte der christlichen Erziehung*, 45–52, and for Tertullian, Neymeyr, *Die christlichen Lehrer*, 106–7.

[55]For Clement, see *Strom.* 1.2.2; 1.9.1; 1.13.2; for Origen, see Eusebius *Hist. eccl.* 6.15.1, and footnote 13 above.

[56]See Neymeyr, *Die christlichen Lehrer*, 86.

We then, the little ones, guarding ourselves from the blasts of heresies, which puff up to swollen vanity, and not entrusting ourselves to fathers who admonish us wrongly, we then reach perfection, when we are the church and have received Christ, its head.[57]

From this and many other passages it becomes clear that Clement's concept of church has a strongly polemical orientation. When he speaks about the gatherings of heretics, he is eager to use the plural ἐκκλησίας,[58] in order to deny their claim to be ἐκκλησία in the singular, the one and true church, in which the just assemble.[59] Clement repeatedly accentuates the unity and authenticity of the church against the many heretical groups.[60] Only in the church does knowledge exist:

> If there is a demonstration of proof, one should also agree to search and learn through the scriptures themselves by way of demonstration how the heresies (αἱρέσεις) went astray, and only in the truth and in the old church does the most genuine gnosis and the truly best way of thinking (αἵρεσις) exist.[61]

[57]*Paed* 1.18.4: Ἡμεῖς δὲ οἱ νήπιοι τοὺς παραφυσῶντας εἰς φυσίωσιν φυλαξάμενοι τῶν αἱρέσεων ἀνέμους καὶ μὴ καταπιστεύοντες τοῖς ἄλλως ‹ἡμᾶς› νουθετοῦσι ‹πατράσι› τελειούμεθα τότε, ὅτε ἐσμὲν ἐκκλησία, τὴν κεφαλὴν τὸν Χριστὸν ἀπειληφότες. There seems to be a corruption in the text, which has ἡμῖν and πατέρας; Stählin solves the problem by changing ἄλλως into ἄλλους and νουθετοῦσι into νομοθετοῦσι. I suggest ἡμᾶς for ἡμῖν and πατράσι for πατέρας. For the edition of Stählin, see note 27.

[58]*Strom.* 7.98.2: ἥπερ μετατίθενται ὑπὸ φιλοτιμίας τῆς αἱρέσεως καὶ τῆς πολυθρυλήτου κατὰ τὰς ἐκκλησίας αὐτῶν πρωτοκαθεδρίας, δι᾽ ἣν κἀκείνην τὴν συμποτικὴν διὰ τῆς ψευδωνύμου ἀγάπης πρωτοκλισίαν ἀσπάζονται ("[they endure everything and move every log, as the expression goes. . .] rather than withdraw themselves because of the pride in their heresy and their notorious desire to occupy the first seat (cf. Matt 23:6) in their assemblies; because of this they embrace the first couch of their drinking party by having an agape meal—but falsely called so").

[59]Ibid., 7.107.2–3: ὧν οὕτως ἐχόντων συμφανὲς ἐκ τῆς προγενεστάτης καὶ ἀληθεστάτης ἐκκλησίας τὰς μεταγενεστέρας ταύτας καὶ τὰς ἔτι τούτων ὑποβεβηκυίας τῷ χρόνῳ κεκαινοτομῆσθαι παραχαραχθείσας αἱρέσεις. ἐκ τῶν εἰρημένων ἄρα φανερὸν οἶμαι γεγενῆσθαι μίαν εἶναι τὴν ἀληθῆ ἐκκλησίαν τὴν τῷ ὄντι ἀρχαίαν, εἰς ἣν οἱ κατὰ πρόθεσιν δίκαιοι ἐγκαταλέγονται ("Things being as they are, it is evident that, compared to the original and most true church, these later heresies and those which came still later than the former, have been fake innovations. From what has been said it has become clear then, in my opinion, that the true, the truly old church is one in which those are enrolled who are just according to a divine plan").

[60]Ibid., 7.100.7: Καὶ δὴ τριῶν οὐσῶν διαθέσεων τῆς ψυχῆς, ἀγνοίας, οἰήσεως, ἐπιστήμης, οἱ μὲν ἐν τῇ ἀγνοίᾳ τὰ ἔθνη, οἱ δὲ ἐν τῇ ἐπιστήμῃ ἡ ἐκκλησία ἡ ἀληθής, οἱ δὲ ἐν οἰήσει οἱ κατὰ τὰς αἱρέσεις ("Since there are three dispositions of the soul, ignorance, presumption, and knowledge, those in ignorance are the pagans, those with knowledge the true church, and those with false presumptions the sectarians").

[61]Ibid., 7.92.3: ἀποδείξεως δ᾽ οὔσης ἀνάγκη συγκαταβαίνειν εἰς τὰς ζητήσεις καὶ δι᾽ αὐτῶν τῶν γραφῶν ἐκμανθάνειν ἀποδεικτικῶς, ὅπως μὲν ἀπεσφάλησαν αἱ αἱρέσεις, ὅπως δὲ ἐν μόνῃ τῇ ἀληθείᾳ καὶ τῇ ἀρχαίᾳ ἐκκλησίᾳ ἥ τε ἀκριβεστάτη

The use of αἵρεσις here twice in the same sentence is striking: first to mean "heresy," and then "way of thinking" or "school of thought." It is the only occasion on which Clement equated αἵρεσις with his church, and he clearly does so only as a play on words, in order to make a point, since elsewhere αἵρεσις is a word that Clement uses to characterize his opponents.[62]

To distinguish the church from other gatherings, Clement claims that the true church bases itself on its right interpretation of scriptures, the legitimacy of its rule and tradition, and its guardianship of liturgical celebrations.[63] (He makes a noteworthy early critique of improper eucharistic and baptismal practices.) In another passage delineating his view on the church, Clement says:

> In addition, we know that the name "heresies" has to be used as a contrast to the truth, from which the "sophists" tore off a part to damage people and kept it buried in their human techniques of sophistry. They plume themselves as being prominent, but more in a "school" (διατριβή) than in a church.[64]

The language here denotes Greek philosophical schools; elsewhere Clement uses the word διατριβή specifically to indicate them.[65] The so-called sophists, however, are no outsiders; they are either individuals or a group within the Christian community of whom Clement disapproves. His exclusivist concept of ἐκκλησία was central for the way he perceived his own com-

---

γνῶσις καὶ ἡ τῷ ὄντι ἀρίστη αἵρεσις.

[62]Clement uses αἵρεσις also for Greek philosophical schools, but more usually for heretical schools. Another word with the same meaning is σχολή, which Clement seems to apply only to heretical schools and not to Greek schools, see *Strom.* 3.92.1 (for Tatian); 4.71.1 (for Heracleon); both texts name Valentinus as the founder of the "school."

[63]See *Strom.* 1.96.1: "καὶ τοῖς ἐνδεέσι φρενῶν παρακελεύομαι λέγουσα," φησὶν ἡ σοφία, τοῖς ἀμφὶ τὰς αἱρέσεις δηλονότι, "ἄρτων κρυφίων ἡδέως ἅψασθε, καὶ ὕδατος κλοπῆς γλυκεροῦ," ἄρτον καὶ ὕδωρ οὐκ ἐπ' ἄλλων τινῶν, ἀλλ' ἢ ἐπὶ τῶν ἄρτῳ καὶ ὕδατι κατὰ τὴν προσφορὰν μὴ κατὰ τὸν κανόνα τῆς ἐκκλησίας χρωμένων αἱρέσεων ἐμφανῶς ταττούσης τῆς γραφῆς. εἰσὶ γὰρ οἳ καὶ ὕδωρ ψιλὸν εὐχαριστοῦσιν ("and 'I encourage,' wisdom says, 'speaking to those who are without sense' [Prov 9:16], clearly those who are associated with heresies, 'touch the secret loaves with pleasure and the sweet water of theft' [Prov 9:17]; scripture clearly does not apply the words 'bread and water' to any others than the heresies who use bread and water in their offering not according to the rule of the church. For some even celebrate the eucharist with plain water.")

[64]Ibid., 7.92.7: καὶ ὅτι τῶν αἱρέσεων ἀνάγκη τὴν ὀνομασίαν πρὸς ἀντιδιαστολὴν τῆς ἀληθείας λέγεσθαι γινώσκομεν ἀφ' ἧς τινὰ ἀποσπάσαντες ἐπὶ λύμῃ τῶν ἀνθρώπων οἱ σοφισταί ταῖς ἐξευρημέναις σφίσιν ἀνθρωπικαῖς τέχναις ἐγκατορύξαντες· αὐχοῦσι προΐστασθαι διατριβῆς μᾶλλον ἢ ἐκκλησίας. On this passage, see Alain Le Boulluec, *La notion d'hérésie dans la littérature grecque, IIe–IIIe siècles* (2 vols.; Paris: Études Augustiniennes, 1985) 389, 413.

[65]See, for example, *Strom.* 1.39.5; 1.63.2; 1.79.3; 5.57.3.

munity; he did not wish to compare it to any other establishment or tradition such as a "school" or "school of thought."

Clement was, however, by no means unbiased in his claim to represent the one, undivided church.[66] His opponents obviously might have made the same claims. This rivalry reflects a period in which communities struggled for existence, identity, and dominance. Within these groups there were also diverse factions competing for influence. Even if some of these groups were not inclined to think in institutional terms,[67] they still could claim to possess the exclusive path to knowledge or salvation. Clement certainly saw them as making such claims.[68]

This competition may explain Clement's avoidance of the term διδασκαλεῖον to characterize his own community. As in Irenaeus, the term commonly characterized a heretical religious group. Clement may not have wanted to invite comparison with other "schools," whose claims he considered false. He may, for the same reason, have avoided words such as σχολή, διατριβή, or αἵρεσις to characterize his church.[69]

Clement was not the only member of the Alexandrian tradition to be reticent about naming its educational activity. Origen also fails to connect the word *didaskaleion* with his own teaching, at least in the works for which the Greek text has survived. The word occurs once as a descriptor of the "venerable school of the Pythagoreans."[70] Elsewhere he uses the word *school* metaphorically, for example, when he speaks about paradise. He characterizes this as an "auditorium and school," in which the souls learn about things on earth and things to come.[71] Whether the term

[66]Lampe (*Die stadtrömischen Christen in den ersten beiden Jahrhunderten* [Tübingen: Mohr, 1987] 313–14) distinguishes between the terminology that Christians used to characterize themselves within their community (the term "church" functions in this sense for Clement) and that which they used to present themselves to the outside world.

[67]Klaus Koschorke, *Die Polemik der Gnostiker gegen das kirchliche Christentum* (Leiden: Brill, 1987) 67–71.

[68]Alain Le Boulluec has studied these heresiological debates, tracing recurrent patterns of accusations in the works of Justin, Hegesippus, Irenaeus, Clement, and Origen. He also attempts to define whether these accusations are directed to real or fictitious opponents; see Alain Le Boulluec, *La notion d'hérésie.*

[69]For the equation of Christian groups with philosophical schools or other societies, see Robert Lewis Wilken, "Kollegien, Philosophenschulen und Theologie," in Wayne A. Meeks, ed., *Zur Sozologie des Urchristentums* (Munich: Kaiser, 1979) 165–93.

[70]*Cels.* 3.51. The same text is included in idem, *Philocal.* 18, 22.

[71]*Princ.* 2.11.6: Puto enim quod sancti quique discedentes ex hac vita permanebunt in loco aliquo in terra posito, quem 'paradisum' dixit scriptura divina, velut in quodam eruditionis loco et, ut ita dixerim, auditorio vel schola animarum, in quo de omnibus his, quae in terris viderant, doceantur. . . ("For I think that the holy ones when they depart from this life will stay in some place on earth, which holy scripture called 'paradise,' as in some place of learning, and, so to speak, auditorium or school for the souls, in which they may be taught about all that they had seen on earth. . .").

diaskaleion denoted the Alexandrian instruction even in Origen's time remains to be seen, since the primary information on this comes once again from Eusebius.[72]

The uncertainty about a formal title for the school persists, for Eusebius himself is inconsistent in his terminology when dealing with the education of the Alexandrian church. He applies a multitude of terms to the same functions quite indiscriminately. The term *didaskaleion* is common, but in a series of variations: διδασκαλεῖον τῶν ἱερῶν λόγων ("school of the sacred words"),[73] τὸ διδασκαλεῖον τῆς ἱερᾶς πίστεως ("the school of the sacred faith"),[74] τὸ ἐν ᾽Αλεξανδρείᾳ κατηχητικὸν διδασκαλεῖον ("the catechetical school in Alexandria"),[75] τὸ κατ᾽ ᾽Αλεξάνδρειαν διδασκαλεῖον ("the school in Alexandria"),[76] τὸ τῆς κατηχήσεως διδασκαλεῖον ("the school of instruction").[77] Many other terms, however, seem to be interchangeable with those that incorporate *didaskaleion*: ἡ τῶν πιστῶν διατριβή ("the school of the faithful"),[78] ἡ διατριβὴ τῆς χατηχήσεως ("the school of instruction"),[79] ἡ τοῦ κατηχεῖν διατριβή ("the school of instruction"),[80] ἡ διατριβή ("the school"),[81] ἡ σχολή ("the school"),[82] τὸ κατηχεῖν ("the instruction"),[83] ἡ κατ᾽ ᾽Αλεξάνδρειαν κατήχησις ("the instruction in Alexandria"),[84] τὸ ἔργον τῆς κατηχήσεως ἐπὶ τῆς ᾽Αλεξανδρείας ("the work of instruction in Alexandria"),[85] τὰ συνήθη τῆς κατηχήσεως ("the customary activities of instruction").[86] Even when Eusebius speaks about instruction in the period after Origen's departure from Alexandria—that is, in the mid-third century, in the time of Heraclas and Dionysius—he employs the term διατριβὴ τῆς χαταχήσεως along with phrases modifying διδασκαλεῖον.[87] This flexible vocabulary may well indicate that there still was no fixed name for the school.

[72]Nautin (*Origène: Sa vie et son oeuvre*, 39 n.6) notices that in the passage about Origen becoming head of the catechetical school at the age of eighteen (*Hist. eccl.* 6.3.3), Eusebius used his own words, which were not based on Origen's report.

[73]Eusebius *Hist. eccl.* 5.10.1 (Pantenus).

[74]Ibid., 7.32.30 (Pierius).

[75]*Antiquorum martyriorum collectio (fragmenta)*, (PG 20) 1524, 1.18 (Origen).

[76]Eusebius *Hist. eccl.* 5.10.4 (Pantenus).

[77]Ibid., 6.3.3 (Origen); 6.26.1 (Origen and Heraclas).

[78]Ibid., 5.10.1 (Pantenus).

[79]Ibid., 6.29.4 (Heraclas and Dionysius).

[80]Ibid., 6.3.8 (Origen).

[81]Ibid., 6.3.1 (Origen), and 6.4.3 (martyrs from the school of Origen; Heraclides and Heron).

[82]Ibid., 6.4.3 (martyrs from the school of Origen; Serenus).

[83]Ibid., 6.3.1 (Origen).

[84]Ibid., 6.6.1 (Pantenus, Clement, Origen).

[85]Ibid., 6.8.1, 3 (Origen).

[86]Ibid., 6.14.11 (Origen).

[87]Ibid., 6.29.4 (Heraclas and Dionysius); 7.32.30 (Pierius); see notes 79 and 74 above.

The nomenclature of the school aside, it seems clear that teaching and scholarship within the penumbra of the church was a long-established activity in Alexandria well before Origen. Eusebius's characterization of the early school's curriculum as consisting of interpreting scripture and teaching catechism, corresponds closely to Clement's activities as they emerge from his writings. Eusebius's claim that Clement engaged in catechetical instruction seems, therefore, amply justified. In general, Eusebius's measured comments on the Alexandrian succession and school are verifiable, right down to the ambiguity of its terminology.

Modern scholarly discussions of these early Alexandrian teachers have often drawn comparisons with Justin Martyr to illustrate how an "independent" Christian teacher would operate. In a compelling study, however, Peter Lampe has provided a new view of Justin's position in the Roman setting.[88] He bases his work not only on literary, but also epigraphical and archeological sources that give his reconstructions a fresh perspective.[89] He views the Christian communities around the year 160 as fragmented groups that were scattered around the city in various house churches but that maintained some sort of relationship with one another. He points out that the *Acts of Justin* shows how Justin conducted teaching activities from his house; even the name of the place where Justin lived, "above the bath of Myrtinus," survives, although its actual location remains unknown.[90] Lampe characterizes the group around Justin as a variant of the house church, namely a house church around a teacher, and thus a school church with common religious activities, such as meals. He also suggests that each of these Christian communities at Rome, including the one around Justin, could have had its own officials. He includes not only Justin but also Tatian, Cerdo, Apelles, and some Valentinians in this category of teachers around whom Christian groups gathered.[91]

Peter Lampe's reconstruction of the situation in Rome is attractive because it overcomes some traditional stumbling blocks. Applying a model

[88]Lampe, *Die stadtrömischen Christen.*

[89]Georg Schöllgen ("Probleme der frühchristlichen Sozialgeschichte," *JAC* 32 [1989] 23–40, with thanks to François Bovon for the reference) who reviews the work by Lampe, is too harsh in his critique. He avers that there are "too many unknowns" on which Lampe bases himself. In Schöllgen's view, it would have been better if Lampe had selected more limited sources of another city, such as Carthage, with more homogeneous information. In his criticism of Lampe's "methodological sloppyness" [sic] Schöllgen even goes so far as to call the dissertation "a failure," although he does concede that the book provides an almost unexhaustible source of material. From my point of view, the book is, on the contrary, an important and original attempt to bring very diverse materials into a new perspective, and Rome with its relative wealth of information seems a sensible and logical choice of subject. The wealth of material that this study contains more than compensates for any shortcomings.

[90]Lampe, *Die stadtrömischen Christen*, 238.

[91]Ibid., 316–18.

along the lines of that sketched in Rome for Justin and his companions gives the situation in Alexandria an interesting twist. It clarifies how various groups meeting in private houses could perceive themselves as churches. It also gives insight into how instruction coincided with other liturgical functions, a reality to which others have pointed in the practices of Origen.[92] The union of liturgical and didactic functions is, of course, best fulfilled by a priest, and this seems to have been the situation of both Clement and Pantenus. In a letter preserved by Eusebius, Alexander, bishop of Jerusalem, a friend and former pupil of Clement, calls him a presbyter.[93] Furthermore, Clement refers to his mentor Pantenus as a presbyter.[94] Although much scholarly effort has been dedicated to dismissing any ecclesiastical significance to the term, there seems to be no compelling reason not to translate it "priest."[95] The argument against a straightforward interpretation

[92]Auf der Maur and Waldram, "Illuminatio Verbi Divini."

[93]Alexander in a letter to the church in Antioch, see Eusebius *Hist. eccl.* 6.11.6.

[94]See Clement, *Prot.* 113.1 (πρεσβύτεροι); *Ecl. proph.* 50.1 (πρεσβύτης); *Fragm.* 22 (3.201.26; Eusebius *Hist. eccl.* 6.14.2–4, ὁ μακάριος πρεσβύτερος); *Fragm.* in 1 John 1:1 (3.210.1, presbyter); also *Strom.* 1.11.2 (the true Sicilian bee), and *Ecl. proph.* 56.2 ("our Pantenus"). In another letter Alexander calls Pantenus and Clement μακάριος ("blessed") and ἱερός ("holy"), see Eusebius, *Hist. eccl.* 6.14.9 (cf. Clement *Fragm.* 22 above). Origen only terms Pantenus a predecessor: "τὸν πρὸ ἡμῖν πολλοὺς ὠφελήσαντα Πάνταινον..." (see a letter of Origen in Eusebius, *Hist. eccl.* 6.19.13).

[95]The words πρεσβύτης, πρεσβύτερος, or πρεσβύτεροι occur often in Clement's writings. Several meanings in addition to "older, venerable person" in a general sense, are distinguishable: (a) As indicated in the previous note, "presbyter" sometimes stands for Pantenus. Theoretically, Clement could have been referring to any old man or men, but combining the term with a philosophical concept or a biblical interpretation makes an allusion to Pantenus very likely. In most of these cases, Eusebius had already interpreted the term as a reference to Pantenus, a link that modern scholars have generally accepted. Eusebius also informs us that in the lost *Hypotyposes* Clement mentioned his teacher by name and referred to his interpretations of Scripture (*Hist. eccl.* 5.11.2; 6.13.2). In this context, Méhat brought up another rather extensive passage, *Strom.* 6.106–7, in which Clement gives a eulogy of the perfect gnostic, whom he calls πρεσβύτερος. Méhat argued that this "presbyter and true servant of the will of God" represents Pantenus as well (Méhat, *Étude sur les "Stromates" de Clément d'Alexandrie*, 56–58). b) The word πρεσβύτεροι can also refer to the Israelites of scripture, or to the Jews in their relationship with the law (*Paed.* 1.59.1, 1.84.2, 3.75.3; *Strom.* 3.90.20. (c) The word can also mean "people in the immediate circle of the apostles," who received oral traditions in contrast to written texts (*Ecl. proph.* 11.1; 27.1, 4). The same usage appears in the fragment of Papias, preserved in Eusebius (*Hist. eccl.* 3.39.4). For Clement, the transmission of church traditions from the apostles is an important instrument for the right interpretation of scripture and is a protection against "heretical" teaching. It seems unjustified to conclude from these passages in the *Eclogae* that Pantenus could have left no written works, as Neymeyr and Scholten suggested, since the passages do not refer to Pantenus (Neymeyr, *Die christlichen Lehrer*, 45 n. 52; Scholten, "Die alexandrinische Katechetenschule," 36–37, n. 126). (d) In addition to the aforementioned texts in which Clement alludes to Pantenus, the word is used as "priest" in the church, often in combination with other titles, such as ἐπίσκοπος ("bishop"), διάκονος ("deacon"), χήρα ("widow"), or λαϊκός ("layman"); some texts com-

of πρεσβύτερος is even based in part on an emendation of the Clementine text by Stählin.[96] Adapting the reconstruction of Lampe for Alexandria around the time of Clement's residence there reinforces the idea that these men had a liturgical role in a Christian community. It even raises the possibility that Clement and Pantenus could have been the center around which a community congregrated. Furthermore, there is evidence that presbyters may have had a position of particular strength in Alexandria in Clement's time, since in one of his letters, Jerome remarks that at the beginning of the third century the Christian communities there were represented by a group of presbyters, who elected one of themselves episcopus: in a certain sense, first among equals.[97] The application of ἐπίσκοπος and πρεσβύτερος to the same

pare the earthly functions in the church to the heavenly hierarchy; see *Paed.* 3.63.1; 3.97.2; *Strom.* 3.90.1; 6.106.2 (three times); 6.107.2, 3; 7.3.3; *Quis div. salv.* 42.4. This last passage gives an interesting insight in Clement's usage, since he calls the same person at first ἐπίσκοπος and then πρεσβύτερος. For Clement, at least in his rendering of the story of Saint John and the robber, the distinction between ἐπίσκοπος and πρεσβύτερος is not all that clear.

[96]See *Paed.* 1.37.3: Πῶς οὖν οὐ ταύτη νοεῖν τὸν ἀπόστολον ὑποληπτέον τὸ γάλα τῶν νηπίων, εἴ τε ποιμένες ἐσμεν οἱ τῶν ἐκκλησιῶν προηγούμενοι κατ᾿ εἰκόνα τοῦ ἀγαθοῦ ποιμένος, τὰ δὲ πρόβατα ‹ὑμεῖς›, μὴ οὐχὶ καὶ γάλα τῆς ποίμνης τὸν κύριον λέγοντα τὴν ἀκολουθίαν φυλάττειν ἀλληγοροῦντα ("How should we not suppose that the apostle meant the milk of the little children here, if, according to the image of the good shepherd, we who preside over the churches are shepherds and you the sheep; does he not want to preserve the coherence of the allegorical language when he says that the Lord is milk of the herd [cf. 1 Cor 9:7]?"); for a discussion of Stählin's emendation [ἐσ]μὲν for ἐσμεν and related textual problems, see Méhat, *Étude sur les "Stromates" de Clément d'Alexandrie*, 55 and n. 54; I prefer to read ὑμεῖς, since this "slip of the pen" (ἡμεῖς for ὑμεῖς) occurs very frequently and is easy to explain; see *Strom.* 4.4.1; 4.33.4; 4.87.4. The first to question Clement's priesthood was Hugo Koch ("War Klemens von Alexandrien ein Priester?" *ZAW* 20 [1921] 43–48), but his arguments were disputed by Friedrich Quatember, *Die christliche Lebenshaltung des Klemens von Alexandrien nach seinenmPädagogus* (Vienna: Herder, 1946). Modern scholarship has partly accepted the idea of Clement's status as a priest; see Pierre Nautin, *Lettres et écrivains chrétiens des IIe et IIIe siècles* (Paris: Cerf, 1961) 117–18, 140; Méhat, *Études sur les "Stromates" de Clément d'Alexandrie*, 55–58; Neymeyr, *Die christlichen Lehrer*, 48–49 (for the period in Jerusalem). Others, such as van den Broek, "Christian 'School' of Alexandria," 43, still sustain Koch's position.

[97]Jerome *Epist.* 146.1.6: "presbyteri semper unum ex se electum et in excelsiori gradu conlocatum episcopum nominabant, quomodo si exercitus imperatorem faciat aut diaconi eligant de se, quem industrium noverint, et archidiaconum vocent. quid enim facit excepta ordinatione episcopus, quod presbyter non facit?" ("The presbyters always appointed one who was elected from their own ranks and put in a higher position as bishop, in the way in which, if this is the case, the army creates an emperor or deacons elect from themselves someone whom they have known as industrious and whom they call archdeacon. For what, except for the ordination, does a bishop do that a presbyter does not?") Everett Ferguson (in a letter) points out that Clement has the rather unusual pairing of πρεσβύτερος and διάκονος without ἐπίσκοπος (see *Strom.* 3.90.1; 7.3.3); this might be another indication for the prominence of the role of the presbyter. For a discussion of the early organization of the Alexandrian

person in Clement's *Quis dives salvetur* seems to indicate that the terms were still interchangeable in his time and environment, just as they had been in Rome for *1 Clement* and *Hermas*.[98] Lampe maintains that in the Roman context ἐπίσκοποι were πρεσβύτεροι with particular functions, one of which was to represent the Roman Christian community as a whole to outside churches.[99] This presbyterial format, however, was about to change. A more centralized system was just around the corner or had already begun to function in Clement's time.[100] Scholars have suggested that the power struggle known from Origen a generation later could have had antecedents in the Alexandria of Pantenus and Clement. It may have been one of the reasons for the latter's departure from the city.[101]

■ Philo

At last it is possible to consider how Philo fits into this picture of a Christian teaching tradition. How could it be that the famous Jewish biblical philosopher connects with and is even saved from oblivion by an obscure group of Christians, over a century and a half after his death? As is well known, Clement and Origen were acquainted with Philo's works. They used his biblical interpretations and followed his Platonic ways of thinking. This combination, in which the Platonic underpinnings corroborate their biblical explorations, may represent their greatest debt to Philo.[102]

church, see Everett Ferguson, *Ordination in the Ancient Church: An Examination of the Theological and Constitutional Motifs in the Light of Biblical and Gentile Sources* (Ph.D. diss., Harvard University, 1959); idem, "Origen and the Election of Bishops," *CH* 43 (1974) 26–33. For a listing of ancient sources and further bibliography, see Roelof van den Broek, "Juden und Christen in Alexandrien im 2. und 3. Jahrhundert," in Jacobus van Amersfoort and Johannes van Oort, eds., *Juden und Christen in der Antike* (Kampen: Kok, 1990) 108 and n. 25.

[98]*Quis div. salv.* 42.4; see above note 95 (end). For Rome, see Lampe, *Die stadtrömischen Christen*, 336–37. Irenaeus shows the same usage, see *Adv. haer.* 4.26.2. The interchangeability, however, does not go both ways: bishops were also presbyters, but not all presbyters were bishops (with thanks to Everett Ferguson for pointing this out).

[99]Lampe, *Die stadtrömischen Christen*, 336–45 suggests that contact among the various house churches was kept by representatives who met in regular conventions. He explains how through the delegation of tasks the presbyterial system became gradually more monarchic, since certain tasks were more important than others. The pressure of conflict may also have been a reason to have more centralized authority.

[100]As recent studies show, the creation of a monarchic episcopacy probably took much longer than previously thought; for the situation in Rome, see the study of Allen Brent, *Hippolytus and the Roman Church in the Third Century: Communities in Tension before the Emergence of a Monarch-Bishop* (vc suppl. 31; Leiden: Brill, 1995).

[101]As Nautin (*Lettres et écrivains chrétiens des IIe et IIIe siècles*, 18, 140) speculates.

[102]For Clement, see Annewies van den Hoek, *Clement of Alexandria and His Use of Philo in the Stromateis: An Early Christian Reshaping of a Jewish Model* (Leiden: Brill, 1988); Runia, *Philo in Early Christian Literature*, 132–56; for Origen, ibid., 157–83; idem, *Philo and the Church Fathers: A Collection of Papers* (Leiden: Brill, 1995) 117–25.

Some scholars have argued that Alexandrian Christianity came out of Judaism and that this Jewish background remained a major influence.[103] This may have been true before the Jewish revolt (115–117) and its suppression by Trajan.[104] By the late second century, however, events had radically attenuated that continuity. In all likelihood, Clement and Origen's link with Philo and other Jewish Hellenistic or Jewish Christian sources was primarily a literary one. Clement does not reflect living contacts with Jewish scholars,[105] although Origen does to some extent, particularly in his later years in Caesarea. Even Christian authors of the time of Hadrian and the Antonines reveal no clear signs of a relationship with a Jewish or Jewish Christian ambience. The fragments of the works of Basilides and Valentinus show that they had primarily a Greek intellectual training. Such writers may have served as a link between Philo and the later Christian Alexandrian tradition, but the nature and extent of this transmission remain uncertain.[106] Although Clement does not always view predecessors such as

[103]See Albertus F. J . Klijn, "Jewish Christianity in Egypt," in Birger Pearson and James E. Goehring, eds., *The Roots of Egyptian Christianity* (Philadelphia: Fortress, 1986) 114–75; also Roelof van den Broek, "Jewish and Platonic Speculations in Early Alexandrian Theology: Eugnostos, Philo, Valentinus, and Origen," in Pearson and Goering, *Roots of Egyptian Christianity*, who uses the Jewish gnostic writing *Eugnostus the Blessed* from the Nag Hammadi Corpus to elucidate the nature of God in the writings of Philo, Valentinus, and Origen. For a discussion of his arguments and particularly of the problem of dating, see Christoph Markschies, *Valentinus Gnosticus?* (WUNT, 65; Tübingen: Mohr/Siebeck, 1992) 320–22. This issue is also discussed by Pearson ("Christians and Jews in First-Century Alexandria," in George W. Nickelsburg and George W. MacRae, eds., *Christians Among Jews and Gentiles: Essays in Honor of Krister Stendahl on His Sixty-fifth Birthday* [Philadelphia: Fortress, 1986] 206–16) in relation to the *Epistle of Barnabas* and the *Teachings of Silvanus*; these writings, however, are plagued by uncertainties as to both place of origin and date.

[104]The revolt started in the summer of 115 and ended around August or September of 117, the beginning of Hadrian's reign. Jews from all over the diaspora, including not only Egypt, but also Cyrenaica, Cyprus, Mesopotamia, and possibly Judea were involved; see Joseph Mélèze-Modrezejewski, *Le Juifs d'Egypte: De Ramsès à Hadrien* (Paris: Éditions Errance, 1991) 161–81, 203. Cf. Eusebius, *Hist. eccl.* 4.2.1–5.

[105]Revealing in this respect is a look at Stählin's index (*Clemens Alexandrinus vierter Band: Register* [GCS 39; Leipzig, 1936]) 100 s.v. Ἑβραῖος. Only on a few occasions do the words Ἰουδαῖος or Ἰουδαῖοι seem to refer to living people.

[106]See Winrich Alfried Löhr (*Basilides und seine Schule* [WUNT, 83; Tübingen: Mohr/ Siebeck, 1996] 332–33), who gives an assessment of Basilides and his circle in Alexandria. Birger Pearson has raised the possibility that Basilides and Isidor were in charge of the Alexandrian school before Pantenus; see his *Gnosticism, Judaism and Egyptian Christianity* (Minneapolis: Fortress, 1990) 210. In this context it is noteworthy that Basilides is not a "heavy user" of Septuagint texts nor of the Pentateuch in particular, see ibid., 328. Any discussion about a possible connection with Philo should take this diverse orientation into consideration. Markschies (*Valentinus Gnosticus?*, 323, 404) cautiously suggests that Valentinus could have been an intermediary between Philo and the later Alexandrian Christian writers. See also the recent article of Gilles Quispel, "The Original Doctrine of Valentinus the Gnos-

Basilides and Valentinus in a negative light, he obviously does not consider them his predecessors. Their role as mediators becomes even more questionable in light of their absence from Origen's list of "predecessors," which leaps from Philo to Pantenus and Clement.[107]

Whatever happened around the time of Hadrian, the traditional watershed in Jewish and Christian Alexandria, the living contacts with Judaism seem to have vanished thereafter. The connection with the Hellenistic Jewish intellectual and literary tradition is a different matter. Philo's works were presumably famous and important enough to merit collection by a major library, where anyone of erudition could have consulted them.[108] The question of libraries is urgent, not only in the case of Philo's works but even more so for some other, more obscure writings that both Clement and Origen cite. Some of these sources lack the sophistication and intellectual attraction that Philo would have offered to both Jewish and non-Jewish Greek readers. There seems to be no reason why these minor texts should have been part of a library accessible to the general public.[109]

It seems likely, then, that there existed a Christian library or libraries that preserved not only texts for liturgical readings, but also works that served the intellectual needs of biblical interpreters like Clement and Origen. It is revealing to see how seriously and meticulously these scholars dealt with scriptural interpretations. Their working techniques often come down to questions of commas and periods. They asked themselves whether they should pause in a sentence, or why a particular preposition appears. If the preposition was unusual in Greek—and there were occasional "Aramaisms" to overcome—their next question would be what implications such an oddity

---

tic," *VC* 50/4 (1996) 339–42.

[107]Origen identifies Philo three times by name and mentions him as a predecessor on thirteen other occasions at least; see Runia, *Philo in Early Christian Literature*, 160–62. In a letter that Eusebius preserved in *Hist. eccl.* 6.19.13, Origen calls Pantenus a predecessor. Origen alludes to Clement as a predecessor at least four times; see Annewies van den Hoek, "Origen and the Intellectual Heritage of Alexandria: Continuity or Disjunction," in Robert J. Daly, ed., *Origeniana quinta* (Leuven: Peeters, 1992) 47–50. The passages are: *Comm. in Matt.* 12.31; 14.2; *Comm. in Joh.* 2.25; *Comm. Rm* 1.1. Compare also the remarks of Alexander in a letter to Origen (in Eusebius *Hist. eccl.* 6.14.8), in which the former mentions the friendship that both he and Origen received from their predecessors Pantenus and Clement; also Harnack, *Geschichte der altchristlichen Literatur*, 2. 4 n. 6.

[108]See also Eusebius's remark that citizens of Rome admired Philo's words so much that they placed them in libraries (*Hist. eccl.* 2.18.8). It remains unclear whether Eusebius refers only to the *Legatio ad Gaium* or to other Philonic writing as well.

[109]Many obscure writers or texts occur, especially in Clement; see the indices of quotations in the Stählin editions. It is of some significance that Clement cites his "gnostic" opponents rather literally; this also shows that he had their works, or excerpts from them, at hand, see Annewies van den Hoek, "Techniques of Quotation in Clement of Alexandria: A View of Ancient Literary Techniques," *VC* 50 (1996) 233 and 237 (table).

had for the meaning.[110] These exegetes assumed that everything in biblical language had a high purpose and was explicable, if not straightforwardly in literal terms, then along the allegorical paths of the spirit. Thus every minute detail of the scriptural text proved meaningful for the interpretive eye. This tradition of meticulous reading and interpretation is a very characteristic feature of Alexandrian Christian writing.[111] Rabbinic interpretative techniques could have been influential in developing this approach. The problem is, however, that the Christian writers were Greeks without a Jewish upbringing or even, in the case of Clement, much contact with a living Jewish tradition. Their knowledge of Jewish biblical interpretations, therefore, must have derived primarily from their reading, while the world of Greek grammarians provided them with some other tools.

The question of a Christian library is related to that of the existence of a scriptorium, which would have preserved, enlarged, and disseminated the library's collection. The hypothesis of a major Christian scriptorium in Alexandria has merit because the textual transmission of not only the Philonic corpus but also the epistles of Paul and other early Christian writings trace back to second century Alexandria.[112] It seems likely that such an enterprise of collating, editing, and copying texts would have had links to a school of biblical scholarship, but whether such a scriptorium originated in Pantenus's time or even earlier remains unclear.[113]

Alexandrian Christian writers named Philo as part of their own tradition, and it is clear that they meant by that much more than that someone had stumbled upon some interesting leftover scrolls.[114] Origen, in fact, identi-

[110]See Clement, *Strom.* 4.70–73; Origen, *Comm. in Joh.* 2 (21) 137; Annewies van den Hoek, "Clement of Alexandria on Martyrdom," 331 and n. 32.

[111]Related to the question of accurate reading is Origen's adaptation of the system of marginal signs; see Leighten Reynold and Nigel Wilson, *Scribes and Scholars* (2d ed.; Oxford: Clarendon, 1974) 43. For the importance of the Bible for Clement's thinking, see Claude Mondésert, *Clément d'Alexandrie: Introduction à l'étude de sa pensée religieuse à partir de l'écriture* (Paris: Éditions Montaigne, 1944).

[112]For the Pauline corpus, cf. Gunther Zunz, *The Text of the Epistles: A Disquisition upon the Corpus Paulinum* (London: Oxford University Press, 1953) 271–72; for works of Philo, see Dominique Barthélemy, "Est-ce Hoshaya Rabba qui censura le 'Commentaire Allégorique'? À partir des retouches faites aux citations bibliques, étude sur la tradition textuelle du Commentaire Allégorique de Philon," in *Philon d'Alexandrie* (Paris: CNRS, 1967) 60; for various papyri, see Colin H. Roberts, *Manuscript, Society and Belief in Early Christian Egypt* (London: Oxford University Press, 1979) 24; for NT MSS, Kurt Aland and Barbara Aland, *The Text of the New Testament* (Grand Rapids: Eerdmans, 1987) 59.

[113]See Joseph de Ghellinck (*Patristique et Moyen Age: Études d'histoire littéraire et doctrinale* [Paris: Brouwer, 1947] 264), who refers to the Ptolomaic example for any subsequent libraries in Alexandria; see also Dominique Barthélemy, *Études d'histoire du texte de l'Ancien Testament* (Fribourg: Éditions universitaires, 1978) 203–17; Guglielmo Cavallo, *Le biblioteche nel mondo antico e medievale* (Rome: Laterza, 1993) 67.

[114]Runia (*Philo in Early Christian Literature*, 135), who refers to Barthélemy ("Est-ce

fied Philo as one of his predecessors even more explicitly than he did Clement.[115] This tribute has special significance, since Origen's original and independent thought rarely made use of material from other writers. When he does quote others, he is uncommonly scrupulous in acknowledging his debt, and Philo is among the few meriting citation.[116] The work of Philo seems thus to have been a fixture in the libraries of both Clement and Origen. May one presume that Philo's works were already standard assets in Alexandrian libraries of previous decades? Unfortunately, this remains an open question. Origen saw to it that this bibliographic tradition continued to spread, for when he moved to Caesarea taking his books and scrolls with him, his collection included Philo.[117] His library was to become the basis of that of Pamphilus and Eusebius, and some of the extant medieval manuscripts of Philo were copies of texts transmitted through the Caesarean library.[118]

The first documented Christian library was in Jerusalem, founded by Clement's pupil, Alexander.[119] There is no explicit evidence of a Christian library in Alexandria at that time, but since Alexander studied there before going to Jerusalem, it seems plausible that he found his model in that city.[120] As just mentioned, Origen had a private collection of books, some of which he sold because he could not or did not want to keep up with Greek literature (and he even expresses pleasure at the financial benefits he

---

Hoshaya Rabba," 60).

[115]See above, note 107.

[116]Another example is Hermas, whom Origen quotes nineteen times, almost always mentioning his name, see Annewies van den Hoek, "Clement and Origen as Sources on 'Noncanonical' Scriptural Traditions During the Late Second and Earlier Third Centuries," in Gilles Dorival and Alain Le Boulluec, eds. *Origeniana sexta: Origène et la Bible/Origen and the Bible* (Leuven: Peeters, 1995) 98–99.

[117]Harry Y. Gamble (*Books and Readers in the Early Church* [New Haven: Yale University Press, 1995] 157) points out that one can establish the disposition of materials within the library of Caesarea from Eusebius's way of using them. Gamble refers to an interesting study by Hugh Jackson Lawlor (*Eusebiana* [Oxford: Clarendon, 1912]), who tried to reconstruct the Philonic scrolls on the basis of Eusebius's report.

[118]See Leopold Cohn and Paul Wendland, "Prolegomena," in iidem, *Philonis Alexandrini opera quae supersunt* (Berlin: Reimer, 1886) iii–iv. It is also significant that a complete papyrus codex, probably dating to the late third century, was discovered with two of Philo's works at Coptos in a Christian setting and that the text is related to the Caesarean Philonic text tradition; see ibid., xli–xliii; Runia, *Philo in Early Christian Literature*, 23, 298.

[119]Eusebius *Hist. eccl.* 6.20. See Giorgio Pasquali, "Biblioteca," *Enciclopedia Italiana di scienze, lettere ed arti* 6 (1938) 942–47; and the excellent recent study by Gamble (*Books and Readers*, 154).

[120]Not only Alexander but also Pamphilus studied in Alexandria. He was a student at the catechetical school under Pierius, who was called "Origen, the younger"; see Jerome, *De viris illustribus*, 76; Photius, *Bibliotheca*, 119. When Pamphilus came to Caesarea, he expanded the library on the basis of Origen's personal collection.

derived from the sale).[121] His patron Ambrose provided Origen with scribes to produce his manuscripts. Whether others such as Clement had their own libraries or depended upon those of a patron or upon a communal collection is a tantalizing question that remains unanswered for lack of evidence. The preservation of books is pivotal in the discussion of Philo and the Christian tradition in Alexandria. The books that Clement wrote in Alexandria show that he had access to the majority of the Philonic treatises.[122] In the last three *Stromateis* and the other works written after leaving the city, however, the number of citations from Philo drops off considerably; only a few literal quotations from the *Quaestiones in Genesim* remain.[123] It thus seems likely that other libraries were less well furnished and that the presence of books influenced authors' abilities to cite, no matter how highly developed their memory was. Unfortunately, one cannot answer the question of how the Philonic corpus and other Jewish texts ended up in Christian libraries.

In the absence of hard information, one can only speculate about the way in which Philo's manuscripts were transmitted in the later first and second centuries. One among a multitude of possibilities is that some hellenized Jewish groups who studied the scriptures and Jewish-Greek writing in general could have "converted" to Christianity, while keeping their "ancestral" scrolls.[124] Another scenario could be that, during or after the sup-

[121]See Eusebius, *Hist. eccl.* 6.3.9.

[122]Van den Hoek, *Clement of Alexandria and His Use of Philo*, 210.

[123]Pointed out by Runia, *Philo in Early Christian Literature*, 144; for the material, see van den Hoek, *Clement of Alexandria and His Use of Philo*, 197–208.

[124]See Robert M. Grant ("Theological Education at Alexandria," in Birger Pearson and James E. Goehring, eds., *The Roots of Egyptian Christianity* [Philadelphia: Fortress, 1986] 180), who suggests a connection with a community such as the Therapeutae. This group appears in Philo's *De vita contemplativa*, and Philo apparently had a close relationship with it. The Therapeutae lived outside Alexandria, supposedly to the west—between Lake Mareotis and the sea—but not very far from the city. Lake Mareotis, the present Lake Mariut, seems to have been substantially larger in Antiquity; see William Smith and George Grove, *An Atlas of Ancient Geography: Biblical and Classical* (London: Murray, 1875) map 33. Eusebius portrayed the Therapeutae as early Christians, an obviously erroneous reconstruction of the group, at least, for Philo's lifetime; see Eusebius, *Hist. eccl.* 2.17.3–24. In Late Antiquity a number of Coptic monasteries existed in that region, the remains of which still seem to be visible. Interestingly, in my Greek course at Harvard, Sister Lois, a Coptic nun, commented on Philo's description of the landscape and climate in *De vita contemplativa*, saying that it fitted the situation of her priory on the north coast very well. This priory is located between 39 and 40 kilometers from Alexandria on the main road to Salum on the Libyan border. The dwellings of the Therapeutae were presumably somewhat closer to Alexandria but in the same region; François Daumas ("La 'solitude' des Therapeutes et les antécédents égyptiens du monachisme chrétien," *Philon d'Alexandrie* [Paris: CNRS, 1967] 349) locates them to the west of modern El Dikheila. In a recent publication G. Peter Richardson ("Philo and Eusebius on Monasteries and Monasticism: The Therapeutae and Kellia," in Bradley H. McLean, ed.,

pression of the Jewish revolt, Christians (among them Jews and non-Jews) might have appropriated or rescued (depending on the perspective) existing book collections.[125] Since both Judaism and Christianity of this period in Alexandria are shrouded in obscurity, one hypothesis is as valid as another.[126]

■ Conclusions

Although it is important to read Eusebius critically, this does not mean that one should dismiss all of his claims. Exchanging Eusebius's alleged reconstructions for equally hard to prove modern versions of them is risky.[127] There is, after all, considerable external support in other ancient authors for

Origins and Method: Toward a New Understanding of Judaism and Christianity [Sheffield: JSOT Press, 1993] 334–59, with thanks to David Runia for the reference) discusses the connection between the Therapeutae and Eusebius, who spent some time in Egypt during the persecutions of Diocletian. He points out that Eusebius could well have interpreted Philo's description of the Therapeutae on the basis of his own experiences in the Egyptian desert. I disagree with Richardson about the possible location of the Therapeutae, who places them on the south shore of Lake Mareotis on the basis of Philo's decription ὅπερ ἐστὶν ὑπὲρ λίμνης Μαρείας κείμενον (MS M has ἐπί instead of ὑπέρ). Citing LSJ, s. v. ὑπέρ, Richardson argues that ὑπέρ with a genitive means "beyond" or "farther inland" in this case. The first meaning that LSJ offers, however, is "over" or "above," namely "on higher ground" and even "on the shore"; see Pindar *Nem.* 765; also Herodotus *Hist.* 6.105. The second meaning "above" or "farther inland" does occur in a geographical context, but LSJ does not fail to notice that in Hellenistic Greek this meaning is more common with an accusative. Indeed, Philo distinguishes between ὑπέρ with a genitive and with an accusative. ὑπέρ with the genitive occurs most commonly in a metaphoric sense: "for," "because of," "concerning," or "in defense of" (passim); on a number of occasions the word has a local meaning, such as ὑπὲρ γῆς "above ground," see *Sacr.* 25; *Her.* 226; *Fuga* 57; *Abr.* 140.1; *Mos.* 1.175; *Dec.* 56.2. When on rare occasions ὑπέρ means "above" in the sense of "beyond," Philo uses the accusative, see *Legum allegoriae* 1.2; *Som.* 1.54; *Spec.leg.* 86.4. Because of other information in Philo's text as well, a location closer to Alexandria seems more likely, first because Philo says explicitly that the Therapeutae live around or near Alexandria: περὶ τὴν Ἀλεξάνδρειαν (*Vita cont.* 21). He also indicates that the location is on a rather low hill, ἐπὶ γεωλόφου χθαμαλωτέρου, which could correspond to the calcareous dunes, and he says that the sea is close by, τοῦ πελάγους ἐγγὺς ὄντος (Ibid., 22). The pleasant sea breeze that he describes would not be noticeable thirty or more kilometers inland. Moreover, the dunes between the lake and the sea are notably higher than the lowlying area south of Lake Mareotis; a depression south of the lake is indicated on the road map of Egypt (Vienna: Freytag & Berndt, 1986, scale 1: 1.000.000). These "literary" observations confirm the actual survey of the area by Daumas, "La 'solitude' des Therapeutae," 350–55.

[125]See also Barthélemy ("Est-ce Hoshaya Rabba," 60), who makes Pantenus's school responsible for the rescue of the Philonic books.

[126]Gregory Sterling presented some other plausible scenarios to the 1996 SBL meeting in New Orleans; his paper entitled "'The School of Sacred Laws': The Social Settings of Philo's Treatises," will appear in *The Studia Philonica Annual,* forthcoming.

[127]The work of Hornschuh ("Das Leben des Origenes," 1–25, 193–214) shows how tricky it is to attempt to determine which part of Eusebius's account is historical and which is not.

Eusebius's account of the school of Alexandria. Both Clement and Origen speak of a continuous tradition, in which they place themselves. The term *didaskaleion* can denote not only an actual locality but also a school tradition. It remains unclear, however, whether the term was in use during their time. When Eusebius speaks of a succession, he is not so far off because he seems to reflect the intention that is implicit in the statements of the very people he describes. Clement calls Pantenus his mentor, and Origen mentions predecessors, among whom are Pantenus, Clement, and (most surprisingly) Philo.

The idea that the schools in the time of Pantenus and Clement were not "official" but "private" undertakings by independent teachers clarifies little. First, the terms *official* and *private* do not easily apply to a situation in which any Christian religious gathering was illegal and thus "unofficial" on its face. Characterizing such a meeting as a school may well have taken away some of its illegitimate edge.[128] Scholars have often cited the situation in Rome at the time of Justin Martyr as comparable, but the relationship of his school to the Christian community is far from clear. Reversing previous views, recent scholarship has asserted that Justin's school itself represented a Roman church community. A similar argument could well be made for the situation in Alexandria in Clement's day.

That the διδάσκαλοι and πρεσβύτεροι continued the role of the elders in the Jewish community is another hypothesis that seems dubious. In the remote past of the first century this may have been the case, but in the almost equally obscure present of the late second century not much of a living Jewish tradition remained, at least not in the sources considered here. Charismatic διδάσκαλοι continued to exist; Origen portrayed them as wandering teachers who went from village to village.[129] Clement and Pantenus do not fit that description; they seem to have had sophisticated messages and operated in one city. That they were laymen rather than ecclesiastical officials is unlikely, since in Clement's time an elaborate system of baptismal instruction seems already to have been in place, and this kind of instruction was part of his curriculum. Both Pantenus and Clement are called πρεσβύτεροι, a term that designates not only an aged person but also indicates a function in the church. Clement uses the same term to describe the church's ministries.[130]

Philo and the Christian school are closely related and, in a sense, they are inseparable. The Philonic corpus owes its preservation to the Christian tradition of Alexandria and its extension via Origen in Caesarea. The link

---

[128]Wilken, "Alexandria: A School of Training for Virtue," 191; and Lampe, *Die stadtrömischen Christen*, 313.

[129]Origen *Cels.* 3.9.

[130]See *Paed.* 3.63.1; *Strom.* 3.90.1; 6.107.2; 7.3.3; *Ecl. proph.* 42.9; cf. note 95 above.

with Philo was no longer with a living Jewish tradition but with a literary heritage. One might never have known any of Philo's works were it not for the Christian Alexandrian tradition, but then again, one might never have heard of a Christian Alexandrian tradition were it not for Philo.

Journal of Ecclesiastical History, Vol. 47, No. 2, April 1996

Justification by Faith in Augustine and Origen

by † C. P. BAMMEL

O rigen and Augustine might be thought to represent opposite extremes in Pauline exegesis. In working out his characteristic understanding of Pauline theology Augustine developed emphases which were different from those of Origen. In his early works of Pauline exegesis of 394–6 a central point for Augustine is the relationship between works of the law and grace. Origen's *Commentary on Romans* develops many Pauline themes, but he takes a more historical approach than Augustine, and a prominent emphasis for him is the relationship between Jews and Gentiles in the divine dispensation.[1] Augustine is an independent thinker, who digests his reading and does not plagiarise. It is not always easy to identify his use of earlier writers. The example to be discussed in the following paper is of particular interest, since it gives us the opportunity of seeing Augustine's reaction to Origen on the central point of justification by faith at a period just before the outbreak of the Pelagian controversy.

Augustine's sermon on Psalm xxxi[2] appears to have been written at a time when he had been reading Origen's *Commentary on Romans* in the abridged Latin version by Rufinus. He uses the fact that the first two verses of this psalm are quoted in Romans iv. 7–8 as an excuse for devoting the first part of his sermon to a discussion of Rom. iv. 1ff. It is apparent from his words at the beginning of the first and second sections

---

It is with great sadness that the Editors of this JOURNAL report the death of the author between submission of this article and its publication.

[1] For comparison of Augustine and Origen in their interpretation of Romans see C. P. Bammel, 'Augustine, Origen and the exegesis of St Paul', *Augustinianum* xxxii (1992), 341–68, and 'Die Juden im Römerbriefkommentar des Origenes', in H. Frohnhofen (ed.), *Christlicher Antijudaismus und jüdischer Antipaganismus*, Hamburg 1990, 145–51. Both these articles are reprinted in C. P. Bammel, *Tradition and exegesis in early Christian writers*, Aldershot 1995. For a study of the characteristic emphases in Origen's exegesis of Romans see Theresia Heither, *Translatio religionis: die Paulusdeutung des Origenes*, Cologne–Vienna 1990, and the review of that book in *Journal of Theological Studies* n.s. xliv (1993), 348–52.

[2] *Enarratio ii in Ps. 31*, CCL xxxviii. 224–44.

that he had given instructions for the passage from Romans to be read out to the congregation.[3]

Augustine starts his sermon with a description of the contents of the psalm as he sees it: 'the grace of God and our justification with no antecedent merits of ours but with the mercy of our Lord God going before us'. He then sketches two opposite pitfalls, on the one side the assumption that, so long as one has faith, God will forgive one however one behaves and whatever sins one commits, on the other side a self-confidence in one's own obedience to the commandments which results in the sin of pride.

Augustine then turns to the Epistle to the Romans, stating that Paul's quotation there gives evidence that the psalm is concerned with that grace by which we are Christians. He then quotes Rom. iv. 1–2 ('Quid ergo dicemus inuenisse Abraham patrem nostrum secundum carnem? Si enim Abraham ex operibus iustificatus est, habet gloriam, sed non ad Deum') and goes on to give a description of pagans who glory in their own works and therefore refuse to be converted. Abraham, he says, was different. At this point comes the passage where Augustine is most obviously using Origen's commentary on Rom. iv. 1–8. Both Fathers are fascinated by the logical progression of Paul's argument here. Origen comments on Paul's dialectical skill and reproduces his argument as follows:[4]

1. 'If the person justified by works does not have glory before God,
2. but Abraham, it is agreed, has glory before God,
3. then it follows that Abraham is justified not by works but by faith (so that necessarily he has glory before God).'

It is worth noting, first, that Origen's second premiss is added by him, not being present in Paul's text, and second that his form of the argument corresponds exactly to Aristotle's recipe for a syllogism in his *Analytica priora*.[5]

The corresponding passage in Augustine is more elaborate. It retains Origen's premisses (1 and 2) and conclusion (3), but states the second premiss (2) several times and makes the first premiss (1) specific to Abraham (following Paul), rather than general: 'It is certainly known to us and obvious that (2) Abraham has glory before God; (1) but if

---

[3] Ibid. 1. 4: 'praecedens hunc psalmum lectio'; 2. 2–3 'apostolus Paulus; unde ipsam lectionem uobis legi uoluimus'.

[4] *De Römerbriefkommentar des Origenes*, ed. Caroline P. Hammond Bammel, ii, Freiburg 1996, iv. 1. 18–21: 'Nam (1) si is qui ex operibus iustificatur non habet gloriam apud Deum, (2) Abraham autem constat habere gloriam apud Deum, (3) ergo non ex operibus sed ex fide iustificatus est Abraham ut necessario habeat gloriam apud Deum.' For the sections of Origen's commentary that will be considered here some Greek fragments survive, but we will concentrate on Rufinus' translation, since this is the version that Augustine used. For the Greek fragments see Jean Scherer, *Le Commentaire d'Origène sur Rom. III. 5–V. 7*, Cairo, 1957.

[5] See also Benson Mates, *Elementary logic*, Oxford 1972, 204ff. and 213ff. (on Stoic logic).

Abraham is justified by works, he has glory but not before God; (2) but he has glory before God; (3) therefore he is not justified by works.'[6] That Augustine follows Origen in this passage was noticed by Schelkle.[7] He did not however carry the comparison further. If one reads the rest of the relevant part of Augustine's sermon together with Origen's *Commentary on Romans* in Rufinus' abridgement a number of parallels emerge. They are on the whole points which Augustine could have thought of for himself. They do not prove anything individually, but taken together I think that they give evidence of Augustine's reading of Origen, and in this case of his appreciative reading and agreement with what he read.

Before we proceed further the question arises whether the dating of Augustine's sermon is compatible with an influence from Origen's *Commentary*. In an earlier article I have argued that Rufinus' translation of this work could have reached Augustine between about 407 and 411 and that its influence is indeed apparent in his earlier anti-Pelagian treatises of 411–12, of which the *De peccatorum meritis et remissione* shows a positive influence from Origen, whereas the *De spiritu et littera* gives evidence of a more critical reaction.[8] There have been various attempts to date Augustine's sermon on Psalm xxxi. Zarb[9] placed it between 411 and 413, arguing that its emphasis on grace has the Pelagians in view and that the opposition to those who say works are unnecessary so long as one has faith associates it with the *De fide et operibus* of 413. Against this De Blic[10] argued that there is no textual similarity to the *De fide et operibus* and that the opponents envisaged as enemies of true humility are not the Pelagians but pagans, philosophers and Donatists. He therefore concluded that the sermon was preached before 411 (but after 396, because it has a 'doctrine trop ferme' to be dated before the *Quaestiones ad Simplicianum*). On the other hand Rondet, in a discussion which makes no reference to De Blic's careful article, took up Zarb's view again and noted a number of links with works dated around 412.[11] The most striking of these is with *De*

---

[6] *Enarratio* 2. 20–31: 'Quia enim fatemur, et ipsa est fides nostra de sancto patriarcha, qui placuit Deo, ut dicamus eum et nouerimus ad Deum habere gloriam, ait apostolus: Certe notum est nobis et manifestum, quia (2) Abraham ad Deum habet gloriam; (1) at si ex operibus iustificatus est Abraham, habet gloriam, sed non ad Deum; (2) ad Deum autem habet gloriam; (3) non ergo ex operibus iustificatus est. Si ergo non ex operibus iustificatus est Abraham, und iustificatus est? Sequitur, et dicit unde: Quid enim scriptura dicit? id est: Unde dicit scriptura iustificatum Abraham? Credidit autem Abraham Deo et reputatum est illi ad iustitiam. Ergo ex fide iustificatus est Abraham.'
[7] Karl Hermann Schelkle, *Paulus Lehrer der Väter: die altkirchliche Auslegung von Römer 1–11*, Düsseldorf 1956, 124. As Schelkle points out, Augustine understands this passage quite differently in his *Expositio quarundam propositionum ex epistula ad Romanos* 20, on Rom. iv. 2. [8] Bammel, 'Augustine, Origen', 341, 343, 358–63.
[9] S. Zarb, *Chronologia Enarrationum S. Augustini in Psalmos*, Malta 1948. This work was unfortunately not available to me.
[10] J. De Blic, 'La date du sermon de saint Augustin "in psalmum 31"' (ML 36, 257–75)', *Gregorianum* xvii (1936), 407–12.
[11] H. Rondet, 'Chronologie des "Enarrationes in Psalmos"', *Bulletin de littérature ecclésiastique* lxi (1960), 281–4.

peccatorum meritis ii where Proverbs iv. 27 ('ne declines in dexteram aut sinistram') is applied to the two opposite errors of pride at one's own righteousness and the expectation that one will not be punished for one's sins.[12] He dates the sermon to 412 or 413. The disagreement with De Blic's observations can perhaps be resolved by the argument that in 412/13 the Pelagian controversy was not sufficiently far advanced for Augustine to have been thinking in terms of a group of opponents who deserved to be attacked for their lack of humility. Alternatively we could date the sermon to 411 just before the beginning of the Pelagian controversy. The positive use made of Origen's *Commentary on Romans* would point to the sermon having been written at much the same time as or shortly before the *De peccatorum meritis*, in 411 or 412 rather than 413,[13] and indeed the parallel use of Proverbs iv. 27 in the sermon and in *De peccatorum meritis* ii gives the impression that the version in the sermon is earlier.[14] According to a title in two of the manuscripts the sermon was delivered at Carthage. This would have been possible in 411, when Augustine was preaching at Carthage in the summer months both before and after the conference with the Donatists, or (though I think this less likely) in autumn 412.[15]

There seems to be no need to assign the sermon to the same date as the *De fide et operibus*. That work is concerned with three questions: should persons living in sin with no intention of reform be admitted to baptism; should ethical instruction be given only after baptism or beforehand; will the baptised person who retains his faith but refuses to change his life none the less be saved? Of these only the third question concerning the need for good works after baptism overlaps with the contents of the sermon, and this is a question which arises naturally from a reading of Paul and which Augustine could have thought of for himself prior to the specific enquiry which prompted the *De fide et operibus*.[16] The same problem caused concern to Pelagius, when he was writing his Pauline commentary at Rome in the years before 410.[17] Augustine read Pelagius' commentary between writing

---

[12] *De peccatorum meritis et remissione*, ii. 35, 57, CSEL lx. 125. 24–126. 1; *Enarratio*, CCL xxxviii–xl. 31. 2, 1. 41–52.

[13] When he wrote the *De spiritu et littera* Augustine was reacting more critically to his reading of Origen's *Commentary on Romans*: Bammel, 'Augustine, Origen', 361–2.

[14] In the *De peccatorum meritis* ii. 35. 57 only one of the two opposite errors (that of claiming to be without sin) is relevant to the context. Augustine appears to be repeating an idea which he had developed more relevantly in the sermon.

[15] On the timing of Augustine's visits to Carthage see O. Perler, 'Les voyages de saint Augustin', *Recherches augustiniennes* i (1958), 5ff., with the chronological table at pp. 14–15.

[16] It arises most obviously from the disagreement between Paul and James; Rondet, 'Chronologie', 282 n. 10, points out that in about 411 Augustine wrote a commentary on James, which is now lost. He describes it in his *Retractationes* 2. 32 immediately before the *De peccatorum meritis*. In fact Augustine had anticipated much of what he says in the sermon in his *De diversis quaestionibus* 76 on James ii. 20, where he had argued that there is no real disagreement between the two apostles, on the grounds that Paul's words 'sine operibus' refer to works prior to faith (CCL xlivA. 218ff.).

[17] *In Romanos* iii. 28: *Pelagius's expositions of thirteen epistles of St Paul*, ed. A. Souter, Cambridge 1926, 34: 'Abutuntur quidam hoc loco ad destructionem operum iustitiae,

bks i–ii and bk iii of *De peccatorum meritis*.[18] It provides confirmation for a dating of the sermon before bk iii (that is, before this reading of Pelagius) that his treatment of the problem in *De fide et operibus* shows an influence of Pelagius which is not yet present in the sermon.[19]

Having confirmed that the likely dating of Augustine's sermon on Psalm xxxi fits with his use of Origen's *Commentary on Romans*, let us look at the part of the sermon dealing with Rom iv. 1–8 and note the parallels with Rufinus' version of Origen. The initial idea of the two opposite pitfalls of negligence and boasting has a parallel in Origen's section on Rom iii. 27–8, but Augustine depicts the two extremes much more drastically. Origen mentions the danger of negligence at bk ii. 6. 53–5 and the danger of boasting (prompted by Rom iii. 27) at bk iii. 6. 7off.,[20] but does not present them as opposites in the manner developed by Augustine. He goes on to quote 1 Corinthians i. 31 ('qui gloriatur in Domino glorietur'),[21] which Augustine quotes immediately after his citation of Rom. iv. 1–2.[22] After the passage quoted above, which expounds Paul's argumentation in Rom. iv. 1–2 and is clearly dependent on Origen, Augustine again emphasises the danger of supposing that faith alone without good works is sufficient and refers to the Epistle of James as correcting a false understanding of Paul and commending Abraham's works (James ii. 21).[23] Origen refers to the same verse for the same purpose.[24] Augustine continues with the words 'Laudo superaedificationem operis, sed uideo fidei fundamentum; laudo fructum boni operis, sed in fide agnosco radicem.'[25] These pictures of faith as the foundation on which works are built, and of faith as the root which brings forth the fruit of good works, appear also in Origen.[26]

---

solam fidem [baptizato] posse sufficere adfirmantes...'. The Pelagian work *De malis doctoribus* is also directed against those who think that having faith means that they can sin with impunity (see, for example, iii. 1–2, PL Suppl. 1, 1421).

[18] He states this himself in *De peccatorum meritis* iii. 1. 1 (p. 129).

[19] Pelagius' brief section quotes 1 Cor. xiii. 2, Rom. xiii. 10 and James ii. 26. In the *De fide et operibus* Augustine introduces this problem at xiv. 21 (CSEL xli. 61), and quotes first Gal. v. 6 (a verse which he makes much use of in the sermon), and then 1 Cor. xiii. 2 and Rom. xiii. 10 in quick succession (p. 62), and later also James ii. 26 (xiv. 23, p. 64, 16–17). In the sermon his quotations of Rom. xiii. 10 and 1 Cor. xiii. 2 are widely separated by other quotations and discussion (5. 8, p. 227 and 6. 15–16, p. 229).

[20] *De Römerbriefkommentar*, 249 ('Sed fortassis haec aliquis audiens resoluatur, et bene agendi neclegentiam capiat, si quidem ad iustificandum fides sola sufficiat'), 250–1.

[21] *Commentarium* iii. 6. 86–7 (*De Römerbriefkommentar*, 251).

[22] *Enarratio* 2 (p. 225).

[23] Ibid. 3. 9–16: 'dico de ipso Abraham, quod inuenimus etiam in epistola alterius apostoli...Iacobus enim in epistola sua, contra eos qui nolebant bene operari de sola fide praesumentes, ipsius Abrahae opera commendauit, cuius Paulus fidem'.

[24] *Commentarium* iv. 1. 69–72: 'Propterea ergo et in alio scripturae loco dicitur de Abraham quia ex operibus fidei iustificatus sit quia certum est eum qui uere credit opus fidei...operari.'   [25] *Enarratio* 3. 17–19.

[26] *Commentarium* iii. 6. 64 (works which are not built on the foundation of faith – 'supra fundamentum fidei' – cannot justify their doer); iv. 1. 113–18 ('fides...tamquam radix...surgant ex ea rami qui fructus operum ferant').

In the next section of his sermon Augustine states that works done prior to faith are empty,[27] however praiseworthy they may appear to men. He then states that it is the intention that counts, and elaborates the pictures of runners running or helmsmen steering in the wrong direction. Origen had developed the idea that works are seen and praised by men, and faith only by God,[28] and emphasised the importance of intention at several points in his commentary.[29]

In sections 5–6 Augustine provides quotations from St Paul which show the need for works after faith, in particular Galatians v. 6 ('Fides quae per dilectionem operatur').[30] He emphasises the centrality of charity (Rom. xiii. 10), or rather of faith, hope and charity (1 Cor. xiii. 13). Paul states that a man is justified by faith without works because there is no merit in the works done by the unbeliever. The pagan sets his hopes either on the wrong source or on the wrong goal. Good works are not good unless they grow from the root of faith.

Origen writes of the association of faith, hope and charity in his section on Rom. iv. 18–22 and, like Augustine,[31] he is interested in the order in which the three are listed in 1 Cor. xiii. 13.[32] He agrees that works cannot give justification without faith,[33] although in general he takes a more favourable view than Augustine does of the prospects of Gentiles who obey the natural law.[34]

In section 7 Augustine moves on to consider Rom. iv. 4 ('Et ei qui operatur, merces non imputatur secundum gratiam, sed secundum debitum'). He notes the contrast between 'gratia' and 'debitum'. Remission of sins is given free, whereas works deserve condemnation (since all have sinned). For the wages of sin is death (Rom vi. 23). God gives not the deserved punishment, but undeserved grace. Origen too in discussing this verse contrasts 'gratia' and 'debitum'.[35] He goes on to state explicitly that 'debitum' should be taken in a negative sense as the punishment deserved by sin, quoting Rom vi. 23 and other verses in

---

[27] Cf. Origen's words at ibid. ii. 6. 64, quoted in the previous footnote.
[28] Ibid. iv. 1. 29–56. [29] Ibid. ii. 1. 7–14; iv. 4. 105–13.
[30] This verse is not quoted by Origen and would be less effective in Greek, since 'quae operatur' renders not 'ἐργαζομένη' but 'ἐνεργουμένη'.
[31] *Enarratio* 5. 52f.: 'illo ergo loco a fide coepit apostolus'.
[32] *Commentarium* iv. 6. 44–7: 'Et puto quod prima salutis initia et ipsa fundamenta fides est; profectus uero et augmenta aedificii spes est, perfectio autem et culmen totius operis caritas, et ideo maior omnium dicitur caritas.'
[33] Ibid. iii. 6. 62–6: 'Ubi uero fides non est quae credentem iustificet, etiamsi opera quis habeat ex lege tamen quia non sunt aedificata supra fundamentum fidei quamuis uideantur esse bona tamen operatorem suum iustificare non possunt, quod eis deest fides.' He also states (ibid. iv. 5. 106–10) that complete obedience to the natural law is not enough; faith is necessary for justification.
[34] See, for example, ibid. ii. 7. 10–18, 30–3; Bammel, 'Augustine, Origen', 362 nn. 89–90.
[35] *Commentarium* iv. 1. 150–2: 'in fide quidem gratia sit iustificantis, in opere uero iustitia retribuentis'; see also 174ff.

support.[36] Augustine is clearly influenced by this negative understanding, though he does not agree entirely. He states that good works deserve the kingdom of heaven (*Enarratio* 7. 15), but assumes that in fact his own hearers and indeed all mankind are sinners (7. 1–3, 15–17). Towards the end of section 7 Augustine states that if you boast of your own deserts, God sees what is in you (7. 26–8). This emphasis, that God sees into the heart, is present also in Origen's discussion of Rom. iv. 1–8.[37]

After a short section in which he urges his hearers to pay attention, Augustine goes on to expound the opening verses of the psalm, which are quoted in Rom. iv. 7–8. Both Augustine and Origen[38] comment on the fact that the psalm is entitled 'intellectus Dauid' or 'intellegentiae'. Augustine, however, does not imitate Origen, but uses this title in order to reiterate the main points he wishes his hearers to grasp.[39] Stimulated by the word 'dolus' in Psalm xxxi. 2b (not quoted in Rom. iv), he then cites Jesus' words about Nathanael from John i. 47–8, and interprets this of the human race, which was 'sub conditione carnis' ('sub arbore fici') and in bondage to the 'impietas propaginis' and on which Christ took pity ('uidi te'). This allegorical passage, though not taken from Origen, is reminiscent of the manner of Origen, and uses the words 'in iniquitate conceptus sum' from Psalm l. 5 in a way that is characteristic of Origen.[40]

Augustine's exposition of Psalm xxxi. 1–2a (= Rom. iv. 7–8: 'Beati quorum remissae sunt iniquitates, et quorum tecta sunt peccata. Beatus uir cui non imputauit Dominus peccatum') at the end of section 9 differs from Origen's, in that he takes the three statements as equivalents and does not follow Origen's idea of three stages, the second stage of which consists of 'covering' earlier bad deeds with new good deeds.[41]

In sections 10–12 Augustine examines the parable of the Pharisee and the publican from Luke xviii, using the Pharisee as an example of boasting. The same is done by Origen in his section on Rom. iii. 27–8 (*Commentarium* iii. 6. 72ff.), and both authors quote Proverbs xx. 9 as a warning against boasting.[42]

The rest of Augustine's sermon is concerned with the exposition of the remaining verses of Psalm xxxi and does not challenge comparison with Origen's commentary, although it is interesting to note that there are numerous quotations from the Epistle to the Romans.

The comparison with Origen of the first part of Augustine's sermon on Psalm xxxi shows that Augustine found much to agree with in his reading of Origen and picked up a number of ideas from him. He did not, however, treat Origen as an authority and he felt free to differ from his

---

[36] Ibid. iv. 1. 152ff.   [37] Ibid. iv. 1. 33–5.   [38] Ibid. iv. 1. 218–23.
[39] *Enarratio* 9. 4ff.; the emphasis on understanding in section 8 looks forward to this section.
[40] See *Commentarium* v. 9. 133–4, 162–3; vi. 12. 51. These are passages which influenced Augustine when he was writing his *De peccatorum meritis*: Bammel, 'Augustine, Origen', 359, 366.   [41] *Commentarium*, iv. 1. 224–36.
[42] Ibid. iii. 6. 92–3; *Enarratio* 12. 22.

interpretations. In order to complete the comparison we should look briefly at the differences as well. Most of the parallels with Augustine come from Origen's sections on Rom. iii. 27–8 and Rom. iv. 1–8 (*Commentarium* iii. 6; iv. 1), so it will be sufficient to look at these sections.

Naturally enough Origen, writing a commentary, examines all Paul's words phrase by phrase, whereas Augustine, preaching to a congregation, picks out and elaborates the main points that he considers relevant for his hearers. Origen pays attention to the context of Paul's words and Paul's historical situation, showing how Paul attempts to mediate between Jewish and Gentile believers.[43] He has a strong interest in the interpretation of Paul's references to various laws, the Old Testament law, the natural law, the law of works, the law of faith and so on.[44] When he reaches the verses about Abraham he takes an interest in the details given about Abraham in Genesis.

It may be worth picking out a few of the points made by Origen that Augustine does not follow. On Rom. iii. 27–8 Origen looks for examples of persons saved by faith alone without works and cites the robber crucified together with Christ, the sinful woman of Luke vii. 37–50 and the many cases where Christ says 'Your faith has saved you'. Interestingly Augustine uses this example of the robber crucified with Christ (and also the case of the convert who dies immediately after baptism) in another sermon.[45] In the sermon on Psalm xxxi he is concerned not with the rare cases of those who are justified by faith with no preceding or following good works, but rather to show that all works prior to faith are worthless, whereas faith itself must necessarily result in works.

In his section on Rom. iii. 29–30 (*Commentarium* iii. 7) Origen has a discussion of the phrases 'ex fide' and 'per fidem' in Rom. iii. 30, in which he concludes that those who are justified 'ex fide' are perfected by doing good works and those who are justified 'per fidem' start off with good works. Augustine found this distasteful, as is apparent from his remarks on the verse in question in the *De spiritu et littera*.[46]

In the section on Rom. iv. 1–8 Origen first outlines the context of Paul's remarks, and comments on the logic of Rom. iv. 2, and then states that there are two justifications (ways of being counted righteous), one through works, whose glory is in itself and before men, and one through faith, whose glory is before God, who sees the heart. The latter, however, cannot be combined with unrighteousness. He who truly believes will do works of faith and justice and all goodness and have glory both in secret before God and openly before men. After considering why Paul calls Abraham 'our father according to the flesh', Origen goes on to examine the passage from Genesis from which Paul quotes in Rom. iv. 3 and to list Abraham's earlier acts of faith. He concludes from various biblical verses

---

[43] *Commentarium*, iii. 6. 3–20; cf. iv. 1. 11–16.   [44] Ibid. iii. 6. 108–13; iv. 1. 11–14.
[45] Sermo ii ('de Abraam ubi temptatur a Deo'), 9. 229–41, CCL xli. 16.
[46] See Bammel, 'Augustine, Origen', 362, 368.

that it is possible to have faith in part or perfect faith. He also questions whether not only faith but also other virtues can be counted for righteousness, and he notes that not every case of belief described in the Bible is counted for righteousness.[47] Much of this must have seemed to Augustine to distract from the main point of Paul's words. For Augustine justification by faith applies to the transition made from law to grace or from the letter to the spirit at the point of conversion or baptism, when the believer with no antecedent merits is received and justified by God's mercy.[48] To suggest that one needs a number of acts of faith or that one can count faith as one among other virtues does not fit with this picture. Origen sometimes appears to agree with Augustine – for example at *Commentarium* iii. 6. 56–60 he states that the pardon given at the time of receiving justification is for past sins not future sins, clearly thinking of a single moment as at conversion or baptism – but he also likes to speak in terms of a gradual progress towards perfection in virtue.[49]

Moving on to Rom. iv. 4–5 Origen gives the negative interpretation of the wages for works which has already been mentioned, and he emphasises that whereas Paul states that the wages of sin is death, he describes eternal life not as the wages of righteousness but as the grace of God.[50] He then repeats his reference to the robber on the cross as an example of an unbeliever justified by faith alone. He comments on Paul's quotation from Psalm xxxi and conjectures that Paul understood that those who have reached the age of distinguishing between good and bad must necessarily have either unrighteousness or righteousness. It follows therefore that righteousness is imputed to the one who has believed in God and whose sins have been forgiven, even if he has not yet done works of righteousness. This faith, when it has been justified, begins to produce the fruit of works. After this he goes on, as has already been described, to interpret the quotation from Psalm xxxi in terms of three progressive stages, an interpretation rejected by Augustine. Finally he explains the difference between 'iniquitas' and 'peccatum' (Rom. iv. 7).

What exactly do Origen and Augustine understand by justification by faith? By the words 'by faith' they understand 'by faith alone without works'. Augustine is particularly keen to emphasise that justification is without antecedent merits[51] and that works before faith are useless.[52] Origen too, as we have seen, states that works of the law which are not built on the foundation of faith cannot give justification.[53] Origen (in Rufinus' version at least) sometimes seems to speak as if faith or

---

[47] In his *De spiritu et littera* xxxii. 55ff. (CSEL xl. 212ff.), Augustine asks what kind of faith is commended by the apostle.

[48] Cf. the opening words of his sermon: 'Psalmus gratiae Dei et iustificationis nostrae nullis praecedentibus meritis nostris, sed praeueniente nos misericordia Domini Dei nostri.' [49] See also below pp. 233f.

[50] Contrast Augustine at *Enarratio* 7. 15: 'Bonis [operibus] quid debetur? Regnum caelorum.' [51] Cf. ibid. 1. 1–2: 'nullis praecedentibus meritis nostris'.

[52] Ibid. 4. 1ff.: 'ea enim ipsa opera quae dicuntur ante fidem...inania sunt'.

[53] *Commentarium* iii. 6. 62–7; Scherer, 'Le commentaire d'Origène', 166, lines 4–6.

conversion were a merit which deserves to be counted for righteousness,[54] but he also states that there is no work which could demand reward from God,[55] and in a later section he explicitly states that faith itself is a gift of God given by grace through the Holy Spirit, written by the Spirit in the human heart.[56] Both Origen and Augustine are also concerned to argue that justification should be followed by good works, although Origen does quote the example of the crucified robber, who is saved without any opportunity of performing works.

The concept of 'justification' is not unproblematic. The Greek verb δικαιοῦν translated by justify (Latin 'iustificare') means to count as just. That this is how Paul understands it is indicated by the context in Romans iv with its talk of λογίζεσθαι εἰς δικαιοσύνην and of forgiveness of sins.[57] Rufinus' translation of Origen does not have an explicit discussion of the meaning of the word, but it is used in a way that can be correctly understood.[58] The association of justification with forgiveness of sins (*Commentarium* iii. 6. 56–9; iv. 2. 21–5) suggests that the sinner is counted as just. In the section on Rom. iii. 25–6 (*Commentarium* iii. 5) Origen speaks of justification in the context of Christ's propitiation for the remission of sins[59] and of God's judgement in the age to come.[60] Augustine, however, both in this sermon and elsewhere understands 'iustificare' as meaning 'make just'. He states this repeatedly. Thus particularly clearly in his Sermon ccxcii *In Natali Joannis Baptistae* against the Donatists he asks, 'Quid est justificare?' and answers 'Iustum facere'. The Donatist when performing a baptism says, 'Ego iustifico'.[61] In his *Expositio quarundam propositionum ex epistola ad Romanos* Augustine writes on Rom. iv. 4: 'Deus per gratiam dedit, quia peccatoribus dedit, ut per fidem *iuste uiuerent*, id est, bene operarentur. Quod ergo bene operamur iam accepta gratia, non nobis sed illi tribuendum est, qui per gratiam nos iustificauit',

---

[54] *Commentarium* iv. 1. 146–7: 'ex multis partibus fidei in unum coaceruata perfectio quae mereretur ad iustitiam reputari'; iv. 1. 228–9 and iv. 3. 20–1: 'fidei meritum'; Scherer, 'Le commentaire d'Origène', 178. 15 ('τῇ ἀξίᾳ δικαιώσεως πίστει'), 186. 16–19.

[55] *Commentarium* iv. 1. 153–5: 'uix mihi suadeo quod possit ullum opus esse quod ex debito remunerationem Dei deposcat'; Scherer, 'Le commentaire d'Origène', 184. 8–12 ('οὐδὲν ... ὡς ὀφείλων δίδωσιν ἀλλὰ πάντα ὡς χάριν δωρεῖται').

[56] *Commentarium* iv. 5. 17–34, 60–75; Scherer, 'Le commentaire d'Origène', 204. 14–205. 8.

[57] See, for example, C. H. Dodd, *The Epistle of Paul to the Romans*, London 1932, 51. Of course the Old Testament background must also be taken into account. See Albrecht Ritschl, *Die christliche Lehre von der Rechtfertigung und Versöhnung*, ii, Bonn 1882, 304ff., 321ff.

[58] Origen himself is clear. See Scherer, 'Le commentaire d'Origène', 162, lines 14–16: 'τοῖς πιστεύσασιν εἰς τὸν Ἰησοῦν ἢ εἰς τὸν Θεὸν διὰ τοῦ Ἰησοῦ λογίζεται ὁ Θεὸς τὴν πίστιν εἰς δικαιοσύνην, καὶ οὕτω δικαιοῖ τὸν ἐκ πίστεως Ἰησοῦ. See also ibid. 184, lines 6–7: ἥντινα πίστιν οὖσαν δικαιοσύνην λογίζεται εἰς δικαιοσύνην ὁ Θεός'.

[59] *Commentarium* iii. 5. 23–6: 'Deus enim iustus est et iustus iustificare non poterat iniustos; ideo interuentum uoluit esse propitiatoris ut per eius fidem iustificarentur qui per opera propria iustificari non poterant.'

[60] Ibid. iii. 5. 237–9: 'Si uero sustentet et patiatur [Deus] in praesenti saeculo recte erit iustus iudex in futuro. Iustificat ergo eum qui ex fide est.'

[61] Section 6, PL xxxviii. 1324A.

and on Rom iv. 5: 'Quod autem ait, "Qui iustificat impium", hoc est ex impio *pium facit... quia ideo iustificatus est ut iustus sit.*'[62] In his sermon on Psalm xxxi Augustine states, 'If the unbeliever is justified, he *becomes just* instead of an unbeliever.'[63] His deepened study of the Epistle to the Romans in the years 411–12 caused Augustine once to question this understanding of justification. This is in his *De spiritu et littera.* After repeating his usual understanding of the word in the earlier sections of this work,[64] he queries what its meaning is in xxvi. 45,[65] where he is discussing the problematic verse Rom ii. 13, 'factores legis iustificabuntur'. He first states, 'quid est enim aliud "iustificat" quam "iusti facti", ab illo scilicet qui iustificat impium, ut ex impio fiat iustus?' He then, however, goes on to qualify this: 'aut certe ita dictum est "iustificabuntur", ac si diceretur "iusti habebuntur", "iusti deputabuntur"', and quotes Luke x. 29 ('he, however, wishing to justify himself') in support. Subsequently Augustine reverts to his previous understanding of justification. In the immediately following sections of the *De spiritu et littera* he writes of justice being written by God's grace in the inner man who has been renewed, and of the law of God being written anew in the minds of believers through grace, and he describes this writing as justification.[66] His interpretation of justification as making just is reiterated in later works, for example *Enarratio in Ps 118 Sermo 26* ('iustificat impium, hoc est, per gratiam suam ex impio facit iustum'),[67] or *Retractationes* 2. 33 (59). 10 on *De peccatorum meritis et remissione* ('de gratia dei qua iustificamur, hoc est iusti efficimur').[68] It must be admitted that Augustine's understanding of the actual words 'justification' and 'justify' is incorrect. This is perhaps less important than one might expect, mainly because the context in which Paul speaks of justification also includes references to the remission of sins and to faith being counted for righteousness, so that it is likely that the concept of the believer being counted as righteous will often be touched on within the same complex of ideas.

Is justification something that takes place at one moment, at conversion or together with forgiveness of sins at baptism, or is it a process? Romans iv. 5, with its mention of the 'impius' (naturally understood as the unbeliever who believes), suggests conversion. In the case of Abraham it takes place at a particular occasion of his placing his faith in God, as recorded in Genesis xv. 6, although Origen regards this as the culmination of a number of acts of faith on Abraham's part.[69] The New Testament examples quoted by Origen are of faith being placed in Jesus' power to

[62] *Expositio* 15–16, CSEL lxxxiv. 9–10.
[63] *Enarratio* 6. 26–7: 'Si iustificatur impius, ex impio fit iustus.' See also ibid. 24. 6–7: 'Unde iusti? Non meritis uestris, sed gratia illius. Unde iusti? Quia iustificati.'
[64] *De spiritu et lettera* ix. 15, CSEL lx. 167. 7–8: 'iustitia dei...qua induit hominen, cum iustificat impium'; x. 16, p. 168. 17: 'iniustus, ut iustificetur, id est ut iustus fiat'.
[65] CSEL lx. 199. 10–12, 23–6.
[66] *De spiritu et lettera* xxvii. 47, p. 201, 24–5; xviii. 48, p. 202, 24–9.
[67] *Enarratio – Ps 118* 1, 37–8, CCL xl. 1753.   [68] *Retractationes*, CCL lvii. 117.
[69] *Commentarium* iv. 1. 101–36.

save, heal and forgive sins.[70] When applied more generally to the convert to Christianity the association with forgiveness of sins would suggest the occasion of baptism.[71] At *Commentarium* iv. 1. 200ff. Origen writes of the conversion and renunciation of evil which comes when one reaches the age of being able to distinguish between good and evil. This is associated with belief in God, forgiveness of sins and justification.[72]

For Augustine, who virtually always takes justification to mean 'making just', it must be a process. Yet this process has a beginning, either at conversion or in baptism. Conversely for Origen justification (i.e. one's faith being counted for righteousness) marks the beginning of a process of progress in justice and good works, as he describes in *Commentarium* iv. 1. 211–18, 227–36. Augustine associates the beginning of justification with 'that grace by which we are Christians' (*Enarratio* 2. 1–2), with conversion (6. 47–9) and with forgiveness of sins (7. 11, 17–20; 21. 9–10). The process of being made just involves a change of direction (4.7ff.; 6. 52–7), and a cleansing of one's love, so as to love God and neighbour (5. 26–33). Faith works, i.e. carries out good works, by means of love (6. 1ff.; 7. 20–1), but these good works must be ascribed to the grace of God (9. 9–11).[73]

In the treatises which (assuming our dating to be correct) were written shortly after the sermon on Psalm xxxi Augustine works out his understanding of the process of justification in much more detail. Thus in the *De peccatorum meritis* ii. 7. 9[74] he points out that the remission of sins given at baptism is only the beginning of a renewal in the inner man according to the divine image, which is finally completed at the resurrection of the dead. In the *De spiritu et littera* he reiterates the observation that it is by the spirit that believers are justified (made just).[75] To compare Augustine's and Origen's teaching on conversion and the spiritual life would however require a lengthy book rather than a short article.[76] Our task was to look at Augustine's *Sermon on Psalm 31* on justification by faith and the influence on it of his recent reading of

---

[70] Ibid. iii. 6. 27–52.　　　　　　　[71] Cf. ibid. iii. 6. 53–60.

[72] Cf. Scherer, 'Le commentaire d'Origène', 186, lines 10–12: 'Δικαιοῖ οὖν τὸν ἀσεβῆ διὰ τῆς πίστεως μεταθέμενον ἀπὸ τῆς ἀσεβείας ὥστε λογίζεσθαι τὴν μεταθεῖσαν αὐτὸν ἀπὸ τῆς ἀσεβείας πίστιν εἰς δικαιοσύνην.'

[73] In a later sermon, *Sermo* clviii (sections 4ff., PL xxxviii. 864f.), Augustine explicitly asks the question whether we are already justified. Those who are baptised, whose sins are forgiven, who are 'iustificati a peccatis', who have faith, have 'aliquid iustitiae'. Yet conflict with the flesh, the world and the devil still remain. If we say that we have no sin we deceive ourselves. So it is necessary to progress in justice ('Iustificati sumus: sed ipsa iustitia, cum proficimus, crescit'). [74] CSEL lx. 79. 19ff.

[75] For example *De spiritu et littera* iii. 5, p. 157. 10–11, 13–16; ix. 15, p. 167. 11–12; xiii. 22, p. 176. 14–17; xvi. 28, p. 181. 24ff.: 'hic autem spiritus dei, cuius dono iustificamur, quo fit in nobis ut non peccare delectet'; xviii. 31, p. 184, 12–14.

[76] Augustine's ideas on justification have often been discussed in connection with those of the reformers. To the bibliography in Angelo di Berardino, *Patrology* 4, Westminster, Maryland 1988, 444, may be added G. R. Evans, 'Augustine on justification', *Studia Ephemeridis 'Augustinianum'* xxvi (1987), 275–84.

Origen. We found considerable agreement between the two Fathers, although Augustine is more selective than Origen in emphasising what he regards as being of prime importance. Augustine seems also to have been selective in his reading. On getting hold of a copy of Rufinus' version of Origen on Romans he seems first to have looked at the particular parts which attracted his interest at the time, rather than studying the work right through.[77] His consultation of Origen's *Commentary on Romans* marks the beginning of a new phase of intense preoccupation with the study of the Pauline epistles. This is of importance for the development of his thought. It makes itself apparent in his earlier anti-Pelagian works, the *De peccatorum meritis* and the *De spiritu et littera*.[78] The treatment of justification in the *Sermon on Psalm 31* is a small foretaste of these more important works.

---

[77] On Augustine's selective reading see L. Doutreleau, *Didyme l'Aveugle, Traité du Saint-Esprit*, Paris 1992, 126.   [78] See Bammel, 'Augustine, Origen', 358ff.

SL 23 (1993) 158-76

Baptism Portrayed as Martyrdom in the Early Church

by

Gordon Jeanes*

I. Baptism and Dying with Christ

In recent decades liturgists have been exploring how baptismal rites before the fourth century talked about regeneration, after the pattern of John 3:5, more than about dying and rising with Christ in the words of Paul in Romans 6:3ff. The shift in emphasis from the one understanding of baptism to the other was probably general throughout the Church in both East and West,[1] but is seen particularly clearly in the Syrian rites of baptism, where the earlier rites are based on a *mimesis* of Jordan rather than of Calvary, and where the shift also goes hand in hand with changes in the pattern and understanding of baptismal anointing. Gabriele Winkler describes the earlier form of the prebaptismal anointing in Syria as "the ritualization of the entry into the messianic kingship of Christ which is made through the coming of the Spirit at this anointing";[2] in the later rites "the entire ritual assumed a more and more purificatory character,"[3] in which "the preparation as a whole is viewed as a drama-like battle with Satan."[4]

The reason for the change in emphasis is less clear than the simple fact that it happened. Sebastian Brock suggests that it was due to a suppression of the Jewish origins of Christianity, and a hellenization of its rites.[5] Edward Ratcliff

---

* The Revd Gordon Jeanes, an Anglican priest, is the Cuming Fellow in Liturgy and Chaplain of St Chad's College, University of Durham, 18 North Bailey, Durham DH1 3RH, England.
[1] Cf. my paper at the Oxford Patristics Conference 1991, "Paschal Baptism and Rebirth: A Clash of Images?", forthcoming in *Studia Patristica*, in which I seek to show that even a paschal context for baptism by no means prevented its being understood in terms of John 3:5 rather than Romans 6.
[2] "The Original Meaning of the Prebaptismal Anointing, and its Implication," *Worship* 52 (1978) 43.
[3] Ibid., 42.
[4] Ibid., 39.
[5] "The Transition to Post-Baptismal Anointing in the Antiochene Rite" in B. D. Spinks (ed.), *The Sacrifice of Praise* (Rome 1981) 220.

158

believed it was due to the development of the Church of the Holy Sepulchre in Jerusalem, that Cyril of Jerusalem reinterpreted the meaning of the rites on the basis of the site, and that the influence of Jerusalem had its effect far and wide.[6] Winkler doubts Ratcliff's thesis, and believes that the reinterpretation of the rites was "because of the inner change of dynamics within the rite itself. Once baptism moved away from its original essence, being the *mimesis* of the event at the Jordan, and shifted at the same time toward a cathartic principle, it was inevitable that all rites that preceded baptism proper became subordinated to a process of thorough cleansing."[7] And the reason for the new emphasis on purification, Winkler believes, was the extension of the periods of preparation for baptism, over years and even to one's deathbed.[8] Ruth Meyers looks for an explanation in the large number of converts to the Church after the peace of Constantine. "With such a great number of catechumens would come a need to attest to the sincerity of a person's conversion."[9]

In this paper we are concerned first of all not with the cause of the change in the baptismal liturgy but with the source from which it acquired its imagery. It will be suggested that the language of the combat with Satan and other motifs that we see in the rites and in the baptismal catecheses were not invented out of thin air, as it were (even if such a thing were possible), but were taken over from the history and literature of the martyrs. Then, in the light of this, we may see that the cause of the change can be described as a synthesis of the opinions of Winkler and Meyers. Meyers is right to put the change in the rites in its historical context. Winkler has a real insight into the development of liturgy when she opposes the idea of particular factors such as Jerusalem having such a massive influence, but speaks of an "inner change of dynamics." This change of dynamics, however, cannot be viewed in the baptismal rites in isolation, but in the change of dynamics in the Church as a whole. The age of the martyrs was past, the imagery and language of martyrdom was, as it were, "up for grabs," and also what the martyrs stood for, the radical challenge of the gospel to the world, was a kind of "no man's

---

[6] "The Old Syrian Baptismal Tradition and Its Resettlement under the Influence of Jerusalem in the Fourth Century" in G. J. Cuming (ed.), *Studies in Church History* 2 (London 1965) 19-37 (esp. 28ff.) = A. H. Couratin and D. H. Tripp (eds), *E. C. Ratcliff: Liturgical Studies* (London 1976) 135-54.

[7] "The Original Meaning," 42, n. 63.

[8] Ibid., 40.

[9] "The Structure of the Syrian Baptismal Rite" in P. F. Bradshaw (ed.), *Essays in Early Eastern Initiation,* Alcuin/GROW Liturgical Study 8 (Nottingham 1988) 32.

159

land" which needed to be occupied if the witness of the Church was to be continued. In part that was taken up by the monks, but just as every Christian might have been called to be a martyr, so in the new rites of baptism every Christian now had to speak personally the language of the martyr's rejection of the world and engage in combat with Satan.

II. General Similarities

General similarities between baptism and martyrdom are commonly known and well acknowledged. They have their basis in the saying of Jesus associating his death with his baptism.[10] Tertullian spoke of martyrdom as a second baptism,[11] and Hippolytus in the *Apostolic Tradition* could assure catechumens that the martyrs receive baptism in their own blood.[12]

In the fourth century, looking back on the age of martyrs, John Chrysostom's notions of martyrdom are revealing. They have been studied by Gus Christofis,[13] who includes a discussion of martyrdom as baptism. Martyrdom is, as we would expect, a baptism, and it confers forgiveness of sins.[14] Whereas baptism is in the likeness (ὁμοίωμα) of the death of Christ, the martyr is conformed (συμμορφούμεθα) to his death.[15] The death of the youngest of the Maccabee youths—he jumps into a cauldron—is compared to baptism.[16] In a sermon delivered in Easter week to the neophytes in a church of the martyrs in Antioch, Chrysostom makes a direct comparison of the neophytes with martyrs.[17] Here the point of the comparison is that both martyr and neophyte die to the world and their lives are hidden with Christ in God. Chrysostom develops the comparison with regard to the Christian life, particularly prayer and almsgiving, but here he tells us nothing about the baptismal ceremonies.

---

[10] Luke 12:50.
[11] *De Baptismo* 16. Cf. R. Jacob, "Le martyre, epanouissement du sacerdoce des Chrétiens dans la littérature patristique jusqu'en 258," *Mélanges de sciences réligieuses* 24 (1967) 76-9.
[12] *Apostolic Tradition* 19, ed. B. Botte, *La Tradition apostolique de saint Hippolyte* (Münster 1963) 40.
[13] "The Notions of Martyrdom According to St John Chrysostom" (M.A. Thesis, Durham 1984).
[14] *In S Lucianum Martyrem* 2 (*PG* 50:522).
[15] *De SS. Bernice et Prosdoce* 6 (*PG* 50:639).
[16] *In Sanctas Maccabeos* II.6 (*PG* 50:625).
[17] Stavronikita 7; English translation from P. W. Harkins, *St John Chrysostom: Baptismal Instructions*, Ancient Christian Writers 31 (Westminster MD/London 1963) 104-18; discussed by E. Mazza, *Mystagogy* (New York 1989) 123.

160

A physical connection between baptism and martyrdom is suggested by J. G. Davies.[18] He places some importance on the similarities between baptisteries and tombs or *martyria;* one perhaps should not hypothesize too much from what may be coincidentally suitable forms of building.[19] But Davies also mentions the attachment of baptisteries to *martyria,* and concludes: "in an age when martyrdom was a thing of the past, the candidate for initiation was nevertheless assured by the positioning of the baptistery that he could share in and receive the fruits of the death of Christ, the supreme martyr."[20]

From general similarities, let us move to actual instances of parallels.

III. The Courtroom and Judgment

We have the most explicit link between baptism and martyrdom in Gennadius of Marseilles. Gennadius compares the catechumen who receives initiation with the martyr: in each the sacraments of baptism are fulfilled. One confesses their faith before a priest, the other before their persecutor; one is sprinkled or dipped in water, the other is sprinkled with their blood or consumed by fire; one receives the Holy Spirit through the laying on of a bishop's hand, the other becomes a dwelling place of the Holy Spirit, because it is not the martyr who speaks but the Holy Spirit who speaks through them.[21]

Gennadius is a late writer (*fl.* 470), but we may begin with him because he is so explicit. A century earlier, Zeno of Verona, (writing our earliest surviving Latin sermons in the 370s) presents the paschal baptism as a courtroom scene, in which the initiand is tried and then executed. The execution is described graphically, and although no blood is shed the old person is said to have definitely died.[22]

For us, the courtroom motif, the sinner before God condemned and sentenced to death, all sound like modern popular evangelicalism. But the present writer's suspicion is that for Zeno and his contemporaries, the courtroom was the same as for Gennadius a century later, that of the confrontation between the gospel and the world, between the martyr and the judge.

[18] *The Architectural Setting of Baptism* (London 1962) 17-18.

[19] For the temptation to classify ancient buildings, see the comments of Cyril Mango on *martyria* in his *Byzantine Architecture* (London 1986) 44-56.

[20] *Architectural Setting,* 18.

[21] *De Eccles. Dogmat.* 74. (*PL* 58:997); see J. D. C. Fisher, *Christian Initiation: Baptism in the Medieval West* (London 1965) 54-5.

[22] *Sermon* 1.42 in B. Löfstedt (ed.), *Tractatus,* Corpus Christianorum Series Latina 22, Turnhout 1971.

161

Two passages stand out in Zeno; both seem to be loosely based on Tertullian. Tertullian tells the imprisoned Christians that they have already left the prison of the world, the *saeculum*. The world has worse darkness, chains and dirt than can any physical prison, and they have left the world.[23] Zeno also presents the world as the prison when he tells the newly baptized, "Rejoice, you now owe nothing to the world. You are freed of earthly chains and bonds. Terror and filth are past."[24]

And, in the second passage, as far as Tertullian is concerned, the pagan sinner fears the court, but with the Christian it is different: "If pointed out, they pride themselves on it; if accused, they do not defend themselves; when examined they confess of their own accord; when condemned they give thanks."[25] Zeno likewise says of baptism: "It is a new kind of judgment, in which the guilty, if they deny the crime, are condemned; if they acknowledge it, they are acquitted."[26]

The contradiction between the judgment of the world and of God was (and is) a Christian commonplace. Pierre-Marie Gy has explored the ambivalence of the Christian term *confessio* in the language of penance in the Middle Ages. *Confessio* has its ambivalence rooted in the Hebrew *hôdâ(h)*, 'confession of sin' and 'glorification of God'.[27] But Gy puts the force of the ambivalence in the language of the pagan courtroom:

> The pagan governor summons me before him and questions me: "Are you a Christian?" I reply, "Confiteor." He understands this to mean, "I confess I am guilty," and decides my head should be cut off. But when I say "Confiteor," I am conscious of having confessed my faith, borne witness to the faith. Other Christians will say I am a confessor of the faith, perhaps a martyr.[28]

Upside-down judgment is found in all sorts of ways in the divine courtroom. "You will judge the judges," Tertullian tells the martyrs,[29] and: "The

[23] *Ad Martyrs* 2.1-2.
[24] *Sermon* 2.29.1.
[25] *Apologeticum* 1.12.
[26] *Sermon* 2.10.2. For the connection with Tertullian, cf. Löfstedt's note on the text.
[27] Cf. Christine Mohrmann, "Linguistic Problems in the Early Christian Church," *Études sur le Latin des Chrétiens* 3 (Rome 1965) 185: "This double meaning finds its fullest literary exploitation in St Augustine's *Confessions.*"
[28] "The Inculturation of the Christian Liturgy in the West," *Studia Liturgia* 20 (1990) 12.
[29] *Ad Martyres* 2.4.

162

world will endure the judgment, not of the proconsul but of God."[30] The martyrs in the *Passion of Perpetua and Felicity* shout, "You judge us, and God judges you."[31]

Cyprian has the same motif of the courtroom. Here is total concentration on the judgment by Christ of the confessor: "Let it be before your eyes, dearly beloved, that he, who alone received all judgment from the Father and who will come to judge, has already brought forth the sentence of his judgment and of his future trial, pronouncing and attesting that he will confess before his Father those who confess and that he will deny those who deny."[32]

There is the hint of a reaction against the proconsul in the claim that Christ alone received the power of judgment. Very different is the treatment by Theodore of Mopsuestia of the courtroom motif in his *Baptismal Homilies,* where the preliminary rites are portrayed as a court case against the devil who appears to be the real villain, and at first the candidate appears to be more weak than evil, and more sinned against than sinning: "When you present yourselves to give in your names, in the hope of finding a dwelling-place in heaven, the exorcisms are, so to say, a law-suit with the devil; you are freed from slavery to him by God's judgment." However attention reverts to the candidates and their own condemnation:

> You stretch out your hands to God in the attitude of one at prayer. For we have fallen into sin and the sentence of death has thrown us to the ground. . . . The rest of your body should remain upright, looking up to heaven. By this attitude you present, so to speak, a request to God, asking him like a petitioner for liberation from your ancient fall and a share in the joys of heaven.[33]

The courtroom motif is a continuity in martyrdom and baptism, as is most clearly seen in the writings of Gennadius. However, he ignores a difference in the motif according to its context. When applied to the martyrs, they are innocent, the faithful witnesses to Christ the only true judge. At the Last Judgment God will vindicate them, and the world will recognize that by condemning the martyrs it has invited judgment on itself.

---

[30] Ibid., 2.3.

[31] *Passio Sanctarum Perpetuae et Felicitatis* 18.

[32] *Ep.* 58.3; English translation from Sister Rose Bernard Donna, *Letters,* Fathers of the Church 51 (New York 1964) 165.

[33] *Baptismal Homily* 2.1-4; English translation from E. J. Yarnold, *The Awe-Inspiring Rites of Initiation* (Slough 1972) 176-8.

163

In the context of baptism in Zeno and Theodore, and in the later tradition of penance as outlined by Gy, the candidate accepts the verdict and judgment of God, and only by doing so receives his gracious love and forgiveness. The basic motif remains the same—the perfect judgment of God. But whereas the martyr is the faithful confessor of Christ, the candidate preparing for baptism comes in from the world and still shares in its guilt until that guilt is confessed and forgiveness is received.

IV. The Contest with Satan

The contest with Satan was an ever-growing feature in the baptismal rites in both East and West. In the West, anti-demonic rites had a place in initiation at least from the time of Hippolytus. The East, however, saw the introduction of such rites only much later, and the transformation of the rites has been well documented by such scholars as Gabriele Winkler, Sebastian Brock and, in particular detail, by Henry Ansgar Kelly.[34] Here we pick up only one or two features of the baptismal rites which seem to overlap with details in the stories of martyrdom.

1. Athlete and Soldier

The picture of the martyr as athlete and soldier is extremely common[35] and goes back to the beginning of Christianity, and even to Jewish times when a Maccabean martyr was compared to an athlete (4 Macc. 6:9-10). In Paul's writings there is the athlete who is the runner in the race (1 Cor. 9:24-7), but closer to our theme is the blending of racing and conflict in 2 Tim. 4:7-8: "I have fought the good fight, I have finished the race, I have kept the faith. From now on there is reserved for me the crown of righteousness, which the Lord, the righteous judge, will give me on that day."

The martyr athlete is more wrestler than runner, and is set to combat in the gladiatorial games, only the combat is against Satan. This is quite explicit in the vision of Perpetua:

We came to the amphitheatre, and [I was led out] into the centre of the arena. . . . Then out came an Egyptian against me . . . to fight with me. My clothes were stripped off . . . and my seconds began to rub me down with oil (as they are wont to do before a contest). [Perpetua fights and

---

[34] *The Devil at Baptism,* Ithaca NY/London 1985.
[35] Cf. Gerald Bonner, *The Warfare of Christ* (London 1962) 36-48.

164

wins.] Then I awoke. I realised that it was not with wild beasts that I would fight but with the Devil; but I knew that I would win the victory.[36]

The parallel is only too clear in Ambrose: "We arrived at the baptistery. . . . You were rubbed with oil like an athlete, Christ's athlete, as though in preparation for an earthly wrestling-match, and you agree to take on your opponent. . . . The question was put to you, *Do you renounce the devil and his works?*[37]

John Chrysostom explains the anointing with chrism on the forehead (which happens after the renunciation of Satan and adhesion to Christ) thus:

> The priest knows that henceforth the enemy is furious, grinds his teeth and goes about like a roaring lion when he sees those who were formerly subject to his sovereignty in sudden rebellion against him, not only renouncing him, but going over to the side of Christ. Therefore, the priest anoints you on the forehead and puts on you the sign [of the cross], in order that the enemy may turn away his eyes. For he does not dare to look you in the face when he sees the lightning flash which leaps from it and blinds his eyes. Henceforth from that day there is strife and counterstrife with him, and on this account the priest leads you into the spiritual arena as athletes of Christ by virtue of this anointing.[38]

Why does Chrysostom say that the seal on the forehead will make the devil turn away his eyes? The idea of dazzling one's opponent in combat by a polished helmet or shield is perhaps sufficient to explain it, but we find the idea of dazzling in the stories of the martyrs. First and foremost the proto-martyr Stephen's face "was like the face of an angel."[39] No one could withstand the face of the martyr. On the day of the games, Perpetua went out "as the beloved of God, as a wife of Christ, putting down everyone's stare by her own intense gaze."[40] John Chrysostom assured his congregation that the

---

[36] *Passio Sanctarum Perpetuae et Felicitatis* 10; English translation from M. Musurillo (ed.), *The Acts of the Christian Martyrs* (Oxford 1972) 118-19.

[37] *De Sacramentis;* English translation from Yarnold op. cit., 101.

[38] Stavronikita 2.23; English translation from Harkins, op. cit., 51-2.

[39] Acts 6:15. Cf. W. H. C. Frend, *Martyrdom and Persecution in the Early Church* (Oxford 1965) 85: "He was therefore manifesting the glory of God in the form reserved for the Righteous who participated in Judgement; at the end, he was under the direct inspiration of the Holy Spirit."

[40] *Passio Sanctarum Perpetuae et Felicitatis* 17-18.

165

blood of martyrs made their bodies shine brighter than the heavens, and that demons could not look on them or they would be blinded.[41]

The devil, as we know, is like a roaring lion, and the beasts in the arena had difficulties facing and swallowing Christians.

We ourselves also were present as these things happened. . . . The man-devouring beasts for a long time did not dare to touch nor even to approach the bodies of the dear to God, but rushed upon the others. . . . The holy athletes alone, although they stood naked and waved their hands to draw them to themselves (for they were ordered to do this), were not touched at all, but sometimes, as [the beasts] rushed upon them, they were held back, as it were, by some divine power. . . . Thus, you would have seen a youth, not fully twenty years old, standing without fetters and spreading his hands in the form of a cross, and, with a mind undaunted and unmoved, most leisurely engaged in earnest prayer to the Deity, and not at all changing his stand or retreating from the place where he had taken his post, while bears and leopards breathing anger and death almost touched his very flesh, but somehow by a divine and mysterious power just checking their mouths and running again to the rear.[42]

On occasion John Chrysostom uses the motif with regard to the eucharist: the devil flees from one who has just received communion. However, we are not necessarily dealing with a generally used image, for Enrico Mazza is categorical that it is derived from the use of the theme in initiation.[43]

2. Imitation of Christ

The young man spreading his hands in the form of a cross (εἰς σταυροῦ τύπον) was acting out voluntarily not just the form of prayer but the martyr's imitation of Christ naked upon the cross. Among the martyrs of Lyons,

Blandina was hung on a stake and was offered as food for the wild beasts that were let in. [They did not touch her.] Since she seemed to be hanging in the form of a cross, and by her firmly intoned prayer, she inspired

---

[41] *In S. Julianum Martyrem* (*PG* 50:669-70).
[42] Eusebius, *Historia Ecclesiastica* 8.7; English translation from R. J. Deferrari, *Fathers of the Church* 29 (New York 1956) 176.
[43] *Mystagogy,* 117-19.

166

the combatants with great zeal, as they looked on during the contest and ... saw through their sister him who was crucified for them.[44]

Imitation of Christ was central to the tradition of martyrdom.[45] And when Cyril of Jerusalem explains the symbolism of the rites of initiation to the candidates, he includes the idea of imitation: "Stripped naked, in this too you were imitating, Christ naked on the cross, who in his darkness 'disarmed the principalities and powers' and on the wood of the cross publicly 'triumphed over them.'"[46]

This whole lecture of Cyril's is one of great interest in the history of the baptismal liturgy, but the line that Cyril takes in interpreting scripture is not without difficulty. He uses as his scriptural reading Rom. 6:3-14, on being baptized into Christ's death, but in the passage quoted above, moves from Romans to Col. 2:15 to include the triumph over the principalities and powers. We are in the traditional picture of the combat with evil. And Cyril opposes those who believe that baptism confers only remission of sins and adoption (essentially up to his time the classic view of baptism) and maintains that "it further implies a share by imitation in the true suffering of Christ"[47]—not just Christ's death, but his suffering as well. Edward Yarnold comments that "it says much for the importance Cyril attached to symbolism that the symbolic effect of baptism, i.e., the share in Christ's suffering, seems to him more important than the forgiveness of sins or the adoption it confers."[48] One might add that Cyril seems to attach at least as much importance to the suffering of Christ as his death:

> We did not really die, we were not really buried, we did not really hang from a cross and rise again. Our imitation was symbolic, but our salvation a reality. Christ truly hung from a cross, was truly buried, and truly rose again. All this he did gratuitously for us, so that we might share his sufferings by imitating them, and gain salvation in actuality.

---

[44] Eusebius, *Hist. Eccl.* 5.1; English translation from R. J. Deferrari, *Fathers of the Church* 19 (New York 1953) 282.

[45] E.g., Irenaeus, the martyr is he "who tried to follow in Christ's footsteps": *Adv. Haer.* 3.18.5 (*PG* 7:936); Ignatius, *Rom.* 6.3; Polycarp, *Phil* 8.2; Clement of Alexandria, *Strom.* 4.7.43.4; 2.20.104; *Passio Sanctarum Perpetuae et Felicitatis* 18; Cyprian, *Ep.* 38.2 (calls Christ's death a martyrdom); Origen, *Comm. in Ioh.* 6.54; Origen, *Exhortation to Martyrdom* 50; for Chrysostom see Christofis, "The Notions of Martyrdom," 33-5, and R. Jacob, "Le Martyre," 166-9.

[46] *Myst. Cat.* 2.2; English translation from Yarnold, op. cit., 74.

[47] Ibid., 2.6.

[48] *Awe-Inspiring Rites*, 77, n. 18.

167

What transcendent kindness! Christ endured nails in his innocent hands and feet, and suffered pain; and by letting me participate in the pain without anguish or sweat, he freely bestows salvation on me.[49]

John Baldovin sees the problem here: "the analogy [Cyril] draws between the candidate's baptism and the sufferings of Christ is somewhat weak, because the burial and the sufferings are not exact parallels."[50] The parallel, weak in Cyril's own exposition, gains its strength from the parallel between the suffering of the martyr and that of Christ. Imitation of Christ's death, for Cyril, was imitation of his suffering and of his triumph over evil. This was the same imitation as that which the martyr aspired to, but now it is effected sacramentally.

3. The Confession of Faith

One feature of the fourth-century catecheses that always puzzled the present writer was the way in which the commentators would speak of a heavenly audience at the time of the renunciations. The renunciations were often separated from the actual act of baptism by a considerable distance of time and space, and it seemed a strange emphasis to make at this particular point alone. Chromatius of Aquileia explains the renunciations thus:

> And so before you came to baptism, you were asked whether you renounced the world and its pomps and works. And you replied that you renounced it, and thus you came to the grace of eternal baptism. Your words are kept with God. Your reply is written in heaven. You promised to God your word of faith (*fidem*), you promised it in the presence of the angels, because angels attend on us when our word of faith is demanded of us.[51]

And John Chrysostom says,

> Then the priest has you say: "I renounce thee, Satan, thy pomps, thy service, and thy works." The words are few but their power is great. The angels who are standing by and the invisible powers rejoice at your

---

[49] *Myst. Cat.* 2.5; ibid., 76-7.

[50] *Liturgy in Ancient Jerusalem,* Alcuin/GROW Liturgical Study 9 (Nottingham 1989) 18. Mazza, *Mystagogy,* 158, claims that the idea of participation by imitation in the sufferings of Christ is based on Romans 6, though, as we have seen, that passage speaks only of his death.

[51] *Sermon* 14.4; ed. J. Lemarié, *Chromace d'Aquilée: Sermons* 1 (Paris 1969) 244, lines 79-86.

168

conversion, receive the words from your tongues, and carry them up to the common Master of all things. There they are inscribed in the books of heaven.[52]

Mazza has noticed the role of the angels here and quotes the above passage of Chrysostom. He believes that the role of the angels is as intermediaries like that of the angels in the eucharistic liturgies of the Roman Canon and the Alexandrian anaphoras.[53] Obviously they are functioning in some way as intermediaries here, but Mazza does not address the question: Why at the renunciations?

An explanation might be found in the way in which Chrysostom describes the confession under torture of the martyr St Julian: "his voice jumped from his holy tongue, ascended into heaven, the angels saw it and stepped aside, the archangels marvelled at it, while the Cherubim and the other heavenly powers uninterruptedly guided it, until it arrived at the kingly throne of God."[54] The apotaxis is not necessarily to be seen as more important than the syntaxis. But the angels attend on it just as they had attended on the martyr's apotaxis of the world. Chromatius has them attend as witnesses; in Chrysostom's rhetoric their mediatorial role is set aside by the glory of the martyr's confession which wins direct access to the heavenly throne, but that speaks of the role normally expected of them.

There is a difference between the role of angels at martyrdom and baptism. The martyr tradition has a triumphant tone to the confession, but in the context of baptism, the recording of the words in heaven has a less glorious side. Chrysostom says in another instruction: "Therefore let us say these words: 'I renounce thee, Satan,' knowing that we shall be called to account for them on that Day of Judgment."[55]

This motif of the angels watching and recording the faithful confession of the martyr lies behind other bishops' comments on the renunciation (and they make the point only at the renunciation). Cyril of Jerusalem says: "Now realise this: all that you say, especially at that most awesome moment, is written in God's books."[56] And Ambrose: "Your guarantee is binding, not

---

[52] Stavronikata 2.20; English translation from Harkins, op. cit., 51.
[53] *Mystagogy*, 125.
[54] *In S. Julianum Martyrem* (*PG* 50:671).
[55] Montfaucon 2.52; English translation from Harkins, op. cit., 189.
[56] *Myst. Cat.* 1.5; English translation from Yarnold, op. cit., 70.

169

on earth, but in heaven,"[57] and, "Your words are kept not in the tomb of the dead but in the book of the living."[58] It could be, as has been suggested,[59] that here Ambrose is copying Cyril, but it is more probable that we are dealing with a common theme known throughout the Mediterranean, that the combat with the Devil was witnessed by God's angels. For we find that quite explicitly in Cyprian: "God looks on us fighting and battling in the assembly of faith; his angels look on, and Christ looks on. How great is the dignity of the glory, how great is the happiness to fight with God as protector and to be crowned with Christ as judge?"[60]

V. Minor Motifs

Of course it is not the case that a common use of imagery necessitates a dependence of baptism on martyrdom. In two motifs, the image of making bread, and the spiritual marriage, I would suggest merely a continuity of thought.

1. The Image of Making Bread
The idea of being made into bread was already a theme in martyrdom. Ignatius of Antioch writes to the Romans: "Suffer me to be eaten by the beasts, through whom I can attain to God. I am God's wheat, and I am ground by the teeth of wild beasts that I may be found pure bread of Christ."[61] Polycarp, likewise, when burnt was "not as burning flesh, but as bread that is being baked, or as gold and silver being refined in a furnace."[62] And Tertullian's description of "the Lord's threshing floor" concerns martyrdom: "To God alone it belongs to judge, and this is his winnowing fan which even now cleanses the Lord's threshing floor—his Church, winnowing the mixed heap of the faithful and separating the wheat of the martyrs from the chaff of the cowards."[63]

---

[57] *De Sacramentis* I.ii.6; English translation from Yarnold op. cit., 102.

[58] *De Mysteriis* 5.

[59] E. J. Yarnold, "Did St Ambrose Know the Mystagogic Catecheses?" *Studia Patristica* 12 (1975) 184-9.

[60] *Ep.* 58.8. Cf. *Ad Fortunatum*, Preface 4, where martyrdom is described as "the baptism in which the angels baptize."

[61] *Rom* 4.1; English translation from Kirsopp Lake, *The Apostolic Fathers* (London/Cambridge MA 1959) 1:231.

[62] *Mart. Polycarp* 15; English translation from Kirsop Lake, op. cit., 2:333.

[63] *Flight in Time of Persecution* 1.4; English translation from E. A. Quain, *Disciplinary, Moral, and Ascetical Works,* Fathers of the Church 40 (New York 1959) 276.

170

74

But the Lord's threshing floor is rather different in the famous passage in Augustine where the baptismal candidates are pictured as grain being made into bread:

> Remember, you did not exist, and you were created: you were carried to the Lord's threshing floor. . . . When you were set aside as catechumens you were stored in his barn. You gave in your names: you began to be ground with fasting and exorcism. After that you came to water, were moistened and made one. You were cooked then, when the ardour of the Holy Spirit came near, and now have been made the Lord's bread.[64]

This kind of treatment of baptism is by no means unique to Augustine. Similar passages are to be found in Zeno[65] and Gaudentius of Brescia.[66] No doubt it was a Western commonplace.

The passage of Tertullian quoted above is typical of his disdain for the ordinary faithful who are branded as cowards—chaff. But Zeno has a purification of the wheat in his picture of the making of bread, and there the various weeds and chaff represent the sins and impurities rooted out by the preliminary rites of baptism. Augustine has none of this—explicitly—but his description of the catechumens as being brought to the threshing floor, their being ground up and set aside, has less romance and more force when read in the context of passages such as those of Ignatius and Tertullian.

It could be said that the influence of the imagery goes both ways: from eucharist to martyrdom as well as from martyrdom to baptism and eucharist. Polycarp's martyrdom is portrayed as a sacrifice, and the image of bread, or gold or silver, fits in with that. Ignatius hopes that he "may be found a sacrifice through these instruments" (i.e., the wild beasts), and so the same connection applies. But while the imagery of the eucharistic bread is applied to martyrdom, the liturgical imagery of being broken, ground, and purified would seem to gain its force from the tradition of martyrdom.[67]

2. The Picture of Spiritual Marriage

In John Chrysostom we have the opportunity to see how a single writer uses one theme, the picture of the spiritual marriage, with regard to both martyrdom and baptism.

---

[64] *Miscellanea Agostiniana* 1 (Rome 1930), Sermon 6.1, 30; English translation from E. C. Whitaker, *Documents of the Baptismal Liturgy*, 2nd edn (London 1970) 106.

[65] *Sermon* 1.41.

[66] *Tract II in Exodum.*

[67] Zeno has a treatment of wine, similar to that which we have described of bread, in which again the element of martyrdom is introduced (*Sermon* 2.11).

171

The martyr through imitation of Christ's death becomes intimately united with him. This marriage is described as "more spiritual" than an earthly wedding, and in it God is married to human souls. The martyr's soul is the spiritual bride and the blood is offered as the dowry.[68]

A very similar treatment of the theme of the spiritual marriage is found in one of Chrysostom's sermons of baptismal instruction. Again we have "a spiritual marriage," but here the "Bridegroom hurries to save our souls."[69] Concerning the dowry for the wedding, Chrysostom quotes Eph. 5.25-7, and comments:

> Did you see the magnitude of his gifts? Did you see the ineffable bounty of his love? *Just as Christ also loved the Church and delivered himself up for her.* No man would ever have allowed himself to do this, namely, to pour out his blood for the woman who was going to be his bride. But the kindly Master, imitating his own goodness, has accepted this great and marvellous sacrifice because of his solicitude for her, that by his own blood he might sanctify her; that, having cleansed her by the bath of baptism, he might present her to himself a Church in all her glory. To this end he poured forth his blood and endured the cross. . . .[70]

The dowry gift here is Christ himself giving himself for the bride. But Chrysostom goes beyond the quotation of Ephesians to focus on the shedding of the blood, just as the martyr's dowry gift might strictly be said to be oneself, but focuses on the blood. However, the baptismal candidate can offer only the dowry of "the obedience and the agreement which will be made with the Bridegroom."[71] The agreement is that of the syntaxis, the promise of adhesion to Christ.[72]

These sermons do not show an explicit or necessary connection between baptism and martyrdom, but the similarity is clear enough, and in the context of the other themes we are justified in seeing a common and continuous strand of thought, appropriately changed to fit the context of martyrdom or baptism.

VI. Baptismal Symbolism and the Martyr Literature

If this thesis is correct, it might be supposed that baptismal imagery would find its way into later literature about the martyrs. The present writer has not

---

[68] See Christofis, "The Nature of Martyrdom" 39.
[69] *De Eleazaro et Septem Pueris* (*PG* 63:525).
[70] Stavronikita 1.15; English translation from Harkins, op. cit., 28.
[71] Ibid., 1.17 (Harkins, op. cit., 29).
[72] Ibid., 1.16. Cf. Papadopoulos-Kerameus 3.25-6 (Harkins, op. cit., 168-9).

172

attempted a systematic survey of the literature, but a cursory reading has produced a good example in the Martyrdom of Dasius. Herbert Musurillo in his commentary summarizes a number of reasons for believing that the *acta* are late and spurious,[73] but that by no means hinders our study; indeed we are concerned more with the literature of later times than of the Church before Constantine.

In this account we have a quasi-liturgical confession of faith (sounding more like a syntaxis than an apotaxis) by which the martyr opposes and overcomes the devil, and a quasi-liturgical sealing of the forehead against the devil:

> The blessed martyr Dasius said, "I confess I am a Christian as I have confessed many times before and I obey no one else but the one unde-filed and eternal God, Father, Son, and Holy Spirit, who are three in name and person but one in substance. So now by this triple formula I confess my faith in the Holy Trinity, for strengthened by it I can quickly conquer and overthrow the devil's madness." . . . [When overthrowing the idols] He fortified his forehead with the seal of the precious cross of Christ, by whose power he so mightily resisted the tyrant.[74]

This example is reassuring rather than startling. The baptismal imagery is strong enough to be clearly recognizable, and indeed it would be strange if it were any stronger. But this account could only be written in a Christian ambience which took it for granted that in baptism, just as in martyrdom, one's confession of faith was a contest against the devil.

In a paper delivered at the 1991 Oxford Patristics Conference, John Petruccione drew a parallel between the martyr and the baptized Christian in the writings of Prudentius.[75] The imagery of the blood of the Passover, lamb on the doorposts is applied to both instances. In the case of the martyrs, their blood is pictured as having been daubed on the gates of the city in which they were killed, and drives the demons away from the city purified by their expiatory deaths.[76] In another passage, writing against the Jews, Prudentius portrays the Passover blood as the baptismal seal of the sign of the cross, which defends the individual against death and provides escape from the

---

[73] *The Acts of the Christian Martyrs,* xl-xli.
[74] Ibid., 277, 279.
[75] "The Martyr Death as Sacrifice: Prudentius, *Peristephanon* 4.9-72." I am very grateful to Dr Petruccione for allowing me to consult a copy of his paper.
[76] *Peristephanon* 4.65-8.

173

devil's power.[77] Petruccione points out that the imagery in the latter case is applied to individuals rather than, as in the former case, to a community. As always in the literature we have examined, the imagery is applied sensitively and with theological accuracy to each case. The basis is Christ the true Passover lamb. The efficacy of the martyrdom is one with Christ's grace with regard to the city. The ordinary Christian is the individual recipient of the same grace.

VII. Reflections

By way of a conclusion, the subject invites reflections on two aspects of this historical study: the problem of inculturation and the relation of liturgy and doctrine.

With regard to inculturation, the historical process by which the language of dying with Christ entered into the baptismal liturgies has been reliably dated to the fourth century and later. If this paper is correct in seeing the influence of the martyr tradition on the liturgies, then we have to acknowledge that the tradition became a liturgical language only after it had, to all intents and purposes, ceased as a current actual issue. It was only when martyrs were a thing of the past that the language of martyrdom could be applied to the initiation of every Christian. But this is not just a matter of respect for the martyr élite. The image in order to be freed for the common language has to be a step removed from the reality. (To give an example, the image of the Good Shepherd, even in a shepherding community, works only if you forget that the shepherd sooner or later fleeces the sheep.)

The passing away of the age of the martyrs freed the image of martyrdom for the liturgy. Also, this image was bound up with an essential feature of the gospel, its radical challenge to the world, and while the martyr tradition was by no means the only embodiment of the challenge (there was also, for example, the ascetic tradition), it did carry much of its force. When martyrdom was a real, however unlikely, prospect, it was through those individuals and their *acta* that the challenge was focused. The baptismal liturgy in those days did not need to emphasize the death image because it was fostered elsewhere. Indeed, it may be that the real possibility of martyrdom was not the thing of which to remind baptismal candidates. But as the Church became part of the establishment, we see the martyr image and the challenge of

---

[77] *Apotheosis* 355-61.

174

the gospel pass over from the individual confessing their faith before the judge to the baptismal candidate opposing Satan and dying with Christ in the font, and to the ascetic in the desert, putting self to death.

The process suggested here can be paralleled by Gerald Bonner's investigation of the theme of spiritual warfare:

With the triumph of Constantine and the end of the period of persecution, the idea of the spiritual combat might have dropped out of use, if there had not immediately become available another class of men to whom it could be applied now that the martyrs were no more, namely the monks. . . . The victory won in the arena when, by shedding his blood, the martyr proclaimed and made manifest the victory of Christ and the rout of Satan could no longer be looked for; but it was still possible to win victories over the devil by rejecting his temptations, and by carrying the war into his own territory [the desert]. . . . The monastic profession, then, becomes a substitute for martyrdom, and to the monk are applied the epithets formerly bestowed upon the martyr. He is both the athlete and the soldier. . . . The spiritual combat, introduced into Christian thought by St Paul, transferred by necessity to the physical plane in the age of the martyrs, has now once more moved back to the realm of the spirit.[78]

The reflection on liturgy and doctrine is this: can we apply the relation, *lex credendi* and *lex orandi,* to the changes outlined in the baptismal rites and imagery? Can we claim to see the influence of the former on the latter? If by *lex credendi* we mean formal or academic theology as opposed to popular uncritical belief, we cannot, for there is no influence to be seen of councils, controversies, or scholars. But nor do we seem to have here the influence of any *conscious* belief, critically informed or otherwise.

As far as we can tell, the shift in meaning and imagery in early baptism, across the whole of the Mediterranean, was not the conscious initiative of any individual or individuals. Indeed, it seems to have occurred over such a wide area and over such a long period of time (a couple of generations from the Peace of Constantine to the time of Ambrose and Chrysostom), that we cannot presume that the participants were aware of it being such a shift. Each bishop individually by degrees amended his rite according to the atmosphere that the Church breathed. No doubt each borrowed from neighbors or influential sees, but the motivation for the borrowing was the new atmosphere breathed.

[78] *The Warfare of Christ,* 48, 50, 52.

175

In this context, we must conclude that the changes in the liturgy were not due to the isolated influence of Romans 6. It was not as if they suddenly realized that this verse was omitted from the liturgy and worked to include it. Rather the change in the liturgy was the response to a wide spread of concerns, and Romans 6 provided the appropriate picture. In witnessing to the truth about God over against the world, the martyrs were true not only to Paul's portrayal of dying with Christ but also to his conviction of the "rightness of God" over against the *saeculum*. It is by God's grace that they come to follow Christ and to make the Great Confession, and at the last judgment God will vindicate that Confession. But while they were true to Paul's portrayal, they had not Paul as their model, but Jesus. Their response was simply the same as Paul's to that example. Although the baptismal liturgies used Romans 6 about dying with Christ as a scriptural illustration, the real motivation came directly from the response of the martyrs in their vocation to follow after Christ the supreme martyr and only judge.

This is not so much *lex orandi, lex credendi* as *lex orandi, lex vivendi:* the law of prayer in relation to the law of the Christian Church living the gospel, often intuitively, unreflecting, unconsciously, and sometimes even getting it right. It took a long time for the new pattern of church life to establish itself. But by the time of Ambrose and Chrysostom we see a new relationship established between gospel and *saeculum* in diverse but connected ways: the magnificence of establishment, but also the monks, nuns, and ascetics, the new shape of the baptismal liturgy, and also the relations of bishops like Ambrose to the Emperor.

Liturgy and life, *lex orandi, lex vivendi,* were a seamless robe, and changed and adapted as one, naturally rather than by conscious deliberation. Of the writers we have surveyed, only Gennadius explicitly acknowledges a link between baptism and martyrdom in the use of imagery. Zeno was aware of it, and presumably Chrysostom, but the present writer doubts if any were aware of the process of cause and effect in the development of Christian life and baptism that was happening around them. This was the result of *lex vivendi*. It is interesting that only in the twentieth century have liturgical scholars (the agents of the *lex credendi*?) realized something of what happened in the fourth.

176

On Rebaptism: Social Organization in the Third Century Church

J. PATOUT BURNS

The dispute between Cyprian in Carthage and Stephen in Rome over the rebaptism of converts from schismatic communities should be understood as a consequence of the particular and different problems which each church faced after Decius' edict requiring participation in the Roman cult. A social analysis shows that in each case, the ritual of reconciliation of the lapsed was central to defining and controlling the church's boundary. Cyprian focused on the unity of the church in one communion while Stephen upheld the authority of a single bishop over the baptized. In defending the prerogative of his church, the African refused to acknowledge the efficacy of baptism performed in schism and the Roman insisted upon its validity.

The controversy between the churches of Rome and Carthage over the status of baptism performed in heretical or schismatic Christian communities resulted from differences in the impact of the Decian persecution on the Christians of these two cities of the Empire. After crumbling under the imperial assault, the church of Carthage was rescued through the organizational and oratorical efforts of its extraordinary bishop, Cyprian. By correspondence and speeches, first from exile and then in Carthage, he forged a new understanding of the purity and strength of the church which was adopted and supported by his colleagues throughout Roman Africa. But the bishops of Rome rejected that African ideal of the church because it violated what they considered a well established tradition deriving from the apostles themselves.

Surviving records of the conflict are extraordinary for the period: some eighty-two letters which Cyprian wrote and received over eight years, his treatises, the minutes of a decisive meeting of the African bishops, a brief

Journal of Early Christian Studies 1:4 367–403 © 1993 The Johns Hopkins University Press.

record in Eusebius' *Church History*, a contemporary biography of Cyprian, and the *acta* of his martyrdom.[1] However, this historical record is seriously unbalanced. While Cyprian's theory of the nature of the church and of its sacramental action is fully developed and defended, the argument for the traditional position can be discerned only second-hand through Cyprian's responses. As a consequence, perhaps, historians of thought have not been able to explain the ultimate success of the traditional practice and the failure of Cyprian's scripturally based and persuasively argued innovation to take root outside Africa.

This investigation of the historical and theological problem will use the tools of cultural anthropology developed by Mary Douglas.[2] The rituals of baptism and reconciliation of penitents, which were the focus of the controversy, can be studied as purification rites through which individuals crossed the boundary by which Christians segregated and protected their church from the encompassing culture of imperial Rome. Douglas' theory proposes a correlation between a community's trust in the efficacy of its rituals of purification and the experienced success of its internal organization.[3] Using these methods, significant differences can be discerned between the churches in Carthage and Rome which will elucidate the differences in their baptismal practices.

The essay begins with an historical overview of the controversy and then proceeds to analyze the effects of the Decian persecution on the Christian church in Carthage and Rome. Material from the first section will of necessity be repeated in the second and third. The exposition will not employ the technical language of the theory which guides the investigation.

1. The works of Cyprian are complete in CSEL 3.1–3; a number of the treatises are in CCSL 3, 3A. The fullest contemporary treatment of this period is found in the introduction and accompanying notes of G. W. Clarke's *The Letters of St. Cyprian*, ACW, vols. 43, 45, 46, 47 (New York: Newman Press, 1984–89). Maurice Bevenot's translations *St. Cyprian: The Lapsed, The Unity of the Catholic Church*, ACW, vol. 25 (New York: Newman Press, 1957) also contains helpful information.

2. Mary Douglas, *Cultural Bias* (London: Royal Anthropological Institute of Great Britain and Ireland, 1978); *Natural Symbols* (New York: Pantheon Books, 1982); *Purity and Danger: An Analysis of the Concepts of Pollution and Taboo* (London: Ark Paperbacks, 1984). These studies were originally published in the reverse order. Though a number of attempts to explicate the theory have been made, the most successful brief introduction remains that of Sheldon R. Isenberg and Dennis E. Owen, "Bodies Natural and Contrived: The Work of Mary Douglas," *Religious Studies Review* 3 (1977): 1–17.

3. Generally referred to as group and grid. High group indicates that a community has a well defined boundary which segregates its members and restricts their significant social interaction to their colleagues within the community. High grid denotes both the differentiation of roles assigned by the group to its members and the success of this system in meeting the expectations it creates.

I. A BRIEF HISTORY OF THE CONTROVERSY

In December 249, the Emperor Decius, three months after defeating the Emperor Philip at Verona, and wishing to consolidate his position as well as to secure the good fortune of his reign, decreed that every citizen should join him in offering homage to the eternal gods upon whose graciousness the peace and prosperity of the Empire depended.[4] Each person was apparently required to appear before a locally established commission, to testify that he had always been a worshiper of the immortal gods and to demonstrate his piety in its presence by pouring a libation, offering sacrifice and eating the sacrificial meats.[5] While Decius required participation in the Roman ceremonies, he did not specify the renunciation of other religious practices or loyalties.[6] Both continuing Christian practice and the clergy's access to the imprisoned recusants were apparently tolerated.[7] One of the imperial objectives seems to have been the elimination of the divisions of religious exclusivism.[8]

Christian bishops were targeted for early action when enforcement began in January 250: Fabian of Rome died in prison,[9] Cyprian of Carthage withdrew into exile,[10] and Dionysius of Alexandria was hunted

---

4. The edict itself has not survived. See Clarke, *Letters* 1:27–28 for evidence that the requirements may have extended to those who were not citizens as well.

5. For the current state of scholarship on the *libelli*, see Clarke, *Letters* 1:26–27, 134 n. 135. A striking witness to the process of compliance is provided in *epp.* 8.2, 21.3 (CSEL 3.2:487, 531). In *ep.* 43.3 (CSEL 3.2:591), Cyprian made an oblique reference to the five commissioners who supervised the procedures in Carthage.

6. The certificate provided to those who complied with the edict does not mention the renunciation of any other religious loyalty. The two accounts of the martyrdoms of bishops during the subsequent persecution of Valerian do not require them to disavow Christianity but only to participate in the Roman cult. See the *acta proconsvlaria*, 3–4 (CSEL 3.3:cxii-cxiii) for interrogation and sentencing of Cyprian and Eusebius, *h.e.* 7.11 (SC 41:179–185), for Dionysius of Alexandria.

7. The clergy had full access to the imprisoned confessors, including the holding of services in the prison; Cyprian, *epp.* 5.2, 12.1,2 (CSEL 3.2:479, 502–503). Christians were apparently witnesses to the death under torture of some of the confessors; *ep.* 10.2 (CSEL 3.2:491). For the full evidence, see Clarke, *Letters* 1:132 n. 118.

8. G. W. Clarke, "Some Observations on the Persecution of Decius," *Antichthon* 3 (1969): 63–76. On the Jewish exemption from the edict, see Clarke, *Letters* 1:131 n. 117. Christians were disliked as a separatist group which did not participate in common rituals, see *ep.* 7.1 (CSEL 3.2:485). This resentment was the principal danger to the presbyters visiting the confessors in prison and to the Christians in the city; *epp.* 5.2, 6.4, 40.1 (CSEL 3.2:479, 484, 587).

9. The death of Fabian is first noted in Cyprian's *ep.* 9.1 (CSEL 3.2:489), in response to a lost eulogy of the Roman clergy.

10. Cyprian defended his conduct to the Roman clergy in *ep.* 20.1 (CSEL 3.2:527). This letter gives a summary of the progress of the persecution and the Christian response

---

down.[11] When imperial commissions were established in various cities during the late winter and spring, many Christians voluntarily complied with the edict either by actually offering sacrifice[12] or by using bribery to obtain the certificate which attested to their having done so.[13] By the time the deadline for compliance with the edict arrived, a major portion of the laity and some of the clergy had obeyed.[14] Those who persistently refused the commissioners' demand were imprisoned and brought to trial; some were released and others sent into exile.[15] During the spring of 250, the authorities introduced torture into the interrogations of Christian confessors and deprived them of food, water, fresh air and light in an attempt to force them to recant.[16] Although none were executed, some died under this regimen, the first martyrs of the persecution.[17]

---

to it through the summer of 250. Throughout his exile, Cyprian insisted that he had withdrawn because of the danger which his presence, as both a notable and the leader of the Christian community, posed for the community itself. See *epp.* 7.1, 14.1–2, 43.4 (CSEL 3.2:485, 509–510, 593).

11. Eusebius, *h.e.* 6.40 (SC 41:143–145). He was subsequently rescued by other Christians.

12. Cyprian later charges that many Christians in Carthage eagerly complied with the edict as soon as it was promulgated; *ep.* 11.8 (CSEL 3.2:501), *laps.* 7–9 (CCSL 3:224–225). *Epp.* 15.4, 24.1 (CSEL 3.2:516, 537) imply that some involved their dependents as well. For evidence of compliance at Rome, see *ep.* 8.2 (CSEL 3.2:487).

13. Those who obtained certificates either did so in person or through an agent by a payment. Some later asserted that they had explained to the imperial commissioners that they were Christians and could not comply with the edict. They regarded the payment as a fine or bribe. In so doing, some Christians were able to exempt and to protect their families and dependents. Similarly, some of the sacrificers seem to have protected others by their compliance. On the different attitudes, see *epp.* 21.3, 55.13–14,26 (CSEL 3.2:531, 632–633, 644).

14. See *epp.* 14.1, 11.8 (CSEL 3.2:509–510, 501). Cyprian later indicated that the majority of the Christians at Carthage had failed to honor their commitment to Christ, *laps.* 4,7 (CCSL 3:222, 224).

15. Cyprian expected their torture and deaths. *Ep.* 6.1–2 (CSEL 3.2:480–481). The problems addressed in *ep.* 13 make it clear that many of the confessors had been released and rejoined the community; see also *ep.* 14.2 (CSEL 3.2:511,). The punishment of exile is also indicated in *ep.* 13.4 (CSEL 3.2:507). *Ep.* 19.2 (CSEL 3.2:526) indicates that some of the exiles had suffered confiscation of their property.

16. *Epp.* 10.1–2, 12.1, 20.2, 21.4, 22.2 (CSEL 3.2:490–491, 502, 527–528, 532, 534). When the Roman confessors write to Cyprian for the first time, they note that they have been held for eight months already, apparently without formal trial; *epp.* 31.1,5, 37.1 (CSEL 3.2:557, 580). The experience of Celerinus in Rome is recounted in *ep.* 39.2 (CSEL 3.2:582).

17. For death under torture in Carthage, see *epp.* 11.1, 10.1–2, 12.1, 22.2 (CSEL 3.2:496, 490–491, 502–503, 534–535). In Rome, the presbyter Moyses seems to have died under these conditions; in *ep.* 55.5 (CSEL 3.2:626–627), Cyprian referred to him as a martyr.

While the imperial prosecution continued, the Roman clergy urged the fallen, both sacrificers and certified, to begin purifying themselves through repentance.[18] Reconciliation and readmission to communion were delayed, however, until the end of the persecution, except for the traditional giving of peace to dying penitents.[19] Confessors in prison fully supported the clergy's insistence on sustained repentance.[20]

At Carthage, imprisoned confessors responded differently to the pleading of Christians who had failed. In expectation of their martyrdom, the confessors granted letters of peace to the lapsed, promising to intercede with God and win forgiveness for their sin. Once a martyr died and entered heaven, the lapsed presented his letter to the clergy requesting, or demanding, readmission to the communion of the church on the strength of the martyr's intercession before God.[21] The bishop of Carthage, however, ordered the lapsed to undertake penance[22] until God had granted peace to the church as a whole.[23] Cyprian initially recognized the authority of the martyrs by allowing the presbyters to give peace to those dying penitents who had their letter of intercession.[24] Shortly thereafter he extended this

18. The letter of the Roman clergy to Cyprian, written by Novatian, rejects any distinction between those who sacrificed and those who acquired certificates by other means; *ep.* 30.3 (CSEL 3.2:550–551).

19. This policy is enunciated in *ep.* 8.2–3 (CSEL 3.2:487) and repeated in *epp.* 30.8, 36.1 (CSEL 3.2:556, 573). In *ep.* 30.8 it is identified as the common practice of the bishops in the area. In a similar way, the comfort of baptism was to be extended to a catechumen in danger of death; *ep.* 8.3 (CSEL 3.2:487).

20. The Roman confessors urged restraint on their brethren in Carthage, *ep.* 28.2 (CSEL 3.2:545–546). Their following of the policy of delay is also indicated in the letter of the Roman clergy, *ep.* 30.4 (CSEL 3.2:552), and in their own letter to Cyprian, *ep.* 31.6,7 (CSEL 3.2:562–563). Celerinus' appeal to the confessors in Carthage attempted to evade this policy; *ep.* 21.3 (CSEL 3.2:531).

21. Cyprian became aware of this problem in the spring 250. He treated it in *epp.* 15–17. *Ep.* 16.3 (CSEL 3.2:519) indicates that the death of the martyr is necessary for the validation of the letter of peace. See *ep.* 21 which requests such a letter of peace. One of the martyrs, Paulus, authorized another of the confessors, Lucianus, to grant peace in his name after his death to whoever asked; *ep.* 22.2 (CSEL 3.2:534).

22. *Ep.* 16.2 (CSEL 3.2:518–519) specifies the procedures which must be followed in the reconciliation of a penitent. Cyprian reminded his clergy and people of the seriousness of the sin of apostasy; *epp.* 16.2, 17.2 (CSEL 3.2:518, 522). Still, he seems to be assuming that forgiveness can be given, at least at death; *epp.* 17.3, 18.2 (CSEL 3.2:523, 524).

23. Cyprian seems to have regarded the persecution as God's chastisement of the church for its sinfulness. He insisted that peace was not to be granted to the lapsed until God had granted peace to the church itself, presumably after its adequate purification. see *epp.* 13.6; 11.3–7 (CSEL 3.2:508–509, 497–501).

24. He referred explicitly to the intercessory power of the martyrs: *ep.* 18.1 (CSEL 3.2:523–524). He instructed that catechumens were also to be allowed the peace of

concession to all dying penitents, bringing his church's practice into line with that of Rome where the letters of martyrs were not available.[25] With the persecution still raging, he reminded the impatient, and apparently impenitent, lapsed that they could immediately reenter the communion of the church by recanting their apostasy before the imperial commissioners.[26] Finally, he joined the Roman clergy in pledging that general consultations would be held after the persecution to establish a policy for restoring the repentant to communion.[27]

In Carthage, contrary to Roman practice, clergy and sinners refused to follow the agreed policy. Although some confessors agreed that the peace they granted should be delayed until God had granted peace to the whole church,[28] the lapsed pressured the clergy to restore them to communion upon the death of the martyr who had promised to intercede.[29] Five presbyters freely admitted the lapsed into the church's communion in open defiance of the bishop's order.[30]

As his exile stretched to a full year, Cyprian worked to regain control of the church, finally succeeding in late winter 251. With the assistance of confessor clergy from other areas who sought refuge in Carthage[31] and the

---

the church, through baptism, if they were in danger of death; *ep.* 18.2 (CSEL 3.2:524).

25. His policy had caused conflict in Carthage between those who had letters of peace and those who did not; *ep.* 19.2 (CSEL 3.2:525). In *ep.* 20.3 (CSEL 3.2:528–529), he broadened the dispensation. For the Roman practice, see n. 19.

26. *Ep.* 19.2 (CSEL 3.2:526). Were this serious, it would be a rare instance of exhortation to voluntary martyrdom. The Romans envisage an involuntary second arrest following repentance; *ep.* 8.3 (CSEL 3.2:487). In Carthage, some of the lapsed were arrested a second time, refused to comply, and were exiled with loss of goods; *epp.* 24, 25 (CSEL 3.2:536–538).

27. *Epp.* 17.3, 30.5 (CSEL 3.2:519, 553).

28. For the arrangement worked out by the confessors expecting to become martyrs, see *ep.* 22.2 (CSEL 3.2:534–535). *Ep.* 23 (CSEL 3.2:536) indicates that the bishop was allowed some discretion in actually granting the peace.

29. *Epp.* 19.2, 20.3 (CSEL 3.2:525, 528). Cyprian commented on the difficult position of the clergy in *epp.* 26.1 and 27.2 (CSEL 3.2:539, 542), and reported that some clergy have been forced to grant the peace in *ep.* 27.3 (CSEL 3.2:542). He noted and rejected the demand of the lapsed: *ep.* 33.1 (CSEL 3.2:566). See also *ep.* 35.1 (CSEL 3.2:571–572) in which Cyprian reported this conflict to the Roman clergy.

30. *Epp.* 14, 15.1, 16.1,4, 34.1, 42, 59.12 (CSEL 3.2:512–513, 514, 517, 520, 568–569, 590, 679–680)

31. He added some of the confessors, such as Celerinus and Aurelius, to the clergy; *epp.* 38, 39 (CSEL 3.2:579–585). He was able to call upon some of his own clergy as well as refugees, including the confessor bishop Caldonius and the confessor presbyters Rogatianus and Numidicus, to enforce his directives; see *epp.* 40, 34, 41, 42 (CSEL 3.2:585–586, 568–571, 587–590).

support of the Roman clergy,[32] he excommunicated the rebels.[33] Thereafter, he regarded the renegade clergy and their supporters among the confessors, the faithful and the fallen, as a schismatic communion cast away from the true and faithful church.[34]

After Easter 251, the imperial action had ceased and popular resentment of the Christians had so subsided that Cyprian could return to Carthage to resume direct governance of the community.[35] His first order of business was a division of the community into standing and fallen, faithful and apostate. Cyprian identified all the standing as confessors: not only those who had withstood imperial interrogation and torture but those who had taken flight and all others who had allowed the edict's deadline to pass without obeying.[36] In contrast, all who had sacrificed, acquired certificates without sacrificing, or who had even intended to comply if apprehended, he charged with idolatry imploring them to seek the forgiveness of God and the peace of the church through penance.[37] By offering immediate reconciliation, he explained, rebel clergy had prevented the lapsed from offering the satisfaction which provided their only hope for salvation.[38] Cyprian branded the schismatic leaders as agents of Satan and warned that splitting the church was unforgivable, a sin more grave than apostasy.[39]

32. *Epp.* 30 and 36 from the clergy and *ep.* 31 from the confessors buttressed Cyprian's lagging authority.

33. *Epp.* 34.1,3, 41.2, 42 (CSEL 3.2:568–570, 589–590). This action was taken in spring 251, when Cyprian was in better control of the situation in Carthage; a year earlier he could only threaten suspension of the offending clergy, see *ep.* 16.4 (CSEL 3.2:520).

34. *Ep.* 43 (CSEL 3.2:590–597), directed to the whole Christian people in Carthage, levels the charge of schism. The laxist party included five of the eight presbyters still in Carthage, some of the confessors, and a significant portion of the laity who had not lapsed. Cyprian's supporters were apparently a minority of the community; see *vnit. eccl.* 12,20–23 (CCSL 3:257–258, 263–266), and Clarke, *Letters* 2:214 n.2.

35. Decius himself was not killed until June of that year. The imperial action had apparently ceased earlier but Cyprian remained in exile because of the fear of popular action upon his return. See *ep.* 43.4 (CSEL 3.2:593).

36. This division of the community grouped the fugitives, such as Cyprian, and all those who had escaped detection in Carthage with the public heroes; *laps.* 2,3 (CCSL 3:221–222). Any who had lacked this firm intention to confess (should it have been required) were invited to repent of their failure; *laps.* 28 (CCSL 3:236–237) and *ep.* 55.13–14 (CSEL 3.2:632–634).

37. *Laps.* 7–9,27–28,36 (CCSL 3:224–225, 236–237, 241–242).

38. *Laps.* 15–16,34 (CCSL 3:228–230, 240). The same charge was made in *epp.* 43.2–3, 59.12–13 (CSEL 3.2:591–592, 679–681) and *vnit. eccl.* 1–3 (CCSL 3:249–251).

39. *Vnit. eccl.* 19, 23 (CCSL 3:263, 265–266). Bévenot indicates that chapter 19, like

When the bishops of Africa met in Carthage for the first time after the persecution, probably in the spring 251, they determined that those who sinned only by acquiring certificates and had been practicing penance might be admitted to communion upon the consideration of individual cases. The sacrificers, however, were to continue the regimen of repentance with the understanding that they would be admitted to communion as death approached.[40] This synod also confirmed the excommunication of the laxist party led by the five rebel presbyters in Carthage.[41]

At this same meeting, the Africans had to address another troubling development: a disputed episcopal election in Rome. After the death of Bishop Fabian the Roman church had decided not to elect a successor, thus being governed only by its presbyters throughout the persecution. In March 251 a majority of the clergy with the assent of the people and the attending bishops of neighboring cities elected Cornelius bishop. On grounds which remain obscure, the presbyter Novatian organized a dissenting group which included many confessors, arranged his own ordination as bishop, and established a rival communion.[42] The complex process of deciding between the rival candidates resulted in a lingering uneasiness between Cyprian and Cornelius.[43]

At a synod in Rome during the summer of 251, Cornelius and his episcopal colleagues adopted a policy for reconciling the lapsed which paralleled that of the Africans.[44] In practice, however, Cornelius made two exceptions. Bishop Trofimus and the entire congregation which he had led into apostasy were readmitted into communion though at least some had been guilty of sacrifice.[45] In addition, amnesty was granted to some confes-

---

chapter 4, of this treatise underwent a subsequent revision. Both versions survived. See his, "Hi qui sacrificaverunt," *JTS* 5 (1954): 68–72.

40. Cyprian reported these decisions in *ep.* 55.6,17 (CSEL 3.2:627, 636).

41. *Ep.* 45.4 (CSEL 3.2:603) reports the decision to Cornelius.

42. In *epp.* 52.2 and 54.3 (CSEL 3.2:618–619, 622–623), written after some of the confessors abandoned Novatian, Cyprian indicated that the parties divided over the policy of reconciling of the lapsed. For the support of the confessors, see *epp.* 49.1, 54.2 (CSEL 3.2:609–610, 622). Cornelius' account of the events is preserved in Eusebius, *h.e.* 6.43.5–20 (SC 41:154–158).

43. The African bishops' process of deciding to support Cornelius is detailed in *epp.* 44, 45, 48 (CSEL 3.2:597–603, 606–608). Cyprian later considered Cornelius altogether too willing to entertain the Carthaginian rebels' complaints against him; *ep.* 59.1–2,18 (CSEL 3.2:666–668, 688–689).

44. Cyprian recounted the agreement in *ep.* 55.6 (CSEL 3.2:627–628).

45. Cyprian argued the Italian bishops had no real options in this case; *ep.* 55.11 (CSEL 3.2:631–632). Cyprian expressed his horror of lapsed clergy in *epp.* 65.1–2,4, 67.3,9 (CSEL 3.2:722–725, 737, 742–743).

sors who had joined Novatian and supported his claim to the episcopacy; they were admitted to Cornelius' communion without either confession or penance.[46] Although Bishop Trofimus was accepted as a layman, the schismatic presbyter Maximus resumed his place in the clergy. Novatian's party not only rejected this lenient policy of reconciling the certified lapsed but refused to grant peace to penitents even at the time of death.[47]

The Novatianist party extended itself into Africa by appointing another of the former Roman presbyters as a rigorist bishop in Carthage.[48] Five laxist bishops also established a competing church, under the leadership of Privatus, the deposed bishop of Lambaesis, and including the rebellious clergy of Carthage.[49] Cyprian was under attack from both sides: by the rigorists for destroying the purity of the church in admitting the certified to communion; by the laxists for jeopardizing the salvation of the sacrificers in excluding them from communion. With characteristic vigor Cyprian counterattacked on both fronts.[50]

When the African bishops met again in May 253, Cyprian warned that a renewal of the persecution had been prophesied and proposed that all sacrificers who had already submitted to penitential discipline under the direction of the bishops should be admitted to communion immediately.[51]

46. Cornelius provided a detailed defense of this decision to Cyprian in *ep.* 49 (CSEL 3.2:608–612). The confessors themselves claimed to have been deceived by Novatian; *ep.* 53 (CSEL 3.2:620). Cyprian congratulated Cornelius and the confessors on their reunion without comment on the procedures adopted: *epp.* 51, 54 (CSEL 3.2:614–616, 621–624).

47. Novatian apparently sent letters to African bishops attacking Cornelius' practices. The charges can be reconstructed from Cyprian's responses to accusations drawn from that letter in his *ep.* 55 (CSEL 3.2:624–648). Cornelius was charged with entering into communion with idolaters: bishops who had sacrificed (10), Trofimus and his congregation (11), sacrificers (12), and those who received certificates (14–15). Cyprian's letter implies that Novatian denied reconciliation to all the penitent lapsed, even at the time of death (17–18,26,28).

48. Another Maximus, *ep.* 59.9 (CSEL 3.2:676). Earlier references to this individual as a supporter of Novatian appear in *epp.* 44.1, 50.1 (CSEL 3.2:597, 613). See Clarke, *Letters* 2:226, 278, 3:249 for his identity.

49. Cyprian detailed the background of each member of this group for Cornelius. Fortunatus, the laxist bishop of Carthage, had been one of Cyprian's presbyters. See *ep.* 59.10 (CSEL 3.2:677–678).

50. He defended himself against the double charges in *ep.* 59.15–17 (CSEL 3.2:684–687).

51. *Epp.* 57.1, 68.5 (CSEL 3.2:651, 748). We may speculate that the pressure from the laxist church influenced this decision. In arguing for it, Cyprian asserted that the sacrificers needed the strength which only the bishops could provide to face the coming challenge; *ep.* 57.4 (CSEL 3.2:653–655). He admitted to having perceived no such need during the prior persecution when the lapsed were urged to regain the communion of the church by publicly confessing their faith; *ep.* 19.2 (CSEL 3.2:526). The peace was

While allowing each bishop to act as he judged best, the Africans adopted this policy and urged it on the Romans.[52]

Cornelius was arrested in Rome a month later, escorted by his congregation in a massive display of support.[53] Apparently convinced of the truth of Cyprian's predictions, Cornelius adopted the African policy before his death in exile a few weeks later.[54] His successor Lucius, himself elected in exile, confirmed this practice upon return to the city.[55] In May 254 Lucius was in turn succeeded by Stephen who proceeded to disagree with Cyprian on every other issue arising from the persecution.

Stephen ignored appeals from Bishop Faustinus of Lyons for support in deposing Bishop Marcian of Arles who followed Novatian's denial of reconciliation to all penitent lapsed even at the time of death. Cyprian wrote to Stephen insisting that he come to the assistance of these penitents who would be lost eternally once they died outside the church's communion. Stephen's response to Cyprian's entreaty is unrecorded.[56]

Next, two Spanish bishops who had been deposed for acquiring certificates of compliance during the persecution and for other engagements with the Roman cults gained Stephen's support for their efforts to be reinstated. The replacement bishops appealed to their African colleagues to intervene on their behalf. Cyprian and his colleagues directed the Spanish congregations to stand fast in rejecting the apostates, asserting that Stephen had not only violated a policy accepted by his predecessors but would pollute himself and his church by entering into communion with idolatrous bishops.[57]

---

to be extended, of course, only to those who had submitted to the authority of the bishops.

52. *Ep.* 57.5 (CSEL 3.2:627), however, asserts that any bishop who does otherwise will have to answer to the Lord for his severity. The laxist charges of cruelty had taken their toll.

53. *Ep.* 60.1–2 (CSEL 3.2:691–693). Cyprian interpreted this public display by the penitents as a confession of faith by which they reversed their failure and earned the peace; *ep.* 60.2 (CSEL 3.2:693).

54. On Cornelius' death, see *ep.* 61.3 (CSEL 3.2:696); on his adoption of the lenient policy, see *ep.* 68.5 (CSEL 3.2:739).

55. *Ep.* 68.5 (CSEL 3.2:739). On the exile, see *ep.* 61.1 (CSEL 3.2:695).

56. *Ep.* 68 (CSEL 3.2:744–749), written late in 254 or early in 255. Cyprian argued that a bishop who dissented from this common decision of his colleagues could not be participating in the same Spirit (3,5). The Novatianist in Arles apparently posed no threat to Stephen's authority in Rome.

57. *Ep.* 67, esp. 9 (CSEL 3.2:742–743). Cornelius had admitted Trofimus, a sacrificer, but only as a layman. Cyprian allowed that Stephen might have been deceived by the petitioner but that would neither excuse his violating established procedure by overruling the local church nor protect his communion from pollution; *ep.* 67.4–5 (CSEL 3.2:738–740).

These exchanges set the stage for the bitter conflict between the Roman and African churches over the status of baptism performed in heresy or schism. The African church had earlier followed the practice of accepting converts originally baptized in a separate community such as that of Marcion or Montanus with only the imposition of the bishop's hands.[58] In a council held some twenty years earlier, however, the Africans had decided that henceforth they would require such converts to submit to baptism.[59] The establishment of Novatianist and laxist churches, affirming Trinitarian faith and dissenting only in penitential discipline, now revived the question of rebaptism in Africa.[60]

In response to inquiries and objections from throughout Roman Africa, Cyprian wrote a series of letters in his own name and with his colleagues in Proconsular Africa defending the practice of rebaptism.[61] The question may already have been under consideration for some time when Stephen was elected bishop of Rome in May 254.[62] A meeting of bishops in Carthage the following spring responded to an inquiry from their colleagues in Numidia on the same question.[63] The following spring, 256, a council of seventy-one African bishops meeting in Carthage discussed the issue and affirmed their existing practice. In reporting their decision to Stephen, however, they allowed that other bishops might act differently within the unity of the church.[64]

58. Tertullian disputed the practice in *bapt.* 15 (CCSL 1:290).

59. The question of custom and the change made by the Africans appears in *epp.* 70.1, 71.2, 73.13 (CSEL 3.2:767, 772–773, 787). Reference to the council under Agrippinus appears in *epp.* 71.4, 73.3 (CSEL 3.2:774, 780). Though Cyprian tried to hide the fact, Firmilian of Caesarea in Cappadocia explained that, unlike the Asians, the Africans had actually changed their practice in the council; *ep.* 75.19 (CSEL 3.2:822–823). For a full discussion of the council under Agrippinus, see Clarke, *Letters* 4:196–199.

60. The identity of faith appears as an argument for the efficacy of Novatian's baptism in *ep.* 69.7 (CSEL 3.2:756); the argument is pushed back to Marcion in *ep.* 73.4–5 (CSEL 3.2:781–782).

61. The treatise *On Rebaptism* may have been written in Africa before Cyprian's death. See J. Quasten, *Patrology* 2:368.

62. The earliest letter, *ep.* 69, in which Cyprian's position is already well developed, must be dated after the death of Cornelius in June 253 but before spring 255, the latest date for *ep.* 70, which presents a more elaborate argument. For the dating, see Clarke, *Letters* 4:173–174.

63. *Ep.* 70 (CSEL 3.2:766–770). This meeting was held in 254 or 255; the later date is judged more likely by Clarke, *Letters* 4:192–193.

64. *Ep.* 72.1 (CSEL 3.2:775–776). This letter also indicates that Stephen may have been admitting schismatic clerics to office, contrary to all established policy; *ep.* 72.2 (CSEL 3.2:776–777). Along with it went copies of the letter sent by the council to the bishops of Numidia (*ep.* 70) and Cyprian's subsequent letter to Quintus in Mauretania (*ep.* 71).

Stephen responded decisively to the letters sent from the bishops of Africa.[65] He rejected the African innovation and claimed that his church's practice of receiving persons baptized in heresy as penitents by the imposition of hands had been established by the apostles themselves.[66] When a delegation of African bishops was sent to Rome to resolve the conflict, Stephen not only refused to receive them, but forbade the customary hospitality and insulted Cyprian, thereby signaling a break in communion between the two churches.[67]

This Roman challenge did not pass unanswered. Cyprian called an unusual meeting of African bishops on 1 September 256 circularizing influential bishops outside Africa with dossiers of relevant correspondence.[68] Whatever differences may have existed among the African bishops in the earlier stages of the conflict had been resolved by the time of their vote. They unanimously affirmed the rebaptism of heretics and schismatics, echoing Cyprian's arguments in their individual *sententiae*.[69]

No record of the subsequent course of the controversy between Cyprian and Stephen has survived. When Stephen died early in August 257 he was succeeded by Sixtus, with whom the Africans enjoyed better relations.[70] At about the same time Cyprian was sent away from Carthage in the initial stages of the Valerian persecution. A year later he made formal confession of Christianity and was executed on 14 September 258.

The practice of rebaptism continued to be disputed even within the African church. After the Diocletian persecution it became one of the means by which the Donatist Church identified itself with the heritage of Cyprian in opposition to the Catholic Church in Africa which followed the

65. The vehemence of Stephen's response may be explained, in part, by his receipt in the same packet of a copy of the letter to the Spanish congregations (*ep.* 67), in which he is strongly criticized. For the conjectural dating, see Clarke, *Letters* 4:139–140, 142–144.

66. Stephen's letter has been lost (or destroyed); his position is reported in Cyprian's letter to Pompeius, *ep.* 74.1–3 (CSEL 3.2:799–801).

67. The reference to excommunication can be found in *ep.* 74.8 (CSEL 3.2:805–806), as something well known to the addressee. Firmilian of Caesarea reported that Stephen had broken communion with the bishops of Asia as well on this same issue; *ep.* 75.24,25 (CSEL 3.2:825, 826). He added that Stephen had characterized Cyprian as a false Christ, a false apostle and a deceiver; *ep.* 75.25 (CSEL 3.2:827).

68. We may presume that Firmilian of Caesarea was not the only bishop whose support Cyprian sought.

69. The record of the voting is to be found among the works of Cyprian: *sententiae episcoporvm numero LXXXVII* (CSEL 3.1:435–461).

70. Cyprian reported Sixtus' martyrdom, 6 August 258, in *ep.* 80.1 (CSEL 3.2:840). The *vita Cypriani* (14) characterizes him as peace loving (CSEL 3.3:cv).

Roman practice of accepting schismatics and heretics through the imposition of hands.[71]

II. THE CHURCH IN CARTHAGE

This study focuses on the social significance of differences in baptismal practice between Carthage and Rome. The African bishops asserted that converts who had originally attempted baptism in a rival Christian communion must be baptized upon entering the Catholic church with the true baptism of Christ and in the power of the Holy Spirit. Their theological argument was essentially social: because the church of Christ is one and indivisible, only one of the three rival communities could be the true church and only that one possessed the Holy Spirit and the power to sanctify. To concede legitimacy to any rituals performed by competitors would be to abandon their own claim to be the one true church. Yet even as the Africans affirmed the truth of their own practice and its theological foundations they realized that they were attempting to change a widely established custom followed until recently even in Africa.[72] Therefore they allowed other churches to continue the contrary practice within the harmony of the one communion.[73]

If a reasoned argument was presented by the Roman bishop for the practice of admitting converts baptized in heresy or schism by the imposition of hands in penitence it has evaded historical research.[74] Still the record does testify that Stephen not only insisted on the traditional discipline but demanded that the other churches observe it as well.[75] Both Cyprian and Firmilian of Caesarea indicate that he broke communion with bishops who refused to accede to this demand.[76]

71. On which, W.H.C. Frend, *The Donatist Church* (Oxford, 1952).
72. See n. 59 above.
73. *Epp.* 72.3, 73.26 (CSEL 3.2:777–778, 798–799).
74. Stephen's letter to Cyprian, to which reference in made in *ep.* 74.1 (CSEL 3.2:799), did not survive. The only contemporary treatise arguing for the Roman position is *de rebaptismo* which seems to have been composed in Africa, see n. 61. Of the three arguments which might be assigned to Stephen in *ep.* 74, only one, an appeal to the practice of heretics in *ep.* 74.4 (CSEL 3.2:802), had not already appeared in the discussions in Africa. The appeal to tradition in *ep.* 74.2 (CSEL 3.2:802) is found in *epp.* 71.2, 73.13 (CSEL 3.2:772, 787); the appeal to the Name of Jesus in *ep.* 74.5 (CSEL 3.2:813), repeats *ep.* 73.14,16 (CSEL 3.2:788–790). On the African situation of the earlier correspondence, *epp.* 69, 70, 71, 73, see Clarke, *Letters* 4:173–174, 191–195, 206–207, 218–221.
75. Stephen appealed to a tradition which had been observed by the heretics as well as the orthodox; *ep.* 74.2,4 (CSEL 3.2:799–800, 802).
76. See n. 67 above.

By analyzing the conflict between the Novatianist, Catholic and laxist communions in Africa, this section of the study will attempt to specify the social significance of Cyprian's baptismal practice. In the following section, an attempt will be made to extend the investigation to Rome and to determine why Stephen insisted that converts from schism must not be rebaptized.

Christians in Carthage identified themselves as a social group by a common commitment to Christ as the source of eternal life which each member made individually in the baptismal ceremony of initiation.[77] Eucharistic celebrations ritualized that membership, promising a future share in the heavenly banquet.[78] To attain and retain membership, a Christian was required to reject participation in every other religious cult and to follow moral standards based on the teachings of Christ.[79] Carthaginian Christians believed that sharing in the church's communion at the time of death was a necessary and, normally, an adequate condition for attaining the heavenly kingdom of Christ.[80]

Thus the community understood itself as an extension of Christ's heavenly kingdom into the earthly realm. To serve as the gateway from earth to heaven it had to be purified from those elements of Roman society which opposed Christ's rule: idolatry and moral corruption.[81] Thus the baptismal ritual of initiation had to protect the communion by purifying each new member from the evil which had been contracted in living outside the group boundary. The efficacy of this ritual and indeed all the sanctifying power of the community depended in turn on the integrity of its members.

---

77. Cyprian listed the effects of baptism in *ep.* 74.5 (CSEL 3.2:803). See also *ep.* 70.2 (CSEL 3.2:768).

78. *Ep.* 55.6 (CSEL 3.2:627–628).

79. Cyprian threatened excommunication not only for idolatry but for violation of moral and disciplinary standards; *epp.* 1.2, 4.4, 52.3 (CSEL 3.2:466, 475–477, 619).

80. Provision was made to reconcile the dying, even with their course of repentance unfinished; see n. 25 above. Cyprian had to argue that the peace of the church would not save alone, without repentance and satisfaction; *laps.* 14–15 (CCSL 3:228–229). Only the repentant lapsed, however, were portrayed as trembling at the judgment; *ep.* 55.20 (CSEL 3.2:638).

81. This purity was particularly important among the clergy, *ep.* 67.3 (CSEL 3.2:737–738), see also *laps.* 15–16,35 (CCSL 3:228–230, 240–241). Limits on that purity among the laity, in the matter of sexual irregularity, had already begun to be tolerated; *ep.* 55.20–21,25–27 (CSEL 3.2:638–639, 643–645), and Clarke, *Letters* 3:194.

94

Sacrilege or moral corruption within the ranks would jeopardize the salvation of all.[82] To maintain its holiness, therefore, the community used another ritual to cleanse those members who deviated after being baptized.[83] That ritual of purification began with excommunication of the offending member, an exclusion from the communion ritual which prevented the spread of contagion.[84] To gain readmittance, the sinner must then publicly acknowledge the sin and make satisfaction to God by asceticism and good works under the supervision of the bishop. Only then was the cleansed sinner ceremonially readmitted to the communion, by the imposition of the bishop's hands.[85] A penitent in danger of death, however, was readmitted immediately even with the course of satisfaction incomplete.[86] This exception was made because Carthaginian Christians believed that anyone dying outside the peace of the church would not even be judged by Christ and could not attain an eternal reward.[87]

In order to establish and maintain its segregation from the evils of the Roman world, the Christian church used purity codes which it could readily verify—standards defined by actions or behaviors rather than by intentions.[88] Since the moral codes set forth in its foundational documents referred specifically to intention, the church's discipline did make provision for moral attitude, at least as an intensifier or mitigator of behavior.[89] The church did not, however, fear pollution from deceitful sinners hidden within the communion.[90] Christ himself would finally judge the intentions

82. *Epp.* 64.3, 73.19, 74.2 (CSEL 3.2:718–719, 793, 800).

83. Thus the need for satisfaction which delayed the admission of the sacrificers. For this concern, see *ep.* 55.11–12 (CSEL 3.2:631–632).

84. *Epp.* 4.4, 67.9 (CSEL 3.2:476, 742–743).

85. The ritual can be constructed from *epp.* 15.1, 16.2, 17.2, 57.3 (CSEL 3.2:514, 518–519, 522, 652–653). Firmilian of Caesarea reminded Cyprian that the penitent won forgiveness from the Lord by satisfaction, not from the bishop; *ep.* 75.4 (CSEL 3.2:812).

86. *Epp.* 18.1, 20.3, 55.13 (CSEL 3.2:524, 528, 632); catechumens were offered baptism, *ep.* 18.2 (CSEL 3.2:524).

87. *Epp.* 55.29, 57.1,3, 68.3,4 (CSEL 3.2:647, 650–653, 745–747). If they recovered, such Christians remained in the communion; *ep.* 55.13 (CSEL 3.2:632).

88. Generally, the decalogue functioned in this way: *epp.* 4.1–3, 13.4,6, 14.3, 11.6, 55.27 (CSEL 3.2:472–475, 506–509, 512, 500, 644–645).

89. Sometimes to excuse, as in *ep.* 55.6 (CSEL 3.2:627–628); but an appeal to intention was more generally used to credit a person with achievement in excess of actual performance; *epp.* 10.5, 12.1, 55.9, 56.2 (CSEL 3.2:494, 504–505, 630–631, 649). The single instance of accusation is in *laps.* 28 (CCSL 3:236–237).

90. *Ep.* 55.18 (CSEL 3.2:636). Even persons who had been admitted irregularly were allowed to remain in the communion, *ep.* 64.1 (CSEL 3.2:717), as were those who may never have been baptized properly, *ep.* 73.23 (CSEL 3.2:796).

of the heart of each communicant; he did not require the bishop to separate out all the deceivers.[91]

The purity code which defined the boundary of the church set limits but did not fully restrict social intercourse to Christians alone. The majority of the faithful participated in the economic and family life of the dominant culture.[92] They inherited property and attempted to maintain, enlarge and bequeath a patrimony.[93] Some had nonchristian spouses.[94] Certain classes, however, such as dedicated virgins, widows and the poor, received their livings within the community.[95] Clergy, in particular, were not only salaried but required to abstain from other financial engagements.[96] Despite the significance of these special roles for the community's sense of its identity,[97] most Christians expected to live both as Romans and as Christians. In normal times, they seem to have succeeded.

The Decian edict struck at the identity of the Christian community by disrupting its balance of separation and engagement. In requiring that every citizen fulfill a religious obligation to worship the divine protectors of the Empire, the government did not attempt to suppress other religious practices.[98] It did, however, attack the cultic exclusivity essential to Christianity. Faced with this conflict between their commitments, many Christian laity protected their involvement in the Empire by sacrificing or otherwise obtaining the required certificate.[99] Some more prominent persons, including Cyprian, voluntarily went into exile, abandoning their property to confiscation by the state.[100] Among the lower classes, many quietly declined to cooperate, hoping to avoid the notice of the authorities or

91. *Epp. 54.3, 55.18,20* (CSEL 3.2:622–623, 636, 638), *laps.* 27 (CCSL 3:236). Cyprian claimed that Christ had not authorized the bishops to separate the wheat from the tares; *ep. 55.25* (CSEL 3.2:643).

92. According to *ep.* 2 (CSEL 3.2:467–469), the profession of acting was still forbidden.

93. They were thus vulnerable to the persecution; *ep.* 11.1 (CSEL 3.2:496), *laps.* 4,6,11,35(CCSL 3:222–224, 226, 240–241).

94. *Laps.* 6 (CCSL 3:223).

95. *Epp.* 7, 5.1, 12.2, 14.2 (CSEL 3.2:484–485, 479, 504, 510).

96. On clerical salaries, see *epp.* 1.1, 39.5, 34.4 (CSEL 3.2:465–466, 584–585, 570–571); on abstaining, see *ep.* 1.2 (CSEL 3.2:466–467), *laps.* 6 (CCSL 3:223–224).

97. Cyprian treated the suspected infidelity of the consecrated virgins as adultery against Christ, indicating their symbolic role; *ep.* 4.4 (CSEL 3.2:475–477).

98. See Clarke, *Letters* 1:24; *ep.* 5.2 (CSEL 3.2:479) indicates that the clergy had access to the confessors.

99. See nn. 12, 13 above.

100. *Epp.* 13.5, 19.2, 24.1, 25.1 (CSEL 3.2:508, 526, 536–537, 538).

delation by their neighbors.[101] Among those who were interrogated by the imperial officers, some broke their commitment to Christ while others upheld it even unto death.[102]

The assumption that Christians could live as Romans had been shaken and in some cases shattered. What then were the expectations of the Carthaginian Christians, the standing and the fallen, in this new situation? The words of Christ in Matthew 10.32–33 seem to have been particularly significant: he would acknowledge before the Father in heaven those who had acknowledged him before kings and governors but he would deny those who had denied him.[103] To some this was a promise; to others a terrible threat. All believed that the martyrs were even then enjoying the crown of victory in heaven.[104] Confessors were so honored in the church on earth that some, presuming they would certainly be saved, flaunted both moral standards of the community and laws of the Empire.[105] Many sacrificers and certified sought ways to escape the terrible rejection threatened by Christ.[106] Yet even to plead for mercy before the judgment seat of Christ they had to be readmitted and die within the communion of the church.[107] The bishops insisted that only the ritual of penance and satisfaction could lead to the peace of the church and, by implication, the mercy of Christ.[108]

The reconciliation of the fallen, however, was to be delayed. Since the persecution was a divine punishment to purify the church of sinfulness,[109] Cyprian explained, no one whom God had purged could be readmitted before the cleansing was complete and God had granted peace to the church as a whole.[110] Because withholding all hope of reconciliation

---

101. *Laps.* 3 (CCSL 3:222). In *laps.* 10–12, (CCSL 3:226–227) Cyprian indicated that some had stayed behind for fear of losing their property by going into exile. Cyprian remained in exile, he claimed, to prevent new rounds of denunciation of the faithful; *epp.* 14.1, 20.1, 43.4 (CSEL 3.2:510, 527, 593).

102. See above, nn. 15–17. Others failed; *ep.* 56.1 (CSEL 3.2:648), *laps.* 13 (CCSL 3:227–228).

103. This text is cited in *epp.* 12.1, 16.2, 59.12, 58.3, (CSEL 3.2:503, 518, 680, 659) and *laps.* 7,20 (CCSL 3:224–225, 232). The Romans used it as well in *epp.* 30.7, 31.2 (CSEL 3.2:555, 558).

104. *Epp.* 10.4, 22.2, 31.3, 58.3 (CSEL 3.2:493–494, 534–535, 559, 658–659).

105. *Epp.* 13.2,4–5, 14.3, 11.1 (CSEL 3.2:505–508, 512, 496); this forms part of the argument in *unit. eccl.* 20–22 (CCSL 3:263–265).

106. *Epp.* 15–17, 20.2 (CSEL 3.2:513–524, 527–528).

107. *Epp.* 55.29, 57.1,3,4,5 (CSEL 3.2:647, 650–656).

108. *Epp.* 15.1, 16.2, 17.2, 30.6, 55.5 (CSEL 3.2:513–514, 518–519, 522, 554, 626–627), *laps.* 16 (CCSL 3:229–230).

109. *Ep.* 11.4–6 (CSEL 3.2:498–500), *laps.* 1,7,21 (CCSL 3:221, 224, 233).

110. *Epp.* 16.2–4, 17.1, 22.2 (CSEL 3.2:517–520, 521, 530–531).

would drive the fallen to return in despair to their former life in the Empire,[111] Cyprian directed that the fallen should undertake penance and await the results of the general consultation at end of the persecution. In the meantime, reconciliation should be given only to penitents actually in danger of death.[112]

The conflict which arose at this juncture indicates some lack of confidence in the efficacy or efficiency of the ritual of reconciliation. Since idolatry was a sin directed against God rather than an offense against another human and since it violated one's baptismal oath to Christ, some believed it beyond the church's power to forgive.[113] Those still standing tended to view the fallen as carriers of a deadly contagion which threatened to pollute the entire communion, to destroy the church's relationship to God, and thus to shut off its access to the heavenly kingdom.[114]

The fallen sought a more secure escape from their guilt, a way which did not require life-long penance and offer only death-bed reconciliation. They besought the confessors to win for them the mercy from Christ into whose presence they would be immediately translated by dying as martyrs under torture or in prison.[115] In response the confessors not only promised to intercede before God but provided the necessary intervention with the clergy—a letter recommending or directing that the petitioner be granted the peace of the church without submitting to the full course of penance.[116] These letters became efficacious only upon the death of its issuer as a martyr.[117]

In an attempt to contain this practice Cyprian negotiated with confessors in prison and clergy still in Carthage. The letters, he urged, should specify petitioners by name, should be based on a judgment of their sincere

111. *Ep.* 55.6,17 (CSEL 3.2:627, 636).
112. See nn. 22–25 above.
113. Tertullian had asserted as much of adultery and idolatry, *pud.*, esp. 21–22 (CCSL 2:1326–1330). Some of the African bishops had continued to deny readmittance to adulterers until recently; *ep.* 55.21 (CSEL 3.2:638–639) and see Clarke, *Letters* 3:194–195. Cyprian himself introduced this consideration to limit the authority of the martyrs; *epp.* 16.2, 17.2, 59.16 (CSEL 3.2: 518, 522, 686), *laps.* 17–18 (CCSL 3:230–231).
114. This charge was leveled at Cornelius, in Italy and Africa, when he admitted sacrificers, *ep.* 55.10–11 (CSEL 3.2:631–632); see also *epp.* 15.2, 16.2 (CSEL 3.2:514–515, 518).
115. *Epp.* 15–17 (CSEL 3.2:513–524); *ep.* 20.2 (CSEL 3.2:527–528) links the problem to the beginning of torture; *ep.* 21.4 (CSEL 3.2:532) requests such intercession.
116. *Epp.* 22.2, 27.3, 36.2 (CSEL 3.2:534–535, 543, 574).
117. *Ep.* 16.3 (CSEL 3.2:519–520). Note that some of the letters were issued by an authorized agent after the death of the martyr; *epp.* 22.2, 27.1 (CSEL 3.2: 534, 540–541).

repentance, and should request that peace be given only after the persecution had ended.[118] While continuing to assert martyrs' power to free the fallen from the guilt of idolatry, confessors agreed that reconciliation should be delayed and allowed the bishop to judge the conduct of the lapsed during that intervening time.[119] Many lapsed, however, continued to insist on immediate admission to communion.[120]

Some presbyters in Carthage acceded to the demands of the lapsed.[121] After first threatening these dissenting clergy, Cyprian excommunicated them.[122] In response Felicissimus, the local leader of the opposition, announced that anyone who followed Cyprian would be excluded from his communion. Thus a rival church was established into which the lapsed were freely admitted upon recommendation of the martyrs.[123]

When he returned from exile in spring 251, Cyprian faced division within the church in Carthage. He addressed the assembled community, systematically defining its new situation after the persecution. Martyrs and their agents could not disregard that divine law requiring satisfaction which was itself the foundation of such authority as they enjoyed: if Christ did not intend to punish deniers he might not plan to reward confessors.[124] Furthermore martyrs' prayers were not always heard and their intercession was reserved for Christ's own judgment at the end of time not the judgment of bishops.[125] Turning on the rebellious clergy, he characterized them as agents of Satan bent on completing the imperial commissioners' work by preventing the fallen from repenting.[126] Sinners' only hope for salvation, he warned, was to submit to the bishop's judgment and offer satisfaction to God. Despite Christ's threat the scriptures show that God would be merciful to the lapsed who humbled themselves.[127]

The success of the laxist church in Africa forced bishops to take a more lenient stance in requiring satisfaction than they might otherwise have pursued. They offered readmission first to the certified and then to sacri-

---

118. *Ep.* 15.3–4 (CSEL 3.2:515–516).
119. *Ep.* 23 (CSEL 3.2:536).
120. See n. 29 above. Some submitted; *ep.* 35.1 (CSEL 3.2:571).
121. See n. 30 above.
122. See n. 33 above.
123. *Epp.* 41.1–2, 43.2–3 (CSEL 3.2:587–589, 591–592). See also n. 34 above.
124. *Laps.* 20 (CCSL 3:232–233); the same point was made by Cyprian in *ep.* 28.2 (CSEL 3.2:545–547) and by the Roman confessors and clergy in *epp.* 31.8, 36.2 (CSEL 3.2:564, 573).
125. *Laps.* 17–19 (CCSL 3:230–232), see also *ep.* 15.3 (CSEL 3.2:515).
126. See nn. 38, 39 above.
127. *Laps.* can be read as an argument for the efficacy of penance as much as for its necessity, e.g. 29,32,36 (CCSL 3:237, 239, 241–242).

ficers who had submitted to penance, upon examination of individual cases.[128] Two years later, the bishops offered to admit repentant sacrificers on the same terms. The rigorists and laxists, however, continued to hold adherents.[129]

The counteroffensive Cyprian launched against both opponents turned on the relation between the boundary identifying and separating the church from the demonic realm, and the differentiation of roles within its communion. He focused on the office of bishop as the foundation on which a local church is established, and on the rights of penitents suspended from sharing the eucharist.

Cyprian's ecclesiology was founded on the belief that only one communion could actually provide access to God: as God is one, so is the church leading to God. While admitting a certain level of diversity in practice among local churches, he absolutely rejected the legitimacy of competing communions and rival bishops, particularly within the same city.[130]

The true bishop was chosen by God through election by the community; by ordination he was joined to a college whose jointly held authority had been passed down from the apostles.[131] Once a bishop had been established by God, his could be the only true communion in a city.[132] Anyone who rebelled against the authority of God's bishop and the unity of Christ's church was guilty of schism, a crime worse than idolatry since not even martyrdom could expunge it.[133] In the light of this ecclesiological exclusivism, the policy of extending peace to all penitents in anticipation of a renewal of persecution can be seen as an assertion that the church's communion was the sole gateway to heaven, even for martyrs.[134]

As he recognized only a single church, Cyprian also upheld an extreme position in determining its membership. He asserted that no one could

128. See nn. 40, 51 above.
129. Communion with the confessors and martyrs was apparently attractive: *epp. 43.2,5, 51.2* (CSEL 3.2:591, 594, 615), *vnit. eccl. 22–23* (CCSL 3:265–266). The effects of Novatianist propaganda are evident in *epp. 55, 66.*
130. *Vnit. eccl. 8,23* (CCSL 3:255, 266). This is the point of his appeal to Peter as the symbol of the unity of the church in *vnit. eccl. 4–5* (CSEL 3.2:251–253), and elsewhere, *epp. 43.5, 45.1* (CSEL 3.2:594, 600).
131. *Epp. 43.5, 45.3, 55.8, 68.3,5* (CSEL 3.2:594, 602, 629–630, 746, 748).
132. *Epp. 3.3, 33.1, 52.4, 55.24, 66.1,8* (CSEL 3.2:471, 568–569, 619–620, 642, 727, 733), *vnit. eccl. 8,17,18* (CCSL 3:255, 261–263). The same claim was advanced for Cornelius, based on the priority of his election and regularity of his ordination; *epp. 45.3, 55.8* (CSEL 3.2:602, 629–630).
133. *Epp. 55.17,29, 60.4* (CSEL 3.2:636, 647, 694), *vnit. eccl. 14* (CCSL 3:259–260).
134. The martyrs had to be prepared in the church's communion rather than confessing Christ as penitents; *epp. 54.1, 55.17, 57.4* (CSEL 3.2:621, 636, 653–654).

attain salvation outside the communion of that one church. Thus he warned bishops who followed a rigorist policy that God would hold them responsible for the souls of penitents whom they condemned by refusing death-bed reconciliation.[135]

The insistence of the lapsed on immediate reconciliation and the popularity of the laxists' decision to admit the apostates, even at the risk of the purity of the church, show that Cyprian's view was widely shared in Africa.[136] In contrast, rigorists must have believed that Christ might forgive what the church could not and thus that the peace of the church was not required for the salvation of a baptized penitent.[137] Stephen's decisions to tolerate a rigorist bishop in Arles and to break communion with a major portion of the episcopate indicate that he may not have shared Cyprian's understanding of the necessity of the church's communion for salvation.[138]

The Africans, then, identified the church by means of its eucharistic communion: catechumens and penitents were marginal but definitely outsiders.[139] Novatianists, and perhaps Romans in general, defined the church more broadly by means of baptism: once baptized, a sinner could be saved by persevering in penance.[140] Thus the dispute could be characterized as a conflict over the rights and privileges of penitents as a class of persons within the church.

The conflict over the appropriate purity and boundary of the church turned, therefore, on the significance of institutional differentiation and the relation of status in the church to divine governance. A review of the various classes of membership and their roles in the church is therefore necessary.

---

135. *Ep.* 68.4.2 (CSEL 3.2:747).

136. The necessity of communion for salvation was never at issue between Cyprian and the laxists.

137. Otherwise their exhortations to repentance would surely have fallen on deaf ears, as Cyprian argued they would in *ep.* 55.28 (CSEL 3.2:646–647).

138. *Ep.* 68.1,4 (CSEL 3.2:744, 747), seems to indicate multiple attempts to enlist Stephen's assistance in removing Marcian. Cyprian and Firmilian of Caesarea report that he had broken communion with the Africans and the Asians; *epp.* 74.8, 75.6,24–25 (CSEL 3.2:806, 813–814, 825–826). Dionysius of Alexandria confirmed this report; Eusebius, *h.e.* 7.5.3–5 (SC 41:169–170).

139. Thus Cyprian could allow converts from schism who had been admitted in the past without proper baptism to attain salvation through the communion; *ep.* 73.23 (CSEL 3.2:796). He explained that catechumens might be saved through martyrdom because of their faith; *ep.* 73.22 (CSEL 3.2:795–796). But he sincerely believed that the excommunicate were lost, whatever their intentions; *epp.* 68.3–4, 70.2 (CSEL 3.2:745–747, 768–769).

140. A parallel might have been the reduction of the clerical penitents to the lay state; *epp.* 55.11, 64.1, 72.2 (CSEL 3.2:632, 717, 776–777).

The Christian community at Carthage was divided into three major groups, each with its particular privileges and obligations: clergy, laity, and the marginal. The bishop, presbyters, deacons, readers and other officers of the community comprised the clergy. The laity included some specific subgroups, such as dedicated virgins, widows, and the poor supported by community funds. Catechumens, penitents and the excommunicate were at the margin but still had certain membership rights.[141] Members did not claim roles for themselves; the community itself ascribed these stations to individuals through a variety of rituals, among them ordination, dedication, baptism, admission to penance, reconciliation, and formal excommunication. Positions could not be achieved or claimed by individuals; they were assigned by clergy and laity through established procedures.[142]

Successful functioning of such a system of assigned roles, however, depended on the experienced satisfaction of the expectations which it created. Rights and responsibilities of each station had to be internalized and respected by the community as a whole. When members' expectations were met, class organization reinforced the group coherence guaranteeing its proper identity. When obligations were neglected with impunity and rights were ignored without redress, when the anticipation of rewards and punishments was frustrated, then the system of differentiation broke down and the very identity of the group was called into question. A functioning authority might maintain the integrity of the system by shifting achievers and offenders to more appropriate categories: confessors could be ordained as clergy, lapsed clergy be returned to the lay state, sinful laity become penitents, rebels be excommunicated. In the absence of such an authority and the appropriate internal categories for reclassification, however, deviants could only be unmasked and expelled by the group as a whole.[143] When such a breakdown in discipline occurred therefore, the

141. The hearers and penitents, for example, were to be admitted to peace in danger of death; *epp.* 18.1–2, 20.2–3, 55.17, 68.1 (CSEL 3.2:524, 528, 636, 744). The excommunicate also had a certain right to be accepted as penitents and admitted to peace before death; *ep.* 68.1 (CSEL 3.2:744). Schismatics, however, forfeited this right; *epp.* 35.1, 57.3, 69.6 (CSEL 3.2:571, 652, 755).

142. Cyprian consulted the entire body of the faithful in the selection of the clergy, *epp.* 29.1, 38.1, 39.1 (CSEL 3.2:548, 576, 581–582) and the admission of the schismatics to penance; *ep.* 59.15 (CSEL 3.2:684–685). He asserted that the laity had the right to refuse and to depose a bishop who had proven unworthy; *ep.* 67.4–5 (CSEL 3.2:738–739). Fundamentally, he asserted that Novatian in Rome and Fortunatus in Carthage were claiming for themselves an office which had already been given to another; *epp.* 55.8, 59.5 (CSEL 3.2:629–630, 671–673).

143. Cyprian had to make such an appeal for control of the confessors and the lapsed by face-to-face pressure during the persecution; *epp.* 14.3, 15.3, 17.3 (CSEL 3.2:512, 515, 522).

identity of the group was threatened and the danger of pollution from the outside became acute.

The internal differentiation of the Christian community at Carthage was already under pressure before the persecution began. Cyprian's election as bishop had been disputed by a group of the clergy; this tension persisted, eventually turning into rebellion.[144] Furthermore, some clergy had not respected the restrictions of their office: deacons were apparently consorting with consecrated virgins and presbyters assumed financial responsibilities incompatible with their office.[145]

When persecution broke out, the bishop voluntarily withdrew and attempted to direct his endangered community from his unexposed position even as he required that the other clergy stay at their posts.[146] A large number, perhaps even the majority, of the laity readily violated their baptismal commitment.[147] Conflict arose within the clergy over the bishop's directives for the care of the imprisoned and relief of the impoverished.[148]

The persecution also strained the social order by creating new roles whose responsibilities and rights had to be agreed upon. First confessors and then martyrs appeared. These honors were not assigned by the community; they were granted by God or achieved by the individuals.[149] Both roles carried the claim to extraordinary privileges without attendant obligations through which the community could exercise control.[150] Some of the first confessors to be released violated community behavioral standards with impunity.[151] Martyrs' letters of peace proved even more destabilizing: they allowed those who had voluntarily denied Christ to share communion with confessors who had suffered for their faith and faithful who were still in danger for not complying with the edict.[152] While some confessors remained in forced exile and others of the faithful were in voluntary exile, those who sacrificed or bought certificates retained their

144. *Epp.* 14.4, 16.1, 43.1 (CSEL 3.2:512–513, 517, 591).

145. *Epp.* 1.1, 4.1–2 (CSEL 3.2:465, 472–474).

146. He judged that his presence was a danger to the community as a whole; see n. 10 above. On the status of other clergy who had withdrawn, see *ep.* 34.4 (CSEL 3.2:570–571)

147. *Epp.* 14.1, 11.1,8 (CSEL 3.2:509, 495–496, 501–502), *laps.* 4,7 (CCSL 3:222–225).

148. *Epp.* 11.1,6, 12.1,2 (CSEL 3.2:496, 500, 502, 504).

149. The bishop, in contrast, was established by God through the vote of the community; the bishop chose the other clergy in consultation with the people. On the disciplinary implications, see *ep.* 3.1,3 (CSEL 3.2:469, 471).

150. *Epp.* 13.4, 14.3, 15.3, 17.3 (CSEL 3.2:506–507, 512, 515, 522–523).

151. *Epp.* 13.4,5, 14.3 (CSEL 3.2:506–508, 512).

152. *Ep.* 31.8 (CSEL 3.2:564). In addition, the fallen who did not have letters from the martyrs resented the admission of those who did; *ep.* 19.2 (CSEL 3.2:525).

property and had regained their status as Christians.[153] Some penitents who were admitted to communion on their deathbeds recovered to enjoy the peace of the church, while their healthier fellows continued in penance and danger outside the communion.[154] Presbyters and deacons had usurped the right of the bishop to admit or exclude from communion.[155] The differentiation of roles, with the attendant rights and privileges of each class, had broken down and the community's identity was in danger.

Even from his exile Cyprian worked to restore discipline and a sense of identity in the community. Once he had secured the support of the Roman clergy[156] he commissioned a group of confessor clergy to excommunicate the rebels and take over the governance of the community.[157] He insisted that all the fallen, both sacrificers and certified, must submit to exclusion from communion.[158]

Upon returning to Carthage Cyprian set about rebuilding the internal structures of the community by dividing the entire community into only two categories: the standing and the fallen. Among the standing he grouped confessors, voluntary exiles like himself, and those faithful who had declined to obey the edict.[159] The fallen encompassed both those who had freely sacrificed and those who had obtained certificates by any other means, regardless of their reasons for acting.[160] Some among the faithful confessed they had prepared to sacrifice had it been required of them; these too he ranked among the fallen, though with a lesser degree of guilt.[161] Those fallen who had refused to submit to penance were declared excommunicate; the others were recognized as penitents and promised eventual reconciliation.[162] Schismatics were branded as pagans, enemies of Christ and the church.[163]

Cyprian claimed for the bishop authority to act as God's vicar in judging

---

153. *Ep.* 19.2 (CSEL 3.2:528).
154. *Epp.* 55.13, 64.1, 56.2 (CSEL 3.2:632, 717, 648–649).
155. *Epp.* 16.1, 41.1 (CSEL 3.2:517, 587–588).
156. His own status was in question because of his withdrawal, *epp.* 9.2, 20.1 (CSEL 3.2:489, 527), and not secured until he had received *epp.* 30 and 31, which he then forwarded to Carthage, *ep.* 32.1 (CSEL 3.2:565).
157. *Epp.* 41, 42 (CSEL 3.2:587–590). On the identity and role of this group, see Clarke, *Letters* 2:202–203, 208–209.
158. *Epp.* 20.3, 36.1 (CSEL 3.2:528–529, 573).
159. *Laps.* 2–3 (CCSL 3:221–222).
160. *Laps.* 8–13,27 (CCSL 3:225–228, 236).
161. *Laps.* 28 (CCSL 3:236–237), see also *ep.* 55.14 (CSEL 3.2:633–634).
162. *Laps.* 30–36 (CCSL 3:237–242).
163. *Laps.* 34 (CCSL 3:240), *ep.* 65.5 (CSEL 3.2:725).

on earth with jurisdiction even over sins against God.[164] To confessors he assigned the privilege of offering the first opinion when the laity advised the bishop on assigning penance to individual sinners.[165] The martyrs, he explained, would have the same right to counsel mercy when Christ judged at the end of time.[166]

To deal with the problem of admitting into the communion those tinged with idolatry, Cyprian reversed the Novatianist argument. He asserted that Christ reserved to himself the separation of secret sinners from true saints within the communion; no bishop could presume to usurp God's prerogative.[167] To respond to the rigorist concern, he specified that the purity of the clergy, not of the community as a whole, was required to secure the church's identity and the spiritual power of Christ in its rituals.[168] Anyone who violated the ban on contact with demonic rites and other sins against God was forbidden to exercise a position of leadership in the community and lead its prayer.[169] After appropriate satisfaction had been made, however, clerics who had sinned against God might be readmitted among the faithful.[170] In practice any Christian sinner could be admitted among the penitents and even among the faithful, at least as death approached.[171] In these measures, Cyprian responded to the threat to the community's boundary by restoring its internal differentiation of roles and stations.

This program of restoration also attempted to restructure and satisfy expectations of members of the community. Confessors and martyrs were honored without jeopardizing clerical authority. The fallen were reintegrated into the community through efficacious rituals of purification. The bishop sought the advice of clergy and faithful in choosing candidates for ordination and in admitting the fallen to penitence, then communion.[172] Responsibility for the purity and identity of the community would be exercised by its actual members: neither martyrs in heaven nor laxists in

164. *Epp.* 59.5,15,16, 57.1, 66.3 (CSEL 3.2:671–672, 684–686, 650, 728–729) *laps.* 14–19,29,32 (CCSL 3:228–232, 237, 239).
165. *Epp.* 59.5,15, 15.3, 16.4 (CSEL 3.2:671–672, 684–685, 515, 520).
166. See n. 125 above.
167. *Ep.* 55.25 (CSEL 3.2:643–644).
168. Cyprian solved the problem of the boundary of the church by realigning its internal differentiation; *epp.* 65.2, 67.2–3,6 (CSEL 3.2:723–724, 636–637, 741). Origen reported a similar discipline in *Cels.* 3.51 (SC 136:122–123).
169. *Epp.* 55.11, 64.1, 65.1–3, 67.1,6, 72.2 (CSEL 3.2:632, 717, 721–724, 735–736, 741, 777).
170. *Laps.* 29 (CCSL 3:237).
171. *Epp.* 55.17,26–27, 59.15 (CSEL 3.2:636, 644–646, 684–685).
172. *Epp.* 38, 39, 40, 59.15 (CSEL 3.2:581–586, 684–685).

schism were conceded authority to grant admission into the church communion.

The Decian persecution initially challenged the Christian church's sense of its own identity as an extension of the Kingdom of God, separated from the realm of demonic idolatry. The community's failure to maintain its commitment to Christ provoked a crisis in which roles were confused and expectations were frustrated. To reestablish the church's boundary, Cyprian had to rebuild its internal structure: to establish the bishop's relation to God and the community; to specify different responsibilities of the clergy and the laity for the holiness of the church; to assert penitents' obligation to make satisfaction and right to receive peace. By accepting and following this internal discipline, the community reasserted control of its boundary and established both the efficacy and the necessity of the rituals of excommunication and repentance which protected its identity.

So, even before the question of the efficacy of baptism performed in one of the rival communions arose, Cyprian had already established the foundations of the African position: identification of the schismatics as anti-Christian, and the true church's exclusive right to control the boundary which separated it from the demonic realm populated by pagans, heretics and schismatics. Thus when the controversy broke out, both Cyprian's response and its eventual success in Africa were predictable.

Cyprian's written statements on the working of the ritual of baptism do not present a carefully integrated and elaborated theory of its efficacy. Although he specified that the Spirit operates in the washing, he also explained that this divine gift was actually communicated through imposition of the bishop's hands.[173] Yet in defending the efficacy of baptism given to the dying by sprinkling, he asserted that the Spirit is communicated fully by the washing itself.[174] He also asserted that efficacy of the ritual depended upon the faith of the recipient, and then had to argue that the schismatics did not truly share the Catholic creed.[175] Nor did he distinguish the imposition of hands in penance from the second stage of the baptismal ritual. As a consequence he did not clearly understand Stephen's

173. *Epp.* 70.1, 73.9, 74.5,7 (CSEL 3.2:767, 784, 802–805). This follows Tertullian, with the modification that the Spirit instead of an angel operates in the washing; *bapt.* 6–8 (CCSL 1:282–283).

174. *Ep.* 69.12–14, and esp. 15 (CSEL 3.2:760–765); in *ep.* 70.3 (CSEL 3.2:769), the African bishops argued that baptism was indivisible; but in *ep.* 73.9 (CSEL 3.2:784), Cyprian explained a succession of actions with different agents. He also shifted positions on the efficacy of the baptism of John; compare *ep.* 69.11 (CSEL 3.2:759), to *ep.* 73.24–25 (CSEL 3.2:797).

175. For the effects, *epp.* 69.12,16, 73.22 (CSEL 3.2:761, 765, 795–796). On the common faith, *epp.* 69.7, 73.4–5 (CSEL 3.2:756, 781–782).

reception of schismatic converts as penitents rather than inadequately baptized converts.[176]

In fact, of course, Cyprian's refusal to recognize the efficacy of baptism performed in a rival communion was based not upon an analysis of the various parts of the ritual but upon his belief in the unicity of the true church: the one communion founded by Christ upon the first bishops and continued through their united successors.[177] Outside that one communion were enemies of Christ, utterly deprived of the power of the Spirit.[178] Since the one church could not be divided into rival communions, he reasoned that to concede baptism to the schismatics would be to renounce his community's own claim to be the church of Christ.[179] The church's unicity and its exclusive claim to sacramental efficacy shine through the descriptive images with which Cyprian argued: enclosed garden and sealed fountain,[180] passover lamb and house of Rahab,[181] fortified camp of God's army,[182] seamless garment of Christ,[183] Paradise with its four rivers,[184] the ark of Noah.[185] Over and again, Cyprian identified the rejection of schismatic baptism with the defense of the oneness of the church.[186]

After the debacle of the Christian response to the Decian edict, Cyprian attempted to rebuild the shattered church at Carthage. He presented a coherent view of the true church as a tightly bounded unity, definitively segregated and under attack from the demonic realm which encompassed both false Christians and true pagans. He worked to reestablish the church's internal differentiation of orders and classes, adjusting responsibilities and expectations of both the standing and the fallen to fit new realities. Divine power and holiness could be found only within the com-

---

176. *Epp.* 72.1, 73.6,9, 74.5 (CSEL 3.2:771–772, 783, 802–803). See also the earlier *ep.* 69.11 (CSEL 3.2:760). But he did recognize the difference: schismatics who had been baptized originally in the Catholic communion could be readmitted through the imposition of hands in penitence; *epp.* 71.2, 74.12 (CSEL 3.2:772–773, 809).

177. *Epp.* 69.3, 70.3, 71.2, 73.7,11 (CSEL 3.2:752, 769, 773, 783–784, 786).

178. *Epp.* 69.1,5, 72.1, 73.11, 74.3,4 (CSEL 3.2:749–750, 754, 776, 786, 801–802).

179. *Epp.* 69.3–4, 70.3, 73.25 (CSEL 3.2:752–753, 769, 797–798).

180. *Epp.* 69.2, 74.11 (CSEL 3.2:751, 808).

181. *Ep.* 69.4 (CSEL 3.2:752).

182. *Epp.* 73.10, 74.9 (CSEL 3.2:785, 806). This was in fact the most commonly used image, see *epp.* 54.1, 55.17, 59.17, 57.1, 58.8, 61.3 (CSEL 3.2:621, 636, 687, 651, 664, 697).

183. *Vnit. eccl.* 7 (CCSL 3:254).

184. *Ep.* 73.10–11 (CSEL 3.2:785–786).

185. *Epp.* 69.2, 74.11 (CSEL 3.2:751, 809), outside of which everyone drowned, using 1 Pet. 3.20.

186. Explicitly in *epp.* 71.2, 73.2, 74.3 (CSEL 3.2:773, 779–780, 801).

munity, he insisted, and were mediated by its legitimately established officers: everything outside the true church must be judged polluted and evil. Converts from either idolatry or schism must be admitted in the same way, by the efficacious ritual which cleansed them from evil. Cyprian's understanding of the church did not admit the possibility of division into rival communions. In meeting the challenge of the laxists and the rigorists after the Decian persecution, the African bishops came to share Cyprian's views and to apply them to the two rituals which defined the boundary of the church, first to reconciliation of penitents and then to baptism of converts.

The thesis of this study proposes that in denying legitimacy to Christian rituals performed outside their communion, the African bishops were guided by the exigencies of their struggle against the double challenge of the rigorist and laxist communions. The bishops of Rome who disagreed with them may have based their own understanding of the church and the rituals of its competitors on a different social experience. To the rivalry in Rome, the investigation now turns.

III. THE CHURCH IN ROME

Although the Christian community in Rome suffered failures under the enforcement of the Decian edict, it did not experience the general breakdown of discipline which occurred in Carthage.[187] Cyprian's exile resulted in conflict among the clergy of Carthage but in Rome clerical leadership proved effective in maintaining the unity and discipline of the church. After Bishop Fabian's exemplary martyrdom,[188] the council of presbyters ruled the church throughout the persecution. The election of Cornelius as his successor was delayed for two years. Because few Roman confessors died under torture, martyrs' letters of intercession did not pose the threat to clerical authority that they did in Africa. The imprisoned confessors, moreover, agreed with the clergy that the fallen were to undertake penance and that only the dying were to be admitted to peace before a new bishop was elected at the end of the persecution.[189]

Once the persecution had waned and Cornelius was elected bishop, conflict did break out. An episcopal council set conditions for reconciling

187. *Ep.* 8.2 (CSEL 3.2:486–487), from the Roman to the Carthaginian clergy recounts the failures of the Christians and the limited success of the clergy in dissuading those waiting in line to sacrifice.
188. *Ep.* 9.1 (CSEL 3.2:488–489).
189. *Epp.* 30.3–5, 31.6,8, 36.2 (CSEL 3.2:551–553, 562, 564, 573–574). The one recorded attempt to gain a martyr's letter was by a native Carthaginian, Celerinus, on behalf of compatriots in Rome; *ep.* 21 (CSEL 3.2:529–532).

the fallen similar to those established in Carthage at the same time: immediate admission for the certified and continuing penance for the sacrificers.[190] The same council made a singular exception to this general practice, by admitting an entire community and its bishop as though they had only obtained certificates of compliance although they had all sinned together by offering incense.[191] These decisions were rejected by a majority of the confessors. Led by the presbyter Novatian who had been their spokesman during the persecution, they established a rigorist communion from which all the lapsed were excluded.[192] Some, realizing they had been deceived, soon repudiated Novatian's policy and publicly shifted allegiance to Cornelius.[193]

Cornelius deposed and replaced the three bishops who had ordained Novatian a bishop[194] and moved to defend his position. In letters presenting his case to other churches in the Empire, he appealed to his prior service in lower clerical office and the legitimacy of his election; he attacked the irregularity of Novatian's baptism and ordination as well as his cowardice during the persecution. The case was built on procedures properly followed and offices dutifully fulfilled; it did not address the controversial policy of reconciling the lapsed.[195] Gradually, Cornelius' claim was recognized in Rome and throughout the Empire.[196]

The nature of the conflict in Rome allowed Cornelius to assume a much stronger position than Cyprian could in Carthage since the Roman church was not threatened by an influx of unrepentant apostates carrying martyrs' letters of peace. Instead, fallen Christians could be readmitted to commu-

190. See n. 44 above.

191. See n. 45 above.

192. On Novatian's concern, see *epp.* 54.3, 55.25 (CSEL 3.2:622–623, 643–644). *Ep.* 55.5 (CSEL 3.2:627) names him as agent of the confessors.

193. Cyprian had pleaded with them to return and did not challenge Cornelius' decision to allow Maximus to return to his office, though Cyprian would apparently not have allowed this in Carthage; *epp.* 43.7, 72.2 (CSEL 3.2:597, 776). See n. 46 above.

194. The three were excommunicated though one was readmitted as a layman; *ep.* 50 (CSEL 3.2:613) and Eusebius, *h.e.* 6.43.10 (SC 41:156).

195. Cornelius, having passed through all the stages of clerical advancement, had been duly elected and ordained by the people and the surrounding bishops; Novatian had been baptized by sprinkling during illness rather than immersion, refused to serve as a presbyter during the persecution, was illicitly elected and irregularly ordained bishop. See Cyprian's *ep.* 55.8 (CSEL 3.2:629–630), and Cornelius letter to Fabian of Antioch in Eusebius, *h.e.* 6.43.8–9,13–17 (SC 41:155–158).

196. *Ep.* 60.1–2 (CSEL 3.2:691–693) recounts the community's support of Cornelius at the time of his arrest. The Africans' delay in recognizing Cornelius show that the problem was resolved once legates had returned from Rome; *epp.* 44.1, 48.2,4 (CSEL 3.2:597–598, 606–608). In Asia, the process was apparently more drawn out; Eusebius, *h.e.* 6.44–46 (SC 41:159–163).

nion only by submitting to Cornelius' authority: the rigorists refused to accept them and the laxists never established a communion in Rome.[197] In this way Cornelius remained firmly in control of the boundary of his church. Furthermore, his church's large and efficient bureaucracy had continued to function throughout the persecution and remained loyal to him in the subsequent schism. He did not have to replace a major portion of his clergy, as Cyprian did.[198] Despite the persecution and the schism, the governing structures of the Roman church functioned as its members would have expected.

As has been observed earlier, the weakening of the Carthaginian community's internal system of rights and responsibilities endangered its defining boundary. Just the opposite occurred in Rome where the performance of the clergy, the faithful and even the lapsed bolstered confidence in the church's identity and purity. Consequently, Novatian's opposition to the practice of granting peace, first to the certified and then to the sacrificers, did not threaten the sense of holiness shared by Cornelius' community. The people not only approved Cornelius' policies but urged even greater leniency in applying them.[199] They remained confident that the spiritual power of their church would protect them from that disabling pollution which so threatened Novatian and his followers.[200]

The Novatianist challenge was directed at the efficacy of procedures which the church used to cleanse and reconcile fallen Christians. Throughout the conflict Novatian sought to preserve the purity of his communion against the contagion carried by the apostates.[201] Thus he required any

197. Attempts to establish the community are reflected in *epp.* 50, 52.1–2 (CSEL 3.2:613–614, 616–619) between Cyprian and Cornelius. *Ep.* 59.1–2 (CSEL 3.2:666–668) indicates a subsequent attempt to displace Cyprian.

198. The letter to Fabian of Antioch, in Eusebius, *h.e.* 6.43.11 (SC 41:156) details its size: forty-six presbyters, seven deacons, seven subdeacons, forty-two acolytes, fifty-two exorcists, readers, and doorkeepers. Cyprian, in contrast, lost most of his presbyters and did not have enough clerics to handle his correspondence from exile; *ep.* 29 (CSEL 3.2:547–548) and Clarke, *Letters* 2:214. Clarke also provides a complete listing of Cyprian's known clergy; *Letters* 1:42–43.

199. The people approved the readmission of the schismatic confessors without penance and Maximus' return to the clergy; *ep.* 49.2 (CSEL 3.2:611–612). They convinced Cornelius to accept one of the bishops who had ordained Novatian; Eusebius, *h.e.* 6.43.10 (SC 41:156). They rallied behind Cornelius when he was arrested and exiled, *ep.* 60.1–2 (CSEL 3.2:691–693). The peace was extended to the sacrificers during that exile; *ep.* 68.5 (CSEL 3.2:748). If this action took place earlier, it was unknown to Cyprian and the African when they took the step in June 253; *ep.* 57.1 (CSEL 3.2:650–651).

200. The laxists in Carthage relied on the intercession of the martyrs rather than the rituals of the church to secure the sanctity of their community.

201. The letter of the Roman confessors, which was attributed to Novatian in Cyprian's

Christian tainted by idolatry after baptism to continue in penance outside the communion and to be judged by Christ himself.[202] In addition he charged that by admitting apostates Cornelius had contaminated his own communion and destroyed its power to sanctify.[203] As a result, contrary to the traditional practice of the Roman church Novatian rebaptized converts who had been defiled in Cornelius' communion.[204] The Novatianist attack therefore focused squarely on the efficacy of the ritual of reconciling penitent apostates through the imposition of hands. Thus when Cornelius' successor Stephen insisted that converts not be rebaptized, he was fending off the assault against the power of the ritual of repentance to purify sinners and protect the church.

Stephen's views on church unity and on the efficacy of ritual can be discerned only from the writings of Cyprian and his colleagues; none of his own correspondence has survived.[205] Stephen did not share Cyprian's belief that the church of Christ was restricted to a single communion outside which no one could gain salvation.[206] Thus in accepting Novatian's baptism Stephen did not fear that he was abandoning his own claim to be the representative of Peter and his church, the true community of Christ.[207] His other actions as head of the Roman church also show that he did not regard his own communion as the sole gateway to salvation. Stephen tolerated a bishop in Arles who sent dying penitents to face Christ's judgment deprived of the peace of the church.[208] He broke communion with African

---

ep. 55.5 (CSEL 3.2:627), makes clear the danger of pollution and the necessity of purification; the same is true in the contemporary letters of the Roman clergy. See *epp.* 30.2,3, 31.6,7, 36.1,3 (CSEL 3.2:549–551, 562–563, 573, 575). Cyprian understood Novatian's concern in the same way; *epp.* 54.3, 55.25–27 (CSEL 3.2:622–623, 643–646).

202. See nn. 137, 140 above.

203. Cyprian's defense of Cornelius to Antonianus indicates that a letter of Novatian is the source of the charges made against Cornelius; *ep.* 55.2–3 for the context, and 10,12 (CSEL 3.2:624–625, 631, 632) for specific charges.

204. This decision is first reported in *ep.* 73.2 (CSEL 3.2:779), which was written in the May or June 256. It may have been in place since the admission of the certified in 251 or the sacrificers in 253. On the tradition, see *ep.* 74.2 (CSEL 3.2:800).

205. *Epp.* 68 and 72, are addressed to Stephen, by Cyprian and the African bishops, respectively. Cyprian's *ep.* 67.5,9 (CSEL 3.2:730, 733) refers directly and indirectly to Stephen; *ep.* 74.1 (CSEL 3.2:799) discusses positions which were defended by Stephen in response to the Africans' *ep.* 72. Firmilian's *ep.* 75, attacks Stephen on the basis of this lost letter.

206. In *ep.* 74.2 (CSEL 3.2:800), Cyprian reported that Stephen considered his views on the unity of the church as an unwarranted innovation.

207. Firmilian remarked on Stephen's boasting of the privileges of his see; *ep.* 75.17 (CSEL 3.2:821).

208. *Ep.* 68.2–3 (CSEL 3.2:745–746) Cyprian believed that such persons were automatically condemned.

and Asian bishops without fearing that he would thereby jeopardize the salvation of the faithful in these churches or his own.[209] He may have allowed schismatic clergy to retain office upon entering the Catholic communion.[210] Unlike Cyprian, he viewed separated communities as part of the Christian realm whose members Christ might judge worthy of admission to the Kingdom of Heaven.

The question of the proper means of admitting converts baptized outside the one church had been discussed in Africa for some time before the bishops agreed to require rebaptism and reported this decision to their Roman colleague.[211] Stephen's decisive reaction to that communication and to the episcopal delegation subsequently sent from Africa to mediate the resulting dispute can be discerned in the reactions of Cyprian and Firmilian of Caesarea.[212]

The conflict involved a misunderstanding of the ritual of imposing hands by which Stephen received schismatic converts into his communion. Cyprian interpreted it as the second part of the baptismal ritual by which the Holy Spirit was conferred upon a convert baptized outside the church. On this basis, he demonstrated that the practice was incoherent, since the presence of the Spirit was equally necessary for the first part of the ritual, the washing to purify from sin.[213] Stephen, in contrast, identified the ritual as the reconciling of baptized penitents who had sinned by schism[214] and defended the practice as apostolic tradition accurately preserved in the Roman church.[215] In support of the validity of the original schismatic baptism he cited only the power of the invoked Name of Jesus.[216] If Ste-

---

209. *Epp.* 74.8, 75.6,24–25 (CSEL 3.2:805–806, 813–814, 825–826). See also Eusebius, *h.e.* 7.5.2–4 (SC 41:169). It may be noted that Firmilian also assumed that salvation was possible outside the communion, at least for catechumens; *ep.* 75.21 (CSEL 3.2:823).

210. The admonition of the African bishops in *ep.* 72.2 (CSEL 3.2:776–777), provides insufficient evidence for determining his actual practice, though the argument is the same as that used in the case of Marcian of Arles, where Stephen had tolerated deviance; *ep.* 68.4 (CSEL 3.2:747).

211. See nn. 61–64 above.

212. Thus Stephen's own views should be determined on the basis of *epp.* 74, 75, not by reference to intra-African correspondence, *epp.* 69, 70, 71, 73, which preceded his response. For the events, see nn. 65–67 above. For the chronology, see Clarke, *Letters* 4:173–174, 192–193, 206, 212–215, 219–221, 234–235, 248–252.

213. See n. 176 above.

214. Cyprian reported this in *ep.* 74.1–4 (CSEL 3.2:799–802).

215. Cyprian, *ep.* 74.2,4 (CSEL 3.2:800–802); Firmilian confirmed and amplified; *ep.* 75.6–7,19 (CSEL 3.2:813–814, 822–823), claiming an alternate, apostolic tradition. The same argument appeared in *epp.* 71.2, 73.13 (CSEL 3.2:772, 787–788).

216. *Epp.* 74.5 and 75.18 (CSEL 3.2:802–803, 822) attribute this to Stephen; *ep.* 73.4,14 (CSEL 3.2:781, 788), show that it was used in Africa as well. The argument

phen did specify more fully the effects of the baptismal ritual and the mode of the Holy Spirit's operation in a schismatic community, these clarifications have escaped the historical record.[217] In rejecting the practice of rebaptizing converts, therefore, Stephen argued primarily not for the validity of schismatic baptism but for the efficacy of the catholic ritual of reconciliation.[218]

Clearly, the ritual of admitting to communion by the imposition of hands had a different meaning in Stephen's dispute with Novatian than it did in Cyprian's conflict with the laxists. In Carthage, Cyprian had to assert the necessity of the imposition of a legitimate bishop's hands; in Rome, Stephen was required to defend its efficacy. Novatian had asserted that Cornelius and Stephen lacked power to reconcile idolaters through penance and the imposition of hands. In response, Roman bishops proceeded to receive not only the apostates who failed during the persecution but also converts from the rigorist schism by the very ritual whose efficacy they had denied. As Cornelius had insisted that confessors abandoning Novatian acknowledge him the one bishop of the most holy catholic church in Rome,[219] so Stephen required schismatics to entrust their salvation to the ritual of reconciliation by which he received them into communion. The traditional practice of recognizing heretical baptism provided Stephen with the perfect riposte to Novatian's challenge.

Stephen's vehement reaction to the African decision to require rebaptism of schismatics in their own churches was also a function of the centrality of the ritual of reconciliation in his conflict with Novatian. Letters which the African bishops sent in a packet to Stephen after their spring 256 meeting raised issues to which the Roman bishop was sensitive. Informing Stephen of their conciliar decision on rebaptism, the African bishops asserted that imposing hands could not cleanse the schismatics who had been defiled by washing in polluted water.[220] They also instructed him that clergy who had

---

from the identity of ritual and baptismal interrogation, which appears in *epp.* 69.7, 73.4,17–18 (CSEL 3.2:756, 781, 790–791) cannot be securely traced to Stephen. Its appearance in *ep.* 75.9 (CSEL 3.2:815–816) may be dependent upon the copies of these letters sent to Firmilian rather than upon Stephen's letter.

217. The African bishops specified these problems in their letter to Stephen, *ep.* 72.1 (CSEL 3.2:775–776), but the subsequent correspondence contains no indication of his response, *ep.* 74, 75.

218. Contrary to Cyprian's understanding of his purpose in *ep.* 74.4,8 (CSEL 3.2:802,806).

219. *Ep.* 49.2 (CSEL 3.2:611). Cyprian would have required them to acknowledge that there was only one church!

220. *Ep.* 72.1 (CSEL 3.2:775–776), in reference to the baptism performed in schism. Though *ep.* 71.2 (CSEL 3.2:772–773) did include the concession that schismatics who

gone into or been ordained in schism were not to be allowed to hold office in the catholic communion but to be admitted only as laymen. These schismatics, they explained, carried the impurity both of their rebellion and of their responsibility for those of their followers damned when they died in the schism.[221] The Africans sent Stephen copies of directives on rebaptism previously sent to the bishops of Numidia and Mauretania.[222] These conciliar reports may also have been accompanied by a copy of the letter supporting the Spanish congregations. In it, thirty-seven bishops strongly criticized Stephen for disregarding the danger of contaminating the entire communion when he ordered reinstatement of an apostate bishop.[223] The Africans cited Cornelius' practice in support of their warning.[224]

These four letters were read by the Roman bishop in the context of his conflict with Novatian quite differently from the way the Africans wrote them in the midst of their dispute with the laxists. The admonitions to exclude schismatic and idolatrous clergy could be construed as support of Novatian's charge of pollution. Arguments for the necessity of rebaptizing converts could impugn the efficacy of the ritual of reconciliation. The Africans joined Novatian in rejecting the established custom of accepting heretical baptism on the basis of recently discovered truth.[225] Finally, Cyprian's appeal to Peter and Paul, patrons of the Roman See, as models of unity and deference to truth added insult to injury.[226] Stephen broke communion with the Africans, and then with the Asians who upheld their own contrary apostolic tradition.

Stephen's actions in dealing with his episcopal colleagues in Gaul, Spain, Africa and Asia betray the attitude which governed his relations with Novatian in Rome. He defended his episcopal authority and the rituals

---

had originally been baptized in the catholic communion might be admitted by the imposition of hands alone, it did not address this new pollution incurred by rebaptism in schism.

221. *Ep.* 72.2 (CSEL 3.2:776–777).

222. *Ep.* 72.1 (CSEL 3.2:776) indicates that it was accompanied by copies of *ep.* 70 and 71 and identifies their addressees.

223. *Ep.* 67.9 (CSEL 3.2:742–743). The same catenae of scriptural texts are used in *epp.* 67.1, 72.2 (CSEL 3.2:736, 777). For the dating, which remains conjectural, see Clarke, *Letters* 4:139–140, 142–144.

224. *Ep.* 67.6 (CSEL 3.2:741). Stephen may have used Cornelius' reception of the confessor Maximus back into the presbyterate as a precedent to attract Novatian's clergy; see n. 46 above.

225. *Ep.* 71.3 (CSEL 3.2:773–774). Yet they had conceded, in *ep.* 71.2 (CSEL 3.2:772–773), the efficacy of the imposition of hands for cleansing those who had been baptized in the catholic communion before entering the schism.

226. *Epp.* 70.3, 71.3 (CSEL 3.2:769–770, 773–774). Peter was willing to learn from Paul (Acts 15:16, Gal 2:1); Paul to attend to revelation given another (1 Cor 14:29).

through which he maintained discipline in the community by granting admission both to communion and to clerical rank. He never perceived a threat to the purity or identity of his church; he never regarded schismatics at home or dissenters abroad as denizens of the demonic realm from which he must shield his church. Instead, he viewed them as rebels within the kingdom of Christ whom he must discipline and subject to his apostolic authority.

Because its system of rights and responsibilities had held firm and its expectations were fulfilled during the persecution, the Roman community did not fear contamination by apostates and the resulting loss of religious power. Its bishops felt no need to protect their communion from the encroaching pollution of idolatry or sedition. Defending the church's boundaries against imagined incursions from the demonic realm was the work of false bishops like Novatian and, apparently, Cyprian. Secure in his own position, Stephen had only to maintain discipline by asserting his authority. As bishop of Rome he would purify sinners by imposing hands; as successor of Peter he would determine proper procedure for the universal church.

IV. CONCLUSION

The hypothesis of this study states that the difference in the positions of the churches of Rome and Africa on the rebaptism of heretics can be understood through an analysis of the social situations of the two communities after the crisis of the Decian persecution. In Rome, the church's assurance of its identity and its commitment to traditional discipline remained firm during the persecution. Afterwards, Novatian challenged the church to reaffirm its rejection of Roman idolatry and denied its power to cleanse Christians from that sin. In Carthage, both the church's separation from false worship and its internal system of roles and responsibilities were seriously compromised during the persecution. The laxist party compounded the crisis by offering communion to the lapsed without requiring extended penance and episcopal granting of peace. Five years later, the Roman bishop had regained full control of his church's members but the Africans faced entrenched opposition. Their conflicting responses to the question of rebaptizing converts from schism reflected that difference.

The Decian persecution shattered the Christian church in Carthage: most of the presbyters turned against their exiled bishop; confessors flouted traditional discipline; many of the laity failed to uphold their baptismal commitment and then refused to make satisfaction before demanding readmission to communion. The failure of its members to meet the responsibilities of their stations assaulted the very identity of the community. As a result, confidence in the efficacy of the rituals of purification, baptism and penance, was undercut. Penitents were torn between the martyrs' offer of immediate forgiveness and the bishops' demand of penance before peace. Catholic bishops hesitated to deny all efficacy to the rituals of purification performed by their rigorist rivals.

Faced with uncertainty, Cyprian enforced the obligations and claimed the privileges of the church. By restoring discipline within the community, he reestablished the boundary separating the one true church from all its enemies. Thus he rebuilt confidence in the exclusive efficacy of the community's rituals to move converts and penitents across the chasm dividing the Kingdom of Christ from the realm of Satan. To follow the earlier practice of admitting heretics and schismatics without baptism would have been, for the bishop of Carthage, either to accept the laxist blurring of the divide between the godly and the demonic or to concede the rigorist patent on purity and consign himself to exterior darkness. In Cyprian's view, his communion's power to mediate salvation required that it alone control the rituals by which a candidate was separated from Satan and joined to Christ.

In Rome, as has been seen, Novatian's schism upheld the purity of the church by the traditional rituals of baptism and penance. Rigorists insisted that only baptism could protect the church communion against the contagion of idolatry; no bishop was empowered to cleanse baptized penitents from the guilt of that crime against God. Novatian not only refused peace to the fallen, but purified catholic converts by a new baptism. Stephen, and presumably Cornelius, insisted that the ritual of penance, culminating in the imposition of the bishop's hands, effectively cleansed the sinner, thereby protecting the purity of their communion. From the catholic perspective in Rome, the dispute focused on the authority of the bishop to forgive postbaptismal sin.

In their disagreement over the status of schismatic converts, neither Cyprian nor Stephen held baptism itself as the primary issue. Instead, the ritual of reconciliation was foremost in the minds of both bishops. To establish the necessity of the imposition of episcopal hands and thus maintain the boundary and identity of his church, Cyprian denied the schismatics power to baptize as well as to reconcile. To maintain the efficacy of the ritual of reconciliation and thus assert his own episcopal authority, Stephen defended the traditional concession of baptism to schismatics and heretics.

It may have been the traditional practice of the churches of Asia, as Firmilian claimed, to require schismatics and heretics to submit to rebaptism upon entering the catholic communion. But in Africa the practice was not universally accepted at the time of the Decian persecution. Cyprian's successful effort to establish this innovation can best be understood as an integral and essential element of the rebuilding of Christian society in Africa after the devastation visited upon it by Decius' edict.

The fundamental difference between Cyprian and Stephen revealed by this analysis lies in the way each established the boundary separating the realm of Christ from that of Satan. Cyprian recognized a unique church communion as the presence of the heavenly Kingdom of Christ in the world. Outside that church neither did the Holy Spirit sanctify nor did Christ acknowledge any disciples; all who died in that exterior darkness were damned without so much as a hearing. Stephen, without specifying the precise status of heretical and schismatic communities, believed that those who confessed Christ and were baptized in his Name might hope for salvation through his sovereign mercy in the final judgment. The clash of these two ideologies would plague the churches for the next two centuries.

J. Patout Burns is Thomas and Alberta White Professor of Christian Thought, Washington University, St. Louis

Ulfila's Own Conversion

Hagith Sivan
University of Kansas

Ulfila the Goth (ca. 310–383) has gained fame as the Arian apostle to his people.[1] More accurately, he was responsible for the conversion of some Goths to semi-Arianism during the 340s.[2] Yet two distinct traditions exist regarding Ulfila's own religious formation. One is an Arianized version of his life in the reports of Philostorgius and Auxentius, which claims Ulfila as an Arian from birth. The other, a Nicene version gleaned from the works of Socrates, Sozomen, and Theodoret, asserts that Ulfila "converted" from Nicene orthodoxy to Arianism sometime between 360 and 376. How compelling is either biography? If, moreover, Ulfila had remained loyal to Nicene doctrines until at least 360, to what had he converted the Goths in the 340s?

In this article I propose to locate the critical events of Ulfila's religious progression in the late 330s against the background of the diplomacy, court politics, and religious confrontations that followed the demise of Constantine.

---

[1]In this paper, I use the terms Nicene/orthodox(y) and Arian/Arianism in their widest possible senses to denote two basic dispositions toward the trinitarian question. I am, of course, aware of the differences between and inside each, but for the purpose of this paper, these umbrella terms should suffice. For a lengthy exploration of the subject, see Richard Patrick Crosland Hanson, *The Search for the Christian Doctrine of God: The Arian Controversy* (Edinburgh: T. & T. Clark, 1988).

[2]Edward Arthur Thompson, *The Visigoths in the Time of Ulfila* (Oxford: Clarendon, 1966), still provides the most readable introduction to the subject of both the bishop and Gothia. Among more recent contributions the lengthy introduction of Roger Gryson (*Scolies ariennes sur le Concile d'Aquilée* [SC 267; Paris: Cerf, 1980]) to Auxentius's *Vita Ulfilae* is invaluable.

HTR 89:4 (1996) 373–86

I shall endeavor to show that it was indeed an early "conversion" which shaped the course of the bishop's life and fixed his loyalty to a particular brand of Arianism. The treatment of Ulfila's "conversion" in the sources also provides an important test case for understanding the formation of Nicene and Arianized historiographical traditions in Late Antiquity.

■ The Nicene Biography of Ulfila

Nicene historians attributed Ulfila's change of heart to various causes, and they set it within various historical contexts. Although all three are primarily interested in the Gothic mass conversion to Arianism rather than in the beliefs of one individual, they provide invaluable insights into both the bishop and his nation.

Theodoret (ca. 393–466): Theodoret, whose evidence modern historians have largely ignored, introduces a mass Gothic conversion to Arianism into his description of a diplomatic exchange between Goths and Romans.[3] According to him, Eudoxius, the bishop of Constantinople (360–370) and an Arian, suggested to the emperor Valens (364–378), also an Arian, that converting the Goths to the imperial creed would go a long way toward bolstering the peace accord between the Goths and the empire. While the use of religion as a political tool in a peace process appeared reasonable, Valens and Eudoxius encountered unexpected resistance from the Gothic chieftains, who strenuously opposed both peace and conversion. They insisted on loyalty to the Nicene orthodoxy of their fathers, or so Theodoret assures his readers.[4]

At this point in his narrative, Theodoret presents Ulfila as the venerable bishop of the Goths.[5] Eudoxius meets with him and presents him with both an eloquent exposition of the Arian tenets and a generous bribe. These methods of persuasion find their mark, and as a result Ulfila prevails upon his Gothic flock (and presumably their chieftains) to convert from orthodoxy to Arianism under the false impression that no real doctrinal difference between the two positions existed. One might well be suspicious of Theodoret's reconstruction of events. That the Goths may not have fully discerned the more intricate theological differences between the Nicene and Arian camps is credible enough. It is, however, difficult to believe that they could have been completely oblivious to the basics of the theological dispute, especially if they had been orthodox originally, as Theodoret asserts.

---

[3]Theodoret *Historia ecclesiastica* 4.33.
[4]Ibid.
[5]Ibid.

Theodoret's grasp of basic chronology and of Ulfila's own history is also tenuous. He connects the Gothic mass conversion to the crossing of the Danube in 376, a turning point in Gothic history as contemporary sources amply illustrate.[6] He feels compelled, however, to resurrect Eudoxius for the occasion—the bishop had died in 370. Theodoret also chooses to emphasize the Goths' recent orthodox past to the neglect of their deeply-rooted paganism. Above all, Theodoret dates Ulfila's Arian mission among the Goths to the mid-370s instead of its traditional dating to the 340s and thus endows him with a Nicene affiliation prior to his conversion to Arianism.

Socrates (ca. 380–450): Socrates, another orthodox ecclesiastical historian, associates a Gothic mass conversion with internecine disputes between two pagan Gothic chieftains, Athanaric and Fritigern.[7] In this version, Fritigern defeated his rival Athanaric with imperial reinforcements, and subsequently embraced Arianism out of gratitude to the emperor. Here the chain of events clearly leads from Valens to Fritigern to the latter's Gothic followers. Ulfila plays a relatively minor role in this tale as a teaching missionary who undertook to instruct the Goths in their new faith. Ulfila apparently embarked on his missionary task among Fritigern's subjects with such zeal that he provoked Athanaric to initiate a persecution of the Arian Goths in his own domain. These events apparently transpired in the early 370s, before the Goths crossed the Danube in 376.

In his history, Socrates calls Ulfila "a bishop,"[8] and places him in Fritigern's camp as an intellectual apostle who tutored the Goths in both letters and Christianity (in its Arian guise, of course). In his description of the Council of Constantinople of 360, however, Socrates insists on Ulfila's roots in orthodoxy.[9] He asserts that Ulfila had been a Nicene from the very beginning of his career and had only subscribed to Arian tenets when he signed the canons of that council.

Sozomen (late fourth to midfifth century): Of the Nicene historians, Sozomen provides the fullest narrative, according Ulfila a pride of place.[10] He casts Ulfila as the chief of an important embassy that the Goths sent to

---

[6]Ammianus (*Res Gestae* 31.4–5) describes the crossing in graphic and dramatic details. Whether or not the conversion can be as accurately dated has been a subject of much modern controversy. For an excellent survey of both ancient and modern sources, see Zeev Rubin, "The Conversion of the Visigoths to Christianity," *Museum Helveticum* 38 (1981) 34–54.

[7]Socrates *Historia ecclesiastica* 4.33–34.

[8]Ibid.

[9]Ibid. 2.41.

[10]Sozomen *Historia ecclesiastica* 6.37.

Valens in 376 to ask for imperial permission to settle on Roman soil. This mission is well attested in contemporary secular sources, although none of them refers to a bishop as its sole leader or to Ulfila himself.[11] Once on Roman soil, the Goths succumbed to internal disputes, with the aforementioned Athanaric and Fritigern leading the fray. Like Socrates, Sozomen attributes to Fritigern a willing, if politically motivated, conversion to Arianism.[12]

Sozomen also appends to this story a lengthy coda in the form of a miniature biography of Ulfila.[13] Ulfila, hitherto a loyal Nicene, participated in the Council of Constantinople in 360, where he supported the Arians Eudoxius and Acacius without embracing their theological position. Although Sozomen's portrayal implausibly insists upon Ulfila's loyalty to Nicene orthodoxy despite his siding with two notable Arian leaders, it at least has the merit of linking the Goth with Eudoxius during the latter's lifetime. In order to account for Ulfila's ultimate conversion to Arianism, Sozomen reintroduces him to the capital, engages him in religious debates with Arian leaders, and involves him in a mysterious embassy that required access to imperial circles.[14] Ulfila, he claims, converted to Arianism as the only way to obtain the help of Arian leaders in furthering his urgent mission.

In spite of chronological discrepancies and factual inconsistencies, the three Nicene accounts agree on several features of Ulfila's career.[15] These include: (1) the bishop's Nicene leanings prior to his "conversion" to Arianism; (2) his possibly insincere conversion under political duress from orthodoxy to Arianism in 360 or thereabouts; (3) personal contacts with leading members of the Arian faction in Constantinople who were influential at court; and (4) a leading role in a mass Gothic conversion to Arianism

---

[11]Ammianus *Res Gestae* 31.4–5; Eunapius frag. 42 (Roger C. Blockley, *The Fragmentary Classicising Historians of the Later Roman Empire* [2 vols.; Liverpool: Cairns, 1981–83]) are the most important. See Herwig Wolfram (*History of the Goths* [trans. T. J. Dunlap; Berkeley: University of California Press, 1988] 423 n. 2) for a fuller list of ancient and modern sources.

[12]Sozomen *Historia ecclesiastica* 6.37.6–7.

[13]Ibid., 6.37.8–9.

[14]Ibid., 6.37.9; This embassy undoubtedly has no link with the one in 376 which sought land for the Goths within the empire. Sozomen not only clearly distinguishes between the two but makes the earlier one (in the 360s) the occasion for Ulfila's conversion.

[15]Euangelos Chrysos (*Τὸ Βυζάντιον καὶ οἱ Γότθοι* [Thessaloniki: Hetaireia Makedonikon, 1972] 113–14) ascribes the similarities between Socrates and Sozomen to the latter's borrowing from the former. But as Peter J. Heather ("The Crossing of the Danube and the Gothic Conversion," *GRBS* 27 [1986] 298) demonstrates, however, Sozomen used another source in addition. On the relationships among the three historians, see Glenn F. Chesnut, *The First Christian Histories: Eusebius, Socrates, Sozomen, Theodoret and Evagrius* (2d ed.; Macon, GA: Mercer Unviersity Press, 1986).

in the 370s. The Nicene histories, while suspect at various points, thus provide a fairly coherent picture of the missionary, a picture that deserves closer scrutiny.

■ The Arian Biography of Ulfila

The orthodox accounts of Ulfila's life run counter to the conventional scholarly wisdom.[16] The regnant scholarly life of Ulfila derives primarily from the testimony of the Arian Auxentius (second half of the fourth century), who produced a biography of his mentor, as well as from entries in the fragmentary fifth-century *Historica ecclesiastica* of Philostorgius (ca. 368–425), an Arian sympathizer. The modern consensus includes the following elements: Ulfila's birth in 311, consecration as bishop of the Goths by a leading Arian cleric between 337 and 341, and a mission to Gothia in the 340s.[17] These missionary endeavors ended abruptly after seven years, in the wake of persecutions of Gothic Christians. Ulfila and his disciples returned to Roman soil in the late 340s and subsequently settled in Moesia with the blessing of the (Arian) emperor Constantius II. The following decades of the bishop's life remain hazy, although apparently marked by his translation of the Bible into Gothic, and punctuated by attendance at church councils (most notably those of Constantinople in 360 and 383) and by involvement in religious disputes among Christian factions. Ulfila died in 383, not long after the Goths and the Romans signed a major peace agreement which ended seven years of hostilities.

Both Philostorgius and Auxentius imply that Ulfila had been an Arian from the inception of his career, if not from birth. They seem, moreover, to have extensive knowledge about the early stages of the bishop's ministry prior to the 360s, precisely the period about which the Nicene historians are silent. In fact, the surviving fragments of Philostorgius's work cover only the period from Ulfila's birth to his expulsion from Gothia in the late 340s. Auxentius narrates the same period but, omitting about thirty-five years between the return to the empire in the 340s and the 380s, he extends Ulfila's biography through his mentor's participation in the Council of Constantinople in 383 and then to his death. Above all, the two Arian accounts omit a personal conversion, as have all modern accounts.

How likely, one should ask, is the story of such a conversion? Its very inclusion in Nicene narratives credits its authenticity, since Ulfila's aban-

---

[16]See n. 2 above. See also Peter J. Heather and John Matthews, "The Life and Work of Ulfila," in idem, *The Goths in the Fourth Century* (Liverpool: Liverpool University Press, 1991) 133–43.

[17]Auxentius's letter which contains the biography appears in the critical edition by Roger Gryson. An English translation appears in Heather and Matthews, *Goths in the Fourth Century*, 146–47. Philostorgius *Historia ecclesiastica* 2.5.

donment of the orthodox camp for the Arian cause hardly enhanced the glory of the church to which the three Nicene writers belonged. On the other hand, the absence of a conversion story in the Arianized account of Philostorgius lends further credibility to the event, since it is precisely this sort of episode that Philostorgius' ultraorthodox editor, Photius, was likely to omit. Auxentius's own reticence is similarly explicable. He was constructing a biography of an ideal religious leader who had never deviated from his purpose and certainly had never changed his creed. As a result, Auxentius's Ulfila displays a staunch and single-minded adherence to one form of belief throughout his life.[18]

That Ulfila's upbringing was not Arian appears probable on various grounds. Philostorgius calls attention to the existence of Cappadocian Christians among the Goths since at least the end of the third century.[19] Their type of Christianity, although only gleaned from sparse evidence such as the activities of the midthird-century bishop of Caesarea, Firmilian, was of the nature of what later became "orthodoxy."[20] Ulfila would thus have received the rudiments of his religious education in a pre-Nicene version. The participation of one Theophilus, "bishop of the Goths" (τῶν Γότθων ἐπίσκοπος), in the Council of Nicaea[21] and his subscription to its creed indicate that the tenets of orthodox Christianity infiltrated Gothia as early as 325, when Ulfila was only fourteen years old.[22] If there is need to attach a label to Gothic Christianity prior to Ulfila's missionary activities in the 340s, "orthodox" would be considerably more accurate than "Arian."

■ A New Biography of Ulfila

With these considerations in mind, one must allow for the possibility of a personal conversion. The sources of the Nicene presentation of the bishop's life also deserve consideration. How, then, did the Nicene historians arrive at their version of Ulfila's conversion, and why did they date this critical

---

[18]*Semper credidi* ("I always believed") is the phrase that Auxentius uses to explicate Ulfila's credo (*Vita Ufilae* 63). One should note that Auxentius knew his hero only during the late phase of the latter's episcopal career.

[19]Philostorgius *Historia ecclesiastica* 2.5. Socrates (*Historia ecclesiastica* 1.18) claims that Constantine intended to send missionaries to the Goths after he signed a treaty with them in 332. It is unlikely, however, that Philostorgius invented both greater antiquity for Christianity in Gothia as well as Cappadocian connections. See also Hagith Sivan, "The Making of an Arian Goth: Ulfila Reconsidered," *Revue bénédictine* 105 (1995) 280–92.

[20]See Pierre Nautin, "Firmilian of Caesarea," *Encyclopedia of the Early Church* 1 (1992) 324.

[21]Although it is not entirely clear whether Theophilus represented the Danubian Goths or the Crimean Goths at Nicaea, his link with Ulfila points to the former.

[22]Socrates *Historia ecclesiastica* 2.41.

transformation to the 360s? A closer look at Sozomen's account is needed to gain an understanding of these issues.

In order to provide a precise context for Ulfila's conversion, Sozomen involves him in two diplomatic initiatives. In the first, the bishop heads a Gothic delegation dispatched in 376 to obtain imperial permission for the Goths to settle within the empire.[23] Negotiations took place somewhere along the Danubian *limes*, a fact that alone distinguishes it from the second embassy, which Sozomen clearly places in Constantinople. None of the surviving records of the 376 negotiations refers to Ulfila by name, although the success of the Gothic mission and the resultant treaty may have been partly owing to him.[24] One source, however, does acknowledge the presence of bishops among the Goths who migrated across the Danube in 376,[25] and another refers to a priest, a confidant of Fritigern, who conducted delicate negotiations with Valens on the eve of the battle of Adrianople in 378.[26] There is no evidence, however, that Ulfila either joined the crossing hordes or converted to a new creed at this time.

Although Ulfila's mission to Constantinople appears in Sozomen's narrative after the Danubian embassy, its place in the text is misleading. There is no doubt that the former event forms a digression. In fact, Sozomen reports two Ulfilian visits to the capital.[27] One brought him to the council of Constantinople in 360, while the other involved negotiations with the imperial court. The historian offers neither a date nor a reason for the second trip, but states that Ulfila needed the support of leading Arians in the capital in order to gain entry to courtiers useful to him. Sozomen also implicitly dates this episode to the early 360s and clearly connects the mission with Ulfila's own conversion to Arianism.

Sozomen's second embassy calls to mind a similar venture that Philostorgius includes in his narrative.[28] According to the latter, the young Ulfila participated in a diplomatic mission that an unnamed Gothic ruler sent to Constantinople during the reign of Constantine (306–337). Like Sozomen, Philostorgius does not disclose the purpose of this mission, but he does assert that hard on the heels of its appearance on Roman soil, Eusebius of

[23]Sozomen *Historia ecclesiastica* 6.37.5–6.

[24]Ammianus *Res Gestae* 31.2–4; Eunapius frag. 42; Wolfram, *History of the Goths*, 117–18. Heather, "Crossing of the Danube," 316–17.

[25]Eunapius (frag. 48.2) suspects that the Goths pretended to be Christians. He may have been wrong.

[26]See Ammianus *Res Gestae* 31.12.8 on the priest; but Ammianus's account is problematic. The priest appeared *cum aliis humilibus* ("with a few low class men"), an odd company for so critical and delicate a mission, and one hardly calculated to inspire Valens with confidence or a desire to cooperate. The Romans insisted on embassies worth their dignity.

[27]Sozomen *Historia ecclesiastica* 4.24.1–6.37.8; 6.37.9.

[28]Philostorgius *Historia ecclesiastica* 2.5.

Nicomedia, the leading Arian figure of the 330s and bishop of Constantinople between 338 and 341, consecrated Ulfila bishop. One obvious problem with this account is that it contradicts Auxentius's chronology which dates Ulfila's consecration to the early years of the reign of Constantius II.[29] Nor does Philostorgius account for the pivotal role that Eusebius of Nicomedia played in ecclesiastical politics even before his elevation to the see of Constantinople.

Modern scholarly efforts to reconcile the divergent chronologies of Ulfila's life include a proposal to reject the narrative of Auxentius in favor of that of Philostorgius.[30] In this reconstruction, Philostorgius depicts the Gothic delegation as reaching Constantinople in time for Constantine's *tricennalia* in 336. Ulfila was conveniently consecrated at the Council of Constantinople during this visit. Such a reconstruction, however, bristles with problems. To begin with, Ulfila's elevation to a bishopric need not have coincided with a church council.[31] There is, moreover, no evidence for a Gothic delegation to Constantine's *tricennalia*. While perhaps not decisive, the failure of Eusebius of Caesarea's lengthy panegyric on this imperial celebration to allude either to foreign delegations in general or to a Gothic one in particular is highly suggestive. Two further details undermine the credibility of the hypothesis of a Gothic embassy in 336 and Ulfila's consecration at that time. The pagan tribal leader who, according to Philostorgius, had commissioned the embassy to the empire was unlikely to have dispatched Ulfila among his delegates in order to facilitate his promotion to bishop. It is unclear, finally, how the consecrating bishop in 336 could have been Eusebius of Nicomedia, since he became patriarch of Constantinople only in 338.

Philostorgius's dating scheme, therefore, appears misguided. The fact that both he and Sozomen refer to an Ulfilian mission to the imperial court at Constantinople, however, is significant and has been overlooked hitherto. In spite of the chronological discrepancies between Philostorgius and Sozomen, both clearly echo the souvenirs of a single Constantinopolitan mission. When, then, could such an embassage have occurred, and what circumstances would have allowed one of its members to convert from the Nicene to the Arian camp and then receive a bishop's staff? To answer the first question, one must take a brief excursion into the history of Roman diplomacy during the fourth century.

---

[29]Auxentius, curiously, ignores Eusebius of Nicomedia, thus strengthening the impression that the historian was either surprisingly ignorant or highly selective regarding the facts of Ulfila's early career.

[30]Timothy David Barnes, "The Consecration of Ulfila," *JTS* 41 (1990) 541–45.

[31]Compare Heather and Matthews, *Goths in the Fourth Century*, 142–43, who also disagree with Barnes.

The surviving evidence of diplomatic contacts between Goths and Romans indicates that dispatches of delegations were ordinarily a way of responding to an impending crisis or a change of government. On the eve of the battle of Adrianople in 378, for example, the Gothic chieftain Fritigern commissioned a clergyman as head of a delegation to the emperor Valens in an attempt to avert a major confrontation.[32] The death of an emperor also could provoke peoples on the outskirts of the empire to embark on diplomatic missions in order to stave off potential crises. According to Ammianus, the accession of Julian in 361 and the new emperor's warlike reputation led many neighbors of Rome to send embassies posthaste to confirm the peace and to offer fealty.[33]

It is precisely this type of situation that Philostorgius's Gothic mission evokes, and which, therefore, helps to date Ulfila's first Gothic mission to the year 337. Constantine's death in May of that year and the lack of clear arrangements for the imperial succession called into question the validity of previous agreements between Rome and its weaker neighbors. Just five years before his death, Constantine had signed a *foedus* with the Goths which entailed an exchange of hostages and presumably a commitment by the Goths to lend military aid upon demand.[34] The treaty now lay in the hands of his successor(s) who might elect to renege on it.

This is the most likely background for the appearance of a Gothic delegation in Constantinople. One of its delegates was a young polyglot named Ulfila, who knew Greek, Gothic, and Latin. His services would have proven useful in such turbulent times. More importantly, this scenario explains Philostorgius's reference to Constantine, rather than to one of his sons. In light of the confusion at court between May and September of 337, the identity of the new emperor was still unclear when the Gothic delegation reached the imperial capital. The presence of Constantius II in Constantinople soon after his father's death and the conspicuous role that he played in Constantine's state funeral must have helped to create the impression that he was his father's designated successor.[35] The Gothic delegation was perhaps only one of many foreign embassies attempting to gain access to the new ruler of the Roman world. The Goths needed some advantage in their

---

[32]Ammianus *Res Gestae* 31.12.8. This presbyter carried two letters from Fritigern to the emperor: one repeating the terms of the 376 *foedus* ("treaty") between the Roman government and the Goths, the other proposing a strategy for resisting anti-Roman groups. Ammianus states that the man was a close confidant of Fritigern. This claim echoes what all the Nicene ecclesiastical historians assert about the nature of the relationship between the Gothic chieftain and Ulfila. Was the ambassador possibly the venerable bishop himself?

[33]Ibid., 22.7.5.

[34]See Wolfram (*History of the Goths*, 61–63) for details of this arrangement.

[35]Eusebius *Vita Constantini* 70.

diplomatic gambit. That advantage came in the person of the Christian member of the embassy, Ulfila, who suddenly became a valuable tool in the political game to secure the imperial ear.

None of the sources, unfortunately, describes in detail how Ulfila gained entry to the circle of Eusebius of Nicomedia, a trusted confidant of Constantius II. Both Eusebius and Constantius were known Arians. The former probably enticed the young Goth with promises of Ulfila's rapid promotion within the church and of his own intervention on behalf of the Gothic embassy. The price that Ulfila's new *amicus* and patron exacted for his favors was conversion to the tenets of Arianism.[36]

A blend of politics and religion operated in this case on at least two levels. At the level of diplomatic negotiations, Constantius reaffirmed his father's policy of adherence to the treaty of 332. Besides a unique inscription, dating to 354, which bestows on Constantius II the title of *Gothicus maximus*,[37] there is no evidence of a Gothic victory by this emperor.[38] The Goths apparently also kept the peace and—even when menacing the provincials along the frontier—did not suffer from major retaliation until Valens led a Gothic expedition in 368.[39]

At the level of religious commitment, Ulfila exchanged the pro-Nicene creed of his youth for Eusebius's brand of Arianism and consequently gained an episcopal appointment as a reward. The willingness to "convert" for a specific gain is in itself a regular feature of the religious landscape of the period. Ulfila, however, not only experienced a personal conversion under the expert tutelage of Eusebius of Nicomedia, but also embarked on a missionary campaign among his own people beyond the Danube. The pre-

---

[36]Such tactics accord well with the tenor of politics at court during the years of Arian emperors. My reconstruction also can shed light on the prominence that the Nicene descriptions of Ulfila's conversion accord to Eudoxius. In their tale, Eudoxius apparently ensured that all recipients of the grain dole in the capital had to enter communion with the Arians unless they wished to forgo their rations. Not surprisingly, this collusion between church and court brought many new adherents to Arianism. William Telfer, "Paul of Constantinople," *HTR* 43 (1950) 40.

[37]*CIL* 3.3705 (*ILS* 732). See also Adelina Arnaldi, "I cognomina devictarum gentium dei successori di Constantino il grande," *Epigraphica* 39 (1977) 93–95.

[38]Unless, as seems unlikely, the persecution of Christians in Gothia was the result of hostilities with Rome. This assumption derives from an analysis of the *Passio Sancti Sabae*, which seems to record three waves of the persecution of Christians in Gothia, the first resulting in the expulsion of Ulfila. See Rubin, "Conversion of the Visigoths," 44. An inscription dated to 338–340 refers to the Gothic menace along the Danube and to fortifications erected for the security of the inhabitants (*CIL* 3.12483 [*ILS* 724]). A Gothic victory would need to have taken place between 338 and 354, if at all. See Arnaldi, "I cognomina devictarum," 95 n. 18.

[39]Ammianus *Res Gestae* 27.5, and at much greater length, Themistius *Ors.* 8 and 10 (both translated and discussed in Heather and Matthews, *Goths in the Fourth Century*, 13–50).

cise date of his consecration is thus immaterial, since he might have lingered in Constantinople until Eusebius's death in 341.

Many of the transdanubian Goths whom Ulfila indoctrinated in the tenets of Arianism in the 340s probably already had been Christians and thus would have converted, like him, from orthodoxy to Arianism.[40] Whether or not Ulfila managed to extend his mission to the vast majority of his people, who were still pagans, remains unclear. His efforts may have led to his expulsion after only seven years in Gothia. When the bishop returned to Roman soil with his loyal followers, Constantius allowed them to settle in Moesia, where Ulfila apparently completed his translation of the Bible into Gothic. It must have been as a patron of the Arian Goths within the empire, moreover, that the emperor entered the pages of the Gothic calendar.[41] The calendar commemorates the anniversary of Constantius' death, a unique honor which places a Roman emperor in the company of martyrs and apostles.

If Ulfila's conversion was due to a complex combination of factors, so also was the reporting of this change in subsequent historiography. This event, clearly a critical stage in the bishop's theological development, came to feature prominently in Nicene histories. Did it, however, leave any traces in Gothic histories? How influential was Ulfila in Arianizing the Goths? Given the current state of the evidence, it is impossible to reconstruct with accuracy a Gothic version of their past, and especially of the beginnings of Christianity in their midst. The fourth-century *Passio Sancti Sabae* recounts persecutions of Christians in Gothia, probably in the early 370s, and its hero Sabas himself was evidently a Catholic and not an Arian.[42] The Gothic calendar, moreover, provides more information about Gothic martyrs of both Arian and Nicene persuasion, but neither the calendar nor the *Passio* speak of Ulfila's place within Gothic Christianity.

In the late sixth century, the Gothic (orthodox) historian Jordanes referred to Ulfila as the bishop of a group called *Gothi minores* ("Lesser Goths"), dwellers in Moesia whom the author knew to have been in his own time poor and peaceful people who were fond of drinking milk.[43] The passage in Jordanes unfortunately furnishes no clue as to the activities of

---

[40]It is a vexed question whether Ulfila was appointed as a bishop of the Christians in Gothia or as a bishop of the Goths in general. The former appears more plausible. For rival missions in Gothia, see Sivan, "Making of an Arian Goth," 287–88.

[41]For the text and an English translation, see Heather and Matthews, *Goths in the Fourth Century*, 128–30.

[42]See Hippolyte Delehaye, "Saints de Thrace et de Mesie," *Analecta Bollandiana* 31 (1912) 216–21 for the text; Heather and Matthews, *Goths in the Fourth Century*, 111–12 for translation; and Rubin, "Conversion of the Visigoths," 36–37 for discussion.

[43]Jordanes *Getica* 267.

Ulfila and his contemporaries. Jordanes's reticence may lend support to the Arian versions of Auxentius and Philostorgius, who also dissociate Ulfila from the main course of Gothic history. Odd as it may appear, the introduction of Arian Christianity to the Gothic masses by Ulfila in the 370s never entered the extant Gothic historiography.

The search for an explanation of Ulfila's prominence in later writings leads, then, to Arian-Roman traditions—back, that is, to Auxentius and Philostorgius. Neither was writing a Gothic history, but both sought to create an Arianized version of the history of the church. As representatives of an Arian school of historiography they cast the bishop as the pious shepherd of a large group of Goths who fled the persecution at home and came to the empire with the blessing of an Arian emperor (Constantius II). Auxentius probably knew about Ulfila's involvement in a Gothic mission in the 340s from the man himself. But any role that his hero may have played in later Gothic history bore no relevance to the biography which Auxentius reconstructed. Auxentius's successful portrayal of Ulfila as an Arian leader, meanwhile, probably inspired Philostorgius, who presumably had access to the circle of Auxentius, to assign the bishop a prominent role in his own account of the church in the fourth century. A Cappadocian himself, Philostorgius went so far as to ascribe a Cappadocian origin both to Christianity in Gothia and to Ulfila's ancestors. Above all, Philostorgius must have been as aware as the later Nicene historians were of the strength of Germanic Arianism in the early fifth century. Since this was a period of decline for Roman Arianism, he deliberately advanced Ulfila to a position of prominence as the outstanding exemplar of the earliest Gothic Arianism. Philostorgius probably also had access to a source containing information about Ulfila's first visit to Constantinople, his dealings with leading Arians in the capital, and his relationship to the Arian emperor Constantius II.

From the Arian sources, the elevated portrayal of Ulfila moved to the Orthodox historiography. The Nicene historians who, like Philostorgius, puzzled over fifth-century Gothic Arianism were aware of only one Gothic mass conversion in the fourth century. To account for the vibrancy of Gothic Arianism in their own time they, too, resorted to Ulfila. After all, how else could they explain the tenacious adherence of the Goths to Arianism half a century after the deaths of both Valens and Fritigern, the men who had engineered the Gothic conversion in the 370s? As a result, Nicene historiography created its own version of the history of Gothic Arianism.

To both Arian and Nicene ecclesiastical historians, the life of Ulfila thus offered a neat solution to two problems. For the former, he was an early protagonist of their creed who spread the word to a large number of Goths. For the latter, he provided a ready explanation for the tenacity of a creed vanishing from the center of the empire. In the Nicene version, the Goths may have initially converted out of gratitude to Valens, but they were still Arians because of the enormous influence that Ulfila had exerted over them after his own conversion from orthodoxy to Arianism.

■ Conclusion

To summarize, Arianized Greek historiography appropriated Ulfila and elevated him to the rank of a national apostle. Nicene Greek historians did the same, at least partly in response to versions like Philostorgius's. On the other hand, the silence of the Latin church historians regarding Ulfila's role in the Arian formation of the Goths emphasizes the innovative role of the hellenophone historiography which cast Ulfila as the most important Gothic missionary and the fountainhead of Gothic Arianism. The earliest Nicene reference in the West to a mass Gothic conversion appears in the history of Orosius, written in the late 410s. Orosius claims that Valens sent "teachers of the Arian dogma" in response to a Gothic request to dispatch "bishops from whom they may learn the rules of the Christian faith."[44] The context of this passage implies that Orosius is thinking of a period just prior to the battle of Adrianople in 378. Like the Gothic sources, Orosius never refers to Ulfila or to his alleged role in the Christianization of the Goths in the 370s.

Ulfila first appears in the annals of Nicene-Greek ecclesiastical histories when they describe the notoriously pro-Arian Council of Constantinople of 360. The council, which favored the moderate Arians, was a plausible context in which to set the far-reaching conversion from orthodoxy to Arianism. Ulfila's involvement at Constantinople was significant enough to have left a mark on orthodox accounts of the council, as well as to obscure his earlier activities. His uncompromising commitment to Arianism from 360 until his death in 383 obliterated the memory of previous stages of his religious metamorphosis. Since the Arian accounts of Ulfila's life by Auxentius and Philostorgius preferred to focus on Ulfila's earlier life, the Nicene Greek historians had a free hand to construct a history which delayed Ulfila's acceptance of Arianism in order to make him the father of Gothic Arianism in the late fourth century.

The relative obscurity shrouding Ulfila's early decades is not surprising in view of the respectability of the semi-Arianism of such prominent leaders as Eusebius of Nicomedia and Eusebius of Caesarea. Only later, between the Councils of Constantinople of 360 and 383, did the Arian and Nicene sides harden into political and theological extremism. From the vantage point of the triumph of orthodoxy in the fifth century, a whole

[44]Orosius *Historia adversum paganos* 7.33.19. The translation is that of Rubin, "Conversion of the Visigoths," 50–51.

century after Ulfila's own conversion, both Arian and Nicene historians could rearrange the facts to suit their individual purposes. Such a rearrangement proved particularly convincing when it connected Ulfila with Eudoxius and Valens, respectively a controversial Arian figure and a powerful ruler famed for his energetic political machinations.

Taking their cue from the Nicene historiographical fiction about a belated conversion, modern scholars have regarded the Council of Constantinople as a turning point in Ulfila's own allegiance to Arian dogmas.[45] But whether or not he became an extreme Arian in 360, such a date obscures a far more critical transformation. Ulfila's initial conversion from orthodoxy to Eusebian (semi-)Arianism had already occurred by the late 330s. This early conversion, and not merely subsequent events in Gothia or the empire, explains both Ulfila's loyalty to Eusebian Arianism and the special treatment which Constantius II accorded him in the late 340s upon his flight to the empire. Without taking into account this early stage in Ulfila's career, all reconstructions of his activities lack a solid foundation.[46]

[45]See, for example, Heather and Matthews, *Goths in the Fourth Century*, 137–38; Gonzalez Fernandez, "Wulfila y el sinodo de Constantinople del ano 360," *Antiguedad y Cristianismo* 3 (1986) 47–51.

[46]I am grateful to the anonymous reader of *HTR* for useful criticism. My belated thanks go to Zeevic Rubin for introducing me to Ulfila, many, many years ago.

The Prayer of the Heart in Syriac Tradition*

SEBASTIAN BROCK

The crossing of boundaries

It is a remarkable fact that a number of writings on the spiritual life are far more widely read and exert a much greater influence today than was ever the case during the lifetime of their authors. That this is not simply a consequence of the invention of printing can be seen from one particularly striking nineteenth-century example, *The Way of the Pilgrim*, which only achieved its totally unexpected popularity in its English translation, first published in 1930. Writings such as this, indeed, tend to have a delightfully disconcerting way of transcending the boundaries, not only of time and space, but also of language, culture and ecclesiastical allegiance. A notable instance here is provided by the works of an obscure seventh-century monk living in the remote mountains on the borders between modern Iraq and Iran, who wrote in Syriac, and who belonged to a Church considered heretical by the rest of Christendom – works which nevertheless have exercised a considerable influence, in Greek and Arabic translations, on recent monastic revivals in both the Greek Orthodox Church (on Mount Athos) and the Coptic Orthodox Church (in the Nitrian desert between Cairo and Alexandria),[1] not to mention the reasonably wide readership they have had among Western Christians, thanks to a somewhat awkward English translation made in 1923 by the Dutch orientalist A.J. Wensinck.[2]

The reason why such a writer as St Isaac of Nineveh, far removed from us in time and space, should none the less still have an appeal among modern readers is not far to seek. Since the Christian can be understood as living simultaneously in two different dimensions, in sacred as well as in ordinary time and space, wherever the concern is with matters of the spirit, where sacred time and space are operative, the gap in historical time and geographical space that may exist between a particular writer or group of writers and the present day is without any real importance. For where sacred time and space are concerned, what is relevant is the quality of

---

* A paper read at the Fellowship conference 1981.

1. See O.F.A. Meinardus, 'Recent developments in Coptic monasticism', *Oriens Christianus* 49 (1965), pp.79-89, and 'The hermits of Wadi Rayan', *Studia Orientalia Christiana: Collectanea* 11 (1966), pp.294-317 (p.304 for St Isaac).

2. *Mystic Treatises by Isaac of Nineveh* (Amsterdam 1923; reprinted Wiesbaden 1969); a new translation, by Fr Mamas of the Monastery of the Transfiguration (Brookline) is forthcoming. On St Isaac see also my 'St Isaac of Nineveh and Syriac spirituality', *Sobornost* 7:2 (1975), pp.79-89, and 'St Isaac of Nineveh', *The Way* 21 (1981), pp.68-74.

what goes on, not where or when it goes on. That is why writings on the Prayer of the Heart, no matter whether they date from the fourth or the fourteenth century, whether they come from Greece, Iraq, or Russia, are equally relevant to the Christian in twentieth-century England, seeing that they concern a subject which touches on the very essence of our existence.

The location of the heart in sacred space

As far as the topic of the Prayer of the Heart is concerned the concept of sacred space happens to be of more immediate importance than that of sacred time, for we are dealing with what might be called the 'geography of the spirit'. What is the map of this world like? In particular, whereabouts is this heart, where prayer takes place, to be found, and where is it located? We are of course asking the wrong question first for, as we have just seen, with sacred space it is the content which locates things, and not their position in ordinary space. Thus, to anticipate a little, we shall discover that this 'heart', where the prayer of the heart takes place, is to be found wherever there is purity of heart. Accordingly we should begin by asking what is this heart? We should at once avoid thinking of it as being the same thing, let alone in the same place, as our physical heart. Long before medical science discovered the physiological importance of our physical heart, the Israelites had been talking of the heart as the centre of our whole being, and the seat, not only of the emotions (as it still remains for us in popular usage), but also of the intellect, of thought and the will. We have moved this aspect up to the head, and so we get the dichotomy of the heart versus the head, feeling versus reason. For the Hebrews this tension was less marked, seeing that both feeling and reason were understood to originate in the same place, the heart. This all has some important consequences for the later history of Christian spirituality which I should touch on briefly here.

The heart and the mind

Early Christian writers on the spiritual life were heirs to both Semitic and Greek cultures, and each writer has his own individual admixture of elements from each of these traditions.[3] It so happened that there was some Greek backing, among the Stoics, for the Semitic concept of the heart as the seat of the intellect, but for the Platonic and Neoplatonic tradition this is not the case, and Christian writers in this tradition — above all 'Dionysius the Areopagite' — show little or no interest in the heart as the centre of the spiritual life, speaking instead of the *nous,* the mind or intellect (though the Greek term covers rather more than either of these English words imply).

Wherever the influence of the Dionysian writings was strong (and it was strong in both East and West, but above all in the West), the heart is not an important location in the spiritual geography of the human being. It has become separated on this map of sacred space from the intellect (and in some cases more or less replaced by it).

3. On the importance of the heart in early Christian spirituality see A. Guillaumont, 'Le coeur chez les spirituels grecs à l'époque ancienne', *Dictionnaire de Spiritualité* 2. 2281-8.

This is why, in the Western Christian tradition, 'prayer of the heart' usually has a somewhat narrower sense than it has in most of the Eastern Christian tradition, for in the West the heart is simply the seat of emotions, of affective prayer, whereas in the East it has (among certain writers at any rate) retained its biblical role of being the seat of the intellect as well.

A passage from St Bernard's Commentary on the Song of Songs very neatly illustrates the dichotomy that has taken place in the sacred geography of the medieval West: 'There are two kinds of contemplation', he writes, 'one seated in the intellect, the other in the heart's disposition; the one is accompanied by light, the other by warmth; the one consists in perception, the other in devotion'.[4] Popular usage today simply reflects this division described by St Bernard: we speak of the mind being 'illumined', but the heart being 'set on fire'.

The spirituality of the prayer of the heart, then, is going to be richest wherever it is at its most biblical, that is to say, wherever the 'heart' is regarded as the focal point of *every* aspect of the 'inner person', as St Paul calls it (Rom. 7:22), the focal point of the intellect as well as of the emotions and feelings — just as for us today the heart has also become the focal point of our *physical* existence, of the 'exterior person', as well. Indeed the fact that the single term 'heart' can nowadays be used to refer to the focal points of the two different modes of our existence, of both our physical and our spiritual being, might almost be termed providential, for the ancient Hebrew writers, who first used the term 'heart' metaphorically, certainly had no conception of the physiological importance of the heart. There is in fact a great advantage in having this single term to denote the central point of these two modes of existence, for it serves to emphasise the 'wholeness' of the human person, constituted out of body and soul: the 'heart' of the inner man is also the heart of the outer man; neither heart can function properly without the other. Just as modern medical practice is apt to overlook the fact that many illnesses are psychosomatic, so too writers on the spiritual life (and especially those in the Platonic tradition) are apt to forget the other side of the coin, that we have a body as well as a soul; and after all it was the 'body' and not the soul which St Paul (I Cor. 6:19) described as the 'temple of the Holy Spirit within you'. It is not a case of body versus soul, but of body *and* soul: the 'heart' is doubly the centre of the psychosomatic entity that makes up the human person.

How important it is for the *whole* person to be involved in prayer is indicated by the eighth-century East Syrian writer Symeon:

> Prayer in which the body does not toil by means of the heart, and the heart by means of the mind, together with the intellect and the intelligence, all gathered together in deep-felt groaning, but where instead prayer is just allowed to float across the heart, such prayer, you should realise, is just a miscarriage, for while you are praying, your mind is drawing you away to some other business that you are going to see to after praying. In such a case you have not yet managed to pray in a unified manner.[5]

4. St Bernard, *On the Song of Songs* 49 (*PL* 183:1018).
5. Ed. A. Mingana, *Early Christian Mystics* (Woodbrooke Studies 7 [1934], p.58 (tr.), p.313 (text). Translation mine.

The interior heart

Headlines about heart-transplants and other wonders of modern medicine should not lead us to forget about the existence of this other 'interior' heart, and to suppose that it is only the physical heart that is of importance and relevance in twentieth-century society, for this 'interior heart' has by no means disappeared from *homo sapiens* in the course of human evolution over the last two thousand years; it is still capable of having miracles, even more wonderful than heart-transplants, performed upon it, since it is not a human surgeon who is operating, but the Holy Spirit himself. At the other end of the scale, however, there is always the ever-present danger that this 'interior heart' could atrophy through neglect.

The importance of this other heart lies in the fact that it is the innermost point of our being – unlocatable in space – where contact with God is possible. In the Psalter (Ps. 27:8) it is the heart which speaks to God, and since prayer, according to one definition, is 'conversation and encounter with God',[6] then 'prayer of the heart' is basically nothing other than deep communication between the centre of our being and God.

That the heart is the place where prayer takes place is strikingly brought out by the fourth-century Syriac writer Aphrahat, 'the Persian Sage', as he is sometimes called. Aphrahat, who lived in what is today Iraq, has the distinction of having been the earliest Christian writer to have written a work on prayer in general (as opposed to the Lord's Prayer). In the course of this short treatise he offers an intriguing interpretation of Christ's words, 'Enter the chamber and pray to your Father in secret' (Matt. 6:6). Aphrahat comments:

> Why, my beloved, did our Saviour teach us saying, 'Pray to your Father in secret, with the door shut? I will show you, as far as I am capable. He said 'Pray to your Father with the door closed'. Our Lord's words thus tell us 'pray in secret in your *heart*, and shut the door'. What is the door he says we must shut, if not your mouth? For here is the temple in which Christ dwells, just as the Apostle said, 'You are the temple of the Lord' – for him to enter into your inner self, into this house, to cleanse it from everything that is unclean, while the door, that is to say, your mouth, is closed. If this were not the correct explanation, how would you understand the passage? Suppose you happened to be in the desert where there was no house and no door, would you be unable to pray in secret? Or if you happened to be on the top of a mountain, would you not be able to pray?[7]

Thus the chamber to which Christ refers is no longer located somewhere in ordinary space, for it has been interiorised and transferred to sacred space.[8]

---

6. Thus in an anonymous work on prayer in British Library Add.14535 f.22a. The definition is based on Evagrius, *On Prayer* 3, 'Prayer is the converse of the mind with God'.

7. *Demonstration* 4.10 (*Patrologia Syriaca* i.157-60). An English translation of Aphrahat's work on Prayer is forthcoming in the *Annual of the Leeds University Oriental Society*, in a number devoted to Syriac studies.

8. Such an interpretation of the 'chamber' is of course by no means confined to Aphrahat: it already occurs in Origen's treatise On Prayer, and was subsequently adopted by (among others) St Ephrem in the East and St Ambrose in the West.

The functional importance of this interior heart is well brought out by St Isaac of Nineveh. He is answering the question, 'What is the difference between purity of mind and purity of heart?':

> Purity of mind is something other than purity of heart, just as there is a difference between a single limb of the body and the body as a whole. Now the mind is just one of the senses of the soul, whereas the heart controls all the inward senses: it is the senses' own sense, being their very root. Now if the root is holy, then so will all the branches be holy. But this is not the case if it is just one of the branches which is sanctified. The mind just needs a little familiarity with the Scriptures, and a little labour in the matter of fasting and stillness, for it to forget its former occupation and become cleansed, as long as it holds itself back from outside distractions. But it is equally easily defiled again.
>
> The heart, on the other hand, is only purified through great afflictions, and by being deprived of all mixing with 'the world'; it also requires complete and utter mortification. But then, once it has been purified, its purity is not defiled by the touch of insignificant matters, nor is it afraid of severe struggles, for it has acquired a strong stomach that can easily digest all kinds of foods that weak minds find hard to cope with.[9]
>
> For as the doctors say, 'A diet of meat that is difficult to digest makes a sound body all the stronger, since it is digested by an iron stomach'.[10]

This 'purity of heart', then, can only be attained through 'great afflictions'. 'Afflictions' is a term frequently encountered in St Isaac's writings, and by it he seems to understand, not just the ascetic practices of the monastic life, but also all the tiresome externals of everyday life, and learning how to deal with them: in modern terms, all the things one would be only too glad to be rid of – household chores, endless interruptions, missed trains, flat tyres and so on, all the things we continually need to overcome by dint of trying to transfigure them through acceptance, and not allow them to reduce us to frustration, anger and resentment.

With St Isaac's reply in mind, the words of the Sermon on the Mount, 'Blessed are the pure in heart', take on a much deeper meaning and intensity. A 'pure heart' is what the psalmist prayed for; 'purity of heart' is a frequently expressed ideal in Syriac writers, for only it is capable of achieving 'pure prayer'.[11]

There is actually another term, more or less synonymous with 'purity of heart', which is even more characteristic of Syriac writers: *shafyut lebba*, lucidity, limpidity, clarity, sincerity, purity, of heart – the term has several different connotations impossible to capture by a single English word. Like so many things in Syriac Christianity, the terminology goes back to Judaism, not indeed to the Hebrew or Greek Bible, but to the Aramaic interpretative translation known as the Targum. In the narrative of the sacrifice of Isaac (Gen. 22), for example (a chapter of key

9. In biblical and patristic language the interior heart not only has a stomach, as in this passage, but also a face, eyes, and even – in the prayer of repentance of king Manasseh which forms part of the Greek Bible – knees as well.

10. Ed. Bedjan, p.29 (= tr. Wensinck, p.20).

11. 'Pure prayer' is a phrase which is already found in the Syriac Bible (1 Chron. 16:42), though it is absent from the Hebrew, the Greek and other versions.

importance for Judaism), where the Hebrew speaks of Abraham and Isaac going up the mountain 'together', the Palestinian Targum draws out the spiritual perfection of the two patriarchs and renders the word 'together' as 'with a lucid heart'.[12] In the Syriac Gospels (Luke 8:15), it is those with this 'lucidity of heart' who not only hear the word which the sower sows, but also allow it to germinate and bear fruit. The use of the term here is interesting for another reason too, for the parable of the sower is also the source for a rather striking phrase connected with the interior heart which proved very popular with certain writers: 'the earth of the heart' (combining Matt. 13:19 and 23), where the word germinates. As we shall see later on, the 'word' has a *double entente*, for it is both the 'word of the Gospel' and God the Word.

In later Syriac writers 'lucidity of heart' is constantly stressed as the prerequisite for pure prayer: 'One thing really pleases God', says the eighth-century writer John the Elder, 'that the heart should be utterly lucid'.[13] As will become apparent in due course, lucidity of heart is pleasing to God above all because it provides the means for his self-revelation to humanity.

The heart as altar

Aphrahat, like several other early Christian writers, speaks of prayer as an offering or sacrifice, a concept intimated in Psalm 140:2, and made explicit already in the Syriac Bible (Ben Sira 32 (35):8a). Aphrahat knows from biblical passages such as Elijah's sacrifice on Mount Carmel in 1 Kings 18:38, or David's in I Chronicles 21:26, that sacrifices acceptable to God were consumed by fire which descended from heaven, an idea which Aphrahat (along with Jewish tradition) extended to a number of other Old Testament sacrifices, such as that of Abel. Aphrahat uses a whole series of biblical examples of sacrifices to illustrate the need for purity of heart if prayer, which has now replaced sacrifice, is to be acceptable to God, insofar as God looks at the interior disposition of the offerer before responding with fire.[14] Although Aphrahat himself does not go on to connect this fire from heaven directly with the prayer of the heart, this important development is to be found in some later Syriac writers, most notably perhaps in a seventh-century writer, Sahdona or Martyrios (the Greek form of his name). Sahdona develops this idea of prayer as a sacrifice and he emphasises the vital need for it to follow the biblical ordinances concerning sacrifices: that is to say, it should be spotless and without blemish, otherwise it will suffer the same fate as Cain's sacrifice, and be rejected. He continues:

> So, provided the beginning of our prayer is watchful and eager, and with true feeling of the heart we soak our cheeks in tears, and our whole time of prayer

12. There is some reflection of this in homilies on Gen. 22 by the Syriac poets Narsai and Jacob of Serugh. For the term 'limpidity' see G. Bunge, 'Le lieu de limpidité', *Irénikon* 55 (1982), pp.7-18.
13. Letter 51.14 (in *Patrologia Orientalis* 39 [1978]).
14. Aphrahat, *Dem.* 4.2-3.

is performed in accordance with God's will, then our prayer will be accepted in his presence, and the Lord will be pleased with us and find enjoyment in our offering, catching the sweet savour that wafts from the purity of our heart. And he will send the fire of his Spirit, which consumes our sacrifices and raises up our mind together with them in the flames heavenwards, where we shall behold the Lord – to our delight, and not to our destruction, as the stillness of his relevation falls upon us and the hidden things of knowledge of him are portrayed within us, while spiritual joy is granted in our heart, along with hidden mysteries which I am unable to disclose in words to the simple. In this way we establish our body as a living, holy and acceptable sacrifice which, in this rational service, is pleasing to God.[15]

What we have here is a dramatic internalisation of the Eucharistic liturgy. Instead of the bread and wine offered up by the Church, the Bride of Christ, here it is prayer that is the offering, made this time by the individual soul, which also is the Bride of Christ. This offering is made on the altar, not of the Church, but of the heart, and since there is no human priest to utter the epiclesis, God himself sends the 'fire of his Spirit' (phraseology reminiscent of St Ephrem's eucharistic hymns),[16] and raises the mind up to heaven as the fire receives and consumes the offering.

This parallelism between the transfiguring effect of 'pure prayer', and the transformation of the bread and wine into the Body of Blood of Christ at the Eucharist, is a very important one. Syriac writers in the East Syrian mystical tradition of the seventh and eighth centuries in fact use the same technical term for the activity of the Holy Spirit upon the heart when pure prayer takes place as that employed in the eucharistic liturgy at the epiclesis. The word means something like 'overshadowing' (and corresponds to the Greek *epiphoitesis*). Significantly enough it is derived from the verb *aggen* which the Syriac New Testament uses in the Annunciation narrative at Luke 1:35, 'The Holy Spirit shall come upon you, and the power of the Most High shall *overshadow* you'.[17]

The heart, the Eucharist, and now Mary: this new association with the Annunciation introduces yet a further dimension to the theology of the prayer of the heart. In a whole number of different ways Syriac writers bring out the complementarity between the roles of Mary and the Eucharist in the course of salvation history.[18] Mary is the essential meeting point between God and man in the process of the Incarnation, the descent of God to man, just as the Eucharist is the meeting point between man and God in the process of sanctification or (as Eastern tradition, Syriac as much as Greek, expresses it) the divinisation of man, the ascent of man to God. At the same time the sacraments (especially Baptism) continuously 'give birth'

15. Sahdona, *Book of Perfection* ii.8.20 (ed. A. de Halleux, *Corpus Scriptorum Christianorum Orientalium* 252-3).

16. Especially *Hymns on Faith* 10, translated by R. Murray in *Eastern Churches Review* 3 (1970), pp.142-50.

17. On the use of this term in Syriac (and its Jewish Aramaic background) see my 'Passover, Annunciation and Epiclesis', *Novum Testamentum* 24 (1982), pp.222-33.

18. The following is borrowed from my 'Mary and the Eucharist: an oriental perspective', *Sobornost/ECR* 1:2 (1979), p.58.

to Christians, just as Mary gave birth to Christ. In the sacraments the Holy Spirit's activity is assured; what is required is the assent, the co-operation, of the individual, corresponding to Mary's assent at the Annunciation. If that co-operation is given, then the individual Christian too will 'conceive'[19] and Christ will shine forth from his or her heart, just as Mary conceived and Christ 'shone forth'.

Theophanic prayer and the mirror of the heart[20]

Prayer, pure prayer, the product of purity of heart, thus has a theophanic effect: 'prayer reveals the depths of God's presence', writes an anonymous Syriac author;[21] the climax of pure prayer is the revelation of Christ both *to* the heart and *in* the heart. It is important to note the need for the presence of 'true love'in this context: an eighth-century mystic, Abdisho the Seer, states:

> True love [. . .] does not leave anything in your mind apart from the aware-
> ness of God which constitutes the spiritual key with which the inner door of
> the heart is opened – and inside is hidden Christ our Lord.[22]

This theophanic aspect of prayer of the heart is brought out in another way, by means of the imagery of the mirror, always a popular one among Syriac writers.[23] It should be pointed out that mirrors in antiquity were not made of glass but of bronze, and so needed continual polishing if they were to serve their purpose effectively; 'polish this interior mirror of yours' is the repeated exhortation of Syriac writers from St Ephrem onwards. This idea of the mirror is often juxtaposed with the biblical teaching that man is created in the image of God. Since sin has marred this image, it will no longer reflect God properly if held up to the mirror of the heart; but once this image is cleansed (and the potential for this is provided by the Holy Spirit at Baptism), then it will reflect the true likeness of the Creator. Three passages from a very fine writer, John the Elder (or 'the spiritual Sheikh', as he is known as in Arabic), whose letters have recently been published,[24] will illustrate som' ways in which this imagery is employed. The first is in a letter addressed to 'him who is baptised in an utterly mysterious baptism, immersed in God who is hidden in a totally interior way'. In it John draws our attention once again to the profound meaning of the term 'pure in heart':

> God reveals himself to a few, because of their diligence: these people fix
> their eyes within themselves, making themselves into a mirror in which the

19. For St Symeon the New Theologian's striking use of this idea see 'Mary and the Eucharist', pp.58-9; earlier it is found in the Macarian Homilies (ed. Berthold), *Logos* 18.6.12; 27.1.7. In medieval Western tradition it occurs above all in the writings of Meister Eckhart, while in modern times it has been taken up notably by Catherine de Hueck Doherty.
20. I borrow the term 'theophanic prayer' from H. Corbin's *Creative Imagination in the Sufism of Ibn Arabi* (London 1969), p.246.
21. British Library Add.14535 f.23a.
22. Ed. Mingana, *Early Christian Mystics*, p.166 (tr.), p.275 (text).
23. For its use in patristric Greek spirituality see A. Louth, *The Origins of the Christian Mystical Tradition* (Oxford 1981), pp.79-80, 91-3.
24. By R. Beulay in *Patrologia Orientalis* 39 (1978), with French translation.

Invisible makes himself visible; they are drawn to this by God by means of the ineffable radiance which is extended to them and in them from his wondrous beauty, bearing witness to those words of God, 'Blessed are those who are pure in their heart, for they shall see God'.[25]

In another letter he writes:

Cleanse your mirror, and then without any doubt the triune Light will be manifested to you in it; place the mirror in your heart, and you will realise that your God is indeed alive.[26]

The third passage reads:

You are the image of God, O man. Do you wish the image to take on the Likeness of its Model? Then silence all activity of any kind and carry the yoke of your Lord in your heart and wonder at his majesty in your mind continuously, until the image becomes resplendent with his glory, and it is transformed into the Likeness, and you shall become in God a god who has acquired the likeness of his Maker by means of the union which makes like to himself.[27]

Prayer, then, is a process by which God is revealed, reveals himself, to us; he is to be seen in the 'image' which, when cleansed and bright, acts as the mirror by which he is reflected. The aim of the Incarnation is the cleansing of this image in mankind so that God may then be revealed in each individual person; as Christians we thus have the awesome responsibility of being the vehicles of God's self-revelation in the world, a revelation that can only be achieved through this 'purity of heart'.

If a rapid descent from the sublime to the ridiculous may be excused, I would like to point to an apt modern illustration, taken from the kitchen, of what the Fathers understood by this process of cleansing the divine image in which we are created. This image, corrupted by sin, is like an exceedingly greasy saucepan which, with cold water, simply cannot be properly cleansed, however much you try; the provision of hot water and detergent corresponds to the provision of the grace of the Holy Spirit at Baptism: we are now in a position to clean the grease away, and the potential of a shining and bright clean saucepan is there. But it will not just get clean of its own accord: to finish off the job we need to do some scrubbing ourselves. Co-operation between ourselves and the outside agency — whether it be the detergent and hot water in the kitchen, or the Holy Spirit in our lives as a whole — is essential if progress is to be made.

Purity of heart as a state of prayer

Lucidity or purity of heart is not just the pre-requisite for 'pure prayer' of this theophanic nature: purity of heart can itself *constitute* prayer. Let us go back to Aphrahat in the fourth century. Abel's sacrifice was accepted, he says, because of

25. *Letter* 14.1-2.
26. *Letter* 28.2.
27. *Letter* 29.1.

his purity of heart, and this purity of heart, rather than the ensuing sacrifice, is what counts as prayer. In fact there are occasions, Aphrahat points out, when purity of heart definitely leads to action and not to conscious prayer:

> Be careful, my beloved, that you do not let slip some opportunity of 'giving rest'[28] to the will of God by saying 'the time for prayer is at hand: I will pray and then act' − and while you are in the process of completing your prayer, that opportunity for 'giving rest' will disappear; you will thus be incapacitated from doing the will and 'rest' of God, and it will be through your prayer that you will be guilty of sin. Rather, you should effect 'the rest' of God, and that will constitute prayer [. . .]. Suppose you happen to go on a long journey, and, parched with thirst in the heat, you chance upon one of the brethren; you say to him, 'refresh me in my exhaustion', and he replies 'I will pray and then come to your aid'. And while he is praying you die of thirst. Which seems to you the better: that he should go and pray, or alleviate your exhaustion? Or again, suppose you go on a journey in winter and you meet rain and snow and become exhausted from the cold; if once again you run into a friend of yours at the time of prayer and he answers you in the same way, and you die of cold, what profit will his prayer have, seeing that he has not alleviated someone in trouble?[29]

Aphrahat thus makes it clear that purity of heart is no monopoly of the contemplative life: it is just as essential in the active life. In a short but profound work on prayer, the fifth-century writer John the Solitary states that prayer should specifically result in action:

> When you recite the words of the prayer that I have written for you, be careful not just to repeat them, but let your very self *become* these words, manifesting themselves in you as deeds. For there is no advantage in the reciting unless the word actually becomes incarnate in you and becomes action, with the result that you are seen in the world to be a man of God.[30]

We should notice that John's choice of wording once again draws attention to the links between the prayer of the heart and the Incarnation.

This passage from John the Solitary brings me to the last point I should like to make. John here speaks of 'repeating' the prayer, and earlier in the work he emphasises the need for the soul to be 'continuously filled with the remembrance of God'. Now in modern usage the term 'prayer of the heart' is often understood as being synonymous with the Jesus Prayer, the repetition of the Name coupled with a short phrase. In this sense of the term Syriac spirituality seems to have had nothing quite comparable, although short repeated invocations (such as, I imagine, John the Solitary has in mind here) are not uncommon, especially in the East Syrian mystics of the seventh and eighth centuries. But even these do not necessarily contain the name of Jesus. John the Elder, for example, advises the use of the repeated words 'Abba, Abba' in times of fervour; for periods of dryness and emptiness the secret

28. Aphrahat is alluding to Isaiah 23:12: 'This is rest: give rest to the weary'.
29. *Demonstration* 4.15.
30. Published in *Journal of Theological Studies* ns. 30 (1979), pp.84-101 (quotation on pp.99-100).

repetition of the words 'My God, grant me wisdom and strengthen me' are recommended.[31]

What, rather, would seem for them to constitute the characteristic feature of the prayer of the heart is the 'remembrance' or 'recollection' of God, the constant awareness of his presence, 'the practice of the presence of God', as Brother Lawrence calls it. Seen in this light, the 'prayer of the heart' once again turns out to be more a state or disposition, rather than any particular identifiable activity. It is, above all, a loving state of total awareness of God. This is the state where we allow God's presence in our heart to make itself felt, where we allow God to act within us, from the very centre of our innermost being. This divine activity within the human person will invariably have a transfiguring effect, though the nature and intensity of this 'transfiguration' will vary enormously. In very rare cases, such as with St Seraphim of Sarov, it will be very dramatic in its external manifestation. Much more frequently it will act much more imperceptibly, gradually transfiguring the whole course of a person's life: this is what St Isaac no doubt has in mind in the passage quoted earlier, where he speaks of the heart as the root from which the branches of our external life receive nourishment. No doubt we have all had the (very humbling) experience of meeting or coming across someone transfigured in this way; an obvious example of such a person in the world today would be Mother Teresa.

Moreover, where the prayer of the heart takes place, it is not only the individual who is transfigured, for in the eyes of his or her interior heart the whole of creation too is seen in a transfigured fashion.[32] As Philoxenus, in the early sixth century, put it, 'when faith has come, even mean things appear glorious'.[33] Or, closer to home, one need only think of George Herbert's wonderful hymn 'Teach me, my God and King'.

Prayer of the heart, the disposition of constant loving awareness of God, stemming from purity of heart, is quite definitely not just an ideal for those living a contemplative life. It is equally an ideal for each individual Christian, whatever his or her situation may be, seeing that this is one of the means by which God chooses to reveal himself in the world. Mother Teresa's words on her visit to Corrymeela are singularly apposite in this context: 'holiness is not just for the few, it is the duty of you and me'.

A hint of the awe and wonder that surrounds purity of heart is given in a passage from Sahdona's Book of Perfection. It provides us with an appropriate conclusion:

> Blessed are you, O heart that is lucid, the abode of the Divinity; blessed are you, heart that is pure, which beholds the hidden Essence. Happy are you, O flesh and blood, the dwelling place of the Consuming Fire: happy are you, mortal body made out of dust, wherein resides the Fire that sets the worlds

31. *Letter* 36.6-7.
32. St Isaac of Nineveh has a famous passage on this subject (see 'St Isaac and Syriac spirituality', p.71).
33. E.A.W. Budge, *The Discourses of Philoxenus* (London 1894) ii.p 50 (Discourse 3).

alight. It is truly a matter for wonder and astonishment that he, before whom the heavens are not pure, who puts awe into his angels, should take delight and pleasure in a heart of flesh that is filled with love for him, that is open wide to him, that is purified so as to act as his holy dwelling place, joyfully serving and ministering to him in whose presence thousand upon thousand, ten thousand upon ten thousand fiery angels stand in awe, ministering to his glory. Happy is the man of love who has caused God – who is love – to dwell in his heart. Happy are you, O heart, so small and confined, yet you have caused him, whom heaven and earth cannot contain, to dwell spiritually in your womb, as in a restful abode. Happy that luminous eye of the heart which, in its purity, clearly beholds him, before the sight of whom the seraphs veil their faces [. . .]. Blessed indeed are the pure in heart.[34]

34. *Book of Perfection* ii.4.9, 8.

The Spirituality of Chrysostom's Commentary on the Psalms

ROBERT C. HILL

Chrysostom does not figure in traditional lists of spiritual guides from antiquity, nor his *Commentary on the Psalms* among spiritual classics. This may be due to ignorance of it by modern commentators, though aspects of its spiritual teaching could contribute to this omission: the preacher's accent—if preached the commentaries were—on a balance of human effort and divine grace in the process of salvation was thought pelagian by some in the West in the patristic age. No mystic, Chrysostom can be pedestrian in his approach to prayer, and the claim some have made for him as initiator of a lay spirituality is open to question. But there is no doubting the Scriptural fare he provided to his (male) congregations in his classroom.

Of the great texts called into service by Christian commentators from the beginning for spiritual direction or simply moral guidance, a principal one—yielding pride of place only to the Gospels—has been the Psalter. Over thirty of the Fathers are known to have composed commentaries on this book of the Bible,[1] though we are not fortunate enough to have all these still at our disposal or in direct manuscript tradition. One of the better represented is that by John Chrysostom, preacher in Antioch in the late fourth century, from which period of his ministry of the Word the *Commentary* seems to come, and then bishop of Constantinople. Not the whole of the Psalter is included in the text we have;[2] even in the ninth century Photius, bishop of that same see, admitted its incompleteness, leaving the question open as to whether Chrysostom ever

---

1. Marie-Josèphe Rondeau includes eighteen Greek commentaries and sixteen Latin in her survey, *Les commentaires patristiques du Psautier (III–V siècles)*, 2 vols, Orientalia Christiana Analecta, vols. 219, 220 (Rome: Pont. Inst. Stud. Or., 1982, 1985).
2. The Migne reprint in *PG* 55 of the eighteenth-century De Montfaucon edition derives from the seventeenth-century editions of Savile and Fronton de Duc; we await a modern critical edition of the Commentary. Cf. M. Geerard, *Clavis Patrum Graecorum* (CCG) II, #4413.

Journal of Early Christian Studies 5:4, 569–579 © 1997 The Johns Hopkins University Press

commented on every psalm.[3] Beyond the fifty eight in the extant collection of ἑρμηνεῖαι beginning at Ps 4, we have also commentaries on Ps 3 and verses of other psalms that are authentic but not of this collection (if the term "series" begs the question).

Not only does the condition of the *Commentary* leave us with a relatively hefty corpus of patristic material on this important text for spiritual formation. It also has the advantage of coming to us in direct and (compared with Chrysostom's New Testament works) uncomplicated manuscript tradition,[4] and of not being clearly and directly dependent on the work of earlier commentators—a dependence that marks some of the better known Psalms commentaries from antiquity, as Rondeau capably demonstrates. Chrysostom occasionally betrays awareness of other views on a verse; but it is less a tribute to his integrity than an acknowledgment of his ignorance of or disdain for the work of "the scholars" (as he rather pejoratively terms them on occasion) that we do not have to debate the provenance of his teaching on the psalms.

NEGLECT OF CHRYSOSTOM'S COMMENTARY

Yet this lengthy work and its composer have not found widespread recognition in histories of Christian spirituality. This is probably not due to a quibble about the circumstances of its composition/delivery, of which Photius even a millennium ago in Constantinople acknowledged ignorance and which modern scholars have not been able to clarify with certainty;[5] nor would the lack of a critical edition of the text be to blame. Perhaps it has more to do with the extent of the work and its lack of availability in modern languages that accounts for its failure to provide documentation for commentators on Chrysostom's significance in that history of notable guides of the Christian faithful since the New Testament. The treatment

---

3. In the *Bibliotheca* 172–75 Photius admits "we are not yet in a position to know anything about the background of the commentaries on the Psalms [by contrast with the Pauline ones] except to marvel at the force and the other virtues of language" (*PG* 103.504). De Montfaucon quotes a statement of Photius in an unpublished catena to the effect that commentaries on many psalms were missing from the collection at that time (PG 55.19). Jerome, in a letter to Augustine written perhaps at the end of the year 404, does not mention Chrysostom's commentary by name amongst the seemingly exhaustive list of six Greek ones he compiles, though it is possible he includes it implicitly amongst "in paucos Psalmos opuscula" (*Ep* 112.20: PL 22.929).

4. Whereas the Savile edition of the Psalms commentary rests on a handful of manuscripts, R. E. Carter points out that for Chrysostom's New Testament works the *Codices Chrysostomici Graeci* 1–4 considered 824 out of the probably three to four thousand stemming from the Byzantine period ("The Future of Chrysostom Studies: Theology and *Nachleben*," ΣΥΜΠΟΣΙΟΝ: *Studies on St John Chrysostom*, ΑΝΑΛΕΚΤΑ ΒΛΑΤΑΔΩΝ, vol. 18 (Thessaloniki: Patriarchal Institute for Patristic Studies, 1973), 133–35.

5. Cf. my "Chrysostom's Commentary on the Psalms: Homilies or Tracts?" L. Cross (ed.), *Prayer and Spirituality in the Early Church* (Melbourne, 1997).

of "Patristic spirituality" in *The New Dictionary of Christian Spirituality* does not accord a place to the golden-mouthed preacher in a section on "the Golden Age,"[6] nor does he rate a mention in Andrew Louth's classic text, where Origen and Augustine are thought worthy of chapter-length treatment.[7] Charles Kannengiesser is more concessive in acknowledging his contribution to "the spiritual message of the great Fathers," though the Psalms commentary is not cited,[8] as is true of the lengthy article on "Jean Chrysostome" by Antoine Wenger in the *Dictionnaire de spiritualité*.[9] At least Wenger, and more so Louis Bouyer[10] and Gustave Bardy,[11] see this author (if not this work) as significant, and even critical, in the development of Christian spiritual teaching. We need to examine whether the neglect of his *Commentary on the Psalms* in the study of this development is justified, or regrettable and due for amendment.

The reader of this Antiochene's response to the great texts of Christian tradition that have consistently nourished our spirituality, like the Gospels of Matthew and John, the Pauline letters, the Psalms and even Genesis, would soon learn not to look to him as guide through the Cloud of Unknowing, the Dark Night of the Soul or on the Ascent of Mount Carmel. "Mystical" is not the word that springs to mind on our reading Chrysostom's commentary on these spiritual classics of the Bible; "pedestrian" would not be out of place, even "mechanical," generally speaking. Admittedly, on Ps 4 at the beginning of the extant collection, he does lecture on "the art of prayer," and would like to see this as something angelic, infused, impatient even of method:

> The human being who has been taught to converse with God as befits the one conversing with God will from then on be an angel. . . .
> There is no need to take ourselves to a library, nor outlay money, nor hire teachers or orators or debaters, nor devote a great deal of time to learning this oratorical skill. It is instead sufficient to want to do it, and the skills fall into place.[12]

But method is what he upholds even on the art of prayer, and he is equipped to convey it, he assures his listeners. On the opening verse of Ps 4, "God hearkened to my righteousness" (which here he is quoting in commentary on Ps 7.3), he glibly lists qualities of prayer in terms of their efficacy in bringing God to hearken:

6. D. G. Hunter, "Patristic Spirituality," M. Downey (ed.), *The New Dictionary of Christian Spirituality* (Collegeville: Glazier, 1993), 723–32.

7. *The Origins of the Christian Mystical Tradition: From Plato to Denys* (Oxford: Clarendon, 1981).

8. In B. McGinn, J. Meyendorff (edd.), *Christian Spirituality: Origins to the Twelfth Century* (New York: Crossroad, 1986), 61–88.

9. *Dictionnaire de spiritualité* 8:331–55.

10. *The Spirituality of the New Testament and the Fathers* (1960), Eng. trans. (London: Burns & Oates, 1963).

11. "Jean Chrysostome," *DTC* (1924) 18:660–90.

12. PG 55.41–42, 43. It seems preferable to cite the psalms in the numbering of the Hebrew and of modern versions rather than of Chrysostom's Greek text (a form of the Septuagint).

Being heard happens in this fashion: first, of course, worthiness to receive something; then, praying in accordance with God's laws; third, persistence; fourth, asking nothing earthly; fifth, seeking things to our real benefit; sixth, contributing everything of our own.[13]

The items in the list and their order would set alarm bells ringing in some spiritual and theological quarters today, doubtless: the preacher reels off the qualities of prayer to God like a physician writing a prescription, with the supplicant's own worthiness at the top. And in fact this is his favorite model of spiritual direction, a physician curing ailments—not an original metaphor of his, of course, yet reflecting his businesslike approach to the task in hand. Immediately after the above prescription he remarks, "Prayer, you see, is medicine; but if we do not know how to apply the medicine, neither will we gain benefit from it." So learn the rules, follow the prescription.

A RETREAT FROM MYSTICISM?

It is right that theologians generally and not simply today's spiritual directors have some unease about Chrysostom's approach to the spiritual life; as we shall see, this has been true from the time of Augustine, who had to defend his propriety on these scores. What we are seeing in this Antiochene's spiritual or even simply moral direction in the Psalms commentary is symptomatic (if we are to believe Bouyer) of a protest by that school of theology and spirituality against the tendency of the school of Origen "to find Christian dogma under its most metaphysical aspects, or Christian spirituality under its most mystical aspects." In Bouyer's view, "it was the whole orientation of spirituality that was involved," visible in a reaction in monasticism "from mysticism towards a rather moralistic asceticism," with the result in Chrysostom's case, as in his work on virginity, of an "asceticism without mysticism."[14]

We might debate the health of this reaction against "a deceptive 'asceticism,'" as does Bouyer, or attempt to trace it in Chrysostom's case to early ascetic excess. But in the Psalms commentary it is clear he is content not to ascend Mount Carmel,[15] and even in discoursing on the art of prayer to confine his congregation's spiritual aspirations to living the good life in an evil world. This art is acquired by following another itemized prescription:

being of sober mind and contrite spirit, approaching God in a flood of tears, seeking nothing of this life, longing for things to come, making petition for spiritual goods, not calling down curses on our enemies, bearing no grudges, banishing all disquiet from the soul, making our approach with heart broken, being humble, practicing

---

13. PG 55.85.
14. *Spirituality of the New Testament and the Fathers*, 436–44.
15. While Wenger concurs with this view of Chrysostom's lack of mysticism, that he is "habituellement très sobre sur ce sujet," he reminds us of a different spirit infusing the homilies *On the Incomprehensible Nature of God* ("Jean Chrysostome," 337–39). (We noted Wenger's ignorance of the Psalms commentaries.)

great meekness, directing our tongues to good report, abstaining from any wicked enterprise, having nothing in common with the common enemy of the world—I mean the devil, of course.[16]

The world in which his congregation lived and worked out their salvation with fear and trembling was a hazardous one, he told them, peopled with the devil and the demons. It was a world not completely good; Chrysostom would find congenial the sentiments of Wordsworth,

> The world is too much with us.
> Late and soon, getting and spending,
> We lay waste our powers.
> Little we see in nature that is ours.[17]

There is none of the cosmic optimism that one associates with other eastern theologians; in place of optimism there is a dualism, contrasting present life and present realities with future ones. One wonders how much of a service he did his listeners in bidding them despise this world; prayer, he says (still on Ps 4), should encourage this attitude:

> In this way the soul is released from the shackles of the body; in this way the mind is raised on high; in this way our abode is transferred to heaven; in this way one scorns things of this life.[18]

While the preacher himself is a shrewd observer of legal and commercial life, and can speak fluently to his congregation of "interest, contracts, bonds, goods for sale, wills, prices of properties, profits, shops" in opening commentary on Ps 9, the quandary he leaves them in (as does many an unthinking preacher) would have been aggravated by his recommending them later in that psalm to achieve "freedom from all worldly concerns."[19]

Yet we gather from the text that the congregation(s) that assembled for his evening commentaries (seemingly not within a eucharistic context, in a church,

---

16. PG 55.43. Less mechanical is his treatment of the art of prayer at the opening of his commentary on Ps 130 (PG 55.373).

17. W. Wordsworth, Sonnet 18, *Selected Poems* (London: Collins, 1980), 435. We have therefore to qualify Bouyer's claim for Chrysostom as "the precursor if not the initiator of a spirituality for the laity," and this after being "a rather dried-up ascetic, inclined towards a disquieting fanaticism." It was involvement in the exercise of ministry that effected this conversion and made him "full not only of understanding but of sympathy," in Bouyer's view (*Spirituality of the New Testament and the Fathers*, 446). Likewise, Anne-Marie Malingrey seems not to be taking account of the evidence of the Psalms commentary, at any rate, in maintaining: "The majority of Christians are called to live in the world. For them John traces the way" ("John Chrysostom," A. Di Berardino [ed.], *Encyclopedia of the Early Church*, Eng. trans. [Edinburgh: James Clark & Co, 1992], 441).

18. PG 55.42.

19. PG 55.122, 129. Likewise, on Ps 112.8, in a context where he urges his listeners to lift their minds from worldly cares, which "divide the attention and undermine our resolve," he speaks of the spiritual life in terms of capital investment and earning of interest (PG 55.297–98).

but in a teaching setting, a διδασκαλεῖον) comprised men (only), unlettered even in biblical matters, more rather than less affluent (though there were poor people present as well), with perhaps other clergy in attendance on (a rare) occasion. They did not receive any strong endorsement of their lay condition in terms of spiritual status or potential, as priesthood occasionally did; married life came a poor second to the virginity that was presumably not an option for such an audience. On Ps 45.14, "Virgins will be conducted to the king," the preacher began by quoting Paul, "The women who marry will have distress in the flesh" (I Cor 7.28), and then waxed eloquent on the unflattering comparison:

> The married woman, you see, has to worry about children, husband, house, servants, relatives, in-laws, grandchildren, fertility and infertility (time does not allow, in fact, for a description of the troubles of married life), whereas the virgin on her cross is freed from present trouble, lifted above daily cares and the topsy turvy of life; her eyes fixed on heaven, she enjoys the grace of the Spirit and revels in happiness.[20]

If that was not discouragement enough for his lay congregation, Chrysostom on Ps 44.25 concluded a moralistic insert on marriage with the grudging concession, "The reason marriage was allowed, after all, was in case you should exceed proper limits." In both cases he was claiming the support of Paul (even if employing a familiar rhetorical commonplace); and of apostle and preacher both it could be said that it was not their most adequate theology of married life.

VICES AND VIRTUES

Chrysostom finds the psalms fertile soil for discoursing on vices and virtues, and though his listing of them is probably traditional, we look for the marks of personal experience or contemporary social trends. The references in Ps 49 to the futile attempts of the rich to attain everlasting remembrance arouse in the preacher a savage irony about the rich spendthrift who outlays vast sums in such lavish attempts instead of appropriately using resources to meet the needs of the poor. He berates such avarice, waste and neglect, urging his listeners instead to the practice of almsgiving—an acknowledgment that his society had no remedy for structural poverty.

> What could be worse than this folly, to regard tombs as an everlasting home, to take pride in them? Many people, at any rate, have constructed tombs in many cases more splendid than houses. I mean, they go to toil and trouble either for the benefit of enemies or for worms and ashes, outlaying the expense required for this to no purpose. Such, you see, is the attitude of those with no hope in future realities.[21]

---

20. PG 55.202. Of this passage we would have to agree with what Wenger says of Chrysostom's treatise on virginity, that it "traite des inconvénients du marriage d'une manière qui peut scandaliser l'homme d'aujourdhui," even if at variance with his homilies on marriage ("Jean Chrysostome," 346–47).
   (The textual evidence for the setting of the commentaries I have assembled in the introduction to my forthcoming translation and commentary.)
   21. PG 55.231.

From the same sense of desperation to right a social evil he elevates poverty into a virtue: "You well know that wealth is an encouragement to vice in those who do not take heed, whereas poverty is the mother of wisdom,"[22] he says in commenting on Ps 4.7. The virtues of meekness and gentleness receive lengthy encomium in commentary on the phrase in Ps 45.4, "the cause of truth, gentleness and righteousness," resulting in a series of biblical texts and examples illustrating the meekness of David and Moses.[23] The question this gives rise to in the reader is answered to some extent by his obvious personal affinity with the plight of the righteous sufferer—a frequent theme in the Psalms; there is repeated reference by the preacher to the plight of the young men in the fiery furnace from Daniel 3, and to David maltreated by Saul and Absalom, to Noah alone in a vicious generation, to Job, to the Maccabees. We feel prompted to ask: Is he speaking from personal experience of such a lot in life?

The spiritual life is often presented by Chrysostom as a battle, with enemies and foes on all sides, but with God as constantly available ally providing weapons and building ramparts for the willing combatant and worthy petitioner. His metaphor for the process of salvation may change, but the balance is constant: a generous God, a willing and worthy plaintiff. At times he seems not ready to concede the utter gratuity of grace, and was dismissed in later church history by the Reformers for this position;[24] yet a sympathetic reader like Augustine could find other balancing statements—though it should be noted that eastern theology generally is not readily aligned with either. His critics in the West, for instance, would be worried by that listing above from commentary on Ps 7 referring to the opening of Ps 4, "God hearkened to my righteousness" (which a more critical reading would speak of as God's righteousness): the first and last requirements of being heard in prayer Chrysostom gave as "worthiness to receive something" and "contributing everything of our own." We must play our part in salvation, no sitting about waiting for grace to strike; God can be won over. He says also on the words from Ps 6.2, "Have mercy on me, O Lord, for I am weak,"

> We all stand in need of mercy, therefore, but we are not all worthy to receive it. Even if it is mercy, you see, nevertheless he seeks out the worthy recipient.[25]

---

22. PG 55.57.

23. PG 55.191–92. The encomium is repeated with these same exemplars at the opening of Ps 132 (PG 55.379–80).

24. His biographer Dom C. Baur quotes Luther's remark, "Chrysostom is worth nothing in my opinion, he is only a foolish babbler" (*John Chrysostom and His Time* I [1929], Eng. trans. [London-Glasgow: Sands & Co, 1959], 374). Calvin, on the other hand, admired Chrysostom as a preacher, as scholars like David F. Wright and John L. Thompson have reminded me.

25. PG 55.72. On Ps 111.9 he likewise urges his congregation to "give evidence of a way of life that is deserving of grace" (PG 55.289). What seem almost throwaway remarks upholding the balance of divine grace and human effort occur in his commentary on other psalms (PG 55.399, 410, 419, 432).

BALANCING DIVINE AND HUMAN

Some commentators account for this insistence on both divine and human contributions to the process of salvation by recalling his Stoic upbringing.[26] But it also matches his businesslike, mechanical approach to the spiritual life that we have already noted: you can work at it, there are rules to be followed in the divine scheme of things. Furthermore, he would see it consistent with his overall vision of the synthesis of the divine and human[27]—in the person of Jesus, in the inspired Scriptures, where by an act of considerateness, συγκατάβασις, God employs human means for the benefit of limited creatures. He is accustomed to make the parallel between scriptural statement and the historical incarnation, which he refers to as oikonomia, and frequently meditates on the mysteries of the human life of Jesus. He shares the eastern respect for divine transcendence, the word "ineffable" frequently on his lips, accounting for his repeated warnings to his listeners against misunderstanding the anthropomorphisms in the language of the psalms. At the same time, he is unwilling to see human nature devalued. In short, it is the principle of incarnation, in both Scriptural interpretation and spiritual direction.

Chrysostom sees the psalmist himself exemplifying this principle in his own work as inspired composer, προφήτης, producing inspired composition, προφητεία: "As it is the work of a smith to make a tool, a builder to build a house, a shipwright to build a ship, so it is an inspired composer's job to produce inspired composition,"[28] he says in commenting on that opening verse to Ps 45 that so many of the Fathers found a fruitful *locus* for developing their ideas on biblical inspiration.

Not surprisingly in the light of his efforts to retain a balance in the process of salvation, his views have been thought to approximate in some degree to pelagian positions. On Ps 45.13, "All the glory of the king's daughter is within," he remarks, "His reference to her colourful attire was well put: the garment was not of one hue. I mean, it is not possible to be saved from grace alone; instead, there is need also of faith, and after faith virtue, too."[29] He gives the impression

26. So Wenger, "Jean Chrysostome," 337; Bouyer, *Spirituality of the New Testament and the Fathers*, 449.

27. See my "St John Chrysostom and the Incarnation of the Word in Scripture," *Compass Theology Review* 14 (1980): 34–38; "On Looking again at *synkatabasis*," *Prudentia* 13 (1981): 3–11.

28. PG 55.184. See my "Psalm 45: A *locus classicus* for Patristic Thinking on Biblical Inspiration," *Studia Patristica* 25 (1993): 95–100.

29. PG 55.199. Wenger ("Jean Chrysostome," 337) is right to remind us also of the customary doxology concluding many of his homilies (though not so consistent in these commentaries), "thanks to the grace and lovingkindness of our Lord Jesus Christ . . . " "pour laver Chrysostome du reproche de pélagianisme ou de semi-pélagianisme." Maurice Wiles seems unaware of such reproaches in giving Chrysostom a (rare) clean bill of health: "Chrysostom was the one leading Antiochene scholar of that time to remain free of any suspicion of heretical taint" ("Theodore of Mopsuestia

not so much of taking a position on a disputed theological issue as of preserving sequence and balance. What he also insists on in his spiritual theology and morality generally is the need for zeal, enthusiasm, προθυμία; there is no room for quietism.[30] In another of those "binomials" that have been noted in his balanced thinking,[31] the vice of indifference, sloth, neglect, ῥαθυμία, is the capital sin—the sin of the first parents, in fact.[32] On Ps 4.1 he castigates his audience for lack of the kind of attention they show to people of rank: "In approaching God, by contrast, we yawn, scratch ourselves, look this way and that, pay little attention, loll on the ground, do the shopping."[33] We need to be challenged in our spiritual lives, he says, rightly recognizing in the parables of Jesus such a challenge (on Ps 49.4).[34]

It is also in regard to his views on the context of salvation, and not simply the agents, that Chrysostom's theology has been found wanting. Texts of his were thought by Pelagius and his followers like Julian of Eclanum to be grist to their mill in downplaying the Fall and original sin, which Augustine found it necessary to reinterpret in keeping with his own (not invulnerable) view.[35] The evidence of extant Psalm commentaries (that on Ps 51 unfortunately not among them) shows that, despite a plethora of occurrences of terms like "evil," "sin" and "wickedness," the Fall rarely receives mention;[36] Chrysostom, like eastern theology generally, tends to accentuate the healing rather than the affliction. If the historical context of salvation is thus unmarked, on the other hand the Church does not appear to any degree as its vital context. Mention of Mount Sion in Ps 9.11 evokes the briefest gloss from the commentator, "Now, in a spiritual sense

---

as Representative of the Antiochene school," P. R. Ackroyd, C. F. Evans [edd.], *The Cambridge History of the Bible* [Cambridge: CUP, 1970], 490).

30. Cf. Wenger, "Jean Chrysostome," 336: "Les historiens de la théologie et de la spiritualité se sont demandé si Jean, dans cette démarche, n'accorde pas trop au vouloir de l'homme. De fait, il n'a rien d'un quiétiste."

31. Cf. F. Asensio, "El Crisóstomo y su visión de la escritura en la exposición homilética del Génesis," *Estudios Bíblicos* 32 (1973): 223–55, 329–56.

32. Cf. his comment on Ps 141.3 (a rare mention of the Fall: PG 55.436). For a similar diagnosis, cf. also his Homilies 14, 18, 19, 21 on Genesis and notes there in my translation, *St John Chrysostom's Homilies on Genesis*, Fathers of the Church, vols. 74, 82 (Washington: Catholic University of America Press, 1986, 1990). In the Psalms commentary, Eli also exemplifies this vice in his neglect of his sons (Ps 109.14–15: PG 55.261).

33. PG 55.41.

34. PG 55.226.

35. For details, cf. Bardy, "Jean Chrysostome," 676–77. Bardy concludes: "Il n'y a pas, en tout cela, de théorie précise du péché originel." (The Psalms Commentary did not figure in the debate, though, as we have seen, isolated statements from it might have served to document positions ancient and modern.)

36. Cf. the brief reference in his commentary on Pss 136.5–9 (PG 55.400–401), 141.3 (437). In a glowing list of the privileges of the human being on Ps 49.12 (233), no such shadow falls.

Sion refers to the Church."[37] We do not gain from this *Commentary* much impression of features of the contemporary Church or Chrysostom's ecclesiology; it is not a theme that he harps on with his congregation.

A RICH SCRIPTURAL FARE

Chrysostom has a lively sense of his role in providing nourishment for the spiritual lives of his listeners, especially by breaking the bread of the Word to them. Not only does he walk them through the psalms, verse by verse, "with precision," ἀκρίβεια, in true Antiochene fashion, leaving no item without comment[38]—unless, like many a preacher, he has let time get out of hand, and he has to rush towards the end. He also embroiders his comment by frequent, sometimes overwhelming, reference to other parts of the Bible—unless again pressure of time obliges him to reduce such detail, perhaps because of an earlier digression in some direction (like polemic against the Jews). The Gospel of Matthew would be his favorite reference; as Kannengiesser remarks of him, "More than Basil and the two Gregorys, John Chrysostom witnesses to the evangelical ground of their common spirituality."[39] He upbraids his congregation for their lack of familiarity with biblical story (though this *Commentary* has the anomaly of frequent citation of Hebrew original and alternative Greek translations as a puzzling feature, considering the limitations of the audience). As he likes to give the psalms an historical base if possible, he has to supplement their biblical literacy, as in opening commentary on Ps 7, which he sees arising out of Hushai's friendship for David:

> It would be good for you to have such a precise knowledge of the Scriptures and the stories they tell as to make unnecessary for us a longer version in explaining their teaching.[40]

They are not expected to have Bibles, but to pay attention, *akribeia* this time being a virtue on their part. "Let those who are disorderly in Church be ashamed of themselves," he tells them in commenting on Ps 44; it is God who is speaking.[41] When both preacher and listeners apply the necessary precision, a rich spiritual fare is provided and assimilated.

We noted above that the occasion of the commentaries on individual psalms was more likely paraliturgical than eucharistic. Perhaps for that reason there is not much emphasis on the role of the liturgy in the spiritual life of his listeners. The person of Jesus looms large; Chrysostom wishes to give a Christological interpretation of the psalms wherever possible, even if this has been found to be

37. PG 55.130. Of Chrysostom's works generally Bardy remarks that his ecclesiology "n'offre rien d'original" ("Jean Chrysostome," 679).
38. Cf my "*Akribeia*: A Principle of Chrysostom's Exegesis," *Colloquium* 14 (Oct. 1981): 32–36.
39. "The Spiritual Message of the Great Fathers," 75.
40. PG 55.80.
41. PG 55.172.

relatively "superficielle,"[42] and beyond that he shows a close familiarity with and relish in rehearsing the mysteries of Jesus' life, the οἰκονομία being frequently in his mind. Someone who has been found to be conspicuously absent in Chrysostom's biblical commentaries generally is Mary, the mother of Jesus; that is true also of this *Commentary*. In one such litany of the mysteries of Jesus' life in course of commentary on Ps 45, Chrysostom lists as a deprivation suffered "not choosing a queen for his mother."[43] On the phrase "God will come openly" in Ps 50.2, he remarks, "Even the pregnant Virgin did not know the ineffable truth of the mystery"[44]—a comment that arouses the ire of Chrysostom's editor Bernard de Montfaucon, who proceeds to correct the lacuna without fully appreciating the full sense of μυστήριον.

For all that, the congregation, or congregations, that received these numerous commentaries on the Psalms got good value from this preacher, even if he was in his youth, as some didactic inexperience suggests.[45] Some of them went on to extraordinary length, far surpassing Augustine's *breviloquium*. If we knew more of the process of composition and delivery than even Photius in the ninth century could discover, we might understand better why some strike us as rhetorically moving and others desultory and offhand (at least in the form we have them).[46] Photius was also struck by their pastoral thrust, remarking of a certain lack of "interpretation or depth of insight" that "he never at any stage neglected what the ability of the listeners dictated and had relevance to their benefit and welfare."[47] Not all spiritual directors are appreciated for keeping this goal consistently in sight, golden-mouthed or not. At all events, account needs to be taken of Chrysostom's *Commentary on the Psalms* in the history of Christian spirituality, not to mention theology and biblical interpretation.

Robert C. Hill, The University of Sydney

---

42. "Une utilisation incidente et superficielle de l'exégèse prosopologique" is Rondeau's summation of Chrysostom's Christological approach to the psalms considered in ch. 6 of *Commentaires patristiques du Psautier.*
43. PG 55.185.
44. PG 55.242.
45. See my "Chrysostom's Commentary on the Psalms" for evidence of this; Photius took the different view that the text suggests "he completed them while at leisure rather than involved in public affairs" (PG 103.504).
46. The Pilgrim Songs, or Songs of the Steps, as he calls them (Pss 120–34), in particular fail to move him, and he dismisses them briefly, with little obvious relish as indicated by the lack of the customary Scriptural documentation. Perhaps the historical substrate he finds in them, the Jewish people's captivity experience, is an inhibiting factor for him.
47. PG 103.505.

Augustinian Studies 24 (1993) 133-146

Augustine's Distinctive Use of the Psalms in the Confessions: the Role of Music and Recitation

Paul Burns
Vancouver, British Columbia

Augustine cites the Psalms very frequently in the *Confessions*. Consultation with a critical edition or a good translation bears out this observation. When one compares the number of quotations and identifiable allusions to other sources, the total number of references to the Psalms becomes quite remarkable.[1] Throughout the *Confessions* there are 287 references to other books or collections in the whole of the Old Testament; there are 222 citations from the Psalms. This feature is most apparent in the narrative books of the *Confessions,* that is 1 to 9. In the opening two books, for instance, there are 5 references to the rest of the Old Testament and 22 to the Psalms. In Book 9 concluding with the climatic scene overlooking the Garden at Ostia and the death of Monica, there are 3 references to the rest of the Old Testament and 25 to the Psalms. In the final four books of the *Confessions* the proportion shifts in Books 12 and 13 especially with the extended reflection on the first chapter of *Genesis.* But even here there are significant numbers of citations from the Psalms. In Book 13 there are 89 references to the rest of the Old Testament and 40 to the Psalms.

Comparison with the New Testament also reveals Augustine's deep interest in the Psalms. In Books 1 and 2 there are 12 references to the New Testament and 22 to the Psalms; in Book 9 there are 23 references to the New Testament and 25 to the Psalms.

These sample comparisons indicate the relatively high incidence of references to the Psalms in the *Confessions*. A preliminary assessment of the significance of the frequency of references to the Psalms in the *Confessions* might point to Augustine's manifest interest reflected in his

157

commentaries and his homilies from this period. As early as 392 Augustine had begun to put together a collection of homilies and commentaries on the Psalms known as the *Enarrationes in Psalmos*. He was well along in this enterprise in the years of the composition of the *Confessions* 397 to 401. However, a comparison of the approaches to the Psalms in these two works reveals some very distinctive features in the use of the Psalms in the *Confessions*.

In the *Enarrationes in Psalmos* Augustine proceeds through each psalm in a somewhat organized manner. He often comments on the assigned title of each psalm or the mood or spirit of the psalm and then proceeds in order through each verse. In the *Confessions* in only one passage at 9.4 does Augustine proceed in anything like this fashion. But even this passage is dominated by the approach which is distinctive in the *Confessions* and this passage will furnish a starting point for this study. At 9.4 Augustine does comment extensively on Psalm 4 proceeding through a number of verses according to their internal sequence. This is the normal pattern for exegetical or homiletical composition which would follow the internal structure and themes of the Psalms. Here the focus of attention, however, is directed towards a different subject than those in the commentaries and homilies. Moreover the vast majority of citations from the Psalms in the *Confessions* do not occur in this systematic consideration of passages of psalms in the sequence in which they occur in the established text. Passages from the Psalms ranging in length from a single term, to a phrase, to compound clauses are incorporated into the text of the *Confessions*. This requires adaptation of grammatical forms; sometimes word order is changed; diction may be adapted; personal references may be made more specific. In 1955 G. N. Knauer examined the contribution of the Psalms to the diction, structure, and topics in the *Confessions*.[2] I intend to go beyond his detailed account of the evidence to propose that it is Augustine's memory steeped in daily recitation and singing of the Psalms which influenced the way they function in the *Confessions*.

There is also a contrast in the subjects Augustine develops in his exegetical work on the Psalms in *Enarrationes* from the themes associated with the Psalms in the *Confessions*. For in the *Enarrationes* Augustine approaches each psalm with a strong christological and ecclesial focus. He is interested in "the whole Christ" or his view of Paul's "mystical body" as the context for christian growth and salvation. In the *Confessions* the focus is very different although not unrelated to the pastoral objectives of the *Enarrationes*. In the *Confessions* Augustine uses the Psalms to describe and to probe the range of his own emotional experience: anxiety, confusion, sorrow, pain, loss, gratitude, joy, praise. It is as if the traditional focus of typological and allegorical exegesis has shifted from the objective person of Christ and turned inwards to provide models and language of subjective experience. It is as if the very target of formal exegesis has been inverted. But this new personal even psychological focus of the Psalms also provides a theological language and explanation for human experience and creative christian transformation of that experience.

This paper seeks to illustrate this interesting change of focus in Augustine's use of the Psalms. To account for the frequency of citation, the flexible, incorporation and reworking of the text of the Psalms, I propose that Augustine is working from his memory of the Psalms not from a written text. Moreover that memory is deeply affected by the daily experience of singing and reciting in a prayerful and reflective context. This would account not only for the flexible manner of citation but also for the intensely personal application of the Psalms to his own life and the sustained dialogue between himself and God which itself is influenced by the language and themes of the Psalms.

My hypothesis rests on some evidence within the *Confessions* dealing with a number of features of his experience around Milan at the time of his conversion. This evidence is reinforced by testimony from two texts written much closer to that experience, namely the *De Ordine* of 386 and the *De Musica* of 389. That evidence is interpreted against the background of theological and metric shifts in Church music at that period. The most suggestive evidence for my proposal comes from the testimony of Augustine's *Ordo Monasterii* dated in a recent study to the 390's. But then religious music had made an impact on Augustine during the 370's in the Manichaean communities with which he had associated. It is the memory of that relationship which lies behind that passage at *Confessions* 9.4.

Although that passage is the only one in the *Confessions* to treat several verses in sequence, it is also a telling example of the distinctive subject matter that psalms are used to examine treats a whole psalm. Here at 9.4, Augustine proceeds through Psalm 4, verses 2-10 and in this appears to conform to the order of exegesis found in his commentaries. But two related features distinguish his commentary here. There is the application of the language and themes of Psalm 4 to his own personal journey and there is a powerfully evocative reference to the Manichaeans who were so much part of an earlier stage of that journey. Augustine laments that those Manichees could not have watched his face and listened to his words while he read the Psalm and understood what was really taking place.[3] There is clearly very deep feeling here. Suzanne Poque, in a paper delivered in 1986,[4] has suggested that there is a wistful memory of the intimacy of the Manichaean meetings back in Carthage and in Rome and an acknowledgement of loss of intimacy in the larger more formal gatherings of orthodox Christians in Milan. Probably the emotion in this passage is even more complex with the added dimension of regret and frustration over the Manichaean failure to recognize and respond to the full word of God. Nevertheless the depth of emotional feeling in this instance is undeniable.

But an intensely emotional tone permeates the whole passage at 9.4. Augustine sees himself as moving from fear and anxiety through hope to joy.[5] This very personal use of Psalm 4 has been noted by Hermann-Josef Sieben, the German Jesuit scholar in an article published in 1977,[6] on the role of Psalm 4 in the relation between "words" and "feelings" during Augustine's conversion as recounted in *Confessions* 9.4 and 10.33. He recognizes the intense personalizing of the sacred text finding there the identification and the clarification of emotional experiences of different stages of the personal journey. Augustine in a sense discovers himself in the text of this Psalm.[7]

Sieben quite helpfully indicates this distinctive feature of Augustine's use of this Psalm to name his own inner states of experience. To distinguish this type of exegesis from more familiar typological or allegorical methods employed elsewhere, Sieben calls this exegesis "therapeutic". This term accomplishes two things. It certainly designates the fundamental orientation to intense states of feeling. This Sieben develops in his article quite specifically. But the term also designates the means of change or transformation. This Sieben tends to assume rather than to develop in that article. Augustine is definitely charting different stages of experience at this time of his life moving from confusion, anxiety and fear to hope, confidence and conviction concluding with joy, peace and rest. The principles of this personal transformation, the cause of the various emotional responses, are clearly enunciated in the dialogue of Psalm 4. It was God who has been present and at work in Augustine's life right from the beginning and it is God who brings the transformation to completion. And Augustine quotes verse 10 to underline this reality.[8] This feature is enshrined in the very structure of the Psalm and Augustine's use of it. There are two participants in the events of Augustine's life being highlighted in his consideration of this Psalm. And God, who is responsible for initiating each stage, is addressed personally as *pater* in verse 2 and as *domine* in verse 7 as well as in 10. In each case God is being addressed and thanked and praised for being the active agent bringing about each successive stage of Augustine's journey which in turn provokes his own successive emotional responses. Psalm 4 then provides the language and structure for the actual changes, names the agent of the change and identifies the emotional condition in response to each change. Hence Sieben's designation of this kind of exegesis as "therapeutic" has more validity than he himself has specified in that helpful article.

Sieben could have examined this dialogic structure in Psalm 4 as a paradigm for the overall structures of the *Confessions* but in this article he is seeking for historical parallels and confirmation for his understanding of this "therapeutic" exegesis. Sieben looks to Athanasius on the one hand and to Augustine's own writings during his Cassiciacum sojourn on the other.

Initially Sieben's appeal to Athanasius' *Letter to Marcellinus* makes some sense. In response to a request from the Deacon Marcellinus for help in understanding the Psalms, Athanasius lays down an interpretive principle. The Psalms, according to Athanasius, function as a mirror reflecting the actual stages of experience in the participant.[9] Athanasius then goes on to classify the Psalms according to the human need and human emotion which they express. When feeling overwhelmed it is recommended that one should sing Psalms 16, 85, 87 or 140; when feeling wonder at order and harmony in creation it is recommended that one should sing Psalms 18, 23; when trying to express hope in the midst of sorrow, it is recommended that one should sing Psalm 41 and on go the recommendations.

To support his claim for influence of Athanasius' work on Augustine, Sieben cites two passages from the *Confessions*. At 10.33 Augustine expresses reservations about the appropriateness of musical settings for the Psalms and considers a recommendation attributed to Athanasius.[10] Sieben uses this passage merely to argue for a direct influence on Augustine by Athanasius. He neglects other features of this passage to which I shall return to support my hypothesis about the significance of Augustine's daily experience of singing, recitation and reflection on the Psalms.

To establish a possible connection between the writings of Athanasius and Augustine, Sieben is on stronger ground in his use of the reference at *Confessions* 8.6 to the *Life of Antony* written in Greek by Athanasius but translated into Latin by 370.[11] This is an important episode leading up to Augustine's own commitment at the end of Book 8. It is clear that the Latin version of this text had a deep influence on Augustine. Unfortunately there is no clear evidence that *the Letter to Marcellinus* was translated into Latin and had a similar impact. So although Sieben's appeal to this *Letter* cannot be supported by actual historical evidence, the suggestion does at least provide a good parallel illustration of the type of exegesis he has dubbed "therapeutic".

Sieben's other historical proposal is more productive. Sieben seeks to find some use of the Psalms as recorded in the autobiographical account of the *Confessions* in the actual writings from the period under discussion. And he does find an intriguing episode recorded in November 386 in the *De Ordine* 1.22-23.

Here the young, talented, self-absorbed Licentius, son of his benefactor Romanianus, provoked a critical reaction from Monica. He had been singing a psalm with real enthusiasm in the toilet. Monica thought this to be an inappropriate place for such a text and reprimanded him. Licentius answers back with a smart retort; Augustine tries to use the situation to get Licentius to move from trivial interests to higher things. Sieben uses the episode to demonstrate that the autobiographical report on the influence of the Psalms is confirmed at least by this one incident recorded in a Cassiciacum text. Sieben in 1977, unfortunately, was still a little too preoccupied with the long debate over the historical validity or fictional character of the account of Augustine's conversion in the *Confessions*. I think that he has overlooked two features in this episode which are central to my own proposed reconstruction. One of these features deals with Augustine's awareness of the capacity of music to draw the soul from temporal interests to a higher reality; the other feature deals with Licentius' and Augustine's actual experience of religious music for hymns and psalms.

Augustine uses the incident in *De Ordine* 1.22 to encourage Licentius to move beyond his preoccupation with the trivial issues of poetic composition to something more profound. This same attitude to Licentius is developed more fully by Augustine in his *Letter* 26. This is the very thesis which Augustine explores philosophically in Book 6 of *De Musica* which he had completed in 389 (and perhaps emended in 412).[12] In this book he sets out a Platonic approach affirming a correspondence between order and harmony at the level of the senses with principles of order and harmony in the cosmos as well as within the human soul. There is the possibility that hearing music at the level of sense might draw the soul to higher levels of reality and perhaps even to the source of all order, harmony and equality in God.[13] Throughout this consideration there is concern over the tendency to become satisfied with merely the sense of hearing.

De Musica 6 begins with a musical consideration of the musical harmony in *Deus creator omnium* and moves through the various levels of the experience of number and rhythm from hearing to memory to deeper levels of harmony in the universe. Robert J. Forman, in an article on *De Musica* in 1988, finds very strong parallels between the theoretical exposition here and the autobiographical account of the experience overlooking the Garden at Ostia in *Confessions* 9.10. The soul is stretched beyond itself away from sensation through a consideration within memory of "time" and "eternity". *Deus creator omnium* is used in the earlier work to provide the context for a consideration of patterned sound and silence to initiate the progress of the soul or *distentio animi*. In the later work the same hymn is quoted to provide the emotional release for the pent up grief over the death of Monica and leads to the consideration of life after death and the relative triviality of location of burial. In *De Musica*, as well, Augustine express traditional misgivings over the power of the senses to trap the soul and impede its progress. The reservation about the influence of sensual hearing expressed here has already been noted in the passage cited from *Confessions* 10.33.[14] There he considered the sober recommendation attributed to Athanasius, namely that sacred Psalms should be recited in a voice close to a speaking tone rather than a chant. In that passage Augustine admits his own reservations but then notes the almost universal practice is to employ musical chants. When he remembers his own deeply emotional response to singing he sets aside his reservations and acknowledges the value of singing the Psalms. It is this judgement about the possibilities of music which lies behind his counsel to Licentius in *De Ordine* 22-23. References to music appear in almost all the passages from the *Confessions* used by Sieben. But it is the very experience of singing and hearing of hymns and psalms which has been overlooked by Sieben.

The experience of the actual musical setting for the *Psalm* is the reason for Licentius' interest and repetition.[15] The text from Psalm 79 provided Licentius with material for his smart rejoinder to the scolding by Monica. But in the passage it is clear that it is the music more than the actual text that has caught his fancy. Augustine reports that he had overheard Licentius singing that same passage when he himself was at prayer and the singing broke into his personal and sorrowful reflection. Then in the evening after supper Licentius excused himself and went to relieve himself in the toilet and while there he chanted the words quite loudly and that was too much for Monica. Augustine comments that it was the unusual melody which attracted Licentius.

In fact religious music has become a matter of general interest and controversy in the fourth century. There were some cultural factors influencing changes in form and in content which were to render music more popular. This new direction in music was recognized and employed by Arians and Manichaeans. Ambrose, who succeeded Auxentius an Arian as bishop of Milan, no doubt appreciated the impact of religious music on people and encouraged its use for more orthodox purposes in the Church at Milan. Augustine himself was certainly powerfully affected. At *Confessions* 9.4 he is at least aware of the custom of singing psalms; at 9.7 he recalls the customs of singing psalms during vigils at Milan; at 9.12 Adeodatus is calmed after the death of Monica by Evodius' singing of Psalm 100 and in the same passage Augustine is aided in his grief by *Deus creator omnium*; at 10.33 despite his reservations Augustine remembers his own experience of the singing of the Psalms and recommends the continued practice. At 9.6 there occurs the most telling testimony to his respect for the value of religious music.[16] A whole succession of experiences was produced by hearing religious music. The sense of hearing led to conviction of truth, to deep devotional response and tears of joy. No doubt the interest of Licentius in new musical settings for the Psalms, and the powerful impact of religious music on Augustine were rooted in new approaches to religious music in the fourth century.

There were metrical innovations as well as theological issues which were having an influence on religious music and its popularity at this time. In his new study of the history of metrics, Frank Whitman points to the beginnings of a shift from formal classical quantitative verse to more natural accentual verse.[17] He mentions the example of Hilary of Poitiers, a generation earlier than Ambrose. Whitman observes that some features of accentual verse are beginning to affect more classical approaches to scansion. Even in Ambrose's *Deus creator omnium* there are still features of the classical form. But this hymn allows no classical substitutions and keeps to a uniform eight syllable line which is an easier form for singing. Also in Ambrose the themes are moving away from the formal dogmatic instruction of Hilary's compositions to themes which reflect and shape actual religious experience and feeling. Augustine, himself, in 394 composed popular accentual verse in his alphabetical hymn against the Donatists, entitled Psalmus contra Donati.

Hilary and Ambrose are not isolated examples of renewed interest in religious music during the fourth century. Earlier in the century Arius had used popular rhythms for his *Thalia* and this had caused Athanasius considerable concern. While Augustine was probably not aware of Arius' use of popular musical settings for his religious purposes, he was certainly aware of Manichaean Hymns. A considerable corpus of Manichaean Hymns has been recovered in this century.[18] They were probably composed in Syriac, then translated into Greek, then Coptic and Latin as the movement spread west. In 1930 a considerable collection of Manichaean texts was discovered in Egypt and a good percentage of this find consists of 289 Manichaean Hymns in Coptic, now published in C.R.C. Allbery's edition. This collection demonstrates the range of themes and to some extent the role of refrains and responses and doxologies. In a 1985 study of Manichaeism and its sources, Samuel N.C. Lieu suggests that Hymns were probably the one element of the Manichaean canon accessible to the Hearers within the sect. No doubt Augustine became very familiar with Manichaean hymnody in his ten years as a Hearer. In fact two of his own compositions bear testimony to the retentive power of Manichaean hymns. Several phrases in Augustine's *Contra epistolam quam vocant fundamenti* of 396 contain possible parallels with some of the Manichaean hymns in the Coptic collection of Allberry. Then in his *Contra Faustum Manichaeum* of 397 Augustine is able to recall main elements of another Manichaean Hymn, the *Amatorium canticum*. His memory of the Manichaeans during the years of the composition of the *Confessions* continues to be associated with music. At the passage in *Confessions* 9.4, with which this reconstruction began, Augustine wonders about the possible impact of his own conversion experience upon his former Manichaean associates if they could have heard his words and seen his face as he reflected on Psalm 4. He laments that they would not have understood that the words were his own springing from his heart when he was in the presence of God.

It is this experience of religious music that had been overlooked in Sieben's article. Admittedly in the passage on Psalm 4 Augustine had entertained the possibility that his former Manichaean associates could have been present while he was reading (*legere*) that Psalm. But even in that passage there are allusions to singing and recitation of psalms: *cantica fidelia . . . recitare.*

Having come this far it is important to try to recreate the context in which Augustine is likely to have experienced the singing and recitation of the Psalms. That context for Augustine's experience of the Psalms is to be found in the practices of daily prayer.[19] Since the days of Tertullian and later Cyprian there is evidence for the gathering of the people at regular intervals during the day to pray the Psalms. This practice was certainly reinforced for Augustine by his experience in the Church at Milan. Ambrose's own writings and those of his biographer, Paulinus speak of his abiding interest in this custom and of the role of music in this service. Augustine, so argues the Augustinian priest and scholar George Lawless, would have experienced this custom at Cassiciacum, continued it at Thagaste and incorporated it at Hippo.[20] For in his *Enarrationes in Psalmos* 49.23, Augustine refers to his own practice on four occasions each day.[21] Augustine also encourages others to follow the same practice. In *Enarrationes in Psalmos* at 66.3, for instance, he offers a description of the practice of an ideal christian at prayer.[22] In this passage Augustine identifies the content of daily prayer at Church as composed of readings and hymns. He also identifies the activity of the participant who is expected to reflect or "(to)chew over (*ruminat*) what he has heard". Then in *Enarrationes in Psalmos* 30.3.1 Augustine uses the metaphor of a mirror (*speculum*) to illustrate the purpose of "rumination" or reflection.[23] A mirror captures the correspondence between one's personal life and the text of the Psalm. This general instruction of the preacher Augustine is then applied to his own life in the *Confessions* which is designed to mirror the internal life of Augustine for others to do the same with their own lives.

The most telling piece of evidence for my hypothesis is the *Ordo Monasterii*, attributed in the oldest manuscripts to Augustine and restored to that status in the 1987 study by Lawless. He reviews the evidence for a date in the 390's. In the second paragraph of that document is the schedule of daily prayer with some indication of the content of prayer and mode of participation. That passage designates six periods of the day at which to gather for praying with the Psalms. People are to gather at Dawn, Terce or 9.00, Sext or 12.00, None or 3.00, the Lighting of the Lamp and just before bedtime. The number and the sequence of the Psalms is indicated for at least some of these occasions. It would appear that the whole *Psalter* would be completed every week or so. Other elements are referred to in passing: antiphons (*antiphonae*); readings (*lectiones*); concluding prayer (*conpletorium*). Various modes of use are hinted at. There ares references to praying or "doing the psalms" (*orare vel psallere*), recitation (*dicantur*) and to responsorial presentation (*ad respondendum dicatur*). So the Psalms form a major part of Augustine's experience of daily prayer. Unfortunately for my purposes the verbs do not categorically specify that the Psalms are sung. But then again that reasonable possibility is not ruled out. Helpful for my purposes is the reference to a concluding prayer after a Psalm or a set of Psalms. Collections of these concluding prayers have survived from the fifth century and they demonstrate a very important pattern for my case.[24] In those concluding prayers, phrases and themes from the Psalms themselves would be drawn together to express some application to the experience of the congregation and after gathering those themes together the prayer is addressed on their behalf to God. In a way those concluding prayers are models in miniature of what Augustine is doing throughout the *Confessions*. Here the focus of attention is not the experience of the community but his own personal experience which the Psalms help to select, interpret and then address to God.

My proposal then is simply this. Augustine's experience of daily recitation and singing of the Psalms with reflection allowing those texts to illumine his own experience gradually over the years had a profound impact on his self-understanding and ultimately on the themes and structure of *the Confessions*. The regular daily recitation and singing of the Psalms would contribute to their frequency in the *Confessions*; the oral nature of that experience with refrains, antiphons and responses would contribute to the use of fragments without regard to their place in a set written text; the concluding prayers would provide a pattern for the application to a human experience. If this case has any validity then a sentence at the beginning of 9.4, with which we began, takes on a specific relevance. Augustine opens that section by acknowledging that he has left Milan and the profession of Rhetoric and retires to Cassiciacum. Then he gives thanks to God for rescuing his tongue as well as his heart.[25] Thus if my proposal has merit then this reference to *linguam*, "tongue," may have a double significance applying both to content and manner of speech. Here the content is derived from the Psalms and the manner is intense personal reflection supported by experience of prayer, recitation and singing of the Psalms.

Notes

1. The edition of the text employed in this paper is P. Knöll *CSEL* 33 (1896); the translation is R.S. Pine-Coffin, *Saint Augustine Confessions* (Penguin 1961).

2. For a study of the influence of the text of the Psalms in the *Confessions*, consult G.N. Knauer, *Psalmenzitate in Augustins Konfessionen* (Göttingen 1955).

3. *Confessiones* 9.4.8: . . . quam vehementi et acri dolore indignabar manichaeis et miserabar eos rursus, quod illa sacramenta, illa mendicamenta nescirent et insani essent adversus antidotum, quo sani esse potuissent! vellem, ut alicubi iuxta essent tunc et me nesciente, quod ibi essent, intuerentur faciem meam et audirent voces meas, quando legi quartum psalmum in illo tunc otio . . .

4. For a discussion of some of the emotional implications in this passage, see S. Poque, "La Prière du catéchumène Augustin en septembre 386 (*Confesiones* XI,4,8-11)", *Congresso Internazionale su s. Agostino nel xvi centenario della conversione, Att II* (Rome 1987) esp. 83-84.

5. *Confessiones* 9.4.9: Inhorrui timendo ibidemque inferbui sperando et exultando in tua misericordia, pater.

6. Consult Sieben, Hermann-Josef, S.J., "Der Psalter und die Bekehrung der VOCES und AFFECTUS zu Augustinus, *Confessiones* IX,4.6 und X,33" *Theologie und Philosophie* 52 (1977) 481-497 and his "Athanasius über den Psalter, Analyse seines Briefes an Marcellinus" *Theologie und Philosophie* 48 (1973) 157-173.

7. *Confessiones* 9.4.8: Quas tibi, deus meus, voces dedi, cum legerem, psalmos David, cantica fidelia . . .

8. *Confessiones* 9.4.11: . . . sed tu, domine, singulariter in spe constituisti me.

9. See Robert C. Gregg, *Athanasius: The Life of Antony and the Letter to Marcellinus* (Paulist Press 1980)111: And it seems to me that these words (the text of the Psalms) become like a mirror to the person singing them, so that he might perceive himself and the emotions of his soul, and thus affected, he might recite them. . . . therefore when one sings the third psalm, and recognizing his own tribulation, he considers the words in the psalm to be his own . . . (*Letter to Marcellinus* 12).

10. *Confessiones* 10.33.50: Aliquando autem hanc ipsam fallaciam inmoderatius cavens erro nimia severitate, sed valde interdum, ut melos omnes cantilenarum suavium, quibus Daviticum psalterium frequentatur, ab auribus meis removeri velim atque ipsius ecclesiae, tutiusque mihi videtur, quod de alexandino episcopo Athanasio saepe dictum mihi conmemini, qui tam modico flexu vocis faciebat sonare lectorem psalmi, ut pronuntianti vicinior esset quam canenti.

11. For the Latin translations of the *Life of Antony*, consult Evagrius of Antioch and for the more literal version see G. Garitte, *Un témoin important du texte de la Vie de s. Antoine Études de Philologie d'archéologie et d'histoire anciennes* 3 (Brussels 1939).

12. For a consideration of the background to Augustine's *De Musica* with the classical sources such as Aristides Quintianus and Aristoxenus, and the Pythagoreans Nichomachus, Ptolemy and Theo of Smyrna see Henry Chadwick, *The Consolations of Music, Logic, Theology and Philosophy* (Oxford 1981) 78-101 and the articles in *Augustine on Music: An Interdisciplinary Collection of Essays* edited by Richard R. La Croix (Edwin Mellen Press 1988). For the philosophical implications of *De Musica* and the parallels with the Ostia episode in the *Confessions* see especially Robert J. Forman "Augustine's Music: 'Keys' to the Logos" (ibid) 17-27.

13. See R.C. Taliferro "On Music" in *Writings of Saint Augustine* vol 2 *Fathers of the Church* (New York 1947) 358: And this is why, if numbers of this kind, coming to be in the soul given over to temporal things, have beauty of their own, yet . . . this beauty is grudged by a Divine Providence. . . . For such a delight (with physical hearing) strongly fixes in the memory what it brings from

the slippery senses. . . . But when the mind is raised to spiritual things and remains fixed there, the push of this habit is broken. . . . And so with a determined retreat from every wanton movement . . . and with a resorted delight in reason's numbers, our whole life is turned to God, . . . (*De Musica* 6.33).

14. *Confessiones* 10.33.50: verum tamen cum reminiscor lacrimas meas, quas fudi ad cantus ecclesiae in primordiis recuperatae fidei meae, et nunc ipsum quod moveor non cantu, sed rebus quae cantantur, cum liquida voce et convenientissima modulatione cantantur, magnam instituti huius utilitatem rursus agnosco. 10.33.

15. Consult the edition of P. Knöll, *CSEL* 63 (1922)135: "... surrexerunt illi et ego inlacrimans multa oravi, cum audio Licentium succinentem illud propheticum laete atque garrule: *deus virtutum* ... quod pridie post caenam cum ad requisita naturae foras exisset, paulo clarius cecinit, quam ut mater nostra ferre posset, quod illo loco talia continuo repetita canerentur. nihil enim aliud dicebat, quoniam ipsum cantilenae modum nuper hauserat et amabat, ut fit, melos inusitatum." *De Ordine* 1.22.

16. *Confessiones* 9.6.14: quantum flevi in hymnis et canticis tuis suave sonantis ecclesiae tuae vocibus conmotus acriter! voces illae influebant auribus meis et eliquabatur veritas in cor meum et exaestuabat inde affectus pietatis, et currebant lacrimae, et bene mihi erat cum eis. 9.6.

17. Consult Frank Whitman, *A Comparative Study of Old English Metre* (U of Toronto 1993).

18. For a recent survey of the extensive remains of Manichaean documents consult Samuel N.C. Lieu, *Manichaeism in the Later Roman Empire and Medieval China: A Historical Survey* (Manchester University Press 1985). For his report on the extensive finds of Coptic sources by Professor Carl Schmidt in 1930 which have been traced to Medinet Medi near a former Hellenistic military settlement of Narmouthis north of Oxyrhynchos, see pp. 7ff. For his observations on Augustine's recollection of Manichaean Hymns, see pp. 134-135. For a comprehensive study of these excerpts, consult F. Decret, *L'Afrique manichéenne: Étude historique et doctrinale* 2 vols. (Paris 1978) I 107-124 n.2, II 79-88 n.2. For the possibilities of liturgical origin of themes in these excerpts from the Manichaean letter, see comparison with some of the hymns in Allberry's collection proposed by J. Ries, "Une version liturgique copte de l'*Epistola Fundamenti* réfutée par saint Augustin?" *Studia Patristica* X I *TU* 108 (Berlin 1972) 41-49. Lieu also provides parallels to the quotation of the "Hymn of the lovers" in the *Contra Faustum* with extensive translations from *A Manichéan Psalm-Book* I part 2 edited and translated by C.R.C. Allberry (Stuttgart 1938) pp. 136, 2 and 138. For a brief comment on this Hymn, consult F. Decret, *Aspects du manichéisme dans l'Afrique romaine: Les controverses de Fortunatus, Faustus et Felix avec saint Augustin* (Paris 1970) 99-100.

19. For a survey of the evidence for the *Prayer of the Hours* in both East and West, consult the survey in Paul F. Bradshaw, *Daily Prayer in the Early Church* (SPCK 1981).

20. For a discussion of the authorship and the dating for the *Ordo Monasterii* as well as text and translation with a detailed evaluation of evidence for Augustine from Milan, Cassiciacum, Thagaste and Hippo up until 400, consult George Lawless O.S.A. *Augustine of Hippo and His Monastic Rule* (Oxford 1987). His helpful appendix is deeply indebted to the textual work of L. Verheijen, *La Règle de saint Augustin, I, Tradition manuscrite, II Recherches historiques* (Paris 1967).

21. Consult D.E. Dekkers and I. Fraipont *Sancti Aurelii Augustini: Enarrationes in Psalmos CCL* 38, 39 (Turnholt 1956) 49.23: Surgam quotidie, pergam ad ecclesiam, dicam unum hymnum matutinum, alium verspertinum, tertium aut quartum in domo mea: quotidie sacrificio sacrificium laudis, et immolo Deo meo.

22. *Enarrationes in Psalmos* 66.3: Vide formicam Dei: surgit quotidie, currit ad ecclesiam Dei, orat, audit lectionem, hymnum cantat, ruminat quod audivit, apud se cogitat, recondit intus grana collecta de area.

23. *Enarrationes in Psalmos* 30.3.1: . . . et si orat psalmus, orate; et si gemit, gemite; et si gratulatur, gaudete; et si sperat, sperate; et si timet, timete. Omnia enim quae hic conscripta sunt, speculum nostrum sunt.

24. For collections of "prayer collects", consult L. Brou, *The Psalter Collects from V-VIth Century Sources* (1949), J. Pinell, *Liber Orationum Psalmographus* (Barcelona 1972). For comment on their origin and function, see J.D. Crichton, *Christian Celebration: The Prayer of the Church* (1976) pp. 86-87.

25. *Confessiones* 9.4.7: . . . eruisti linguam meam, unde iam erueras cor meum benedicebam tibi gaudens . . .

MARTYR DEVOTION IN THE ALEXANDRIAN SCHOOL: ORIGEN TO ATHANASIUS

by JOHN ANTHONY MCGUCKIN

INTRODUCTION

THE Christian interpretation of fatal persecution was a complex one with distinct ecclesial themes merging with Jewish elements from apocalyptic and biblical literature, as well as Hellenistic motifs such as the constancy of the Socratic martyr. The New Testament understanding of the term 'martyr' is predominantly that of legal witness,[1] although some specific senses of blood-witness are emerging already in the first century[2] and have become common by the second.[3] Varying reactions can be traced in the literature of different parts of the Church: for example, in Rome, Alexandria, Asia, Africa, or Palestine.[4] This paper looks primarily at the Egyptian interpretation as a microcosm of the general development of the role of martyrs, and does so by reference to the writings of the theologians whose works cover the main phases of that process. It highlights the distinction that existed between the sophisticated literary interpretation of martyrdom, and the forms of popular devotion that flourished among the non-literate peasantry. The tension between the two approaches, witnessed in both Origen and Athanasius, is demonstrably resolved by the time of Cyril, who represents the harmonious synthesis of both traditions in the new conditions of Christian political ascendancy in fifth-century Byzantine Egypt. The peculiar circumstances of the Egyptian Church, in particular the unusually radical separation that existed there between town and country (and the class and cultural divisions reflected in that), as well as the specific challenge posed to Christianity by the enduring vitality of the old Egyptian religions in the countryside, both left their marks on the specific form of martyr devotion

---

[1] Cf. E. Gunther, *Martus: Die Geschichte eines Wortes* (Berlin, 1941); H. Strathmann, 'Martus', in G. Kittel and F. Friedrich, eds, *Theological Dictionary of the New Testament* (London, 1964), pp. 474–508.
[2] As, for example, in Rev. 2.13.
[3] *Martyrdom of Polycarp*, 2, PG 5, cols 1029–32: Irenaeus, *Adversus haereses*, 5.9.2, PG 7, col. 1144: Clement of Alexandria, *Stromateis*, 4,4–5, 21, PG 8, cols 1225f.
[4] For a general survey cf. R. Lane Fox, *Pagans and Christians* (London, 1986), pp. 419–92.

in Christian Egypt, but the most noteworthy aspect is arguably the subtext of the theological encomia of martyrdom that seems to have the definite concern of subjugating the popular devotion to martyrs, confessors, and ascetics to the interests of the Church hierarchies.

ORIGEN c. 185–251

Eusebius tells us that in Origen's youth, the Emperor Severus (193–211) 'stirred up persecution in every place'.[5] This is, without doubt, a considerable exaggeration, but there were episodes of local trouble for various churches, especially Alexandria. If the evidence of the *Historia Augusta* is taken,[6] the purpose of the Severan edict was to prevent proselytism, and was aimed at the leaders of the Christian movement, particularly those of higher rank.[7] At Carthage the famous passion of Perpetua and Felicitas dates from this time (202), as probably does Tertullian's treatise on martyrdom.[8] At Alexandria[9] Eusebius speaks, in a very odd phrase, of the martyrdom then of 'Leonides, said to be the Father of Origen'.[10]

Aline Roussell[11] has noticed that the manner of Leonides' death, by beheading, denotes his rank as a Roman citizen at a time before Caracalla's edict (212) extended that privilege widely, and places him in the upper of the three ranks of third-century Alexandrian society: Roman citizens, citizens of the *polis* of Alexandria, and native Egyptians. Eusebius tells us the famous story on this occasion of how Origen's mother prevented his bid for martyrdom by hiding his clothes. The story is largely part of Eusebius' pro-Origen apologetic, for in all probability even if he had run off to join his father no one would have wanted to arrest him anyway. The Severan persecution in 202 was entirely directed at the upper class of Roman citizens. Origen's name (the Son of Horus) denotes his native Egyptian birth, despite all his subsequent Hellenistic education, and

---

[5] Eusebius, *Historia ecclesiastica*, 6.1.1; 8.7, *PG* 20, cols 522, 756.
[6] *Vita Severi*, 17.1 (Aelii Lampridii), in H. Peter, ed., *Scriptores historiae Augustae*, 1 (Leipzig, 1884), pp. 247–99.
[7] Cf. W. H. C. Frend, 'A Severan Persecution? Evidence of the *Historia Augusta*', in *Forma Futuri: Studi in onore di Card. M. Pellegrino* (Turin, 1975), pp. 470–80; *Martyrdom and Persecution in the Early Church* (Garden City, 1964); T. D. Barnes, 'Legislation against the Christians', *Journal of Roman Studies*, 58 (1968), pp. 32–50.
[8] Tr. C. Dodgson, *Library of the Fathers*, 10 (Oxford, 1842), pp. 150–7.
[9] For a general treatment cf. P. Delehaye, 'Les Martyrs d'Égypte', *AnBoll*, 40 (1922), pp. 5–154.
[10] Eusebius, *Historia ecclesiastica*, 6.2.12.
[11] Aline Roussell, 'La Persecution des chrétiens dans Alexandrie au IIIe siècle', *Revue historique de droit français et étranger*, 2 (1974), pp. 222–51. Text discussed in H. Crouzel, *Origen* (Edinburgh, 1989), p. 6.

Roussell suggests he was the child of a mixed marriage between an impoverished citizen, who had taken to the profession of teacher of grammatics, and a native Egyptian woman. In such cases the children of the marriage always assumed the lower of the two ranks involved, and on these grounds Origen would not have qualified for capital punishment even if he had vigorously professed Christianity. This is borne out four years later (206), when Origen accompanied six of his pupils to their executions. On that occasion the Alexandrian crowd found the impunity of the teacher outrageous and nearly lynched him,[12] but there was no official move against him, despite his notoriety as a Christian and the fact that the prosecuting judge, Aquila, generally appears to have distinguished himself for his savagery.

Origen never himself refers to his father's death as a martyr, and is oddly taciturn and vague about the historical realities of the martyrdoms generally in his extant writings. It is clear, however, that Eusebius' account of the martyrdoms in Alexandria in 206[13] was based on what must have been Origen's own *Panegyric* on his executed disciples. In line with Origen's extant writings, we could presume from the outset that this lost text would have celebrated their philosophical constancy: martyrs, that is, in the Socratic tradition, as befitted their profession of the scholar's life.

In the main, Origen's attitude to martyrdom can be summed up as rather low key, despite the fact that in a treatise devoted to the theme, he describes it as the discipleship that received the 'promised hundredfold'. In the persecution of Maximin Thrax (235–8), two of Origen's colleagues were imprisoned, his patron Ambrose and the Caesarean priest Protoctetus. Origen disapproved of Christians volunteering themselves for arrest, and at this period he seems to have withdrawn into hiding, a practice he reminds his readers is sanctioned by the Gospels,[14] but having withdrawn he counsels his arrested friends not to be anxious in undergoing their present trials, which apparently involved their transfer to the court at Mainz.[15] This *Exhortation to Martyrdom* is his most extended treatment of the theme, and while it evidently presents itself as an encomium, its primary function as a philosophical protreptic scales down the enthusiasm until it is almost matter of fact. It is interesting, in this light, to

---

[12] Eusebius, *Historia ecclesiastica*, 6.4.1.
[13] Ibid., 6.4: 'As Origen himself expresses it, after receiving her baptism by fire Heraïs departed this life.'
[14] Mt. 10.23; cf. Origen, *Homilies on the Book of Judges*, hom. 9, *PG* 12, cols 987–8.
[15] Origen, *Exhortation to Martyrdom* [hereafter *ExM*], tr. J. J. O'Meara, *Ancient Christian Writers*, 19 (London, 1954); cf. *ExM*, 41, p. 185.

consider whether the literary sang-froid is part and parcel of the stock tradition of Socratic martyrdom or whether it marks a personal desire on the part of Origen to displace, in some degree, the growing Christian devotion to the martyr ideal. Nowhere in his text does he aver to his own flight. Nor does he apologize for it. His friends, rather, are to be consoled for the misfortune of their arrest, but having thus had their choice taken away from them, he urges them on to the inevitable test of fidelity they will have to undergo. In this way his whole argument is his justification for his flight. What he is suggesting as his sub-text is that the vocation of the wise man, the *didaskalos* who is initiated by the Logos, is no less elevated than that of the martyr. He has no apology to make for defending his own charism by prudent escape. Perhaps not for Origen was the response of the Roman Church which set the martyr above all other saints.

In a sense, Origen cannot quite set the balance between the Socratic virtue of scorning death for the truth's sake and the Christian encouragement of his friends to press on for the sake of the hundredfold reward and their identification with the crucified master. In Origen's text the idea that dominates is how the martyr must be constant, like a true wise man in control of all his fears and steadfast in his profession of the truth. He has some specifically Christian elements, of course, most notably his summaries on how the Church abhors and penalizes apostasy,[16] and his section on the necessity of the disciple to bear the cross.[17] But when he wishes to present a series of exemplary martyrs for their emulation it is to II Maccabees that he turns,[18] not to experiences closer to hand. Despite Eusebius' urgent desire[19] to endow Origen himself with the nimbus of the martyr,[20] it would seem that the latter saw the philosophical vocation which he was bent on pursuing as the highest of all callings, and in a discreet way he is even ready to reinterpret the sacrificial role of the martyr along philosophical lines to sustain his point.

The same kind of philosophical abstraction of martyrdom is witnessed in his *Contra Celsum*, written in about 246. Here he radically restricts the martyr tradition to a Socratic paradigm.[21] Once again the martyrs are the

---

[16] *ExM*, 6–10, pp. 146–50.
[17] *ExM*, 11–21, pp. 151–61.
[18] *ExM*, 22–7, pp. 162–7; cf. Origen, *Commentary on Romans*, 4.10, PG 14, col. 999.
[19] It was designed to offset the rising tide of anti-Origenism among the less educated by the strongest appeal Eusebius could make to popular sentiment in his day—that Origen ought to be venerated as a martyr.
[20] Yet, in the end he suffered heroically, in the Decian persecution, so that Eusebius' devotion was not ill judged.
[21] *Contra Celsum*, 3.8, PG 11, col. 929.

true wise men, undeterred from their profession of truth by the savagery of tyrants. What goes hand in hand with this approach, indeed character-izes it, is its presupposition of intellectual superiority, and social exclusivity. He is determined to dispel every hint of fanaticism or populism from the Church's tradition of martyrdom. So, he tells the reader of the *Contra Celsum*, the Church's martyrs are 'few and easily enumerable'. As in his *Exhortation to Martyrdom*, here the concept of martyr is severely restricted to the one who has died for the truth:[22] the loud implication being that the surviving confessor does not count. In advance he is heading off the kind of problem that Cyprian had to face with the confessors of his own church a few years later.[23] Origen might argue that the blood of the martyrs in heaven would intercede for sinners on earth, but his general doctrine of reconciliation restricts its gift to those whom the Logos has initiated, and he would be unlikely to grant that charism indiscriminately to confessors.[24]

This exclusive and philosophical approach, if this was all there was, would hardly prepare one for the very concrete and populist devotion to the martyrs that had emerged among the common people, and fixed on their physical remains as its focus of devotion even from the second century.[25] Clearly Origen's position is already somewhat disingenuous, and partly designed to suppress popular attitudes he knew to be prevalent. At other times in his writings, particularly when he is addressing the less educated directly, as, for example, in his weekday expositions of the Scriptures in the Caesarean Church, a slightly different attitude can be seen. Here he is more ready to develop on the one brief allusion in the *Exhortation*[26] where he admits the intercessory power of martyrs. In his *Second Homily on Leviticus*, Origen has a remarkable section on the seven remissions of sins.[27] While the first of these is baptism, he describes the

---

[22] *ExM*, 50, p. 195; *Commentary on John's Gospel*, 2.28, *PG* 14, cols 176–7.
[23] For the confessor as a significant power in the Church, cf. Eusebius, *Historia ecclesiastica*, 5.1.45; 5.2.5; 5.18.6 (Montanists), *PG* 20, cols 404f.; Cyprian, *Epistles*, 15–16; 17.2; 20–3; 27; 35–6, *PL* 4, cols 270f.; Eusebius, on Dionysius of Alexandria, *Historia ecclesiastica*, 6.42.5–6, *PG* 20, cols 614–15; Tertullian, *De pudicitia*, 22, *PL* 2, col. 1080; *Ad uxorem*, 2.4.1, *PL* 1, col. 1407; *Ad martyres*, 1.6, *PL* 1, col. 700; *De poenitentia*, 9.4, *PL* 1, col. 1354; *Scorpiace*, 10.8, *PL* 2, cols. 166–7.
[24] Cf. J. McGuckin, 'Origen's doctrine of priesthood', *Clergy Review*, 70 (Aug. 1985), pp. 277–86; ibid., 70 (Sept. 1985), pp. 318–25.
[25] The mid-second-century *Martyrdom of Polycarp* already has a motif of the quest for the ashes as relics, and the third-century *Acts of Thomas* has dust from the martyred Apostle's tomb curing a child.
[26] *ExM*, 30, p. 171.
[27] Origen, *Homilies on Leviticus*, 2, *PG* 12, col. 418.

second as the passion of the martyr. This is ostensibly high praise indeed, in the tradition of Tertullian, where martyrdom is the second baptism. But again there is a sub-text, for these two ways are unrepeatable events, and he immediately goes on to discuss other 'repeatable' ways, such as the third remission being almsgiving, and others such as converting sinners, forgiving the wrong-doer, and abundant charity. This would suggest, once again, that while giving martyrdom a place of high honour, he deliberately qualifies its significance in the ordinary life of the Church. In the Leviticus homily he suggests that the death of the martyr has redemptive value for others beyond its merely exemplarist force. Here, I think, he is touching upon some of the reasons the devotion of martyrs was so prevalent among ordinary Christians. In his *Commentary on Judges* he develops this theme and explains it on the basis of Revelation 6.10, which speaks of the souls of martyrs gathered under the heavenly altar. Origen describes the martyrs as currently assisting in the heavenly sacrifices, and admits that their merits intercede for the faithful on earth and also confound the psychic power of the aerial demons.[28] Both attributes featured largely in the popular, or non-philosophical, devotion to the martyrs, and both explained why it was desirable to be buried next to their mortal remains, so that one could avail of their guidance on the Day of Resurrection, a movement which contributed to centralizing the *martyrium*, and thus the cult of martyrs itself, in the ordinary liturgical experience of Christianity.[29] The stress on the physical, however, made it a movement that Origen did not wish to assist.

Yet even when Origen had completed his literary work, some of the Church's major persecutions lay still in the future.[30] The generation between Origen and Athanasius saw the elaboration of new aspects of the role of martyrs, not least the emergence of the desert hermit as the martyr for a new age when martyrdom was thought to lie definitively in the past. The writings of Athanasius give some interesting evidence on these changes and return us directly to Alexandria, revealing some aspects of the physical cult that relate specifically to the Egyptian way of death.

[28] *Commentary on the Book of Judges*, homily 7, PG 12, col. 981; also in the *Commentary on John's Gospel*, 6.36, PG 14, col. 293.
[29] Cf. H. Delehaye, *Les Origines du culte des martyrs* = *Subsidia hagiographica*, 20 (Brussels, 1912); A. Grabar, *Martyrium: Recherches sur le culte des reliques et l'art chrétien antique* (College de France, Fondation Schlumberger pour les études byzantines), 2 vols (Paris, 1946).
[30] Those of Decius (249–51), Valerian (257), Diocletian [The Great Persecution (303–11)], and Maximin Daia (311–13).

ATHANASIUS *c.* 300–373

In a large body of writings Athanasius' references to the martyrs are surprisingly few.[31] In a sense it is a theme that hardly figures for him except in a stock manner, for their appearance signifies only three or four things as far as he is concerned. In the first place, and it is his main usage, the martyrs are legal witnesses to the truth; that is, he applies the predominant New Testament sense of the word. In addition to this, he continues the high literary theme of the martyrs as being philosophically constant in their fidelity to their tradition. These are his normal approaches. In addition, two other aspects complete the picture, though neither of them is uniquely Athanasian; the first is that the martyrs' courage is one of the signs that the new age of Christ has arrived, and with it a transformation of the old human nature. His several references to women martyrs in particular, as something *contra naturam* being a sign of something *supra naturam*, is indicative of this approach. The last aspect is his habitual designations of the martyrs as a class alongside the 'choir' of prophets and patriarchs. The latter is an evident liturgical usage,[32] but it is largely a literary topos for him.

We gain far more interesting indications if we turn to his specific treatise on the *Life of Antony*. The shift from martyrdom to asceticism is already under way. Indeed, our first conclusion must be that it is Athanasius himself who is clearly encouraging that shift and ensuring its long-term endurance in the Christian tradition. Reading Athanasius we might even forget that the Alexandrian Church, under the soon-to-be-martyred Bishop Peter,[33] has expressed its canonical disapproval of those who eagerly sought physical martyrdom instead of being content to follow the prudent example of the Lord who fled from Herod and had taught his disciples to flee, for there, in Athanasius, this very characteristic is approvingly attributed to the eponymous hero of the narrative.[34] But although Athanasius attributes this as high praise to Antony, we have to

---

[31] He has only sixteen references *in toto*. Cf. G. Muller, who lists them in *Lexicon Athanasianum* (Berlin, 1952), p. 877.

[32] Cf. *De incarnatione*, PG 25, cols 144, 145, 181, 189.

[33] Peter was martyred in 311 after five years in hiding. His *Canonical Epistle* was published in 306 against the background of grave troubles in the internal order of the Church, and the complications of the Melitian schism. *St Dionysius of Alexandria: Letters and Treatises*, ed. and tr. C. L. Feltoe (London, 1918).

[34] *Life of Antony* [hereafter *LA*], tr. R. T. Meyer, *Ancient Christian Writers*, 10 (Westminster, Maryland, 1950); cf. ch. 46, p. 59.

remember how different were his own judgements on these matters, for despite being a man of considerable courage, like Origen, he was a great taker to flight, not one to stand his ground unnecessarily and risk arrest or death. For both littérateurs discretion was certainly the better part of valour, and this meant that for both, their doctrinal work took precedence, was simply more important than the quest for martyrdom. The monk as the new martyr inherited several of the characteristics that went along with the title. Even so, it is extremely odd to find Athanasius labouring to present the illiterate Egyptian Antony as a sophisticated neophilosopher, confounding the pagan professors who come out to consult him in the desert. It would seem that the theme was so firmly established in the martyr tradition that Athanasius could not part with it, however ill-fitting the garment had now become.

In the *Life of Antony* it is often difficult to distinguish Athanasius from his subject.[35] Some of the long discourses attributed to the father of monks are, quite obviously, Athanasian treatises on different themes.[36] Other concerns of the *Vita*, such as Antony's constant obedience to the hierarchy of Alexandria[37] and the perfect Nicene orthodoxy of his faith,[38] are clearly Athanasian ideological devices, regardless of their historical accuracy. None the less, the fact remains that Antony was not a philosopher, or a theologian, or a hierarch of the Church of Alexandria; he was a simple, illiterate man who had lived in the desert and fought demons, until in the eyes of all the rural Christians of Egypt he was a supreme exorcist, seer, healer, and man of God. Such was the locus of spiritual power here that neither Athanasius nor any of his successors in Greek Alexandria could afford the monastic movement to develop independently of them. So it was that Egyptian peasant Christianity, with its heavily phenomenal approach, was rearticulated and brought into line by the Christian urban and literary tradition.

The demonology and consciousness of the body and its mortality are so vivid in the desert literature as to be almost distinguishing marks of the Egyptian Church. Antony, after his initial period of asceticism near to the village, withdraws to a necropolis to begin his real spiritual struggle. There

---

[35] Cf. H. Dorries, 'Die Vita Antonii als Geschichtsquelle', *NachGott*, 14 (1949), pp. 17–29; T. D. Barnes, 'Angel of light or mystic initiate? The problem of the Life of Antony', *JTS*, 37 (1988), pp. 353–68.

[36] The discourse to the monks (*LA*, 16–43) ostensibly spoken by Antony is clearly Athanasius' theoretical excursus on demonology, attributed to one whose own praxis against them was one of his famed attributes while alive.

[37] *LA*, 67, tr. Meyer, p. 76; cf. Athanius, *Letter to Dracontius*, ch. 9, PG 25, cols 531–4.

[38] *LA*, 69–70, tr. Meyer, pp. 78–9.

he is almost killed by the physical beatings he receives from the demons.[39] Returning to the battle, he demonstrates his superiority over demonic powers, and his reputation is secured. The necropolis, with its hieroglyphic designs, was a very useful residence for the desert hermit, but a dangerous and frightful place too, for the demonic figures with jackal heads, which were depicted manipulating the souls of the dead, betrayed those places as the particular haunts of demons who were bent on harrowing their victims in Hell. Such was the instinctive Christian rereading of the Egyptian death legends.

The connection between the body and the spirit was graphic and vital in rural Egypt. In other parts of the *Life of Antony*, incubation healings are described at his cell, and even the pagans came to consult the holy man.[40] We are a long way from Origen's spirituality here, and for the next few centuries Coptic Christianity would be at the forefront of the anti-Origenist movement—frequently to such an extent that hierarchs such as Theophilus and Cyril,[41] themselves no lovers of Origen's memory, had to censure villages and monasteries for their anthropomorphism.

The necropoleis of Egypt obviously contained mummies, which being consecrated to the demons in Christian estimate were themselves seen as vehicles of demonic power. The *Lives of the Desert Fathers* contain stories of monks proving their fearlessness before the corpses, and even of one redoubtable monk pulling a mummy from its niche to use as his pillow during the night. When the demon inevitably began to whisper to him threateningly in the darkness, he pummelled the mummy until he drove it out, thus plumping up his pillow in the process.[42]

It is in this environment that the body of the ascetic who has conquered the demons in life is also endowed with immense power in death. The early signs of incubation ritual around Antony have grown in extent by the time of Cyril of Scythopolis,[43] where such phenomena are freely attributed to the ascetics, living and dead. This development, in turn, had a very close reciprocal relation to the increasing cult of the martyrs' remains. Athanasius in his *Life of Antony* gives us some revealing

---

[39] These are the famous trials of St. Antony, *LA*, 8–10, pp. 26–9.

[40] *LA*, 48, pp. 60–1.

[41] For Theophilus, cf. J. Quasten, *Patrology*, 3 (Utrecht, 1975), pp. 101, 103; for Cyril, cf. *Letter to Calosirius*, in L. Wickham, *Cyril of Alexandria, Select Letters* (Oxford, 1983), pp. xxx–xxxi, 214–21.

[42] Cf. H. Leclercq, 'Momie', in G. Cabrol, ed., *Dictionnaire d'archéologie chrétienne et de liturgie*, 15 vols (Paris, 1907–53); W. H. Mackean, *Christian Monasticism in Egypt* (London, 1920).

[43] Cyril of Scythopolis, *The Lives of the Monks of Palestine* [mid-sixth century], tr. R. M. Price (Kalamazoo, 1991).

information about the connection when he narrates Antony's death scene.[44] He is clearly interested here in suppressing a customary practice in his local church, and his need to invoke the popular authority of Antony to bolster his disapproval gives some indication that he knew he was up against a widespread Christian devotion. Here we witness the cultural gap between Hellenized Alexandria and the peasant Coptic churches of Middle and Upper Egypt:

> The Egyptians have the custom of honouring the bodies of holy men with funeral rites, and wrapping them in linen shrouds, especially the bodies of the holy martyrs. They do not bury them in the earth but lay them on couches, and keep them with them at home, thinking in this way to honour the departed.[45]

Antony tells his disciples to bury his body in secret:[46]

> 'Be diligent in this, and if you have any care for me at all, or any regard for me as a father, do not allow anyone to take my body to Egypt, lest they should keep it in their houses.'[47]

At this juncture the body of the martyr and the ascetic become almost synonymous in a physical *cultus* that focuses on aspects brought together from both traditions—of persecuted martyr and desert ascetic. It focuses on prayers for intercession for the forgiveness of sin, prayers for healing, protection, and release from demonic oppression, as well as petitions for guidance for the future and the benefit of the saint's second sight.

In the following generation the assimilation is not only complete and harmoniously synthesized, but even the patriarch of Alexandria himself has come round to it, and in the instance of Cyril we see the Bishop acting as hierophant and intermediary between the martyrs and the faithful. Cyril, like Ambrose before him, and the Empresses Pulcheria and Eudocia in his own day, have visions and dreams that lead them to discover the

---

[44] *LA*, 90–1, pp. 94–6.
[45] *LA*, 90, p. 94.
[46] The motif of disciples burying the master's body is a common one in the literature, not so the motive Athanasius ascribes to the command. He lays great stress on the secrecy attached to the place: 'To this day only those two disciples know the place of burial', but there were traditions of Hilarion venerating the tomb shortly after Antony's death. In 561 the site was 'acclaimed', and the relics were transferred to Alexandria, hence to Constantinople in 635 after the Islamic invasion, and thence to France after the Crusades. Since 1491 the relics have been kept in the church of St Julien, at Arles, and thence partially distributed to Rome and other European churches in smaller reliquaries, one of which is in the present author's possession.
[47] *LA*, 92, tr. Meyer, p. 96.

sacred remains of 'forgotten' martyrs from the earlier generations and to construct splendid shrines to house them.[48] By the fifth century, then, the cult of the martyrs' and ascetics' relics represented such a clear locus of power, alongside that of the palpable political power of the monks who led the celebration of the cult, that no Byzantine leader of any acumen could afford to be aloof from it.

CONCLUSION

In short, the Christian tradition never failed to honour its martyrs. The devotion to their heroic memory extended first of all to belief in their intercessory power for the forgiveness of sins, and subsequently to an enduring belief in the validity of their heavenly intercessions at the altar of God. The attitude of the literate hierarchy to the martyrs was, however, one that carried with it a degree of ambivalence. In the literary tradition of martyr encomia, we can discern an attempt to offer praises while simultaneously qualifying the power the martyrs (and, by implication, confessors) might be thought to exercise in the affairs of the Church on earth. In the case of Egyptian Christianity, we see the cultural gap between the educated and the rural Christians expressing itself in clearly distinct attitudes to martyr veneration. The writings of Origen and Athanasius witness to the way in which the Church leaders of the third and fourth centuries tried to assimilate and direct popular forms of devotion. By the fifth century the process had been completed, and in such a way that through the physical *cultus* of relics the gap between the Hellenistic philosophical tradition and the common people's quest for the phenomenal had been so narrowed that even hierarchs and members of the imperial household could be found at the forefront of the new forms of devotion.

University of Leeds

---

[48] For Cyril's discovery of the remains of Saints Cyrus and John, the 'healing martyrs' or 'holy unmercenaries', cf. J. McGuckin, 'The influence of the Isis cult on St. Cyril of Alexandria's Christology', *Studia Patristica*, 24 (1992), pp. 191–9; for Ambrose's discovery dream for Saints Gervase and Protasius, cf. Ambrose, Epistle 22, *PL* 16, cols 1019–26; for Pulcheria's dream and discovery of the relics of the forty martyrs of Sebaste, and Eudocia's triumphant *adventus* from Jerusalem with the relics of the protomartyr, cf. K. G. Holum, *Theodosian Empresses* (London, 1982).

How on Earth Could Places Become Holy? Origins of the Christian Idea of Holy Places[1]

R. A. MARKUS

This paper tries to elucidate the way in which the early Christian reluctance to accord holiness to places was overcome in the course of the fourth century. Noting the contrast between the pre-Constantinian and later fourth-century attitudes, it allows for extraneous considerations such as imperial patronage and encouragement of pilgrimage, but seeks the religious roots of this shift in Christian attitudes. The view that the example of Jerusalem and the influence of the Jerusalem liturgy encouraged devotion to sacred places elsewhere is dismissed as inadequate to explain the growth of the cult of holy places and pilgrimage to them. The paper suggests that the new post-Constantinian forms of devotion to the martyrs were an important preparation for the emergence of the idea of holy places. The cult gave place a new significance; it met a felt need to make present in post-Constantinian conditions the past of the persecuted Church. Christianity could not envisage places as intrinsically holy, only derivatively, as the sites of historical events of sacred significance.

An Egyptian sage, sorrowfully foreseeing the time when the ancient cults would be forgotten and their sites deserted, prophesied: "At that time this holiest of lands, the site of shrines and temples, will be filled with the sepulchres of dead men."[2] Augustine quoted this prophecy in the course of his polemical Cook's tour of pagan religion in his *City of God*. "What he [Egyptian Hermes] seems to be lamenting," Augustine says, "is that the memorials of our martyrs would supersede their shrines and their tem-

---

1. This paper is based on various earlier versions given at seminars and lectures at the Universities of Cambridge, Chicago, the Catholic University of America, and at the Conference on "Ancient History at a Modern University" in Sydney, July 1993. This last version is to be published in the proceedings of the conference, whose editors I wish to thank for permission to make use of the paper here.
2. *Asclepius*, 24 (ed. Nock & Festugière, 2.327); quoted by Augustine, *civ.* 8.26.

Journal of Early Christian Studies 2:3, 257–271 © 1994 The Johns Hopkins University Press

ples." Augustine was, of course, wise after the event. He was writing in the second decade of the fifth century; what the Egyptian sage had been afraid of had, in large measure, come to pass. But for this to have come about a huge intellectual and spiritual barrier had needed to be surmounted. What I want to try to elucidate is the way this barrier was overcome.

An earlier generation of scholars of religion would not have seen a problem here. Mircea Eliade, to take the best known example, could see holy places wherever he looked on the rich map of religions: "Every kratophany and hierophany whatsoever transforms the place where it occurs: hitherto profane, it is thenceforward a sacred area."[3] Holy places, Eliade thought, are "centres": centres of religious cosmology, centres of the world, and, derivatively, places where the centre is ritually re-enacted: "Every temple or palace, and by extension, every sacred town or royal residence is assimilated to a 'sacred mountain' ['where heaven and earth meet'] and thus becomes a centre."[4] He took it as self-evident that all religions possessed such places. This assumption caused him to misdescribe observed facts,[5] as well as to overlook the fact that Christianity originally had no holy places and for some three centuries continued to have none. An approach more historical than Eliade's is needed if we are to come to grips with this paradox.

Robert Wilken's fine new book on the holiness of the land "called holy"[6] has brought home to us the laborious and tortuous nature of the road which led to the gradual crystallisation of a Christian concept of a "holy land." Although not primarily concerned with the emergence in Christianity of a concept of holy places, his book naturally does touch on this subject. A "Holy Land" could scarcely have come into being had there not already been a scattering of places in the land which were reckoned to be holy. But there is still a need to consider the emergence of the idea, and the resistance to it, of a holy place.

Eusebius thought holy places were what Jews and pagans had; Christians, he thought, knew better. A formidably thorough recent study[7] has

3. M. Eliade, *Patterns in Comparative Religion*, tr. R. Sheed (London: Sheed & Ward, 1958), 367; cf. Eliade, *Cosmos and History: The Myth of the Eternal Return*, tr. W. R. Trask (1954; New York: Harper, 1959), 12.

4. Eliade, *Patterns*, 375.

5. See Jonathan Z. Smith, *To Take Place* (Chicago: University of Chicago Press, 1987), 1–23.

6. R. L. Wilken, *The Land Called Holy* (New Haven & London: Yale University Press, 1992).

7. P. W. L. Walker, *Holy City, Holy Places? Christian Attitudes to Jerusalem and the Holy Land in the Fourth Century*, Oxford Early Christian Studies (Oxford: Clarendon Press, 1990).

documented Eusebius's extreme reluctance to countenance any talk of "holy places." Moses had promised a holy land to the Jews; Jesus promised to his followers a "much greater land, truly holy and beloved of God, not located in Judaea."[8] In Eusebius's view, place had been important to Jews and pagans; a spiritual religion such as Christianity had no room for physical holy places. If there is a holy city now, it can only be the heavenly Jerusalem.[9] Eusebius could not quite keep up this theological conservatism in the face of Constantine's enthusiasm for the holiness of the holy places in Palestine which he adorned with his grand churches; indeed "more than any other early Christian thinker," Wilken writes, "Eusebius was able to adapt his thinking to the new things that happened in his day."[10] Eusebius belonged to an older Christian tradition. In its first centuries Christianity was a religion highly inhospitable to the idea of "holy places"; by the end of the fourth century it had become highly receptive. A measure of the shift in the extent to which these were accepted is furnished by the striking difference in attitude between Eusebius of Caesarea and, in the next generation, Cyril of Jerusalem. Cyril, bishop of Jerusalem in the middle decades of the century, embraced the new fashion with enthusiasm: "others merely hear," he told his catechumens; "we see and touch."[11] To him Jerusalem was a holy city not just as "a place in which God had occasionally been involved in the past: it was a place with a special quality in the present."[12]

Eusebius had good reasons for being apprehensive about a neighbouring see in his own province. Jerusalem was a minor suffragan see under his metropolitan jurisdiction; through the lavish favours of the emperor Constantine and the vast programme of building, it was beginning to look a dangerous rival which could upstage Caesarea. So Eusebius had ample grounds for denying its claims to holiness; but neither the actions of the first Christian emperor nor ecclesiastical rivalries will by themselves explain the extraordinary sea-change we can detect between him and Cyril within a generation. If Eusebius, late in life, could accommodate himself to the novelties that the emperor's religious convictions ushered into his world, many Christians of the fourth century remained reserved, remem-

8. *Dem. ev.* 3.2.10.
9. *Dem. ev.* 4.12.4; 10.8.64; cf. Walker, *Holy City*, 69.
10. *The Land*, 81. Wilken (see especially pp. 88–91 and n. 27) convincingly modifies the view put forward by Walker (pp. 108–116) that Eusebius's assent to the emperor's views was as grudging and as minimising in its intent as was his use of the emperor's vocabulary.
11. *Catech.* 13.22.
12. Walker, *Holy City*, 329.

bering that faith comes not by sight or by touch, but by hearing (Rom 10.17). Thus Gregory of Nyssa, in the later fourth century, feeling it necessary to excuse a visit to Jerusalem as necessitated by official business, explained that he had believed in all the great things that had happened there long before his visit. "So praise the Lord, you who fear Him, in whatever place you are: for no travelling around will bring you nearer to Him."[13] He had no need to see and touch. And even Jerome, as ardent a Jerusalem-dweller as any, could, on occasion, voice similar sentiments.

It was not only the holy places of Palestine over whose holiness there were mixed feelings. Because of Vigilantius's attack on the cult of relics and holy places in Palestine around 400,[14] even Jerome had to admit that the means now used to honour God were those that had until not long ago been used for honouring the gods, that martyrs were honoured in ways that had been those of idolatry.[15] Ambrose's famous translation of the relics in Milan in 386 and their subsequent cult could still arouse suspicion, and needed defence.[16] The general change of mood is reflected in Augustine's own personal evolution between the years 401 and 422. Reluctant, at first, to countenance the cult of relics, and feeling his way towards an idea of nature subject to its own laws, he allowed little room for miracles in his own times. In his later years, however, he was ready to see daily miracles wrought by the relics of Saint Stephen, recently discovered and brought to Africa, and to make use of them in his pastoral work among his congregations; and he came to accept the prevalent belief in the everyday occurrence of miracles: "the world itself is God's greatest miracle,"[17] he wrote, thus dissolving the idea, barely embryonic, of a nature subject to its own natural laws in the freedom of the divine will. And even when the notion of "holy places" gradually got a foothold in Christian devotion, resistance to taking over pagan holy places lingered: the inhibitions which led the Christians of Gaza to raze the local temple of Baal before building their church on its stones reused in its pavement took almost two centuries to overcome. The principle laid down by Gregory the Great in his famous instruction to his missionaries on the reuse of pagan English sanctuaries gave enlightened recognition to what became widespread practice.[18]

13. *Ep.* 2 (*PG* 46.1013C); cf. Eusebius, *dem. ev.* 1.6.65.
14. See my brief discussion in *The End of Ancient Christianity* (Cambridge: Cambridge University Press, 1990), 148–49.
15. *C. Vigilant.* 7 (*PL* 23.361).
16. Ps.-Jerome, *ep.* 6.11 (*PL* 30.92).
17. *Civ.* 10.12. See my *The End*, 149.
18. See my brief remarks, with references, in *The End*, 154–55.

Such were the hesitations that accompanied the emergence of the cult; but the tide had turned, and turned decisively. Not until the age of the Renaissance and the Reformation would the cult of relics and the idea of pilgrimage to holy places be once again subjected to the suspicion and disapproval they had to overcome in the fourth century.[19] The suspicion and the disapproval are hardly surprising: the cults were not only a novelty, but they cut across the grain of ideas that had been deeply embedded in the consciousness of Christians of an earlier age. We have had some fine studies of the "complicated story" of the fundamental differences and continuities between Christian and earlier, "pagan," religions;[20] what, however, still needs elucidating is the remarkable *volte-face* among Christians on this matter.

It is clear from all the evidence at our disposal that popular enthusiasm ran well ahead of informed clerical opinion on this matter. Despite the reservations of churchmen and thinkers, the cult of the holy places and pilgrimages to them caught on very rapidly.[21] It is easy to understand this in the context of the decades immediately following Constantine's victory over Licinius in 324 which brought him into control of the Eastern provinces. This inaugurated his building activities there, very soon to be followed by much-publicised devotional tourism undertaken by members of the imperial family itself. It can now hardly be open to doubt that here we have a genuine Constantinian revolution. As the most recent and most thorough critical examination of the evidence concludes, "There is no evidence at all that Jewish-Christians, or any other kind of Christians, venerated sites as sacred before the beginning of the fourth century," and that claims made for a continuous Christian or Jewish-Christian cult make sense of the evidence only on a highly questionable set of presuppositions.[22] What began in the 320s and 330s was something quite new. Constantine's building activities, and initiatives by other Christians such

19. On the debates over the letter, including those between the Magdeburg Centuriators, *IVa cent. eccles. hist.* (Basel 1560, cols. 930ff) and Baronius (*Annales*, s.a. 386) see P. Maraval, "Une querelle sur les pélérinages autour d'un texte patristique (Grégoire de Nysse, Lettre 2)," *RHPhR* 66 (1986): 131–46.

20. Especially Sabine MacCormack, "*Loca sancta*: The Organization of Sacred Topography on Late Antiquity," in *The Blessings of Pilgrimage*, ed. R. Ousterhout (Urbana: University of Illinois Press, 1990): 7–40. I owe much to this study, even though it seems to me to fall short in the particular respect I seek to correct in this paper.

21. Eusebius allows us to infer that Christian pilgrimage began very soon, even before he was writing: e.g., *dem. ev.* 1.1.2; 7.2.14 (Bethlehem); 6.18.23 (Mount of Olives); *onomast.* 74.16–18 (Gethsemane).

22. This is the conclusion of the very cogent arguments of Joan E. Taylor, *Christians and the Holy Places: The Myth of Jewish-Christian Origins* (Oxford: Clarendon Press, 1993). The quotation is from her own summary, 295.

as those of the Jewish convert, Joseph of Tiberias (reported by Epiphanius[23]), who wished to build churches in Jewish strongholds in the 330s, were part of the campaign against paganism and Judaism. Christianity would supersede and efface the existing pagan, Jewish, or Samaritan cults in places which had a biblical association. Such places could be "restored" to Christians, who were in imperial eyes their rightful owners.

Was it then simply the imperial initiative, followed almost overnight by popular enthusiasm for the cult of the holy places and for pilgrimage to them, that explains the origin of Christian holy places? That this was in large measure the case can hardly be doubted. It was certainly not a change in Christian views about places: these views seem to have been far more hostile, and remained, to say the least, ambivalent for a considerable time. When scholars have tried to explain this shift—as a few have, though only too rarely—they have usually started from Jerusalem and the other "holy places" in what later became known as "the holy land"; other holy places elsewhere are then seen as having come into being by analogy, imitation, or through influence from Jerusalem. I want to reverse this order. I shall argue that in fact what came first were new feelings associated with other holy places, notably, the burials of martyrs, which brought about the change; that it was not primarily a change of attitude to place so much as to history that was at the bottom of it; and that the attitudes towards holy places in general changed slowly, lagging behind the new cultic practices which had already begun in Jerusalem. The very rapid coalesence of the new cults with the ancient practices of venerating and visiting the burial places of the martyrs should incline us to reflect on the affinity of the two cults, or rather, the cult of two classes of holy place. Could it be that the old practice, long accepted among Christians, came to warrant the new, and suspect practice? and even, soon, to reinforce it, as the affinity between the two came to be more distinctly perceived? I want to explore an affirmative answer to these questions.

The history of place in Christianity is by no means simple. History—understood as narrative of temporal events—had been a fundamental datum of Christian belief from the start: belief in Christ necessarily comprehended, as its very basis, the acts of God, in the earthly life of the incarnate Lord, done in place and time. All the early community's eschatological hopes were founded on this historical faith. Scholarly interest in the biblical revelation led naturally to an interest in biblical places, just as it encouraged chronological awareness. Eusebius's gazetteer to the

23. *Pan.* XXX.11.9–10. On him, see Taylor, 56–57, 227–28, 276, 288–89, 293, 338–40.

Bible, the *Onomasticon*, was a complement of his chronological enquiries: as Dennis Groh has concluded in an important study, "in the *Onomasticon* Eusebius is doing spatially (and alphabetically) what he has already done chronologically in the *Chronicon* and what he will go on to do narratively in the *History* . . . . It is not a religious Palestine of pious Christians that Eusebius envisions but a Christian continuity with the biblical world expressed in contemporary Roman *space* and nomenclature. . . ."[24] Catherine Delano Smith[25] has traced a whole tradition of cartography which has its origins in his interest in mapping. This sort of interest in place and topography belongs to the realm of exegetical and historical studies— shared, as far as the shadowy information we have allows us to conjecture, by a few early scholar-travellers;[26] it does not belong to the history of Christian devotion or pilgrimage. A by-product of the scholarly tasks, this emergence of a Scriptural topography had as little to do with any Christian cult of the holy places as Eusebius's interest in the martyrs mentioned in the *Ecclesiastical history* had to do with any cult of martyrs and their relics. Both reflect a need for the construction of a spatial and temporal understanding of a Judaeo-Christian history within the spatial and temporal coordinates of the Roman world.[27] But the emergence of the idea of a "holy place," that is to say, a place as an object of devotion, of pilgrimage, one sanctified by ritual, that is a different matter altogether.

That the prevailing mood underwent a profound change in the course of the fourth century is not open to doubt. Christians could not entirely forget St Paul's warning that spaces could not be inherently holy: "The God who made the world and everything in it, being the Lord of heaven and earth, does not dwell in shrines made by man" (Acts 17.24), he had said; they themselves were the temple of the living God (2 Cor. 6.16).

24. "The *Onomasticon* of Eusebius and the Rise of Christian Palestine," *StPatr* 18 (1985): 23–31. See also T. D. Barnes, *Constantine and Eusebius* (Cambridge, Mass.: Harvard University Press, 1981), 110.

25. See especially "Geography or Christianity? Maps of the Holy Land before A.D. 1000," *JThS* n.s. 42 (1991): 143–152, and "Maps as Art *and* Science: Maps in Sixteenth Century Bibles," *Imago Mundi* 42 (1990): 65–83. The maps of the division of Judaea into tribal allotments are mentioned in the *Onomasticon*, 2.8–9.

26. On the nature of the early interest shown in Jerusalem and Palestine, see P. Maraval, *Lieux saints et pélérinages d'Orient* (Paris: Cerf, 1985), 23–28. It is clear that pilgrimage in the proper sense began only in the fourth century, though well before Constantine's building programme got under way, as is clear from the evidence of Eusebius, see above, n. 21.

27. For an exceptionally illuminating study of these, see C. Nicolet, *L'inventaire du monde* (Paris: Fayard, 1988); cf. N. Purcell, "Maps, Lists, Money, Order and Power," *JRS* 80 (1990): 178–82.

Their churches were not temples of a divinity, only gathering places for his worshippers. "As this building," Augustine said, preaching at the dedication of a church, "was made for the purpose of congregating us bodily, so that building which is ourselves, is built spiritually for God."[28] It was the community that was holy, not the church that housed it. The building had a sacredness only derivatively. "These temples of wood or stone are built so that in them the living temples of God may be congregated and gathered into one temple of God."[29] Bishops and theologians would continue to remind their readers and hearers that God is wholly everywhere all at once (*totus ubique simul*), that His majesty could not be enclosed in any building or place, that he is worshipped more suitably in our innermost hearts and minds than in any place set aside.[30] But new ways of speech were making their appearance in media which reflect more directly the instinctive habits of imagination: we have inscriptions that speak of "the house of God," "the hall of Christ," and the like; and visual imagery represented the saint in his shrine just as age-old representations showed the dead in his tomb.[31] Before long "*locus sanctus* narratives" would come to adorn churches.[32]

The gulf which separates the two kinds of discourse has been very suitably characterised in terms of a fundamental dichotomy between "locative" and "utopian" orientations in religion.[33] It would be a simplification to describe early Christianity as entirely non-locative, or "utopian," in the vocabulary of the Chicago scholar Jonathan Z. Smith; to do so would be to play down the tension between a variety of features present within the earliest Christian traditions. All the same, there is a clear shift in

28. Augustine, *sermo* 337.2. This is a frequent theme: e.g. Minucius Felix, *Oct.* 3; 32; Tertullian, *de corona*, 9.2.

29. Caesarius of Arles, *sermo* 229.2.

30. E.g., Minucius Felix, *Oct.* 32.2; Augustine, *In Ioh. ev. tr.* X.1. The notion is, of course, a commonplace of earlier apologetic: cf. e.g. *acta Iust.* Rec. B., 3 (Musurillo, 48); Justin, *dial.* 127.2; Theophilus of Antioch, *ad Autol.* II.3.

31. See MacCormack, "The Organization of Sacred Topography" on the iconography. Not all the references given on p. 15, notes 42–43, are to the point; but the Index to Diehl's *ICLV* under "domus", "aedes", "aula", referring to churches furnishes plenty of examples.

32. Cf. H. L. Kessler, "Pictorial Narrative and Church Mission in Sixth-Century Gaul," in *Pictorial Narrative in Antiquity and the Middle Ages*, ed. H. L. Kessler & M. S. Simpson (Washington, D.C.: National Gallery of Art, 1985): 75–91, at 84.

33. Jonathan Z. Smith's distinction is elaborated in several of his essays: *Map is Not Territory* (Leiden: Brill, 1978), 88–103 (esp. 101); 104–128; 172–189; For its widest bearings, see now his *Drudgery Divine* (Chicago: University of Chicago Press, 1990), 121–22. See also Rowan Williams, "Pre-Nicene Orthodoxy?" in *The Making of Orthodoxy*, ed. Rowan Williams (Cambridge: Cambridge University Press, 1989): 1–23 (especially 6, 9–10).

the fourth century towards the "locative" pole on this grid. How are we to account for it?

A good starting point is to be clear about what we mean by a "holy place." In line with most anthropologists, as well as with the author of the "locative"/"utopian" classification, we may adopt the principle that "ritual is, first and foremost, a mode of paying attention. It is a process for marking interest." It "is not an expression of or a response to 'the Sacred'; rather, something or someone is made sacred by ritual."[34] Places thus become sacred through the interest focused on them in ritual. The secret, according to Smith, of the wholesale christianisation of Roman topography from the fourth century on, is to be found in Jerusalem. For it was in Jerusalem that Christian ritual first came to sacralise a place. Here "Constantine created, for the first time, a Christian 'Holy Land,' laid palimpsest-like over the old, and interacting with it in complex ways, having for its central foci a series of imperial-dynastic churches."[35] Here alone, not in Constantinople or anywhere else, could the emperor create an urban space which would be articulated within the topography of the Scriptural narratives: "In Jerusalem, story, ritual, and place could be one."[36]

Constantine, so the argument runs, created the conditions for the sacralisation of the "holy places" by his foundation of the great memorial buildings in Palestine. Ritual processions came quickly to develop around these buildings and related sites, which brought the physical places and the narratives of the corresponding biblical events into close relation. This created a wholly new set of ritual relationships in which place and time, site and commemorated event, were closely integrated; instead of the customary "continuous reading" of the Scriptures, specific passages came to be attached to specific sites and the events associated with them: readings *apta diei et loco*,[37] as the late fourth-century pilgrim to the Holy Places would keep remarking. There you have a fully fledged "holy place." "Story and text, liturgical action, and a unique place are brought together

---

34. *To Take Place*, 103; 105. See also *Imagining Religion* (Chicago: University of Chicago Press, 1982), 54: "A sacred place is a place of clarification (a focusing lens) where men and gods had to be transparent to each other."

35. *To Take Place*, 79. Eusebius, incidentally, reveals the opposition of some conservative—probably pagan rather than "utopian"—critics: ". . . those who in the blindness of their souls are ignorant of matters divine hold the deed [of founding the church of the Holy Sepulchre] a joke and frankly ridiculous, believing that for so great a sovereign to bother himself with memorials to human corpses and tombs is unfitting and demeaning." *Or. de laud. Const.* 11.3 (trans. H. Drake).

36. *To Take Place*, 86.

37. *Pereg. Egeriae* 47.5.

in relations of equivalence . . . . What is important about this development," Smith concluded, "is that it brought about the overlaying of a
temporal system and a spatial system."[38] And once you've got one holy
place, the idea of holy places could spread, and holy places multiply.

This, we are told, is exactly what happened. The physical relationship
between place and event that could be commemorated in the appropriate
readings was, of course, unrepeatable elsewhere; but of the central importance of the Jerusalem liturgy in shaping the wider Church's worship there
is no doubt.[39] Jerusalem set the pattern for other churches; especially, it
seems, in the matter of adopting prescribed sets of readings from the
Scriptures. Specific passages came to be substituted for the older custom of
continuous readings from the Scriptures. (It deserves to be noted, however,
that the traditional *lectio continua* had often been modified, both on the
greater festivals and on the anniversaries of martyrs, by the choice of
readings more appropriate to the particular occasion; so the novelty is
not all that radical.) Jerusalem ritual thus transformed the Church's traditional practice. And, as Dom Gregory Dix powerfully argued, the new
stress on historical events bound to place and time changed the older
eschatologically oriented, ahistorical worship and non-locative religiosity
into a more profoundly place-bound piety; first in Palestine, then elsewhere.

The impetus to enhanced importance being attached to places, on this
argument, came from what was happening in and around Jerusalem. But
there are several difficulties with this argument:

(i) The spread of a Jerusalem-style lectionary, with the readings related
to Jerusalem told in the biblical stories, could certainly have produced an
enhanced sense *in other places* of the significance of places in the Holy
Land; but it is hard to see how such readings could enhance the sense of the
holiness of these *other* places, the places where the stories were being read.
Smith himself seems to be pointing to this in suggesting that the cutting of
the link between the city of Jerusalem and the events commemorated in the
readings is what made the exportation of the new practice possible: "It is
through structures of temporality, as ritualized, that the divisiveness and

38. *To Take Place*, 89, 92.
39. Since Gregory Dix's classic work, *The Shape of the Liturgy*, 2nd ed. (London:
Dacre Press, 1945) the most important on the influence of Jerusalem is Anton Baum-
stark, *Comparative Liturgy*, tr. F. L. Cross (London: Mowbray, 1958); on the lectionary,
J. A. Jungmann, *Missarum sollemnia* (Wien: Herder, 1948), 483–562; for Jerusalem,
R. Zerfass, *Die Schriftlesung im Kathedraloffizium Jerusalems*, Liturgiewiss. Quellen u.
Forsch., 48 (Münster: Aschendorff, 1968), referred to by Smith.

particularity of space are overcome."⁴⁰ The link between the narrative record and the event commemorated survived, but the link with the place of the event was broken. One would have thought this would *deprive* places of any special significance, rather than make them holy.

(ii) The argument that the new practices at Jerusalem and the emphasis they threw on spatially and temporally defined events gave a new orientation to the earlier eschatological nature of worship seems well supported by the evidence. But we must be clear as to the exact meaning of this statement. What this change may well have done was to re-orientate devotion, as Dix thought: "the idea of historical commemoration," he wrote, [was] "virtually an invention of the fourth century . . ."; and, referring to the celebration of martyrs' anniversaries, whose "birthdays," as they had been known in early days, were now their "depositions," he summed up the change thus: "the earthly, not the heavenly, event is now the object of the liturgical celebration; time and history, not eternity, have become the primary interest of the calendar."⁴¹ "Christian ritual, once brought into contact in the fourth century with the *loca sancta* of Palestine, turned from the vertical dimension of the associative to the linear dimension of the syntagmatic, to an emphasis on narrative and temporal relations."⁴² What Smith is here referring to is the growing emphasis on the historical narrative at the expense of the eschatological significance of the central events of the redemption history. Local history was combined with what Dom Gregory Dix in his classic discussion⁴³ called "the old non-historical cycle" of celebrations, that is to say, the cycle of Sundays and the great seasonal festivals.

Now this may be, indeed is, quite true; but this is not to say that earlier Christian worship had not been historical in nature, only that the eschatological significance of the commemorated events was at the focus of worship. But it was events which had always been taken to be historical—and events, as Eusebius, Melito and others had always known, spatially and temporally defined—that were celebrated on Sundays, at Easter, and the other great festivals. The change in the fourth century was not from eschatology to history, but from the eschatological meaning of the historical narratives to their topographical associations.

(iii) But the chief difficulty is the fact that the argument does not answer but rather restates our question: for to say that these sites came to be

40. *To Take Place*, 94–5.
41. Dix, *The Shape*, 28.
42. Smith, *To Take Place*, 88.
43. *The Shape*, 347.

surrounded by ritual is simply to say that they became holy. What we want to know is why, how was it possible that any place should become holy? How could the ancient objections so lose their power? To be sure, emperors had begun to build, decorate and endow grand churches for favoured bishops and their congregations. Large public spaces in the cities of the Empire now became available for the open display of Christian ritual and worship and encouraged display and ceremony;[44] but such things hardly seem enough to account for the change in Christian attitudes. Emperors usually found Christian devotional practice more resistant to their influence even than were their beliefs. The growth of ritual around sacred sites that took place in the later fourth century seems to require more explanation than the mere availability of ritual space. The dynamics of religious change are generally more complicated than is suggested by a simple story of mere betrayal of principles held earlier, or perhaps one told in terms of corruption by power, or by wealth; certainly so in the present case.

What I want to suggest is that we need to give the first importance to the "local," the cult of the martyrs, in bringing about the transformation we are concerned with; and with it, to the notion of sacred time. Christian sacred time did not emerge as a by-product of the creation of the holy places of Jerusalem and Palestine. Rather, I think, the reverse was the case: Christian sacred space and topography were the product of an already fully-fledged sense of Christian sacred time. The great contribution of the fourth century was to intensify a long established system of Christian sacred time; and one of the consequences—very indirectly—was the emergence of holy places and of a sacred Christian topography. I will now sketch how I think this came about.

The first stage was what Dom Gregory Dix called the wholesale "sanctification of time." I have argued elsewhere[45] that the new conditions of a Christianity favoured by emperors, fashionable, prestigious and likely to confer worldly advantage, required a huge spiritual adjustment from its adherents. They needed to be able to see themselves as the true descendants of the persecuted Church and the rightful heirs of the martyrs; and it was just this that had become so difficult. Among the many expressions of this

44. This has been stressed especially for the development of the stational liturgies in Jerusalem, Rome and Constantinople by J. F. Baldovin, *The Urban Character of Christian Worship: The Origins, Development and Meaning of Stational Liturgy*, OrChrAn 228 (Rome: Pont. Institutum Studiorum Orientalium, 1987). E.g. "The new factor in the fourth century . . . was the freedom that Christians now had to worship in a truly public fashion." (265).
45. See *The End*. The next paragraph is in part borrowed from pp. 90–95.

need I here quote only one, one of the earliest, written on the morrow of the revolution that had transformed, almost overnight, the persecuted Church into a triumphant, and soon to be dominant, élite:

> We, although not held worthy to have struggled [*agonizasthai*] unto death and to have shed our blood for God, yet, being the sons of those who have suffered thus and distinguished [*semnunomenoi*] by our fathers' virtues, pray for mercy through them.[46]

To bridge this generation gap, Eusebius and his contemporaries and successors had to convince themselves that, essentially, nothing had changed and that their Church was still the Church of the martyrs. No radical break could be allowed to divide the triumphant Church of the fourth and later centuries from its persecuted predecessor. The past had to be kept alive in the Church's mind, and not only alive, but renewed in the novel conditions of its existence. And it was the cult of the martyrs that more than anything else enabled them to bridge this hiatus. Through this means they were able to annex their lost past; they could affirm the identity of their Church with the Church of the martyrs. In their presence, they could experience the exultation of the martyr:

> No oppressor's sword has been drawn against us; we have free access to God's altars; no savage enemy lies in wait for us . . . no torturer has attacked us . . . no blood is shed now, no persecutor pursues us; yet we are filled with the joy of triumph . . . [47]

—this is how at the end of the fourth century a bishop in the remote North of Gaul could lead his congregation in welcoming the relics of martyrs brought from Italy. The past was reclaimed; the gulf between it and the present abolished.

The way to this "sanctification of time" was neither short nor simple. The new importance of the martyrs was crucial. It is hardly necessary to document here the cult of the martyrs, its ubiquity and the huge momentum given it in the fourth century. Christian worship had always had a temporal dimension. It always gave central significance to the past: in the first place the biblical past, in the second place the past of the persecuted Church. The events of the Lord's incarnation, earthly life, death and resurrection had been central in the development of the annual cycle of worship from the earliest times to which Christian worship can be traced. But the fourth century experienced a powerful, new need for a sense of its continu-

46. Eusebius, *comm. in Ps.* 78.11 (*PG* 23.949A).
47. Victricius of Rouen, *De laude sanct.* 1.

ity with the persecuted Church. This is what is dramatically displayed in the swamping of the liturgical calendar with martyrs' festivals and the development of their liturgy.

Thus Christians of the post-Constantinian era defined their identity, their sense of being the heirs of their persecuted ancestors, in historical terms. But this indirectly contributed to giving place a new importance as well as to historical time. Place was irretrievably involved in celebrating a martyr's "birthday" or "deposition." The cult of the martyrs retained much of the "domestic character of primitive Christian worship."[48] In its origins it had been in the nature of a private, family commemoration; and even when it had begun, before the middle of the fourth century, to spread from the martyr's own church to other churches, the martyr always retained his link with his own church. The celebration of a martyr commemorated a person in a local event, the martyr dying *here*, in his witness to the Lord. In that commemoration Jesus was honoured as the Lord "not only of universal history but of homely local history as well."[49]

The veneration of martyrs thus served to assure the Christians of a local church of its continuity with its own heroic, persecuted, past, and the universal Church of its continuity with the age of the martyrs. In meeting this huge need of fourth-century Christians, however, it also gave a new importance to place. And two further elaborations of the cult served only to enhance and extend this new sanctification of places: the veneration of martyrs' relics, and the integration of this with the normal worship of urban communities in their churches. The commemoration of the martyr had been tied, originally, to a physical place, that of the burial; and the annual celebration of the anniversary, in however simple or intimate a manner, was a place-bound ritual. In this sense the tomb could always count as a "holy place." Like the tomb, relics linked the martyr's commemoration to physical places; but they made possible the multiplication of such places, liberating the possible holiness of places from the immovability of the tomb. The annual walk to the cemetery and the commemoration there would be replaced by a network of urban churches and the regular cycle of their liturgy. The presence of relics turned the churches into "holy places" housing the saint, in a sense they could not be while they housed only the worshipping congregation. A network of "holy places" thus came into being, in which suburban burials, urban churches, and the more remote destinations of pilgrimage came to define a whole sacred topography of the Roman, and now also Christian, world. Places became

48. Dix, *The Shape*, 348.
49. Ibid., 333.

accepted as sacred through their association with God's action made visible in the world, either in His saving work in the land of Palestine, or through the presence, anywhere, of those who bore their witness to Him. The sacredness of space was a reflex, a projection on the ground, of the sacredness of time. A new sacred topography came gradually to organise the Christian perception of space and to overlay the old, pre-Christian meanings.

Christian holy places thus stood in sharp contrast with pagan places redolent of their "fearful dread."[50] "Originally the [pagan] holiness had been impersonal and inherent in the place, in nature";[51] and, we are told, "in pagan Greek the word 'holy' applied to places, but not to people," even though "canny men" would often make use of "uncanny places."[52] In this sense, Christianity was—and, perhaps, is, or ought to be—deeply hostile to allowing any place to become holy.

Christianity, when it finally endowed itself with holy places, did so almost inadvertently, certainly indirectly, as a consequence of identifying itself with a historical past. A scheme of sacred time had long been an essential part of Christian religiosity, faith and worship. It became very much more elaborate, and its hold on Christian minds much more thorough, in the course of the fourth and fifth centuries, for reasons that the conditions of post-Constantinian Christianity allow us to comprehend. A sense of sacred space, and of a sacred Christian topography, was, however, a late arrival on the Christian scene, and one in large measure produced by the enhanced sense of the past, and the need to experience it as present. Places became sacred as the past became localised in the present. It was always the past that really mattered, and it was the impact of past human action that gave places their significance: "You are here to kneel where prayer has been valid."

R. A. Markus is Professor Emeritus of History at the University of Nottingham

50. *religio . . . dira loci*: Virgil, *Aen.* 8.347–54.

51. MacCormack, "The organization of sacred topography", 10. For a sophisticated account of the passage from pagan places of healing (especially at springs) to healing by Christian saints and, eventually, by their relics, see now Aline Rousselle, *Croire et guérir* (Paris: Fayard, 1990).

52. R. Lane Fox, *Pagans and Christians* (Harmonsdworth: Viking, 1986), 253, 204–05. Cf. for instance, J. Helgeland, "Time and Space: Christian and Roman," *ANRW* 2.23.2 (1980): 1285–1305: "As in prophetic and Christian religion the leitmotif was time, so in Roman religion it was space . . . " Somewhat overestimating the speed of the process, however, he goes on to add: "The ink of the New Testament scarcely dried before the shift from time to space had started" (1292).

GROVER A. ZINN, JR.

Exegesis and Spirituality
in the Writings of Gregory the Great

As I proceeded to fashion this essay on exegesis and spirituality in the writings of Gregory the Great, I asked myself from time to time if there might be an image that would suggest the various aspects of this project in a kind of concentrated visualization. The answer came to me one evening in terms of jewels and their settings. The jewels are the numerous passages in Gregory's exegetical writings that present his teaching about the complex set of ideas and disciplines called "mysticism" by modern writers and given the name "contemplative life" by Gregory. The settings in this image are the exegetical contexts and the exegetical processes in which the passages, the jewels, have their original existence and in which they exhibit their full power and insight.

These passages of spiritual teaching that I have imaged as jewels—and I think of such passages as Gregory's analysis of the active and contemplative lives in *Homilies on Ezekiel* 2.2[1] or his consideration of contemplation in book 5 of the *Moralia*[2]—offer examples of carefully crafted teaching on the life of asceticism and prayer. In these passages Gregory also develops his teaching on the higher states of consciousness, including the immediate experience of divine Being, of God—an experience usually expressed by Gregory through the image of a glimpse of the "unbounded light [lumen incircumscriptum]" that is God.[3]

In some notable instances these passages can quite accurately be described as brief treatises on aspects of the contemplative quest. However, simply taking these as "brief treatises" emphasizes a characteristic that may lead one to ignore that they are exegesis as well—or rather that they are exegesis first of all. Indeed, to take an extreme example of this attitude, when Cuthbert Butler, in his book *Western Mysticism*, set out to construct a presentation of Gregory's teaching on the mystical life, he seems to have been only too willing to ignore the fact that he was dealing with works that were first of all works of scriptural exegesis.[4] This becomes very clear from the way in which he presented the pertinent Gregorian texts for his readers. Although he noted that Gregory's teaching is *"embedded* [emphasis mine] in his principal writings,"[5] he never noted that the writings were exegetical. Moreover, in the extracts from Gregorian writings that are used to supply the supporting evidence for his analysis, Butler either suppresses the biblical passages actually mentioned by Gregory or fails to include in his translation passages that draw on or refer to biblical texts, events, or persons.[6] As Susan Schreiner has noted, at one point Butler even declared that the *Moralia* should be read "without any attention to the constant allegorizing."[7] At the very least, this is a rather amazing determination on the part of a scholar to ignore the genre of a writing while resolutely mining its contents in a selective manner for passages that are useful in presenting Gregory's mystical teaching.

Butler's work is an example, perhaps an extreme one, of what I would call the temptation to remove the jewels from their settings. In his analysis we have the individual passages with sparkling insights, moving descriptions, and persuasive presentations of the mystic's quest. But we do not have the setting that provided the matrix for these comments, nor do we have the full interplay of Gregory's thought with the biblical text and with allusions to biblical passages as well.

The medieval tradition had its own way of removing the jewels from their settings, for Gregory's works, especially the *Moralia*, were soon the object of extraction and condensation. In this case the jewels that were removed were the interpretations of individual verses of Scripture. Paterius's work rearranging the comments in the *Moralia* according to biblical books may have made the comments on specific verses more accessible, but it dismembered the body of Gregory's text in order to make the parts, the fragments, more accessible in a new ordering, a new setting if you will.[8] Bede did the same with his extraction of Gregory's comments on the Song of Songs for book 6 of his own commentary on the

Song;[9] so did William of Saint-Thierry when he formed a brief commentary on the Song out of Gregory's comments.[10] But in regard to William's collection of extracts, this must be said: in at least one instance—namely, his extract from the *Moralia* that is keyed to the verse "I sleep but my heart is awake" (Song of Songs 5.2)—William includes enough of the text to reproduce the exegetical process that leads up to Gregory's use of and comment on this verse.[11] William was, at least at this point, willing to keep part of the setting, along with the jewel.

In pursuing the question of the relationship of the setting and the jewels in Gregory's exegesis and spiritual teaching, I would like to begin with a brief examination of the images that Gregory uses to describe either biblical interpretation or the biblical text itself. In doing this, I think we will find that these images convey something about Gregory's perception of the relationship of text, interpretation, and interpreter. Following this, a consideration of several examples of Gregory's exegesis provides the opportunity to see if there are techniques of interpretation that allow him to "embody," as it were, in his practice the metaphors he uses to describe Scripture and its interpretation.

At several points in writings associated with biblical exegesis, Gregory the Great uses striking metaphors to describe either the biblical text itself or the process of interpreting that text. The letter to Leander of Seville that Gregory prefaced to the *Moralia in Job* is particularly rich in metaphorical references to both text and interpretation. The process of exegesis itself is described by means of three different metaphors: the meandering of a river, the serving of a meal, and the construction of a building.[12] In the opening paragraphs of the surviving short fragment of Gregory's commentary on the Song of Songs, there is an arresting statement that describes scriptural allegory as a "kind of machine [quandam machinam]" that lifts up to God the soul that is now in this life placed at a distance from Him.[13] As Ann Matter has noted, the paragraphs in the commentary that follow this statement offer the longest theoretical consideration of allegory in the early Middle Ages.[14] It does seem to me to be of more than passing interest that this lengthy consideration is introduced by a metaphor presenting a biblical sense as a "machine." Somewhat later in the same commentary Gregory likens Scripture itself to a mountain,[15] while in the letter to Leander, Scripture is compared to a river that is both shallow and deep, enabling the lamb to walk and the elephant to bathe.[16]

Each of these instances serves as an eloquent reminder to us, his readers, that Gregory thought about Scripture and its interpretation in light of some specific visual images. The images tend generally to emphasize the dynamic quality of the exegetical task, the multiple levels of interpretation accessible in the text, and, in the case of the machine of allegory, the possibilities of transformation of the interpreter and/or the reader through interaction with the text.

Of the descriptive phrases mentioned above, three have to do with the behavior of the exegete in relation to Scripture: the meandering river, the serving of a meal, and the construction of a building. The first thing I would observe about these is that they are all processes; they have a dynamic quality reflected quite clearly in the mention of flowing, of providing, of building; they are, as it were, images that suggest in various ways that the interpreter is one who has the task of supplying a need or furnishing something that is not only informative but useful and even delightful for the hearer or reader.

If we look more closely at the images of the meandering river and the serving of food, the descriptive phrases will be seen to focus attention much more directly on the need or needs of the readers and hearers or on the ongoing process of interpretation than on the specific way or ways in which meaning is to be extracted from the text itself. These descriptions contain almost nothing that helps us understand the technical aspects of the way in which Gregory expected exegesis to take place or the resources that the interpreter should draw upon in his effort.

In offering a meandering river as a model, Gregory singles out how rivers may overflow their banks and fill low-lying areas and then, as he says, "return to their bed and continue the course of their flow."[17] This kind of natural behavior, Gregory notes, ought to serve as an example for the interpreter, who will take every reasonable opportunity to divert the course of his interpretation, as it were, and provide useful interpretation that will fill a need—a low-lying or empty place, according to the river comparison—in the lives of his readers or listeners. Although the river does wander about, so to speak, it deviates from its course only for a purpose.

In likening the exegetical task to serving what I think of as a kind of buffet luncheon,[18] Gregory tells us that the host (the interpreter of the text) should make it his goal to provide a meal with a delightful dish for everyone, although he should not expect everyone to like every dish. The object is to provide something to please each palate. This strongly suggests a Gregorian perception that there are not only various needs to be met by the exegete, but also varieties of spiritual tastes and diets. This being the case, the interpreter is well advised to have a keen eye not only for his audience but also for the differing spiritual palates of individuals who come from a wide range of social and religious backgrounds and may well vary greatly in their vocations.

The third image in the *Letter to Leander* is the well-known figure that likens the three senses of Scripture to the construction of a building.[19] The historical or literal interpretation is likened to laying down the foundation for the structure. What Gregory calls the typical or allegorical interpretation erects the walls of the edifice. Finally, the tropological or moral interpretation provides color—a fitting appearance—for the building. This, like the other two images already examined, is, I suggest, an image of a dynamic process. The process is one of creating a "construct," if you will. The "construct" is the result of a process of interpreting a sacred text for the edification of Gregory's audience of listeners and readers. As Gregory tells us, he will labor in the fields of the various modes (history, allegory, tropology) to varying extents, as the case may require. The purpose is to produce an effective construct.

As one inspects the food served up at the exegetical banquet, one may come to wonder why some of the dishes are there. Or to put it differently: One of the aspects of the *Moralia* that makes it simultaneously rich and frustrating is the apparent profusion of biblical texts throughout the work. At the same time that Gregory is giving an interpretation of the Book of Job, he continually turns to texts from other biblical books and offers additional interpretations of them. This profusion of texts was, of course, something that made the *Moralia* such a wonderful source for later medieval digests and compendia of exegesis. One could, as Paterius and others did, construct commentaries on the Bible or form other kinds of compendia from materials carved out of the text of the *Moralia*.[20]

In addition, one could also produce handbooks of moral guidance by extracting relevant passages and ordering them topically.[21]

Although these compendia of interpretation and handbooks of moral guidance were useful, they also violated the integrity of Gregory's text and his exegetical project. For these diverse biblical texts that seem to be strewn, with their accompanying exegesis, throughout the *Moralia* were, for Gregory, part and parcel of the interpretation of the Book of Job. They may appear at first glance to be incidental to the major undertaking, the interpretation of Job, and somewhat peripheral to the so-called treatises on contemplation, asceticism, and other topics that spring up repeatedly in the *Moralia* and Gregory's sermons, but they are nonetheless part of the machinery that makes the exegesis move forward. Indeed, I would suggest that they are a controlling element in shaping Gregory's exegesis not only in the *Moralia* but also in other texts, such as the *Homilies on Ezekiel*. Without the "settings," the "jewels" have a far different appearance.

Gregory's comments about the request that initiated the *Moralia* will help us understand his motivation and purpose for including these additional citations from Scripture.[22] Gregory notes that when the brothers who had accompanied him on his official mission to Constantinople asked him to interpret Job with the allegorical sense directed toward the moral significance, they asked a second thing of him as well: that each interpretation be supported by additional scriptural citations, which Gregory calls "testimonies," and that when necessary these testimonies be given a further interpretation. Thus, from this request sprang the proliferation of biblical texts within Gregory's interpretation. And from this proliferation of texts—and Gregory's particular way of using these texts—comes the motive power of the flowing stream and the varied dishes from the productive kitchen. For the diversions and developments in Gregory's exegesis are sparked and also regulated by the testimonies summoned up in connection with spiritual exegesis.

If we turn to Gregory's exegesis, there are any number of instances in which we can see the selection, control, support, and shaping of interpretations through the use of verses from biblical books other than the Book of Job. The testimonies provide for an opening up of the text, an exploration of the multiple possibilities for meaning—but it is an exploration controlled by the broader connections to be found in the text itself.

My first example is drawn from book 23 of the *Moralia*.[23] Gregory is commenting on verse 20 of chapter 33 of Job: "For that soul's bread and food, which previously had been desirable, now became abominable to him in his life." Gregory's first move is to give a generalized reinterpretation of the text: Whatever satisfied the soul earlier is now turned into bitterness. The "whatever" remains undefined, however, and Gregory proceeds to define it by giving a set of meanings for the word *bread* in sacred Scripture. He finds six meanings: *bread* may refer to the Lord himself, spiritual grace, instruction in divine doctrine, the preaching of heretics, sustenance for the present life, and the pleasure of human delight. Each possible deeper meaning for *bread* is then supported by one or more biblical citations that receive further interpretation if needed. Having thus suggested a rather broad array of options for defining and diverting the discourse in a particular way, Gregory chooses one that fits with the deeper meaning he has discerned in the several previous verses. What Elihu means by *bread*, according to Gregory, is the delight of the present life. This then directs Gregory's own discourse back to the topic of the temptations and distresses of life—even in times of seeming peace and quiet—and the fear and loss of joy that can result. Indeed, this passage takes up the middle term of the tripartite schema of conversion–temptation–death that Carole Straw has so eloquently presented in her contribution to this volume.

In this particular instance, Gregory has made available several possibilities for moral allegory and has presented his listeners/readers with some supporting "evidence" for each possible interpretation. From the range of options thus set forth (a banquet, perhaps?), he has picked one. And it is the one that most appropriately serves his ongoing narrative of the spiritual life at this point in the commentary. While it is possible to look at verses and their interpretation as isolated, single units of meaning, that is not how Gregory proceeded in this case; both the base text and Gregory's allegorical narrative/interpretation moved within a wider framework. This framework was developed and supported on the symbolic, spiritual level by the interlocking network of citations from Job and the other books of Scripture. The testimonies helped define the banks that held the discourse along the riverbed; they moved the flow into the low-lying meadows of useful diversions, and they nudged it back to the main channel so that Gregory (and the reader and the text) could move on to the next topic.

My second example is a passage that is central to Gregory's spiritual teaching, for it represents the first full exploration in the *Moralia* of the symbolic meaning of sleep, dreams, and visions in the spiritual interpretation of the Book of Job.[24] Gregory is commenting on Job 4.13, "When sleep usually seizes a person." This verse, along with others that mention sleep and dreams or visions, provides a locus for discussing Gregory's views on what we may call the interiorization of consciousness and the dialectic between the outer and inner worlds of consciousness in the spiritual quest.[25]

Job 4.13 represents the first appearance in the Latin (Vulgate) text of Job of the word *sopor* (sleep). This is the word for the sleep that comes to Adam in Paradise when God forms Eve from his side (see Gen. 2.21). Gregory takes this occasion as the opportunity to give three deeper meanings associated with the word *sleep:* the death of the body (*mors carnis;* supported with a testimony from 1 Thess. 4.13–14); negligent listlessness (*torpor neglegentiae;* supported with two testimonies, Rom. 13.11 and 1 Cor. 15.34); and "a time of peaceful rest in life when earthly desires have been trampled underfoot [calcatis terrenis desideriis quies vitae]" (supported by two testimonies also: Song of Songs 5.2, "I sleep and my heart wakes," and Gen. 28.11–13, from the account of Jacob's sleep and dream at Bethel). The Genesis account allows Gregory to draw upon Jacob's stone "pillow," his dream, and the ladder from heaven to earth.

With the Song of Songs citation Gregory introduces an extended discussion of the figurative meaning of *sleep* for the spiritual life. As Gregory explains, interpreted in this sense, it means "suppressing the clanging noise of the craving for temporal things [se ab strepitu temporalis concupiscentiae comprimit]" while remaining inwardly "awake" for things of the spirit. After discussing the statement in Gen. 3.5 that in Paradise the eyes of Adam and Eve were opened only after eating the forbidden fruit of the tree of knowledge, Gregory turns to consider the idea of sleep as a withdrawal of conscious attention from external noise and distraction in order to focus intently and in a lively way on inward experiences that open to the world of spirit and the divine. In closing his discussion of this reforming and refocusing of consciousness, he alludes again to Song of Songs 5.2: "So [the mind] abandons the clanging noise of earthly actions [terrenarum actionum strepitum deserit], and, intent on virtues through the pursuit of a time of quiet [per quietis studium], it sleeps and remains awake [vigilans dormit]." Gregory then continues, "For the mind is not led to contemplation of inward things unless it is carefully separated from those things that entangle it outwardly [quae exterius implicant]." The succinct sentence from the Song of Songs has enabled Gregory to condense this insight concerning detachment and interiorization of consciousness into a few words from the biblical text, and to use that text as a defining "peg" for his spiritual interpretation of sleep: "I sleep and my heart is awake."

If we reflect on these examples and others that could be offered, it becomes clear that Gregory's allegorical narratives are skillfully executed constructs. Some of the linkages in these constructs may well be obscure, and they may *seem* contrived, but nonetheless they are there. Gregory's elucidation of the meaning of Job is always worked out in a dialogue, if you will, with other texts of Scripture. These other texts, the testimonies, serve a vital purpose of shaping, directing, and/or confirming Gregory's perception of the deeper meaning of the text of Job. While Gregory's numerous "units" of exegesis can be excised from his work and considered in isolation, that act of dismemberment disrupts the "flow" of the river of interpretation and the judicious filling of the voids where instruction is so clearly needed. In terms of his spiritual teaching, which has been my ultimate point of reference in exploring Gregory's exegesis in this essay, Gregory has created a web of interpretation, so to speak, that supports a recurring analysis of particular biblical words, phrases, and images that become symbolic keys providing an entry into reflection on the experiences of spiritual discipline in its manifold aspects.

In conclusion, I shall return to Gregory's prologue to the surviving fragment of his commentary on the Song of Songs and to his characterization there of allegory as a "machine" *(machina)* that lifts the soul nearer to God.[26] How shall we understand this machine? Perhaps a brief glance at the other appearances of the word *machina* in Gregory's writings will provide a field of reference. In the *Moralia* Gregory speaks of the "machine of compunction" and of the power of love as a machine that also lifts one up to God.[27] Finally, in the course of one of the central discussions of the contemplative life, Gregory introduces the idea that contemplation itself is a kind of machine that lifts the mind up to behold exalted and spiritual things—only to have the mind struck with terror by what it sees and what it knows about itself.[28] These various uses suggest that we would do well to ask if allegory, too, is an experience that produces an effect, as well as a technique that results in the knowledge of spiritual things.

Is allegory only a literary fact—the evocation, or the perception, of spiritual truths in a text that speaks of earthly things? It is easy to read Gregory's construction metaphor for the three senses of Scripture in precisely that way: Allegory is the interpretive sense that builds up the knowledge of the faith, the derivative knowledge of God. But the image of the *machina* of allegory suggests something a bit different. It raises the question of whether allegory, as a machine, is an experience analogous to the experience of compunction, the pain or goad that launches a person on a spiritual itinerary. Does the machine of allegory, like the machine of compunction or the machine of love, have the power to move one, to propel one forward on the path of the spiritual quest?

Analyzing a portion of Gregory's sermon 25 on the Gospels suggests that allegory can have this propelling quality.[29] That sermon takes as its text the narrative of Mary Magdalene's return to the tomb and her meeting with the risen Jesus in the garden as recorded in John 20.11–18. Gregory begins the sermon by characterizing Mary Magdalene as a person who has turned from being immersed in sensual pleasures and love of the world to being now ardent in her love of the Lord. Through his interpretation of the Magdalene's discovery of the empty tomb, her report to the disciples John and Peter, and her anguished vigil and search for Jesus at the tomb after the others depart, Gregory creates a vivid image of passionate, even desperate, longing. Indeed, Gregory has added a new element to the interpretation of Mary's distress and her weeping. Her tears are not only tears of sorrow but also, for Gregory, the tears of a woman "inflamed with the fire of her love," for she "burned with desire for Him whom she believed had been taken away."[30]

Having presented Mary as a lover—indeed as one who loves Jesus ardently—Gregory now takes up the task of defining that love. To do so he turns to the Song of Songs. The focus shifts from history to allegory, from the narrative of the Magdalene's experience to the allegorical/spiritual meaning of the narrative of the bride's search for her beloved in Song of Songs 3.1–5: "Upon my bed during the night I sought him whom my soul loves. I sought him and did not find him" (3.1). The link between history and allegory lies in the experience of loss/absence/search. Gregory's interpretation of the bride uses the text from the Song to define, to furnish a "peg," to fix the meaning of the Magdalene's love in a universal framework and perspective. The bride's search, interpreted allegorically, enlarges the image of love sketched historically in the Gospel and relates it to the spiritual quest. The text concerning the bride does more than provide the definition of Mary Magdalene's loving and searching: In turn the figure of the Magdalene provides a powerful example, drawn from sacred Scripture, of the realization in a human life of the spiritual journey exemplified by the symbolism of the bride's longing, searching, and finding.

Here history, allegory, and experience intersect to lift the reader to a new awareness—and experience—of the impassioned quest of the lover who seeks the one who is present yet absent. The Gospel text and the Song of Songs text are brought together in such a way that each serves to heighten the effect of the other. The Song is used to define the Magdalene's love; the figure of the Magdalene expresses, in a biblical narrative of deep personal experience sensitively and profoundly interpreted by Gregory, what might well remain an abstract notion of the spiritual quest if left as only a symbolic interpretation of the bride.[31]

Thus, we see here the interaction of multiple levels of experience and interpretation as Gregory interweaves historical narrative, an exemplary life, and the machine of allegory to produce a new awareness of reality and the spiritual quest.

NOTES

1. *Hom.Ez.* 2.2.7–15 (*CCSL* 142:22–236).
2. *Mor.* 5.29.51–66 (*CCSL* 143:253–66).
3. See, for example, *Hom.Ez.* 2.2.12 and 14 (*CCSL* 142:233.288–89, 234.320); also, *Mor.* 6.37.59 (*CCSL* 143:329.151); 23.21.42 (*CCSL* 143B: 1176.73–74).
4. Butler, *Western Mysticism*, 65–92, where Gregory's views on contemplation are presented.

5. Ibid., 65–66.

6. Ibid., 69–71, for Butler's condensation of *Hom.Ez.* 2.5.8–11. In Butler's translated version all biblical references and allegory have been stripped away. For this passage Butler does note that he is presenting Gregory's teaching "positively, detached as far as may be from the references to the Temple, and in a contracted form" (69). In another instance, however, Butler presents an extended passage (*Hom.Ez.* 2.2.12–14) without indicating that he has left anything out (66–67). Butler has, in fact, omitted the text of Isa. 6.1 that Gregory quotes and then interprets in connection with his exegesis of the verse from Ezekiel.

7. Susan Schreiner, " 'Where Shall Wisdom be Found?': Gregory's Interpretation of Job," *American Benedictine Review* 39 (1988): 321–42, especially 322n.4 (quotation from Butler).

8. Paterius, *Liber testimoniorum* (PL 79:683–916). It is now recognized that only the text from Genesis through the Song of Songs was produced by Paterius. Two other medieval collections of extracts from the *Moralia* that deserve mention are Taio, *Sententiarum libri V* (PL 80:727–990); and Lathcen, *Egloga de Moralia in Iob* (CCSL 145).

9. Bede, *In Cantica canticorum* 6 (CCSL 119B:359–75). On Bede's exegesis of the Song, see Matter, *Voice.*

10. William of Saint-Thierry, *Excerpta ex libris S. Gregorii Papae super Cantica canticorum* (PL 180:441–74).

11. Ibid., 463A. The comment on the verse from the Song is made up of two extracts from *Mor.* 5.31.54, a passage analyzed later in this essay.

12. *Ad Leandrum* (CCSL 143:1–7). The reference to Scripture as a river is in *Ad Leandrum* 2, to Scripture as a meal and as a building, in 3 (all at *CCSL* 143:4).

13. "Allegoria enim animae longe a deo positae quasi quandam machinam facit, ut per illam leuetur ad deum" (*Cant.* 2; *CCSL* 144:3. 14–15).

14. Matter, *Voice,* 94.

15. "Scriptura enim sacra mons quidam est, de quo in nostris cordibus ad intelligendum dominus venit" (*Cant.* 5; *CCSL* 144:7. 93–94).

16. *Ad Leandrum* 4 (*CCSL* 143:6). There are other comparisons elsewhere; for example, see *Hom.Ez..* 2.1.14 and 2.2.7 (*CCSL* 142:219, 229), where Scripture is likened to a measuring rod *(calamus).*

17. *Ad Leandrum* 2 (*CCSL* 143:4.97–100).

18. Ibid., 3 (*CCSL* 143:4).

19. Ibid.

20. See note 8, above.

21. A work made up of extracts from the *Moralia* grouped under topics concerning morality (e.g., "sin," "vices," "punishment of the reprobate," "penitence," "virtues," and "the just") is the *Remediarium conversorum* of Peter of Waltham. See Peter of Waltham, *Remediarium Conversorum: A Synthesis in Latin of Moralia in Job by Gregory the Great*, ed. Joseph Gildea (Villanova, Pa., 1984). The text is translated: *Source Book of Self-discipline: A Synthesis of Moralia in Job by Gregory the Great: A Translation of Peter of Waltham's Remediarium Conversorum*, trans. Joseph Gildea (New York, 1991).

22. *Ad Leandrum* 1 (*CCSL* 143:2).

23. *Mor.* 23.25.49–26.52 (*CCSL* 143B.1181–86).

24. *Mor.* 5.31.54–32.56 (*CCSL* 143.255–59).

25. The most complete study of Gregory's thought and contemplative teaching is Dagens, *Grégoire*. See also P. Aubin, "Intériorité et extériorité dans les *Moralia in Job* de saint Grégoire le Grand," *RechSR* 62 (1974): 117–66. For Gregory's use of pairs of opposites, see Jean Leclercq, *The Love of Learning and the Desire for God*, trans. Catharine Misrahi (rev. ed.; New York, 1984), 27–36; and Straw, *Gregory*, 17–24 and 47–65.

26. See note 13, above. After this definition of allegory, Gregory comments that "by means of earthly words, it [the soul] is separated from earthly things [per terrena verba separatur a terra]."

27. For the "machine of compunction," see *Mor.* 1.34.48 (*CCSL* 143: 50.12–15): "Cum enim mens per quamdam compunctionis machinam ad alta sustollitur, omne quod ei de se ipsa, sub se ipsa est, diiudicando certius contemplatur." For the idea of the power of love as a kind of machine of the mind, see *Mor.* 6.37.58 .(*CCSL* 143:328.118–19): "Machina quippe mentis est vis amoris quae hanc dum a mundo extrahit in alta sustollit."

28. *Mor.* 5.31.55 (*CCSL* 143:258.80–82): "Sed humanus animus quadam suae contemplationis machina sublevatus, quo super se altiora conspicit, eo in semetipso terribilius contremiscit."

29. *Hom.Ev.* 2.25 (*PL* 76:1188–96).

30. Ibid., 25.1 (*PL* 76:1189B–C).

31. Some of the foregoing interpretation of the Magdalene is drawn from Grover A. Zinn, Jr., "Texts within Texts: The Song of Songs in the Exegesis of Gregory the Great and Hugh of St. Victor," *Studia patristica* 25 (1993): 209–15. I also have in preparation a longer study of the use of Song of Songs texts in the writings of Gregory the Great.

The Origins of Monasticism

JAMES E. GOEHRING

In an article published twenty-five years ago on "The Quest for the 'Origins' of Religion," Mircea Eliade began by citing the French proverb "Il n'y a que les détails qui comptent" (Only the details are really important). He used the proverb to observe that "there are instances in the history of culture when details are unexpectedly illuminating."[1] When one narrows the focus from the history of culture to the history of early Christian monasticism, the validity of Eliade's observation remains. Consideration of the details has, in fact, proven to be not only illuminating, but essential to a proper understanding of the subject; for when the details are forgotten or ignored, the origins and development of Christian monasticism are traced down oversimplified and erroneous paths.

The views of Antony as the first monk and of Egypt as the source from which his innovation and its developments spread throughout the rest of Christendom, views still often found in basic accounts of Christian history,[2] are prime examples of such oversimplified and erroneous conclusions. Clean and simple as this "big bang" theory of monastic origins is, the details fail to support it. It is dependent on the selective use of mainstream Greek and Latin sources and as such betrays its foundation in and support of a western "orthodox" view of history. When the net is cast more widely and the sources read more carefully, the nearsightedness of the theory becomes apparent. The *Life of Antony* itself mentions his predecessors.[3] Syriac scholars have established the independent origin and development of monasticism in the Syrian province,[4] and recent evidence has called the "orthodox" origin of certain monastic developments into question.[5]

The tendency towards theoretical oversimplification is controlled by remembering the importance of the details. What follows is neither an exhaustive treatment of early Christian monasticism nor yet another quest for its "origins,"[6] but rather an introductory tour through the details of selected sources. It is a tour designed both to reveal the diversity in the "origins and development" of early Christian monasticism and to underscore the impact of western historiography on its interpretation.

I. The Evidence of Eusebius

Eusebius of Caesarea, in Book 2 of his *Ecclesiastical History*, offers an example of the perfect union of the proclamation of the gospel with the undertaking of an ascetic life. He reports that when Mark preached the gospel in Egypt,[7] "the number of men and women who were there converted at the first attempt was so great, and their asceticism was so extraordinarily philosophic, that Philo thought it right to describe their conduct and assemblies and meals and all the rest of their manner of life."[8] The account of the Therapeutae, a Jewish ascetic community situated above Lake Mareotis in Egypt, which follows, is drawn directly from Philo Judaeus' *On the Contemplative Life*.[9] Eusebius' identification of this Jewish community as Christian is clearly in error, though his belief that they were Christian betrays his view of the immediacy of the ascetic demand in the Christian call. The evidence should neither be used to support Eusebius' knowledge of "organized monastic communities in Palestine" before 300 CE,[10] nor to argue, since he elsewhere mentions no known Christian communities, that such communities did not yet exist.[11] Rather, Christian belief and ascetic practice were so closely connected in Eusebius' theology[12] that the identification of the Therapeutae as Christian seemed only natural to him. The naturalness of the equation is apparent in the fact that some scholars have chosen to discount the Philonic authorship of *De vita contemplativa* rather than the Christian status of the Therapeutae.[13]

Eusebius' placing of this material near the beginning of his history establishes an origin for the ascetic life very early in the spread of the gospel. The demand of an ascetic life lived in separation from the world is, through this account, made part of the earliest impulse of Christian existence and interestingly linked to Egypt. It reveals in the case of Eusebius not so much a quest for the origins of monasticism nor even evidence of a specific knowledge of it, but rather the impact of his theology on his understanding of history. The elite ascetic life, a life above nature and beyond common human living,[14] is so central to his understanding of Christianity that it pushes itself back into his recovery of Christianity's formative years. If the origins are not understood or known, they are in a sense "mythically" created in the beginning with the gospel.

Beyond this most obvious example of a monastic life in Eusebius' *Ecclesiastical History*, one finds little evidence for a particular lifestyle defined as ascetic. There are numerous ascetic individuals who lead ascetic lives, but there is no individual or pattern that is established as an archetype that one should follow. Physical withdrawal (ἀναχώρησις) from the world, which became so central to the definition of monasticism through the later *Life of Antony*, is represented in Eusebius, but it is neither a prerequisite for the ascetic life nor is it indicative solely of the ascetic individual. He reports that Narcissus, the bishop of Jerusalem, escaped from the church to practice his "philosophic life" by retiring "secretly in deserts and obscure parts of the country,"[15] and that Clement of Alexandria had to seek Pantaenus out from his concealment in Egypt (ἐν Αἰγύπτῳ θηράσας λεληθότα).[16] Yet Origen, whose ascetic life is recorded in detail by Eusebius, practiced his "most philosophic manner of life" as a teacher, a profession that necessitated his presence in the world rather than his physical withdrawal from it. Eusebius reports that he astounded his followers by the severity of his ascetic labours. He disciplined himself in fasting, limiting his sleep, which he took on the floor, persevering in cold and nakedness, embracing extreme limits of poverty, walking without shoes, and abstaining from wine and all but necessary food. Following the gospel precept, he even made himself a eunuch for the kingdom of God.[17] This ultimate act of ascetic renunciation was undertaken, according to Eusebius, precisely because of Origen's presence within the world, so "that he might prevent all suspicion of shameful slander on the part of unbelievers (for, young as he was, he used to discourse on divine things with women as well as men)."[18]

Likewise Eusebius knows that many fled to the desert and mountains not to practice the ascetic life, but to avoid persecution. Unlike Jerome,[19] he does not link, through the commonality of the desert, the flight of early Christians to avoid persecution with the withdrawal of the later Christians as desert ascetics. He rather saw such flight as but another form of persecution that resulted in their death "by hunger and thirst and frost and diseases and robbers and wild beasts."[20] The later understanding of the monk as the latter-day martyr is contradicted in Eusebius in the account of Alcibiades who, though he had led a very austere life, was dissuaded from it before his martyrdom by fellow Christians in jail.[21] Rather than a picture of asceticism replacing martyrdom, one finds presented here the suggestion that persecution could hinder or even curtail the ascetic life.

Retreat to the desert has its origin for Eusebius not in the enforced flight of the persecuted, but in the voluntary search for solitude of the philosophical elite.[22] In joining together the powers of Christianity and Rome, he presented Christianity as the new philosophy that demanded among its elite practitioners an ascetic life. The life of renunciation is in fact the new "philosophic way of life" (βίος φιλόσοφος).[23] While this life may be perfected by martyrdom, it precedes the martyr's call.[24] While Eusebius might admit that some desert ascetics discovered the value of solitary life in the desert as a result of their flight from persecution, he certainly does not find in them *the* origin of the monastic life.

For Eusebius, the ascetic life cannot be an accidental discovery. Viewed as the elite form of Christian existence, it is the highest demonstration of the gospel. As the pre-Christian philosophers logically led an ascetic life, so the new Christian elite, e.g., Origen and Narcissus, knowingly undertook a philosophic life, by which Eusebius signifies Christian teaching and ascetic practice. While the dogma shifted from Plato to Christ, the ascetic lifestyle remained the same.

For the historical origins of monasticism proper Eusebius offers little evidence. His linkage of ascetic practice to the philosophic life, while undoubtedly accurate in a broader sense for the intellectual elite, does not explain the rapid swelling of the monastic ranks in the late third and early fourth centuries by individuals of lower social and intellectual status both within the geographical boundaries of Greek culture and beyond. His portrayal is that of a Greek intellectual and represents a philosophically elite, Hellenocentric view of monastic development.

II. The Life of Antony

The literary source most often turned to first to explicate the origins of monasticism among the common people is the *Life of Antony*.[25] According to the author of this heroic *vita*, Antony, after the death of his parents, turned to the ascetic life when he heard in church the call of the gospel, "If you will be perfect, go sell all that you have and give to the poor; and come, follow me and you will have treasures in heaven" (Matt 19:21). About twenty years old at the time, he gave his inheritance away and began his ascetic career in the vicinity of his village. His subsequent successes in the solitary life led to his ever increasing fame as a holy man, which in turn necessitated his withdrawal to ever more remote desert locations in order to regain his lost solitude. From his first village retreat he soon withdrew to more distant tombs, where he struggled with demons and continued to be visited by old acquaintances.[26] At age thirty-five he withdrew further into the desert of Pispir to a deserted fort where he continued to practice the ascetic life by himself for twenty years. Again his friends came to visit him.[27] In the years that followed, his fame became so great that the many who came to imitate his life eventually broke down the door of his abode to get at him. We are told that when he came forth, he appeared "as one initiated into sacred mysteries and filled with the spirit of God." He had conquered the demands of human life, for his body, in spite of the fastings and struggles, appeared the same as it had been before his withdrawal.[28] Many then came to Antony and were taught by him until once again the pressures became too great. In search of the ever fleeting solitude he desired, he set out on a journey to the Upper Thebaid and established his final abode near the Red Sea at the Inner Mountain (modern Deir Mar Antonios).[29] Here too, of course, his solitude could not be maintained as his fame and influence in matters of ascetic practice and Christian theology continued to grow.

Antony became, through this account, the most famous practitioner of the ascetic life. Much as Paul had become the apostle to the Gentiles *par excellence* through the fact that he was the most influential if not the first, so too Antony became the monk *par excellence*. His status as such easily translated into a view of his undertaking as innovative and original. He became not only the monk *par excellence*, but also the first monk from whom all subsequent developments flowed. From the eremitic life of Antony came the coenobitic innovation of Pachomius, and from these springs in Egypt flowed the monastic rivers that watered Palestine and Syria, Rome and the West.

To base a theory of monastic origins and development on the *Life of Antony* is, however, to base it on a literary model. The image of Antony as the father of Christian monasticism is dependent less on the historical undertaking of Antony than on the literary success of the *Life of Antony*. The rhetorical intent and power of the *vita* are still evident today in the centrality given to Antony in monastic history. The *vita* itself, when proper attention is given to the details, rejects the originality of Antony's undertaking.[30] Before embarking himself on an ascetic career, Antony placed his orphaned sister with "known and trusted virgins." He then sought out an individual ascetic whom he might emulate and found one, an old man in a neighboring village, who had lived the ascetic life in solitude from his youth.[31] Precedents thus clearly existed for the young Antony, even according to the *vita*. In addition, in the *vita* one hears of monasteries in Egypt at the time, though they are reported to be few in number. While this reference to monasteries may be anachronistic, their mere mention indicates that the author had no intention of claiming Antony as the "originator" of the monastic enterprise. He is more concerned with Antony's subsequent fame which, by portraying Antony as staunchly anti-Arian, he uses to garnish monastic support for his own ecclesio-political position.[32] His goal is thus served by portraying Antony as famous and hence more visibly "orthodox."

A comparison of the *Vita Antonii* with the letters of Antony and the sayings attributed to him in the *Apophthegmata Patrum* reveals the literary modeling of the Antony of the *vita*. He bears only an indirect relationship with the historical Antony.[33] The image of Antony as the father of Christian monasticism is but a product of Antony's subsequent success multiplied in turn by the success of the *vita*. This success, real and literary,

215

may have added impetus to the monastic enterprise in Egypt and beyond, but it did not originate it. If the *vita* had not been written, it is questionable whether greater claim would have been given to Antony's influence than to that of Macarius the Great (ca. 300–390), Arsenius (ca. 354–412), or Poemen (d. ca. 450).[34] Athanasius, if indeed he wrote the *vita*,[35] mentions him only once in his other writings. While he corresponded with various monks, we know of no correspondence with Antony. Antony's fame is the fame of the *vita*.

III. The Village Ascetics

When one sets Antony aside and turns instead to the "known and trusted virgins" with whom he left his sister and the old ascetic in the neighboring village whom he sought to emulate, another view of the origins of monastic development in Egypt begins to emerge. Here one finds that withdrawal to the desert is not central; the persons involved remained within the village community. An ascetic life, whether practiced alone or in common with like-minded individuals, involved withdrawal from certain social patterns of human existence (family and sex), but not a physical separation from the community. The fact that persons from his village followed Antony to his desert retreats and sought his presence might be interpreted to mean not that they wished to emulate him but that they felt cheated by his departure. In seeking solitude in the desert away from the village, he was taking with him the power of God made available to the village through his presence. The ascetic had a function in the village, and Antony's innovative departure called this function into question.

The existence of these village ascetics is confirmed from other sources. A party of visitors who traveled between Alexandria and Lycopolis in 394–395 CE on an excursion to visit various monks and monastic communities reports that in the Theban city of Oxyrhynchus "the monks were almost the majority over the secular inhabitants."[36] They observed that the old temples were bursting with monks and that no quarter of the city was free from them. They estimated the number within the walls at five thousand. While the details of the account are open to question, the active presence of monks within the city is apparent. These ascetics had not left to make the desert a city, but had remained to turn the city into a virtual monastery.[37]

A documentary papyrus from Egypt dated to June 324 CE and supplying the first known technical use of the term μοναχός for a Christian monk uses the term precisely to describe such a "city" or village ascetic.[38] In this brief document submitted to Dioscorus Caeso, the *praepositus pagi* of the region, Aurelius Isidorus, a private citizen of Karanis, filed a claim against Pamounis and Harpalus, whose cow destroyed his farming efforts and who assaulted him when he attempted to remove the animal from his field. In describing the assault, Isidorus claims that the two would have killed him if not for the intervention of "the deacon Antoninus and the monk Isaac."

This monk, the earliest for whom direct nonliterary evidence is available, is not one who, in a quest for solitude, fled to the desert or mountains where he might avoid the encumbering affairs of the world. Isaac, as a μοναχός, remained an active member of the wider community. The simple inclusion of his title μοναχός in the petition, together with that of the deacon Antoninus, suggests that both the titles and the individuals were recognized in Karanis. The petitioner, Isidorus, undoubtedly hoped to add weight to his claim through his use of the titles.[39]

The monk or μοναχός Isaac represents a type of ascetic termed elsewhere an ἀποτακτικός. According to the documentary evidence, the apotactic movement played a significant role in early Christianity.[40] It is, however, summarily dismissed in the surviving literary sources. Jerome, who labeled such monks *remnuoth*, repudiated them as reprobate or "false" monks in his famous letter to Eustochium. He reports that they live together in small groups within the cities, refuse to subordinate themselves to anyone, quarrel frequently, dress ostentatiously and sigh constantly for the effect, visit virgins, and disparage the clergy. He advises Eustochium to avoid them like the plague, while recommending to her the "true" monks who follow the anchoritic or coenobitic life.[41]

Jerome's vitriolic attack against such "city" monks is not unusual, though his vituperative skill is perhaps unmatched. His judgment against them is necessarily suspect. Their numbers were large. Jerome himself admits that they were the most numerous type of monk in his own province of Pannonia. His universal rejection of them undoubtedly has more to do with their unsubordinated power and perhaps their theology than their corrupt manner of life. The latter is simply part of Jerome's attack against them.[42]

Within the city, the conflict between the monastic and clerical authority met head-on without the buffer of a desert or monastery wall. In another mainstream literary source, the *Letter of Ammon*, the author reports that his priest dismissed as heretical an Alexandrian monk with whom he first considered affiliating himself. The priest sent him instead up the Nile to the Pachomian community.[43] In the literary sources, which represent the successful ecclesiastical party, these "city" monks have lost the struggle for authority and have been dismissed. They are rejected as those who pervert the monastic life for their own gain and are unworthy, in Jerome's view, of even bearing the title of monk. The latter is reserved for those who withdraw from the social world of the village and leave it thereby under the authority of the clergy. The "true" monk lives in isolation alone or in a community behind a wall. The term μοναχός itself becomes limited in the literary sources to these later anchoritic and coenobitic forms of the ascetic life.[44]

In this literary success of the more easily controllable anchoritic and coenobitic forms of monasticism, the "city" monks or *remnuoth* are not only disparaged, but for the most part they are forgotten or ignored. Their significance for the formative stages of monastic history was thus lost. While the ecclesiastical rhetoric of Jerome and others that carried the day continues to affect the presentation of monastic history, the documentary evidence has begun to challenge their control of that history. The *remnuoth* or ἀποτακτικοί are reclaiming their rightful place. Judge, who wrote the definitive study on the apotactic movement, asserts that

> we must posit an event, or change of fashion, different from and prior to the creation of either eremitism (in its Antonian form) or coenobitism, but perhaps close in time to them, and part of a swift series of developments that led to them. The apotactic movement (as later attested) meets this requirement. It represents the point at which the men at last followed the pattern long set for virgins and widows, and set up houses of their own in town, in which the life of personal renunciation and service in the church would be practiced.[45]

The true significance of the old village ascetic whom Antony encountered before his withdrawal to the desert now becomes clear. He, like Isaac, while setting himself apart from the normal pattern of human existence, remained within the community where he served as a source of inspiration and a known conduit to the divine. It was not an accident that Antony turned to him. Given this understanding of the monk, Antony's subsequent innovation of withdrawal from the village broke the pattern. While in the long run it pleased the ecclesiastical opponents for authority like Jerome, one suspects that in the short run it was viewed by others as desertion. If all who chose the ascetic life fled to the desert, to whom would the villagers turn in time of need?

Documentary evidence likewise helps to explicate the role of the "known and trusted virgins" to whom Antony entrusted his young orphaned sister before he departed on his own ascetic career. A legal document dated to 400 CE records the lease of space on the ground floor and basement of a house by a certain Jew named Jose from two natural sisters, Theodora and Tauris, μοναχαὶ ἀποτακτικαί.[46] While the precise role of these two sisters within the community is not given, their status as μοναχαὶ ἀποτακτικαί sets them apart, and their business transactions suggest their social power and prestige. Since the papyrus comes from Oxyrhynchus, it seems likely that Theodora and Tauris should be numbered among the 20,000 virgins reported living in that city in the *Historia Monachorum*. They outnumbered their male counterparts by two to one.[47]

Two letters from a woman named Didyme of the early fourth century offer tantalizing evidence of an organization of Christian women involved in the daily life of the surrounding community.[48] "Didyme and the sisters" participated in various commercial transactions that include lines of credit and the transfer of goods (grapes, sandals, cakes, a head-band, and an ostrich egg). While it is not clear that their organization should be understood as a monastery in the later sense,[49] it does appear to fit an earlier form of Christian ascetic association in which flight from the world was not primary. Like the μοναχός Isaac, Didyme and the sisters mingle openly in the daily life of the wider Christian community. Their embracing of the "solitary" life does not preclude the using of their talents to help in diverse ways their brothers and sisters in the Lord.

The documentary evidence of these early female and male ascetic associations and roles suggests that Antony's innovation lay not in the idea of withdrawal per se, but in its translation from an ethical to a physical plane. Theodora, Tauris, and Isaac withdrew from the traditional ethical patterns of the family, but not from the social and indeed commercial interactions of the Christian community. They chose a solitary life in place of family and children and viewed it as an opportunity to increase their service to the Lord through their service to their fellow Christians. Antony expanded this concept of withdrawal to include a physical separation from one's fellow Christians through flight to ever more remote retreats.[50]

A careful reading of the Life of Antony reveals that he took time to develop this idea and put it into effect. Judge notes that the term μοναχός appears for the first time in the vita precisely at the moment Antony terminated his self-imposed solitude. It was only then that he "became the centre of public excitement and began to constitute a social movement."[51] Thus even in this most literary of monastic sources, the term monk is linked first to a socially active undertaking rather than to a withdrawal from society. Eventually Antony did outgrow this "social movement" (and with it the original meaning of μοναχός) and withdrew to a distant mountain retreat where he spent the rest of his life, some forty-three years, as a true hermit.

Not all followed Antony in his decision to withdraw further and abandon his newly created social movement. Some chose to remain closer to home in and around the villages. To judge from the accounts of papyri from Oxyrhynchus and Jerome's remnuoth,[52] their numbers were large. Some eventually found an ordered existence in the coenobitic innovations of monks like Pachomius.[53] Others either filtered into developing ecclesiastical structures under the control of the clergy or came under the opprobrium of church officials like Jerome. In either case, as witnesses to a third form of the monastic life, they disappeared from the scene and were forgotten. While more original historically than either the anchoritic ideal of Antony or the coenobitic innovation of Pachomius, the apotactic movement was supplanted by these later developments and forgotten. The original significance of the term μοναχός was lost. In its new meaning of physical withdrawal, Antony, as portrayed in the *vita*, became its first exemplar. Having left the apotactic movement behind literarily, it was a short step to see Antony as the first monk and his innovation as the origin of monasticism.

IV. Pachomius and the Coenobites

The story is much the same with respect to the understanding of coenobitic monasticism as an innovation of the Upper Egyptian figure of Pachomius. It has already been suggested that it arose in Egypt as one of two developments from the earlier apotactic movement. When the latter came under disrepute, the successful movement begun by Pachomius in Upper Egypt came to be associated with the origin of coenobitic monasticism much as Antony had come to be associated with the origin of anchoritic monasticism. It was again to a significant degree the success of the Pachomian *Rule* and the *Life of Pachomius*,[54] both of which had gained wide distribution through their translation into Greek and Latin, that accounted for the assumed preeminence of Pachomius.

The *Life* reports that Pachomius converted to Christianity at about age twenty. As a conscript into the Roman army, he had been housed in prison to await movement towards the front. It was in prison that he first met Christians, who impressed him by the compassion they showed towards him and his fellow conscripts. He promised to convert if he should be freed, and upon his release, he was baptized and undertook an ascetic life as an anchorite under the tutelage of Palamon, a famous ascetic living near the village of Chenoboskeia in Upper Egypt.[55] The ascetic demands were hard, but Pachomius proved capable.

His coenobitic innovation came as the result of a vision. While gathering wood at the deserted village of Tabennesi, he was instructed to remain there and build a monastery. After consulting with Palamon, he undertook the task imposed upon him by the vision. Soon many came to join in his new communal experiment.[56] In time the numbers became too large for the original establishment at Tabennesi, and a second monastery was constructed at the deserted village of Pbow. This second monastery soon functioned as the center of a growing system of monastic settlements scattered along the Nile in Upper Egypt. The *Koinonia*, as it came to be known, served not only a spiritual need, but invigorated the economy of the area.[57] By the time of Pachomius' death in 346 CE, his *Koinonia* numbered some nine monasteries and two affiliated women's houses. Their organization was governed by a common *Rule*, which soon came to be used by coenobitic establishments beyond his organizational control. This development led to the designation of any monastery that used the Pachomian *Rule* as Tabennesiote, which in turn translated, often incorrectly, into the community's Pachomian origin.[58]

The picture of Pachomius' originality is, however, literary rather than historical. According to the *Life of Pachomius* itself, at least three of the original nine monasteries were not founded by the Pachomians but elected to join the Pachomian system. They clearly had an independent origin. There is no indication how long the monastery at Chenoboskeia existed prior to its decision to affiliate itself with the Pachomian *Koinonia*. It is simply reported that it had existed previously under an old ascetic named Ebonh. The monastery of Thmousons, the fourth to join the Pachomian system, likewise had an earlier independent existence,[59] as did the monastery of Thbew, which had been founded previously by a certain Petronius. The latter had withdrawn from his parents' home and gathered like-minded individuals around him who wanted to live in Christ. It was only then that he heard of the Pachomian *Koinonia* and wrote to Pachomius asking that his monastery be accepted into the system. Thbew thus became a Pachomian monastery. The *vita* makes clear through these stories that Pachomius' innovation had little to do with the coenobitic institution itself. It was rather the organizational principle of a *Koinonia* or system of affiliated coenobitic monasteries and the development of a monastic rule that is credited to Pachomius.[60]

Furthermore, it is certain that not all coenobitic communities chose to join his *Koinonia*. When Theodore, Pachomius' most significant successor as general abbot, joined the movement in its early years, he transferred from an existing monastery further down the Nile.[61] There is no indication that Theodore's original community ever desired to join the Pachomian system. Likewise while Shenoute (ca. 348–466) appreciated Pachomius' undertaking and borrowed from his rule, his monasteries had an independent origin and followed their own pattern of development.[62] Meletian and Manichaean communities also remained outside the Pachomian fold.[63]

The theory of a Pachomian origin of coenobitic monasticism must thus be discarded. Attempts to explain his insight through the borrowing of earlier communal experiences or experiments fall into the same trap in so far as they seek to trace the coenobitic development back to a single root. The theory that his efforts to organize disparate monks into a systematic community was a result of his experience in the army would, if it could be maintained, only account for Pachomius' effort and not those of the surrounding communities that joined his system.[64] While the influence of Egyptian temple organization on his *Koinonia* is clearer, once again it helps to explain his particular plans, but hardly the "origin" of coenobitic monasticism.[65]

More recently the awareness of the early presence of Manichaean missionaries in Egypt has offered a possible source of influence for Pachomius' innovation.[66] While their communities existed earlier, there is no direct evidence of their influence on Pachomius. He might as well have heard of Philo's Therapeutae. Furthermore, even if Pachomius had been directly influenced by the Manichaean movement organizationally, it does not establish a single Manichaean origin of coenobitic monasticism. The vast number of monasteries in Egypt in the late Byzantine era simply cannot be traced to a single point of origin. Archaeological evidence from Deir el-Bala'izah suggests, for example, a monastery structure somewhere between the semi-eremitic communities of the Wadi Natrun and the fully coenobitic establishments of Pachomius. Its unique organizational pattern argues against a Pachomian source of inspiration.[67] Finally, it can be noted that when Justinian (482–565) forced a Chalcedonian abbot on the Pachomian community at Pbow, many monks fled to other existing monasteries. That such monasteries existed untouched by Justinian's efforts against the Pachomian *Koinonia* argues for their independence from it.[68]

The possible influence of the Manichaean movement on Pachomius raises the point of the theological nature of the movement. While the surviving literary sources portray it as in close agreement with the mainstream Christian forces exemplified by Athanasius (ca. 296–373), increasing evidence suggests that such careful theological concern and definition is anachronistic, a product of the time when the sources were composed and edited rather than of the historical period they purport to describe. Two major manuscript discoveries made nearby the Pachomian monastery of Pbow raise the question of their origin within the Pachomian system. The Dishna Papers, which include the Bodmer Papyri, include copies of letters from the early Pachomian abbots. This evidence has led James Robinson to claim that the contents of this manuscript hoard represent the remains of a Pachomian library.[69] If true, these contents reveal much about the breadth of Pachomian intellectual activity. As one would expect, biblical texts predominate; but one finds as well apocryphal material, classical texts (including a satyr play), mathematical exercises, tax receipts, and a Greek grammar. While some of this material may have entered the community in the belongings of new members, there appears to have been no effort to weed it out.

The second manuscript collection, the Nag Hammadi Codices, offers an even more startling possibility. This collection preserves a significant number of heterodox texts, many of which are Gnostic in origin and most of which would have been rejected by the Athanasian party. The question of a Pachomian origin and use of these codices has been much debated, and no clear consensus has emerged.[70] The fact that it remains a real possibility in itself underscores a changing view of Pachomian monasticism and its origins. The literary accounts of Pachomian history are no longer assumed to be an accurate reflection of early Pachomian theological concern. They were written to edify future monks and not to record an accurate history for modern scholars. It may well be that the early Pachomians defined their Christianity in terms of their ascetic practice and not in terms of the books they read.[71]

In the case of monastic origins in Egypt, oft presumed to be the source of monastic origins in general, the evidence has revealed a complex situation. The image of Antony and Pachomius as respectively the fathers of anchoritic and coenobitic monasticism is a fiction that grows out of and beyond the depiction of these two figures in the literary sources. While both were influential, their insights were at best innovations and not creations. Antony represents an expansion of the monastic concept of withdrawal from its original ethical plane to include a physical dimension. He withdrew not only from the domestic bonds of family and marriage, but from the social bonds of the village in general. Likewise Pachomius' innovation was not the coenobitic lifestyle itself, but the organization of an affiliated group of monasteries under a common rule. His central monastery of Pbow functioned for the affiliate monasteries in Upper Egypt much as Cluny functioned for its affiliate monasteries in medieval Europe. Both were systems that created fame and power. Neither created it *ex nihilo*, but drew on previously existing coenobitic institutions.

The evidence of the apotactic movement certainly expands our understanding of ascetic practice in Egypt before the appearance of Antony and Pachomius. But it would be wrong to conclude from it that we are now closer to the "origins" of monasticism. The apotactic movement should not serve simply as the "missing link" between early ascetic practices within the home and the later institutionalized forms. Rather it underscores the complexity of the situation, not only in its historical reality, but particularly in the manner in which it has come down to us in the surviving sources. Not only is the available evidence limited, it has been clearly filtered so as to conform with prevailing opinion. The apotactic monk who resided in the village and participated in its social and ecclesiastical affairs was forgotten, or rather repudiated by a later Christianity that had embraced less politically active forms of asceticism. Desert hermits and "imprisoned" coenobites offered a less direct challenge to ecclesiastical and political authority and therefore flourish in the literature that survives, a literature that survives precisely because it represents that ecclesiastical and political authority. The motive behind the silence with respect to the apotactic movement is thus political, and a history of monastic development must take this into account.

V. Egypt and Syria

The complexity of the situation in Egypt is repeated throughout the early Christian world. As the biases of the sources and the earlier selective use of them are taken more and more into account, the diverse origins of monastic practice and its meaning are becoming increasingly clear. Thus the old theory that traced the monastic impulse in all corners of the empire back to an original Egyptian inspiration has proven to be a literary fiction. It too was dependent on a western quest for origins and a Hellenocentric view of the ancient Mediterranean world perpetuated by selective use of the sources and their interpretation.

If one depends chiefly on the *Religious History* of Theodoret of Cyrrhus (ca. 393–458) for an understanding of Syriac monasticism, for example, one cannot help but have a view filtered through Theodoret's selection of the evidence and his adopted Hellenism. To begin with, his evidence is limited by the date of his composition, circa mid fifth century CE. Theodoret knows of individual monks who flourished in the mid fourth century and of coenobitic institutions founded at the same time, but the large preponderance of his evidence dates nearer his own time in the late fourth and early fifth centuries. This compares to a late third century date for Antony (ca. 251–356) and an early fourth century date for Pachomius (ca. 290–346). Given such a data base, one might easily conclude that Syriac monasticism was at least later in date if not directly influenced by Egyptian monasticism.[72]

Even should the monastic enterprise in Syria prove temporally later than its Egyptian counterpart, however, its distinct practices, spirituality, and organization betray its independent origins. The Semitic roots of Syriac-speaking Christianity are clear, and these roots give Syrian spirituality a distinctive flavor unencumbered by the Hellenistic influences of classical Greece and Rome.[73] The Syrian ascetic embarked on a monastic career not to punish or subdue the flesh but to offer the body as a symbol of the faith. The body was not viewed dualistically in opposition to the spirit but as that portion of the person through which the faith might be acted out and become visible.[74] The Syrian monk simply cannot be understood through recourse to the Hellenistic dualism between the spirit and the flesh. While the latter informed Egyptian monastic practice, it ran counter to the purpose of the Syrian ascetic.

If one depends on Theodoret of Cyrrhus, however, one receives just such a Hellenistic image of the Syrian monk. In Theodoret's rendition of the life of Simeon the Stylite (ca. 390–459), his ascetic practices are viewed as evidence of his consummate philosophy.[75] His physical discipline has as its purpose the desire to align his body with the higher purpose of his soul. The influence of the Platonic dualism between spirit and flesh is apparent in

Theodoret's report that Simeon ascended his pillar in order "to fly heavenward and to leave the earthly life."[76] The description of this ascetic life as philosophic unites Theodoret with Eusebius of Caesarea. In Ashbrook Harvey's words,

> For all their differences, Theodoret's *Life of Simeon* represents a harmonious tradition with the fourth century *Life of Antony* of Egypt, and indeed with Eusebius of Caesarea's philosopher martyrs. It is Simeon's acquired dispassion that Theodoret is celebrating. Like Antony, Simeon had first to gain that self-control before achieving the spiritual strength necessary to perform God's work.[77]

Given such a source, it is little wonder that a dependent relationship could be found between the Egyptian and Syriac monasticism. But the Hellenistic veneer is apparent as soon as one compares it with the Syriac *vita*. Here Simeon's actions are understood in the context of the Hebrew prophets, who not only proclaimed God's word, but acted it out.[78] Simeon ascends his pillar not to flee the earthly life, but to serve as a dramatic statement (literal symbol) of the gospel. Again in Ashbrook Harvey's words,

> Simeon became a stylite, then, not in penitence, not to deny his body nor to discipline it, but because through it he could fulfill God's purpose. By public witness of his actions—the prophecy of behavior—he could efficaciously proclaim God's word.[79]

The distinctive nature of the Syrian monastic enterprise is clear. The view that it was theoretically akin to its Egyptian counterpart derived from the uncritical use of selected sources, sources that had themselves already translated the Syriac data into a Hellenized form.

If the beginnings of asceticism had a separate origin in Syria, so too did it develop independently. As the Egyptian anchorites can no longer serve as forerunners of the Syrian hermits, neither can Egyptian coenobitism serve to explain the north Syrian monasteries. Archaeology has shown the distinctiveness of the latter with their greater open space and absence of an enclosing wall.[80] Strong Marcionite and Manichaean presences in Syria[81] might have offered precedents, but, as in the case of Egypt, the connection is not clear. What is clear is that its origins lay not in Egypt.

The more we learn of early Christian monasticism, the more we discover its complexity. While the French proverb, "Il n'y a que les détails qui comptent" (Only the details are really important), may overstate the case, it is fair to say that simplified theories of monastic origins that ignore the details have proven invalid. They were born of that quest for origins with which Western historiography has so long been enamored. But as Eliade points out, "Western man's longing for 'origins' and the 'primordial' forced him finally into an encounter with history";[82] it forced people to consider the details, and the details have dissuaded them from the quest. The monastic sources themselves almost universally agree in placing the origins of monasticism in divine inspiration. Antony and Simeon responded to hearing the gospel, and Pachomius was given a vision. While one may choose to discredit the supernatural nature of this explanation, it shares with the evidence the sense of asceticism as bursting forth simultaneously in myriad places. The "big bang" lies not in one or more historical events, but deep beneath the historical plane of ancient Mediterranean culture. It was the spirit of the times and the new Christian faith that produced the explosion, and as it welled forth from below, it burst onto the plane of history independently throughout the empire. One may still discover influences on specific forms of asceticism and trace various paths of development, but the quest for the "origins" of Christian monasticism should be let go.

Notes

[1]Mircea Eliade, "The Quest for the 'Origins' of Religion," *HR* 4 (1964) 154–69; reprinted in idem, *The Quest: History and Meaning in Religion* (Chicago and London: University of Chicago Press, 1969) 37–53.

[2]Roland H. Bainton (*Christendom: A Short History of Christianity and Its Impact on Western Civilization* [2 vols.; New York: Harper & Row, 1964] 1.104–5 and Jaroslav Pelikan (*Jesus through the Centuries: His Place in the History of Culture* [New Haven and London: Yale University Press, 1985] 110–12) are prime examples of such oversimplified and erroneous conclusions.

[3]*Vita Antonii* 3 (PG 26.843–44); see discussion below.

[4]Arthur Vööbus, *A History of Asceticism in the Syrian Orient: A Contribution to the History of Culture in the Near East* (2 vols.; CSCO 184, 197; Louvain: Secrétariat du CSCO, 1958–1960); Sebastian Brock, "Early Syrian Asceticism," *Numen* 20 (1973) 1–19; R. M. Price, trans., *A History of the Monks of Syria by Theodoret of Cyrrhus* (Cistercian Studies Series 88; Kalamazoo, MI: Cistercian Publications, 1985) xvii–xxiii.

[5]On the relationship between the Pachomian monastic movement and the Nag Hammadi Library, see James E. Goehring, "New Frontiers in Pachomian Studies," in Birger A. Pearson and James E. Goehring, *The Roots of Egyptian Christianity* (Studies in Antiquity and Christianity 1; Philadelphia: Fortress, 1985) 236–52, and Armand Veilleux, "Monasticism and Gnosis in Egypt," in Pearson and Goehring, *Roots,* 271–306. On the significance of the Manichaean influence, see Timothy D. Barnes, *Constantine and Eusebius* (Cambridge and London: Harvard University Press, 1981) 195, who cites L. Koenen, "Manichäische Mission und Klöster in Ägypten," in Günter Grimm, Heinz Heinen, and Erich Winter, eds., *Das römisch-byzantinische Ägypten: Akten des internationalen Symposiums 26.–30. September 1978 in Trier* (Aegyptiaca Treverensia,

Trierer Studien zum griechisch-römischen Ägypten 2; Mainz am Rhein: von Zabern, 1983) 93–108.

[6] The quest for "origins" occurred in diverse fields in the nineteenth century and as such has been shown to be a product of western historiography. Eliade, "The Quest," 37–53.

[7] Birger A. Pearson, "Earliest Christianity in Egypt: Some Observations," in Pearson and Goehring, *Roots*, 132–59.

[8] *HE* 2.16; translation from Kirsopp Lake, J. E. L. Oulton, and H. Lawlor, *Eusebius, The Ecclesiastical History* (LCL; 2 vols.; Cambridge: Harvard University Press, 1926) 1.145.

[9] Leopold Cohn and Paul Wendland, eds., *Philonis opera quae supersunt* (7 vols. in 8; Berlin: Georg Reimer, 1896–1930) vol. 4; F. H. Colson, trans., *Philo* (LCL; 10 vols.; Cambridge: Harvard University Press, 1967) 9.113–69.

[10] Barnes, *Constantine and Eusebius*, 195.

[11] Hermann Weingarten, "Der Ursprung des Mönchtums im nachconstan-tinischen Zeitalter," *ZKG* 1 (1877) 6–10.

[12] Eusebius, *DE* 1.8; Peter Brown, *The Body and Society: Men, Women and Sexual Renunciation in Early Christianity* (New York: Columbia University Press, 1988) 205.

[13] Joseph Juste Scalinger, *De emendatione temporum* (Frankfurt: I. Wechelum, 1593); Ernst Lucius, *Die Therapeuten und ihre Stellung in der Geschichte der Askese: Eine kritische Untersuchung der Schrift De vita contemplativa* (Strassburg: Schmidt, 1879).

[14] Eusebius, *DE* 1.8.

[15] *HE* 6.9.6–6.10.1.

[16] *HE* 5.11.4.

[17] *HE* 6.3.9–13; 6.8.1–3.

[18] *HE* 6.8.2; translation from Lake, Oulton, and Lawlor, *Eusebius, The Ecclesiastical History*, 2.29.

[19] *Vita Pauli* (PL 23.17–30); Karl Heussi, *Der Ursprung des Mönchtums* (Tübingen: Mohr, 1936) 70; Derwas J. Chitty, *The Desert a City: An Introduction to the Study of Egyptian and Palestinian Monasticism under the Christian Empire* (Oxford: Blackwell, 1966) 6–7.

[20] *HE* 6.42.2.

[21] *HE* 5.3.1–3.

[22] Eusebius posits two ways of life given by the Lord to his church: that of the married Christian and that of the elite, who, in their ascetic life, live beyond or above human nature. *DE* 1.8; Brown, *The Body and Society*, 205.

[23] *HE* 6.3.9, 13; 6.9.6; 6.10.1. The same definition of the ascetic life as a practice of philosophy is found throughout Theodoret of Cyrrhus' *Historia religiosa*. P. Canivet and A. Leroy-Molinghen, eds., *Théodoret de Cyr: Histoire des Moines de Syrie* (SC 234, 257; Paris: Éditions du Cerf, 1977–1979); Price, *A History of the Monks*.

[24] *HE* 6.3.13.

[25] PG 26.823–896; Robert T. Meyer, trans., *St. Athanasius: The Life of Saint Antony* (ACW; New York: Newman Press, 1950); Robert C. Gregg, trans., *Athanasius: The Life of Antony and the Letter to Marcellinus* (The Classics of Western Spirituality; New York: Paulist, 1980).

[26] *Vita Antonii* 2–8 (PG 26.841–56).

[27]*Vita Antonii* 10–13 (PG 26.859–64).

[28]*Vita Antonii* 14 (PG 26.863–66).

[29]*Vita Antonii* 49–51 (PG 26.914–19).

[30]Heussi, *Der Ursprung*, 56–58.

[31]*Vita Antonii* 3 (PG 26.843–46).

[32]Robert C. Gregg and Dennis E. Groh, *Early Arianism: A View of Salvation* (Philadelphia: Fortress, 1981) 131–59; but note the anti-Arian stance of the Antony of the letters. Samuel Rubenson, *The Letters of St. Antony: Origenist Theology, Monastic Tradition and the Making of a Saint* (Bibliotheca historico-ecclesiastica Lundensis 24; Lund: Lund University Press, 1990) 44–45.

[33]Hermann Dörries, "Die Vita Antonii als Geschichtsquelle," *Nachrichten der Akademie der Wissenschaften in Göttingen, philologisch-historische Klasse* 14 (Göttingen: Vandenhoeck & Ruprecht, 1949) 357–410; Heussi, *Der Ursprung*, 78–108; Rubenson, *The Letters of Antony*.

[34]The thirty-eight sayings attributed to Antony in the alphabetical collection of the *Apophthegmata Patrum*, while a fair number, do not set him apart numerically at least from a number of other famous monks in the collection. Forty-four sayings of Arsenius are recorded, 47 of John the Dwarf, 41 of Macarius the Great, 209 of Poemen, 54 of Sisoes, and 27 of Amma Syncletica.

[35]Heussi, *Der Ursprung*, 78–86; Timothy D. Barnes, "Angel of Light or Mystic Initiate? The Problem of the Life of Antony," *JTS* 37 (1986) 353–68; Charles Kannengiesser, "St. Athanasius of Alexandria Rediscovered: His Political and Pastoral Achievement," *Coptic Church Review* 9 (1988) 69–70; Rubenson, *The Letters of Antony*, 126–32.

[36]*Historia monachorum in aegypto* 5; translation from Norman Russell and Benedicta Ward, *The Lives of the Desert Fathers: The Historia Monachorum in Aegypto* (London and Oxford: Mowbray, 1980) 67.

[37]Brown, *The Body and Society*, 217.

[38]E. A. Judge, "The Earliest Use of Monachos for 'Monk' (P. Coll. Youtie 77) and the Origins of Monasticism," *JAC* 20 (1977) 72–89.

[39]Ibid., 73–74.

[40]Ibid., 79–89

[41]*Ep.* 22.34 (CSEL 54); F. A. Wright, trans., *Select Letters of St. Jerome* (LCL; Cambridge: Harvard University Press, 1933); Judge, "The Earliest Use of Monachos," 78–79.

[42]This is not to suggest that corrupt monks did not exist in the cities, but only that such corruption was not determined by the monk's residence in the city.

[43]*Epistula Ammonis* 2; James E. Goehring, *The Letter of Ammon and Pachomian Monasticism* (Patristische Texte und Studien 27; Berlin: de Gruyter, 1986) 124–25, 191.

[44]Judge, "The Earliest Use of Monachos," 78–79.

[45]Ibid., 85.

[46]P. Oxy. 3203; Judge, "The Earliest Use of Monachos," 82; E. A. Judge, "Fourth-Century Monasticism in the Papyri," in *Proceedings of the XVI International Congress of Papyrology* (Chico, CA: Scholars, 1981) 613.

[47]*Historia monachorum in aegypto* 5.6; Judge, "The Earliest Use of Monachos," 82–83.

[48]P. Berl. Inv. 13897 and P. Oxy. 1774; Alana Emmett, "The Nuns and the Ostrich Egg" (unpublished lecture).

[49]Emmett, "The Nuns and the Ostrich Egg," 4–5; P. Barison, "Ricerche sui monasteri dell'Egitto bizantino ed arabo secondo i documenti dei papiri greci," *Aegyptus* 18 (1938) 138.

[50]It is not clear to this author whether this innovation is that of the historical Antony or more likely presented as such by his biographer.

[51]*Vita Antonii* 14 (PG 26.863–66); Judge, "The Earliest Use of Monachos," 77. Judge suggests that the monk Isaac may have been influenced by Antony's efforts, since Karanis was but a day's walk from the center of Antony's activities.

[52]See discussion above.

[53]Judge, "The Earliest Use of Monachos," 78.

[54]The *Life of Pachomius* survives in various Coptic, Greek, Arabic, and Latin versions, the interrelatedness of which is complex. For an account of the issues see Goehring, *The Letter of Ammon*, 3–23, and Philip Rousseau, *Ascetics, Authority, and the Church in the Age of Jerome and Cassian* (Oxford: Oxford University Press, 1978) 243–47. The text of the Bohairic version of the *vita* (*Bo*) is found in L. Th. Lefort, ed., *Pachomii vita bohairice scripta* (CSCO 89; Paris: e typographeo reipublicae, 1925; reprinted, Louvain: Secrétariat du CSCO, 1965). The Sahidic versions are found in L. Th. Lefort, *S. Pachomii vitae sahidice scriptae* (CSCO 99/100; Paris: e typographeo reipublicae, 1933; reprinted, Louvain: Secrétariat du CSCO, 1965). The Greek versions (including the *Vita prima* = *G1*) are in François Halkin, *Sancti Pachomii Vitae Graecae* (Subsidia hagiographica 19; Bruxelles: Société des Bollandistes, 1932). The *Rule*, which survives in Coptic and Greek fragments, was translated into Latin and circulated by Jerome. Armand Boon, *Pachomiana latina. Règle et épîtres de s. Pachôme, épître de s. Théodore et "Liber" de s. Orsiesius. Texte Latin de s. Jerome* (Bibliothèque de la Revue d'histoire ecclésiastique 7; Louvain: Bureaux de la Revue, 1932). English translations of all the major texts within the Pachomian corpus are found in Armand Veilleux, *Pachomian Koinonia* (3 vols.; Cistercian Studies Series 45–47; Kalamazoo, MI: Cistercian Publications, 1980–1982). A Greek version of the Life of Pachomius was taken to the Alexandrian Archbishop Theophilus around 400 CE, from where we can surmise it spread. W. E. Crum, *Der Papyruscodex saec. VI—VII der Phillippsbibliothek in Cheltenham: Koptische theologische Schriften* (Strassburg: Trübner, 1915) 12–13; L. Th. Lefort, *Les vies coptes de saint Pachôme et de ses premiers successeurs* (Bibliothèque du Muséon 16; Louvain: Bureaux du Muséon, 1943) 389–90.

[55]*Vita Pachomii: Bo* 7–10; *G1* 4–6.

[56]*Vita Pachomii: Bo* 17–26; *G1* 12–24.

[57]James E. Goehring, "The World Engaged: The Social and Economic World of Early Egyptian Monasticism," in James E. Goehring et al., eds., *Gnosticism and the Early Christian World: In Honor of James M. Robinson* (Sonoma, CA: Polebridge Press, 1990) 134–44.

[58]James E. Goehring, "Chalcedonian Power Politics and the Demise of Pachomian Monasticism," *Occasional Papers*, No. 15 (Claremont, CA: Institute for Antiquity and Christianity, 1989) 17–18.

[59]*Vita Pachomii: Bo* 50–51; *G1* 54.

[60]The organizational principle may be dependent in part on the temple hierarchy and organization in Egypt. Fidellis Ruppert, *Das pachomianische Mönchtum und die*

Anfänge klösterlichen Gehorsams (Münsterschwarzach: Vier-Türme, 1971) 324–26. Manichaean precedents must also be considered (above, n. 5).

[61]*Vita Pachomii: Bo* 29–32; *G1* 33–35. James E. Goehring, "Theodore's Entry into the Pachomian Movement (Selections from *Life of Pachomius*)," in Vincent L. Wimbush, ed., *Ascetic Behavior in Greco-Roman Antiquity: A Sourcebook* (Studies in Antiquity and Christianity; Minneapolis: Fortress, 1990) 349–56.

[62]Johannes Leipoldt, *Schenute von Atripe und die Entstehung des National Ägyptischen Christentums* (Leipzig: Hinrichs, 1903) 34–39; Hans Quecke, "Ein Pachomiuszitat bei Schenute," in Peter Nagel, ed., *Probleme der koptischen Literatur* (Halle-Wittenberg: Martin Luther Universität, 1968) 155–71.

[63]On the Manichaeans see Gedaliahu G. Stroumsa, "The Manichaean Challenge to Egyptian Christianity," in Pearson and Goehring, *Roots*, 307–19, and above, n. 5. On the Melitians, note H. Idris Bell, *Jews and Christians in Egypt: The Jewish Troubles in Alexandria and the Athanasian Controversy* (London: The British Museum, 1924; reprinted, Westport, CT: Greenwood, 1972) 38–99.

[64]Chitty, *The Desert a City*, 22; Leonard Lesko, "Monasticism in Egypt," in Florence D. Friedman, ed., *Beyond the Pharaohs: Egypt and the Copts in the 2nd to 7th Centuries A.D.* (Providence, RI: Museum of Art, Rhode Island School of Design, 1989) 46. It seems unlikely that Pachomius' brief sojourn in the army as a conscript, probably against his will, would have influenced him in the positive direction of modeling his community on the experience.

[65]Ruppert, *Das pachomianische Mönchtum*, 324–26.

[66]See above, nn. 5 and 62.

[67]Peter Grossmann, "Die Unterkunftsbauten des Koinobitenklosters 'Dair al-Balayza' im Vergleich mit den Eremitagen der Mönche von Kellia," in *Le site monastique copte des Kellia. Sources historiques et explorations archéologiques. Actes du Colloque de Genève, 13 au 15 aout 1984* (Genève: Mission suisse d'archéologie copte de l'Université de Genève, 1986) 33–40, fig. 2.

[68]Goehring, "Chalcedonian Power Politics," 1–20.

[69]James M. Robinson, "Reconstructing the First Christian Monastic Library" (paper presented at the Smithsonian Institution Libraries, Washington, DC. September 15, 1986); idem, *The Story of the Bodmer Papyri: The First Christian Monastery Library* (Philadelphia: Fortress, forthcoming).

[70]For the basics of the debate and further bibliography on it, see Goehring, "New Frontiers," 247–52, and Veilleux, "Monasticism and Gnosis," 271–306; also Robert A. Kraft and Janet A. Timbie, reviewers, "The Nag Hammadi Library in English," *RelSRev* 8 (1982) 34–35.

[71]Henry Chadwick, "Pachomius and the Idea of Sanctity," in S. Hackel, ed., *The Byzantine Saint: University of Birmingham Fourteenth Spring Symposium of Byzantine Studies* (London: Fellowship of St. Alban and St. Sergius, 1981) 17–19; idem, "The Domestication of Gnosis," in Bentley Layton, ed., *The Rediscovery of Gnosis: Proceedings of the Conference at Yale, New Haven, Connecticut, March 28–31, 1978*, Vol. 1: *The School of Valentinus* (Leiden: Brill, 1980) 14–16; Goehring, "New Frontiers," 240–52; Clemens Scholten, "Die Nag-Hammadi-Texte als Buchbesitz der Pachomianer," *JAR* 31 (1988) 144–72.

[72]Price, *A History of the Monks*, xix.

[73]Sebastian P. Brock and Susan Ashbrook Harvey, *Holy Women of the Syrian*

Orient (The Transformation of the Classical Heritage 13; Berkeley: University of California Press, 1987) 4–12; Robert Murray, "The Characteristics of the Earliest Syriac Christianity," in N. Garsoïan, T. Mathews, and R. Thomson, eds., *East of Byzantium: Syria and Armenia in the Formative Period* (Washington, DC: Dumbarton Oaks, 1982) 3–16.

[74]"The religious image and the physical action are inseparable and witness to the making literal of the symbol," Brock and Ashbrook Harvey, *Holy Women*, 9.

[75]The following discussion of Simeon and the varied interpretations of his life is dependent on the work of Susan Ashbrook Harvey, "The Sense of a Stylite: Perspectives on Simeon the Elder," *VC* 42 (1988) 376–94.

[76]Theodoret of Cyrrhus, *Historia religiosa* 26.12; Ashbrook Harvey, "The Sense of a Stylite," 379.

[77]Ibid., 380.

[78]Ibid., 382.

[79]Ibid., 382–83.

[80]Jean Lassus, *Sanctuaires chrétiens de Syrie: Essai sur la genèse, la form et l'usage liturgie des édifices du culte chrétien en Syrie, du IIIe siècle à la conquète musulmane* (Paris: Geuthner, 1947) 272–73; G. Tchalenko, *Villages antiques de la Syrie du Nord: Le massif du Bélus à l'époque romaine* (3 vols.; Paris: Geuthner, 1953–1959) 1.19; Price, *A History of the Monks*, xix–xx.

[81]Brock and Ashbrook Harvey, *Holy Women*, 7; Walter Bauer, *Orthodoxy and Heresy in Earliest Christianity* (Trans. Robert A. Kraft et al.; Philadelphia: Fortress, 1971) 1–43.

[82]Eliade, "The Quest," 50.

Withdrawing from the Desert: Pachomius and the Development of Village Monasticism in Upper Egypt[1]

James E. Goehring
Mary Washington College

In a recent article entitled "Le monachisme égyptien et les villes,"[2] Ewa Wipszycka cataloged for the later Byzantine period the abundant evidence of monastic habitation in or adjacent to the towns and villages of Egypt as well as in or on the margins of the cultivated land. Her analysis, which begins after the late third- to fourth-century formative period of Antony, Pachomius, and the Lower Egyptian semi-anchoritic centers in Nitria, Scetis, and Cellia, supplies convincing evidence of the rhetorical selectivity employed in the portrayal of Egyptian monasticism by the authors of the literary sources. In the literary texts, the dominance of monastic sites located in places of solitude generates a monastic geography of physical isolation. While acknowledging this dominance in the literature, Wipszycka draws together the infrequent literary references and the more numerous documentary examples of less physically isolated and more socially integrated monastic centers.[3] The resulting picture of Egyptian mo-

[1]I first delivered a shortened form of this paper at the Twelfth International Conference on Patristic Studies, Oxford, 21–26 August 1995. I wish to thank Richard Valantasis for his helpful comments on the final form of the paper.

[2]Ewa Wipszycka, "Le monachisme égyptien et les villes," *Travaux et mémoires* 12 (1994) 1–44.

[3]Ibid., 3.

233

nasticism is spatially and socially more complex than that derived from the literary sources alone. The significant presence of monastic centers within the inhabited zones (fertile valley, villages, and cities) of Egypt dispels the idea of Egyptian monasticism as a predominantly desert phenomenon. While isolated monasteries flourished in Egypt as a result of the discovery of the desert, Egyptian monasticism was neither in its origins a product of that discovery nor in its subsequent expansion a result of an ensuing flight from the *oikoumene*, or inhabited world, to the newly found isolation of the desert.[4] The growth of monasticism in Egypt did not follow a simple linear path from an ill-defined urban ascetic movement in the later third and early fourth centuries to the withdrawn desert monks of the fourth-century classical period to the large well-defined urban and suburban[5] monasteries of the later Byzantine era. While the discovery of the desert and the growth of desert monasticism intervenes temporally between the early urban ascetics and the later Byzantine monasteries, there is no reason to assume that it formed the necessary link between the two. Ascetic formation within the *oikoumene* developed continuously within the *oikoumene*. While the urban ascetics were not unaffected by the emergence of the desert ascetic movement, neither were they necessarily remade through it. The widespread presence of ascetic communities within the *oikoumene* in the Byzantine period represents, rather, a continuity in urban asceticism that reaches back to the formative apotactic movement identified by E. A. Judge.[6] I do not suggest a simple, direct path of development from the apotactic movement to the Byzantine monasteries, but argue that the practice of ascetic formation never left the *oikoumene*. While it expanded into the desert in the fourth century, it also continued to grow and develop within the inhabited regions of the Nile valley where it first began.

The rhetorical power of the desert image, however, still casts its shadow over the "history" of Egyptian monasticism. The portrayal of the Pachomian monastic movement, which began with the founding of the monastery of Tabennese in 323 CE, offers a case in point. The Pachomian movement,

---

[4]James E. Goehring, "The World Engaged: The Social and Economic World of Early Egyptian Monasticism," in idem, et al., eds., *Gnosticism and the Early Christian World: In Honor of James M. Robinson* (Sonoma, CA: Polebridge, 1990) 130–44; and idem, "The Encroaching Desert: Literary Production and Ascetic Space in Early Christian Egypt," *Journal of Early Christian Studies* 1 (1993) 281–96.

[5]I use the term "urban" loosely to indicate monasteries situated in or adjacent to towns and villages as distinct from true desert cells or communities. In reality, ascetic habitation existed across the full range of geographical possibilities in Egypt. See Goehring, "Encroaching Desert," 281–96.

[6]E. A. Judge, "The Earliest Use of Monachos for 'Monk' (P. Coll. Youtie 77) and the Origins of Monasticism," JAC 20 (1970) 72–89.

which postdates Antony's withdrawal to the desert, is often enrolled without reflection in the desert city formulated by Athanasius in his *Vita Antonii*.[7]
The equation is simple. The seminal *Vita Antonii* defined Egyptian monasticism as a desert movement. Pachomian monasticism is an Egyptian monastic movement. Therefore, Pachomian monasticism is part of the desert
movement. For example, in his article on "The Rise and Function of the
Holy Man in Late Antiquity," Peter Brown distinguished the less remote
desert in Syria from the "true desert" of Egypt. In speaking of Egyptian
monasticism, he asserted that:

> to survive at all in the hostile environment of such a desert, the Egyp-
> tian had to transplant into it the tenacious and all-absorbing routines of
> the villages of the *oikoumene*. . . . Groups had to reproduce exactly, on
> the fringe of the desert, the closed-in, embattled aspect of the fortified
> villages of Upper Egypt. The monastery of Pachomius was called quite
> simply The Village.[8]

Pachomius's monastery of Tabennese, situated on the shore of the Nile in
a village in which the monks built a church for the local inhabitants, has
thus become a fortified desert community.[9]

I shall argue here that the emergence of Pachomian monasticism and the
subsequent expansion and development of the movement is better understood within the context of urban asceticism. Pachomius founded his first
two ascetic communities in deserted villages, and a careful review of the
evidence suggests that the subsequent seven monasteries added to the
koinonia, or community, in his lifetime were also situated in the fertile
valley in or near villages whose names they bore. The Pachomians, who
called themselves ἀποτακτικοι ("renouncers"), supply an important link
from the classical period of Egyptian monasticism between the early apotactic

---

[7]Note that the literary portrayals of the Pachomian movement also postdate Athanasius's
idealization of Antony's withdrawal in his *Vita Antonii*. Text: *PG* 26.825–924; G. J. M. Bartelink,
ed., *Athanase d'Alexandrie: Vie d'Antoine* (SC 400; Paris: Cerf, 1994). English translations:
Robert C. Gregg, *Athanasius: The Life of Antony and the Letter to Marcellinus* (New York:
Paulist Press, 1980); Robert T. Meyer, *St. Athanasius: The Life of Antony* (Ancient Christian
Writers 10; New York: New Press, 1950).

[8]Peter Brown, "The Rise and Function of the Holy Man in Late Antiquity," *JRelS* 61 (1971)
83; compare his later assessment in *The Body and Society: Men, Women and Sexual Renunciation in Early Christianity* (New York: Columbia University Press, 1988) 217.

[9]The same process is seen at work in Derwas Chitty's use of Athanasius's phrase, "The
Desert a City," as the title for his general history of Egyptian and Palestinian monasticism
(*The Desert a City: An Introduction to the Study of Egyptian and Palestinian Monasticism
under the Christian Empire* [Oxford: Blackwell, 1966; reprinted London: Mowbrays, 1977]).
See also the reference to "desert monasteries" in David Brakke, "Canon Formation and Social
Conflict in Fourth-Century Egypt: Athanasius of Alexandria's Thirty-Ninth *Festal Letter*,"
HTR 87 (1994) 398.

movement of the towns and villages and the later urban monasteries of the Byzantine era. They illustrate the continuing draw of the *oikoumene* as a location for ascetic formation and ascetic community. Properly understood, Pachomian monasticism is not a product of the desert, but a form of village asceticism.

Tradition has bestowed on Antony and Pachomius the status of founders of early Egyptian monasticism. They serve as the movement's primary icons. Antony represents the anchoritic model of the ascetic life, Pachomius its coenobitic form.[10] Antony's earlier date has fashioned him as the individual representative of monastic origins. His discovery of the "ascetic" desert marks the beginning of the movement, and the withdrawn anchoritic life becomes its initial form of ascesis. This understanding of the origins of Egyptian monasticism depends in large part, however, on the widespread success of the purposeful biography of Antony published by the Alexandrian archbishop Athanasius. It is Athanasius who links ascetic practice so intimately with the discovery of the desert. In the *Vita Antonii*, he fashions the desert as the *telos*, or final [locational] goal, of male ascetic formation.[11] From his family home within his village, to the outskirts of the village, to nearby tombs, to a deserted fortress in the nearer desert, to the further desert along the Red Sea, Antony's ascetic progress is marked by a movement away from his village, away from the *oikoumene*, into the desert. The desert is the location of Antony's ascetic perfection and the source of this ascetic power.[12] His subsequent returns to the *oikoumene* are simply occasions for using his ascetic power on behalf of an ecclesiastical polity defined by Athanasius. The success of Athanasius's *Vita Antonii* made the desert the *sine qua non* of Egyptian asceticism.[13] True ascetics were desert ascetics. The power of the equation is seen in the tendency of authors to enroll later ascetics, regardless of the location of their cells or monasteries, as citizens of Athanasius's new ascetic city rising in the desert.[14]

[10]Karl Heussi, *Der Ursprung des Mönchtums* (Tübingen: Mohr, 1936; reprinted Aalen: Scientia, 1981) 69–131; Chitty, *Desert a City*, 1–11, 20–29.

[11]Athanasius's portrait of Antony was the most successful, though certainly not the only portrait of the saint. See David Brakke, *Athanasius and the Politics of Asceticism* (Oxford Early Christian Studies; Oxford: Clarendon, 1995); Samuel Rubenson, *The Letters of Antony: Origenist Theology, Monastic Tradition and the Making of a Saint* (Bibliotheca historico-ecclesiastica Lundensis 24; Lund: Lund University Press, 1990); Hermann Dörries, "Die Vita Antonii als Geschichtsquelle," *Nachrichten der Akademie der Wissenschaften in Göttingen, philologisch-historische Klasse* 14 (1949) 359–410.

[12]*Vita Antonii* 14.

[13]The process has much to do with the modern study of early Egyptian monasticism. In the aftermath of Chalcedon and the eventual Arabic domination, knowledge of Coptic developments mostly vanished outside of Egypt. Egyptian monasticism was defined through the monastic texts that had appeared in Greek and Latin: *Vita Antonii*, *Vita Pachomii*, and *Apophthegmata Patrum*.

[14]*Vita Antonii* 14; Wipszycka, "Le monachisme égyptien," 9.

Pachomius too became an inhabitant of this city.[15] Later authors interpret his coenobitic experiment as a secondary development born out of the original anchoritic model. Its origins too were understood to lie ultimately with Antony and the desert.[16] While it is true that Pachomius began his ascetic career as an anchorite under the desert ascetic Palamon, it is seldom acknowledged that his coenobitic innovation occurred through his withdrawal from the desert. In fact, his orientation to the *oikoumene* and its villages was quite distinct from that of Antony. Rather than moving in a direction that led ever further away from the village into the desert, Pachomius, in his ascetic career, never left the fertile Nile valley. He always moved within the sphere of the village, and his innovations occurred precisely through his return to and use of the village.

The Pachomian dossier suggests that Pachomius first came into contact with Christians as an imprisoned military conscript in Thebes around 312 CE.[17] He was amazed at the kindness of strangers who came to the prison to encourage the conscripts and give them food. He struck a deal with God that night in prayer promising to serve him and humankind all the days of his life should he be freed from prison. Released after Licinius's defeat of Maximinus Daia in 313,[18] he proceeded to the village of Šenesēt (Chenobos-

---

[15]The main Coptic and Greek texts of the *Life of Pachomius* have been edited by Lefort and Halkin respectively. L. Th. Lefort, ed., *S. Pachomii vita bohairice scripta* (CSCO 89; Scriptores coptici 7; Paris: e typographeo reipublicae, 1925; reprinted Louvain: CSCO, 1965); idem, *S. Pachomii vitae sahidice scriptae* (CSCO 99/100; Scriptores coptici 9/10; Paris: e typographeo reipublicae, 1933; reprinted Louvain: CSCO, 1965); François Halkin, *Sancti Pachomii vitae graecae* (Subsidia hagiographica 19; Bruxelles: Socété des Bollandistes, 1932). Translations: L. Th. Lefort, *Les vies coptes de saint Pachôme et des ses premiers successeurs* (Bibliothèque du muséon 16; Louvain: Bureaux du Muséon, 1943); Armand Veilleux, *Pachomian Koinonia*, vol. 1: *The Life of Saint Pachomius and His Disciples* (Cistercian Studies 45; Kalamazoo, MI: Cistercian Publications, 1980). Citations from the first Greek life are cited as *G1*. Citations from the Coptic lives are cited as *Bo* (Bohairic) and *S* (Sahidic). The numeral immediately following the S identifies the specific Sahidic version (*S7* = Sahidic life number 7). *SBo* indicates the "complete" version fashioned by Veilleux by filling in *lacunae* in the Bohairic version from the Sahidic and Arabic texts. Following section numbers are those found in Veilleux's *Pachomian Koinonia*. Veilleux follows the sectional divisions for *G1* found in Halkin's *Sancti Pachomii*, and for *Bo*, those found in Lefort's *Les vies coptes*. The *vita* traditions are complex. A history of the debate can be found in James E. Goehring, *The Letter of Ammon and Pachomian Monasticism* (Patristische Texte und Studien 27; Berlin: de Gruyter, 1986) 3–23; for a discussion of the issues, see Philip Rousseau, *Pachomius: The Making of a Community in Fourth-Century Egypt* (The Transformation of the Classical Heritage 6; Berkeley: University of California Press, 1985) 37–48.

[16]Such is already the case in the *Vita Pachomii*; *Bo* 2; *G1* 2.

[17]*Bo* 7–8. His parents are portrayed as non-Christian (*Bo* 4; *G1* 3). Note, however, that Pachomius's sister's name is given as Mary (*Bo* 27; not named in *G1* 32). A recent study of Bohairic chronology (Christoph Joest, "Ein Versuch zur Chronologie Pachoms und Theodoros," *ZNW* 85 [1994] 132–44) argues for a date of 308 CE for Pachomius's conversion.

[18]The traditions do not, for the most part, correctly identify the emperor as Maximinus Daia. See Chitty, *Desert a City*, 7, 17 n. 39; and Veilleux, *Pachomian Koinonia*, 1. 267. Joest's

kion) where he was baptized.[19] He remained in the village and served the people, in part by gathering wood for them from the nearby acacia forests.[20] Eventually, he decided to embrace more fully the ascetic life and apprenticed himself under the old anchorite Palamon, who lived on the outskirts of the village of Šenesēt in a small patch of "interior" desert surrounded by fertile land.[21] Palamon was not a withdrawn desert anchorite of the type represented by the perfected Antony of Athanasius's *Vita Antonii*, but an ascetic who lived on the edge of the village within the fertile valley. He is more akin to the old village ascetic whom Antony first emulated or to Antony himself in his initial ascetic withdrawal to "the places close to the village" (οἱ πρὸ τῆς κώμης τόποι).[22] The fact that Palamon lived in a desert has little bearing on his social connection with the village, since his desert was simply a barren patch of land in the fertile valley adjacent to the village.[23]

Pachomius remained with Palamon for seven years and continued his trips through the acacia forests. The *Vita Pachomii* reports that on one such trip he wandered ten miles south to the shore of the Nile river where he discovered the "deserted village" (Coptic: ΟⲨϮⲘⲒ ΝⲎⲢⲎⲘⲞⲤ; Greek: κώμη τις, ἔρημος οὖσα) of Tabennese.[24] It was the opportunity offered by his chance discovery of the deserted village that led to his decision to remain and build a monastery. Unlike Antony, Pachomius's ascetic vocation was not fulfilled by withdrawing further into the desert. He did not move from his initial location near his village deeper into the desert to distance himself further from society. His ascetic career moved him in exactly the opposite direction. Pachomius finds ascetic perfection in his return to the village, albeit a deserted village on the shore of the Nile.

The religious tradition naturally understands both the discovery of the village of Tabennese and the decision to remain and build a monastery there as directed by God. The spirit led Pachomius to the village and once there, a voice from heaven instructed him to build a monastery. After confirming the vision with his ascetic father Palamon, Pachomius began the construction of the monastery.[25] Shorn of the religious interpretation, how-

---

revised chronology ("Ein Versuch," 144) calls this entire episode into question.

[19]*Bo* 8; *G1* 5.

[20]*Bo* 9.

[21]*Bo* 10; *G1* 6; compare *Bo* 15.

[22]*Vita Antonii* 3.3–4.

[23]L. Th. Lefort, "Les premiers monastères pachômiens: Exploration topographique," *Muséon* 52 (1939) 383–87; Goehring, "Encroaching Desert," 288–89.

[24]*Bo* 17; *G1* 12; on its location, see Lefort, "Les premiers monastères pachômiens," 293–97. Tabennese is the Sahidic spelling for the Bohairic Tabennesi. The Sahidic spellings are used for place names throughout this essay.

[25]*Bo* 17; *G1* 12.

ever, Pachomius's decision to relocate and fashion an ascetic community appears as an innovative idea triggered by the opportunity perceived in the "deserted" village. Ascetics were masters in the reuse of deserted space,[26] and Tabennese, if indeed it was deserted,[27] offered ready space and housing for an emerging ascetic community. Its location on the shore of the Nile made it particularly attractive in terms of the projected needs of such a community. Fertile land for vegetable gardens and the water necessary for their irrigation were immediately available,[28] as were the materials required for the traditional monastic work of basket and mat weaving.[29] Commercial markets for the monks' handiwork were close by,[30] and the Nile offered a ready means of transportation.[31] In fact, the subsequent expansion of the Pachomian *koinonia* into a system of affiliated monasteries spread over 175 kilometers between the towns of Šmin (Panopolis) and Snē (Latopolis) is difficult to imagine apart from the ease of transportation offered by the river. In the later periods of the movement, agricultural holdings outside of the monasteries proper were added,[32] and farming and irrigation regulations became an essential part of the community's rule.[33] As the community grew in size and wealth, its markets expanded[34] and its use of the Nile increased. Eventually, shipbuilding occurred within the monasteries,[35] and monks sailed

[26]Deserted tombs (*Vita Antonii* 8), fortresses (*Vita Antonii* 12), and temples (*Historia monachorum in Aegypto* 5; André-Jean Festugière, *Historia Monachorum Aegypto: Édition critique du texte grec et traduction annotée* [SH 53; Bruxelles: Société des Bollandistes, 1971] 41–43) were all put to use by ascetics. Open spaces within towns and villages likewise offered locations for monastic habitation. Wipszycka, "Les monachisme égyptien et les villes," 3.

[27]See below, pp. 272–74.

[28]*Bo* 23; *G1* 24; compare *G1* 106.

[29]See, for example, *Bo* 22; *G1* 23; *Paralipomena* 9 (Halkin, *Sancti Pachomii Vitae Graecae*, 133–34); *Epistula Ammonis* 19 (Goehring, *The Letter of Ammon*, 139–41)

[30]*Bo* 26; *G1* 28; compare *Paralipomena* 21–22.

[31]Travel often took place by ferry or boat (*Bo* 30), and boats were soon given to the Pachomian communities (*Bo* 53, 56). Communication with Alexandria likewise took place via travel up and down the Nile (*Bo* 28; *G1* 30).

[32]In 367–68 CE, a monk (*apotaktikos*) named Anoubion made payment for taxes on good agricultural land (*apora*) in the Hermopolite nome that belonged to the monastery of Tabennese (*P. Berl. Inv.* 11860A/B). Ewa Wipszycka, "Les terres de la congrégation pachômienne dans une liste de payments pour les apora," in Jean Bingen, et al., eds., *Le monde grec pensée, littérature, histoire, documents: Hommages à Claire Préaux* (Bruxelles: L'Université Bruxelles, 1975) 623–36; compare *G1* 106.

[33]*Regulations of Horsiesius* 55–64; L. Th. Lefort, *Oeuvres de s. Pachôme et de ses disciples* (CSCO 159; Scriptores coptici 23; Louvain: Durbecq, 1956; reprinted Louvain: CSCO, 1965) 98–99; Veilleux, *Pachomian Koinonia*, 2. 217–18.

[34]Note *G1* 113, which mentions two boats returning from a commercial trip to Alexandria where the monks had sold mats to procure foodstuffs and tunics.

[35]*G1* 146; compare *Bo* 204.

not only between the communities in Upper Egypt, but also to and from Alexandria, and possibly to Constantinople.[36] The subsequent growth of the *koinonia's* agricultural and commercial dealings was a natural result of the original village orientation of the movement.[37] A truly desert movement could not have been so active in the common affairs of the society.

Pachomius's success in establishing a monastic community in the deserted village of Tabennese led him to seek out a second deserted village when the time for expansion arose. He built his second monastery at Pbow, a village located approximately three kilometers down river or west of Tabennese in the direction of Šenesēt.[38] One may assume that Pachomius knew the area well, since he had discovered Tabennese while walking from his earlier ascetic abode adjacent to Šenesēt. He could have passed by Pbow on such a trip. Pbow is the only Pachomian community whose actual location is still identifiable today. The remains of its great fifth-century basilica can still be seen on the edge of the modern village of Faw Qibli, which, while not located on the shore of the Nile, lies close to it in the heart of the greenbelt.[39] There is no inner desert surrounding Pbow, only fertile agricultural fields.[40] Moreover, the Pachomian dossier itself suggests that Pbow was near the river. The first Greek *Vita Pachomii* reports that when Theodore died at Pbow, the weeping of the brothers could be heard on the far side of the river.[41] The *Epistula Ammonis* refers to monks from Pbow arriving at an island in the river by boat.[42] Like Tabennese, Pbow was not a desert monastery. It was not even located on the fringe of the fertile valley, but in a "deserted" village in the heart of the greenbelt. Pachomius's use of a second deserted village to expand his community further underscores his commitment to the village rather than the desert. Both his initial innovative idea to create a communal form of the ascetic

---

[36]*SBo* 96, 124, 132; *G1* 113. Compare Roger Rémondon ("Le monastère alexandrin de la metanoia etait-il beneficiaire du fisc ou a son service?" in *Studi in onore di Edoardo Volterra*, vol. 5 [Milan: Giuffre, 1971] 769–81) for a discussion of the involvement of the later Egyptian monasteries in the transportation of the grain tax not only on the Nile, but also between Alexandria and Constantinople.

[37]Goehring, "The World Engaged," 139–41.

[38]*Bo* 49; *G1* 54; on its location, see Lefort, "Les premiers monastères pachômiens," 387–93.

[39]Peter Grossmann, "The Basilica of St. Pachomius," *BA* 42 (1979) 232–36; note the map of the site on p. 234. A color photograph of the remains of the basilica (p. 203) offers a good illustration of its location at the edge of the village, well within the fertile valley.

[40]Egyptian villages were normally surrounded by fertile land (Bagnall, *Egypt in Late Antiquity*, 114).

[41]*G1* 149.

[42]*Epistula Ammonis* 28; compare *Bo* 59–60; *G1* 55, 60, 109, 113. The point of embarkation for the monks from Pbow may have been Šenesēt (*G1* 107).

life and his later development of a system of affiliated monasteries occurred through his discovery and use of deserted villages.

Although the "deserted village" becomes something of a literary *topos* in
the Pachomian tradition,[43] there is little reason to doubt the deserted nature
of the villages of Tabennese and Pbow when Pachomius first stumbled
upon them. It is clear from later sources that vacant buildings and open
land both within and adjacent to the towns and villages of Egypt were
being occupied by the growing ascetic population.[44] Although the question
still remains as to the precise meaning of the term "deserted" (ἔρημος) as
it is applied to the villages, the Pachomian accounts of Tabennese and
Pbow likely fit this pattern. While the Pachomian accounts suggest a completely vacant village akin to the ghost towns of the old American west, it
is possible that the label indicates nothing more than that a sufficient degree of vacancy and open space existed within the villages to enable
Pachomius to establish ascetic communities there.[45] Any population loss
rendered portions of a village vacant and thus made available living space
for ascetics. One need not press the deserted nature of the village too far
to imagine Pachomius's decision to establish his new community there.

While village populations and house occupancy remained relatively stable
in Egypt,[46] tax and census records preserved among papyrus documents
demonstrate that village populations could fluctuate for various reasons and
that, on occasion, the complete desertion of a village did occur. Not all of
the reasons are relevant to the cases of Tabennese and Pbow. The evidence
of village growth and decline in the Fayyum, for example, where the changing reach of the irrigation system and disputes over water determined village viability, has little application to the case of Tabennese or Pbow which
were situated on or near the shore of the Nile.[47] On the other hand, the

---

[43]Note that the author of the Bohairic *Vita* asserts that Šenesēt too was deserted when
Pachomius first arrived (*Bo* 8). The fact that it contained some inhabitants and that Pachomius
was baptized in its church and cared for many of its people during the subsequent plague gives
the author no pause. Pachomius's initial efforts were linked with deserted villages; since he
began his ascetic career in Šenesēt, it too became deserted for the author.

[44]Note the description of Oxyrhynchus in the *Historia monachorum in Aegypto* 5; Wipszycka,
"Le monachisme égyptien et les villes," 3.

[45]This may result from the use of "deserted" to refer to less than complete depopulation,
or it may arise from exaggeration in the *vita* tradition.

[46]Peter van Minnen, "House-to-House Enquiries: An Interdisciplinary Approach to Roman
Karanis," *Zeitschrift für Papyrologie und Epigraphie* 100 (1994) 230–31; compare Lewis,
Life in Egypt under Roman Rule, 65–67.

[47]Neglect of the irrigation system, disputes over water, and the burden of Roman taxation
(including liturgies) all effected village economies and population. J. A. S. Evans, *A Social
and Economic History of an Egyptian Temple in the Greco-Roman Period* (Yale Classical
Studies 17; New Haven: Yale University Press, 1961) 276–77, 282–83; Deborah Hobson,

effect of Roman taxation in all its forms[48] may well apply to the situation of Tabennese and Pbow. Individual flight to avoid taxes and service was common throughout the history of Roman Egypt,[49] and, on occasion, it accounted for a sizable loss in a village's population. Records from the mid-first-century Arsinoite village of Philadelphia illustrate the possible severity of such tax desertion. At the height of the problem in 57 CE, one in every seven or eight men from the village of Philadelphia was a tax fugitive. The situation was so severe that those responsible for the collection of the taxes, which were set for the village regardless of its population, pleaded with the prefect for an adjustment.[50]

While the case of Philadelphia comes from a much earlier period, we know that the problem persisted in the period of Roman rule.[51] As such, it suggests a sequence of events that could account for the vacated property discovered and used by Pachomius in both Tabennese and Pbow. If this were the case, however, it would suggest that the term "deserted," as applied to Tabennese and Pbow in the Pachomian texts, refers to a population loss rather than to the total abandonment of the village. While tax desertion was a significant problem in Egypt, it does not appear that it led to the complete desertion of a village. On the other hand, the problems encountered by a village that experienced considerable desertion in meeting its tax obligations may well explain the local acceptance of the Pachomians' occupation of vacant village property and land. If the Pachomians occupied deserted land and paid taxes on it, their entry into the village would have been a boon to the village economy.[52]

"Agricultural Land and Economic Life in Soknopaiou Nesos," *BASP* 21 (1984) 108; Peter van Minnen, "Deserted Villages: Two Late Antique Town Sites in Egypt," *BASP* 32 (1995) 41–55; Arthur E. R. Boak, "An Egyptian Farmer of the Age of Diocletian and Constantine," *Byzantina Metabyzantina* 1 (1946) 53; compare Bagnall, *Egypt in Late Antiquity*, 138–39.

[48]Lewis, *Life in Egypt under Roman Rule*, 159–84; Bagnall, *Egypt in Late Antiquity*, 153–60, 172–74; Boak, "An Egyptian Farmer," 39–53.

[49]Lewis, *Life in Egypt under Roman Rule*, 163–65, 183–84; Bagnall, *Egypt in Late Antiquity*, 144; Arthur E. R. Boak and Herbert C. Youtie, "Flight and Oppression in Fourth-Century Egypt," in Edoardo Arslan, ed., *Studi in onore di Aristide Calderini e Roberto Paribeni* (2 vols.; Milan: Ceschina, 1956–57) 2. 325–37; Allan Chester Johnson, *An Economic Survey of Ancient Rome*, vol. 2: *Roman Egypt to the Reign of Diocletian* (ed. Tenney Frank; Paterson, NJ: Pageant, 1959) 114–15 (*P. Upps.* 7), 482–83, 546; Rousseau, *Pachomius*, 9–10.

[50]Lewis, *Life in Egypt under Roman Rule*, 164–65; Alan K. Bowman, *Egypt after the Pharaohs: 332 BC–AD 642 from Alexander to the Arab Conquest* (Berkeley: University of California Press, 1986) 77.

[51]Boak and Youtie, "Flight and Oppression," 325–37; Lewis, *Life in Egypt under Roman Rule*, 163–65, 183–84; Bowman, *Egypt after the Pharaohs*, 77; Bagnall, *Egypt in Late Antiquity*, 144; Rousseau, *Pachomius*, 9–10.

[52]Goehring, "The World Engaged," 139–40; Wipszycka, "Les terres de la congrégation pachômienne," 623–36. This may have been the case for Pbow in particular, since the evidence for the Pachomians' revitalization of Tabennese would probably have been known by that time.

A second cause of village decline was plague. While tax desertion had a more limited effect on village population, the outbreak of plague could and did result in village abandonment. Documents from the reign of Marcus Aurelius (161–180 CE) supply an example of the rapid population decline in certain villages as their inhabitants fled an outbreak of plague. In one case, surviving records report a fall in the number of village males from twenty-seven to three to zero.[53] The reality of plague is also apparent in the Pachomian dossier. The Bohairic *Vita* reports that a plague ravaged the village of Šenesēt during Pachomius's initial sojourn there prior to his apprenticeship under Palamon.[54] Pachomius himself died in 346 CE in a plague that decimated the *koinonia*.[55] Another outbreak occurred during Theodore's leadership of the community.[56] Such an outbreak, perhaps even the specific one experienced by Pachomius in Šenesēt, may account for the deserted nature of the villages of Tabennese and Pbow. Plague may have created the opportunity for Pachomius's innovative translation of deserted villages into ascetic villages. This explanation of the term "deserted," which corresponds most closely with the accounts in the Pachomian literary tradition, supports the interpretation of "deserted" as a more extensive population loss in the villages prior to their use by Pachomius.

While we can never know with certainty the degree to which the villages were deserted when first inhabited by the Pachomians, it is clear that they did not remain deserted for long after the Pachomians' arrival. According to the Bohairic *Vita*, the lay population of Tabennese grew so rapidly after the Pachomians entered the village that the monks built a church for the villagers even before they constructed one for themselves. They attended the village church to partake of the eucharist.[57] While less is said of Pbow, one suspects a similar situation.

Archaeological efforts place the monastery on the edge of the modern village of Faw Qibli, and dredge work some 750 meters beyond the monastery in the farmland has revealed the remains of sizable Roman structures.[58] While it may have been the deserted nature of the village that initially drew the Pachomians to it, they did not understand their occupation of the village as exclusive. While they did establish an ascetic village within the village, they also brought the village, as village, back to life. Ascetic withdrawal for the Pachomians occurred within the village, even-

---

[53]Lewis, *Life in Egypt under Roman Rule*, 68 (only males are recorded); van Minnen, "Deserted Villages," 43.

[54]*Bo* 9.

[55]*S7* (Lefort, *S. Pachomii vitae sahidice scriptae*, 87–96); *SBo* 117–23; *G1* 114–17.

[56]*Bo* 180; *G1* 139.

[57]*Bo* 25; *G1* 29.

[58]James E. Goehring, "New Frontiers in Pachomian Studies," in Birger A. Pearson and James E. Goehring, eds., *The Roots of Egyptian Christianity* (Studies in Antiquity and Christianity 1; Philadelphia: Fortress, 1986) 252–57.

tually behind a gated wall. It was never accomplished by spatial separation from the village in the near or distant desert. While undoubtedly controlled to some degree, social interaction between the Pachomians and the non-ascetic village population was part of the Pachomian ascetic life from its inception.

The village pattern inaugurated by the use of Tabennese and Pbow continued in the later Pachomian establishments. While the precise locations of the subsequent seven monasteries added to the *koinonia* in Pachomius's lifetime[59] are not known with any degree of certainty,[60] the evidence suggests that like Tabennese and Pbow, they are best understood as village communities. Like Tabennese and Pbow, two of the later establishments, the monasteries of Šenesēt (Chenoboskion)[61] and Šmin (Panopolis),[62] were clearly named after the village or town with which they were associated. There is every reason to assume that they were located in or near the villages whose names they bore. One may argue that the monastery of Šenesēt was situated in Palamon's "interior desert,"[63] but the location of the "interior desert" adjacent to the village argues for the close association of the monastery with the village. Šenesēt itself, with its "interior desert," was located near the Nile in the greenbelt at a considerable distance from the desert proper.[64]

---

[59]A female monastery was established in the village of Tabennese, although it is never included in the number of monasteries listed in the sources. It is viewed as a sister monastery of Tabennese. *Bo* 27; *G1* 32 (Greek text in François Halkin, *Le corpus athénien de saint Pachôme* [Geneva: Cramer, 1982] 21–22).

[60]Although Lefort's efforts to connect the Pachomian monasteries to specific sites are intriguing, they remain speculative ("Les premiers monastères pachômiens," 379–407). Compare M. Jullien, "A la recherche de Tabenne et des autres monastères fondés par saint Pachôme," *Études* 89 (1901) 238–58; Henri Gauthier, "Notes géographiques sur le nome Panopolite," *BIFAO* 4 (1904) 63–64, 86–87, 94–95; idem, "Nouvelles notes géographiques sur le nome Panopolite," *BIFAO* 10 (1912) 93–94, 103, 121–27; René-Georges Coquin, "Akhmim," in Aziz S. Atiya, ed., *The Coptic Encyclopedia* (8 vols.; New York: Macmillan, 1991) 1. 784.

[61]*Bo* 50; *G1* 54. The monastery of Šenesēt was the third community in the *koinonia*. It had existed independently under the leadership of an old ascetic named Ebonh prior to joining the Pachomian system and was already known as the monastery of Šenesēt when Pachomius accepted it into the *koinonia*.

[62]The monastery of Šmin, the sixth community in the *koinonia*, is not named as such in the main published editions of the *Vita Pachomii* (see above, n. 14). Pages preserved in Toronto, however, include Šmin in a list of Pachomian establishments. Donald Spanel, "A Toronto Sahidic Addition to the Pakhom Dossier (*Fischer A1*, ff. 1–2)," *The Ancient World* 6 (1983) 115–25.

[63]This is the site of the current Monastery of Palamon. René-Georges Coquin and Maurice Martin, "Anba Palaemon," in Atiya, *The Coptic Encyclopedia*, 3. 757; for a photograph that shows the relationship of the monastery to the village, see James M. Robinson, "The Discovery of the Nag Hammadi Codices," *BA* 42 (1979) 208.

[64]Lefort, "Les premiers monastères pachômiens," 383–87.

The Pachomian monastery of Šmin was built on land donated by the bishop of Šmin.[65] The bishop's additional gift of a boat supports the placement of this monastery near the Nile rather than in the desert. Furthermore, the opposition of townspeople to the construction of the monastery makes more sense if the proposed monastery was being built on land valuable to the community. Šmin, a nome (or district) capital, was not a deserted village where land and housing were more readily available. In the nome capitals, land and housing were more valuable and in greater demand.[66] The building of a monastery in such a location was likely seen by some of the inhabitants as adding unnecessary pressure on the town's limited resources.[67]

The locations of the Pachomian monasteries whose names do not correspond to known village names remain more speculative. If the pattern of village monasteries established above is correct, however, there is little reason to place the other monasteries in the desert. The Pachomian sources report that the monastery of Tse was located in the land of Šmin (ϩ Ⲛ ⲦⲔⲀϦ ϢⲀ Ⲩ ⲘⲒ Ⲛ)[68] and the monastery of Tsmine in the vicinity of Šmin (ⲠⲒ Ⲕⲱ ϯ ⲚϢⲀⲘⲒ Ⲛ).[69] While these designations could indicate a desert location, they could equally identify communities situated in or near villages of the same names in the Panopolite nome. The latter alternative follows the pattern established by Tabennese, Pbow, Šenesēt, and Šmin. Unless proof exists to the contrary, it seems most appropriate to assume that the pattern held. While inconclusive, evidence from the *Vita Pachomii* can easily support a village location for these communities.[70]

[65]*S5* (Lefort, *S. Pachomii vitae sahidice scriptae*, 146–47); *SBo* 54; compare *G1* 81.

[66]Deborah W. Hobson, "House and Household in Roman Egypt," *YCS* 28 (1985) 225; Bagnall, *Egypt in Late Antiquity*, 111 n. 11.

[67]While the cause of the townspeople's opposition to the Pachomians is not given, there is no reason to assume that they opposed them on religious grounds alone.

[68]*S5* (Lefort, *S. Pachomii vitae sahidice scriptae*, 145); *SBo* 52; compare *G1* 83; on its location, see Lefort, "Les premiers monastères pachômiens," 403–4. The monastery of Tse was the fifth community in the *koinonia*.

[69]*Bo* 57 (Lefort, *S. Pachomii vita bohirice scripta*, 56); *G1* 83; on its location, see Lefort, "Les premiers monastères pachômiens," 403–4. The monastery of Tsmine was the eighth community in the *koinonia*.

[70]The author of the Sahidic account of the founding of Tse follows it immediately with the story of a gift of a boat to the Pachomians by a city councilor from Kos (Apollinopolis; modern Kous) (*S5* [Lefort, *S. Pachomii vitae sahidice scriptae*, 145–46]; *SBo* 53). The boat is offered so that Pachomius might receive cargo for the monks' use. While the gift of the boat is not linked directly to the monastery of Tse, the placement of the story immediately after the account of the founding of Tse suggests an association between the two in the mind of the author. While the distance between Šmin and Kos (over 150 kilometers along the Nile) militates against an actual connection between the two stories, the very nature of the gift, that is, a boat for delivering cargo to the monasteries of the *koinonia*, underscores the author's understanding of the *koinonia* as a group of affiliated monasteries connected by the river. The gift

There is little evidence for the location of the Pachomian monastery of Tmousons,[71] although once again there is an indication of travel to and from the monastery by boat[72] which suggests its location near the Nile. Lefort's calculation of distances between this community and the others in the Pachomian *koinonia* likewise supports its location in the fertile valley.[73] There is certainly no reason to situate it in the desert. The monastery of Tbewe, founded by Petronius, was located on lands belonging to his wealthy parents.[74] This alone suggests land within the fertile valley, a conclusion further supported by Petronius's father's donation of livestock, carts, and boats to the Pachomians.[75]

Phnoum is the final monastery to enter the system in Pachomius's lifetime and is the only one for which a desert location is even suggested. It was located in the vicinity of the nome capital of Snē (Latopolis). The Greek *Vita Pachomii* locates it simply near the town of Snē (ἄνω περὶ Λατῶν),[76] the Sahidic *Vita* in the district or nome of Snē (ΠΤΟϢ ÑСΝΗ),[77] and the Bohairic *Vita* in the mountain of Snē (ΠΤⲰΟⲨ ÑСΝΗ).[78] If one accepts the Greek and Sahidic reading as correct, then like the other Pachomian establishments, the monastery of Phnoum can easily be located in the fertile valley. It is only if one gives the Bohairic reading primacy that one might place the monastery in the desert of Snē, since the term "mountain" (Coptic: ΤΟΟⲨ; Greek: ὄρος) is commonly

---

of a boat was easily understood and fit readily into the account of monasteries established in the fertile Nile valley; it is hard to imagine an author's use of such a story in an account of desert communities.

[71]*SBo* 51 (equals *Bo* 51 plus missing pages from *S5* [Lefort, *S. Pachomii vitae sahidice scriptae*, 145]); *Gl* 54. The monastery of Tmousons was the fourth community in the *koinonia*.

[72]*Bo* 59; *Gl* 55; but note *Bo* 81, 95.

[73]Lefort, "Les premiers monastères pachômiens," 400; Coquin and Martin, "Dayr Anba Bidaba," in Atiya, *The Coptic Encyclopedia*, 3. 731–32. Lefort suggested Tmousons's possible identification with Dayr Anba Bidaba, a monastery-village located beside a pond in the midst of the cultivated zone some two kilometers west of Nag Hammadi.

[74]*Bo* 56; *Gl* 80; on its location, see Lefort, "Les premiers monastères pachômiens," 399–403. The monastery of Tbewe was the seventh community in the *koinonia*. Petronius, its founder, came from the town of Pdjodj, located in the diocese of Hiw (Diospolis parva). Pdjodj has been identified with the modern village of Abu-Chouche, located on the western shore of the Nile.

[75]While it is not specifically stated that the donation went to his son's community, there is no reason to think otherwise.

[76]*Gl* 83 (Halkin, *Sancti Pachomii vitae graecae*, 56–57).

[77]*S4* 58 (Lefort, *S. Pachomii vitae sahidice scriptae*, 230; idem, *Les vies coptes de saint Pachôme et de ses premiers successeurs*, 303. Lefort choses to translate ⲉⲠⲦΟϢ ÑСΝΗ as "à la montagne de Snê."

[78]*Bo* 58 (Lefort, *S. Pachomii vita bohairice scripta*, 56–57); on its location, see Lefort, "Les premiers monastères pachômiens," 404–7.

translated as desert.[79] Since the Bohairic version was translated from the Sahidic,[80] it seems more likely that the use of the term "mountain" (ⲧⲟⲟⲩ) reflects a scribal shift from the term "district" (ⲧⲟ ⲩ), perhaps under the influence of the growing association of monasticism with the desert. The monastery's proximity to the town of Snē is further suggested by the local opposition that its construction aroused. The bishop himself led the crowd that sought to drive the Pachomians away. It thus seems most appropriate to assume that Phnoum, like the other Pachomian monasteries, was located in the fertile valley near the village of Phnoum in the Latopolite nome.

None of the nine monasteries in the Pachomian system were named after an individual, as was often the case with later singular establishments.[81] In the first half of the fourth century, ascetics had not yet garnered the fame that resulted in monasteries bearing their names. When Ebonh, Jonas, and Petronius joined their ascetic communities to the Pachomian *koinonia*, they were already known as the monasteries of Šenesēt, Tmousons, and Tbewe, respectively.[82] In those cases where the origin of the name of a Pachomian monastery is known, namely, Tabennese, Pbow, Šenesēt, and Šmin, the name derives directly from the name of the village or town with which the monastery is associated. Furthermore, in the two cases where the precise spatial relationship between the monastery and the village or town is clear, namely, Tabennese and Pbow, the monastery was located in or beside the village in the fertile valley. The monastery of Tabennese was the ascetic community located in and thus connected with the village of Tabennese. One suspects that the remaining Pachomian establishments, the precise locations of which are unclear, were similarly called after the villages whose

---

[79]W. E. Crum, "ⲧⲟⲟⲩ," *A Coptic Dictionary* (Oxford: Clarendon, 1939) 440–41; Lefort, "Les premiers monastères pachômiens," 404–7. Even if one accepts the term "mountain," however, the precise location of the monastery remains unclear. The term occurs in papyrus documents in reference to the further or proper desert, to the nearer desert or escarpment at the edge of the fertile zone, as well as to raised arable land that borders the desert (H. Cadell and Roger Rémondon, "Sens et emplois de τὸ ὄρος dans les documents papyrologiques," *Revue des études grecques* 80 (1967) 343–49). Thus even if one accepts the Bohairic reading, there is no assurance that the monastery of Phnoum was located in the desert. A lease contract dated 616 CE (*P. Lond.* 483), for example, refers to a monastery, hamlet and fields located in the mountain of the village of Tanaithis (ἐν τῷ ὄρει κώμης Ταναίθεως). The text refers to livestock and pasturage, and even fish in the waters around the monastery (πιάσαι ὀψάρια ἐκ τῶν παντοίων ὑδάτων τῶν περικύκλωθεν τοῦ αὐτοῦ μοναστηρίου). The monastery of Phnoum may well have existed in a similar location in or near a village of the same name in the Latopolite nome.

[80]Lefort, *Les vies coptes*, lxxviii; Veilleux, *Pachomian Koinonia*, 1. 2.

[81]Peter van Minnen, "The Roots of Egyptian Christianity," *Archiv für Papyrusforschung und verwandte Gebiete* 40 (1994) 84–85.

[82]*Bo* 50–51, 56; *G1* 54, 80.

names they bore. The monasteries of Tse and Tsmine, for example, located in the land or vicinity of Šmin (Panopolis), were likely situated in or beside villages of the same names in the Panopolite nome. The social, commercial, and agricultural efforts of the Pachomian monasteries support such a close and intimate relationship with their neighboring village communities. A careful reading of the Pachomian sources supports this contention.[83] It has already been noted above that the foundation of Tabennese led to such an increase in the village population that the monks built a church for the villagers before they constructed one for themselves.[84] At least in the beginning, they continued to receive the eucharist in the village church. When Theodore's mother came to Tabennese with letters from the local bishop demanding to see her son, she was only permitted to catch sight of him by climbing up on the roof of a nearby house.[85] The monastery of Tabennese was clearly situated in the village.

The monastery of Pbow was likewise situated in the fertile valley where it was effected by the flooding of the Nile. During a plague that ravaged the community, the brothers were distressed because the rising waters cut off their path to the mountain or cemetery in the desert.[86] The Greek *Vita* indicates that the flood normally reached such a height around the monastery that the monks traveled by boat during the flood season.[87] Elsewhere in the sources, one reads of monks working fields on an island in the Nile[88] and gathering fruit from orchards outside the monastery walls.[89] Monks unload a wealthy councilor's gift of wheat from his boat anchored nearby,[90] and in time of famine, they purchase wheat on the local market.[91] Specific monks were appointed to sell the *koinonia*'s handicrafts and make the necessary purchases for the community, practices that underscore the community's contact with the outside world.[92] In the *Regula Pachomii*, while permission is required to leave the monastery,[93] monks may walk about the village at certain times and even visit their families.[94] Permission was also

---

[83]Goehring, "The World Engaged," 134–44.

[84]See above, pp. 273–74; *Bo* 25; *G1* 29.

[85]*Bo* 37; compare *G1* 37. James E. Goehring, "Theodore's Entry into the Pachomian Movement," in Vincent L. Wimbush, ed., *Ascetic Behavior in Greco-Roman Antiquity: A Sourcebook* (Studies in Antiquity and Christianity 6; Minneapolis: Fortress, 1990) 349–56.

[86]*Bo* 180.

[87]*G1* 139.

[88]*G1* 106.

[89]*Regula Pachomii, Praecepta* 76–77.

[90]*Bo* 39; *G1* 39.

[91]*Paralipomena* 21–22.

[92]*Bo* 26; *G1* 28.

[93]*Regula Pachomii, Praecepta* 84.

[94]*Regula Pachomii, Praecepta* 90, 102, 54. In the two cases that refer to monks in the village, Jerome changes the text in his Latin translation to *in monasterio*. See Veilleux, *Pachomian Koinonia*, 2. 189.

required to go to the monastery's shops or stables and to launch a boat or skiff from the harbor.[95] The stables were essential given the gifts of sheep, goats, cattle, camels, and donkeys to the *koinonia*.[96] Extensive pasturage for the livestock would have also been required. The necessary involvement of the Pachomians in agricultural life is underscored by the detailed farming and irrigation legislation in the later *Regulations of Horsiesius*.[97] While the ascetic nature of the movement necessitated its regulation of contact between the monks and the wider society, the location and needs of the *koinonia* made such contact not only unavoidable, but essential. The *Regulations of Horsiesius* simply assert that conversation with seculars whom monks meet on the road be done for the glory of God.[98]

While the ascetic enterprise emphasized withdrawal, the Pachomians practiced withdrawal within the normal sphere of village life. The village monasteries of the Pachomians continued the urban ascetic presence of the earlier apotactic movement, albeit with considerably greater planning and organization. It was not by accident that the Pachomians called themselves *apotaktikoi* rather than monks or coenobites.[99] As the papyrus evidence of the urban *apotaktikoi(ai)* illustrates their legal and social connection with the wider community,[100] so too the Pachomian evidence reveals their legal and social integration within Roman Egypt.[101] A list of tax receipts from 367–68 CE for agricultural land (ἄπορα) in the Hermopolite nome includes a payment by the *apotaktikos* Anoubion, son of Horion, for the monastery of Tabennese.[102] Twenty-one years after Pachomius's death, the monastery of Tabennese, located in the Tentyrite nome, was responsible for taxes on land located at a considerable distance from it in the Hermopolite nome. In the time since his death, his successor Theodore expanded the *koinonia* by founding two additional monasteries near the town of Hermopolis, the capital of the Hermopolite nome.[103] It may be that the older community at Tabennese was legally responsible for land possessed and worked by the younger communities in the Hermopolite nome. Whatever the case, the

[95]*Regula Pachomii, Praecepta*, 108, 111, 118.

[96]*Bo* 56; *G1* 80.

[97]*Regulations of Horsiesius* 55–64.

[98]Ibid., 52.

[99]James E. Goehring, "Through a Glass Darkly: Diverse Images of the *Apotaktikoi(ai)* of Early Egyptian Monasticism," *Semeia* 58 (1992) 28.

[100]Judge, "The Earliest Use of Monachos," 72–89; idem, "Fourth Century Monasticism in the Papyri," in Roger Bagnall, ed., *Proceedings of the Sixteenth International Congress of Papyrology, New York, 24–31 July 1980* (American Studies in Papyrology 23; Chico, CA: Scholars Press, 1981) 613–20; Goehring, "Through a Glass Darkly," 139–41.

[101]Goehring, "The World Engaged," 139–41.

[102]*P. Berl. inv.* 11860A/B; Wipszycka, "Les terres de la congrégation pachômienne," 623–36; Judge ("The Earliest Use of Monachos," 73–74) makes the same point with respect to the *monachos* that appears in a Karanis petition.

[103]*G1* 134.

location of the Pachomian *koinonia* within the legal structures of fourth-century Roman Egypt is clear. There is no reason to doubt that the connection began with Pachomius's innovative move into the "deserted" village of Tabennese. While the land he occupied may have been deserted, as possessable land, his occupation of it would undoubtedly have been noted.[104] Agricultural land would have been taxable from the start of his communal efforts.[105] As his community expanded through the occupation of additional village property and agricultural land, the *koinonia*'s legal and social responsibilities would have increased proportionately. One suspects that the appointment of a steward (ⲞⲒⲔⲞⲚⲞⲘⲞⲤ) at each individual monastery and a great steward (ⲠⲒⲚⲒⲰϯ ⲚⲞⲒⲔⲞⲚⲞⲘⲞⲤ) for the *koinonia* as a whole, as well as the annual financial reckoning in August, for which the leaders of all the individual monasteries came together at the central monastery of Pbow, were necessitated in part by the legal demands of Roman Egypt.[106] Like the *apotaktikoi(ai)* before them, the Pachomians possessed their land and paid their taxes. They too developed and practiced their asceticism within the social and legal framework of the towns and villages of Egypt.

In a similar fashion, the village monasteries of the Pachomian *koinonia* presage the later forms of urban monasticism recognized by Wipszycka in the Byzantine period. The Pachomian monasteries were not located in the distant desert or even on the marginal land where the desert begins,[107] but in or in close proximity to the towns and villages whose names they bore.

---

[104]The question of the legal availability of vacant land and buildings for occupancy by individuals like Pachomius lies beyond the scope of the present essay. In the period in question, the *praescriptio longi temporis* awarded uncontested possession of property to an individual who had been in possession of it for forty years, regardless of how the person actually came into possession of it (Casper J. Kramer and Naphtali Lewis, "A Referee's Hearing on Ownership," *Transactions of the American Philological Society* 68 (1937) 357–87; Roger S. Bagnall and Naphtali Lewis, *Columbia Papyri VII: Fourth Century Documents from Karanis* (American Studies in Papyrology 20; Missoula, MT: Scholars Press, 1979) 173–85; J. A. Crook, *Legal Advocacy in the Roman World* (Ithaca, NY: Cornell University Press, 1995) 104–7). The cultivation of land in this period was often unprofitable (Kraemer and Lewis, "A Referee's Hearing," 366–67). This may account for the lack of opposition to Pachomius's occupation of it. On the other hand, the opposition of local townspeople to his founding of a monastery near the nome capital of Šmin (*G1* 81) may have been occasioned in part by legal concerns over the land in question. Documents do record disputes over vacant property (*SB* 5232; Johnson, *An Economic Survey of Ancient Rome*, 158–59) and complaints about others encroaching on one's land (van Minnen, "House-to-House Enquiries," 244–45).

[105]Urban property was not taxed. See Bagnall, *Egypt in Late Antiquity*, 153.

[106]Goehring, "The World Engaged," 141; Fidelis Ruppert, *Das pachomianische Mönchtum und die Anfänge klösterlichen Gehorsams* (Münsterschwarzach: Vier-Türme-Verlag, 1971) 320–24.

[107]Compare the White Monastery of Shenute. Coquin and Martin, "Dayr Anba Shinudah, History," in Atiya, *The Coptic Encyclopedia*, 1. 761–66.

They were not part of the desert city whose praises Athanasius sang, but rather an expansive development of ascetic practice within the towns and villages of Upper Egypt. Their communities indicate a developmental path from the earlier, less organized forms of urban asceticism represented in the apotactic movement to the later, more structured forms of ascetic practice seen in the urban and suburban monasteries of the Byzantine period. The Pachomian monasteries illustrate the steady and innovative growth of asceticism within the towns and villages of Egypt. They were not a product of the desert movement, but rather serve to challenge the common portrayal of Egyptian monasticism as a predominantly desert phenomenon.[108]

---

[108]Melitian ascetic communities also appear to have been closely connected with villages. *P. Lond.* 1913 refers to a community in the village of Hipponon in communication with the monastery of Hathor in the eastern desert of the Upper Cynopolite nome. See James E. Goehring, "Melitian Monastic Organization: A Challenge to Pachomian Originality," *Studia Patristica* 25 (1993) 388–95.

New Perspectives on the Origenist Controversy: Human Embodiment and Ascetic Strategies

ELIZABETH A. CLARK

The controversy over Origenism that erupted in the last years of the fourth century and the opening years of the fifth has puzzled many students of the period: no single identifiable theological issue seemed at stake. At the center of the Arian controversy lay a debate over the subordination (or nonsubordination) of the Son to the Father; in the fifth-century christological disputes Jesus' "nature" or "natures" prompted disagreement. But what was the focus of the Origenist controversy: the subordination of the Son and the Holy Spirit to the Father? the "fall" of the rational creatures into bodies? the restoration of the Devil? the interpretation of resurrection from the dead?

Although each of these suggestions has limited plausibility, none suffices. Indeed, some evidence casts doubt on whether the alleged errors of Origen's theology mattered much at all to the disputants: even the prosecutors, in the very heat of the controversy, appealed not just to Origen's scriptural erudition but also to questionable points of his speculation.[1] Moreover, many nontheological issues loomed large in the debate, including questions of episcopal jurisdiction, disputes pertaining to the authorship of earlier treatises, and arguments about styles of translation.[2] Such skirmishes make difficult for contemporary scholars the identification of the central battlefield. In addition, the extant evidence pertaining to the ties of kinship, friendship, mentorship, and patronage among the disputants is so abundant that a sociologist employing social network analysis could plausibly argue that no ideational

---

1. For example, Jerome, *Ep.* 85:2–3 (*CSEL* 54:136–137).
2. Epiphanius, *Ep. ad Johannem Episcopum* (Jerome, *Ep.* 51), pp. 1–2 (*CSEL* 54:396–399); Jerome, *Contra Joannem* 10, 40, 41 (*PL* 23:379, 410–411); *Ep.* 82:4, 8 (*CSEL* 55:111, 114–115). Rufinus, *Prologus in Apologeticum Pamphili Martyris pro Origene* (*CCL* 20:233); Jerome, *Ep.* 84:11 (*CSEL* 55:133–134); *Apologia* 1:8–11, 13; 2:15, 23; 3:12 (*CCL* 79:7–11, 12, 48–49, 59–60, 83–85). Jerome, *Apologia* 1:6; 2:11 (2); 3:14 (*CCL* 79:5–6, 45–46, 86–87); Rufinus, *Apologia* 2:36–41 (*CCL* 20:111–116).

Ms. Clark is John Carlisle Kilgo Professor of Religion in Duke University, Durham, North Carolina. This is her presidential address delivered at the annual meeting of the American Society of Church History, 29 December 1989.

253

factors—such as theology—need be introduced to account for the controversy's progress.[3]

Three years' study of the numerous texts pertaining to the controversy,
however, has convinced me that religious issues *do* underlie the debate, issues
lending coherence to the otherwise bewildering assortment of charges and
countercharges. One such theme concerns "the body." This theme, which
achieved prominence during the debates over asceticism in the late fourth
century, intersected the dispute over Origen in surprising ways.

To be sure, previous attacks upon Origen, such as that waged by
Methodius of Olympus early in the fourth century, had also focused on the
notion of "the bodily" in Origen's theology, but for Methodius the status of
the *resurrection* body was the contested point.[4] Although the late fourth and
early fifth-century assailants of Origenism still singled out Origen's teaching
on the resurrection for criticism—a teaching that they misunderstood—the
extensive development of ascetic theory and practice during the course of the
fourth century had served to shift the anti-Origenist focus to themes of
marriage, reproduction, and moral hierarchy based on degrees of ascetic
renunciation.[5] The body present, not the body future, now occupied the
center of discussion.

Concern about the body developed in the Origenist controversy at several
decisive points. For one, theologies of the body based on Origenist and
anti-Origenist views underlay the dispute over anthropomorphism that
disturbed the inhabitants of the Egyptian desert in the closing years of the
fourth century. For another, the anti-Origenist charges relating to marriage
and reproduction that were levelled by Epiphanius of Salamis, Theophilus of
Alexandria, and Jerome resonate with the arguments waged over asceticism a
few years earlier.

The issue feuling debate in Egypt—the issue that marks a distinctively
"Egyptian" contribution to the Origenist controversy—concerned interpreta-
tions of the "image of God": what was it, had humans lost it with the sin of
Adam, and did the concept itself imply that God had human form? The latter

---

3. Using the formula provided by network analysts, I calculate the density of Rufinus's
   network at 78 percent and Jeromes's at 83 percent. "Density" is defined as the number of
   links that actually exist among the persons in the network as a proportion of the total
   number of possible links. See, for example, J. Clyde Mitchell, "The Concept and Use of
   Social Networks," in *Social Networks in Urban Situations: Analyses of Personal Relationships in Central African Towns*, ed. J. Clyde Mitchell (Manchester, 1969). I have attempted
   such a project in "Elite Networks and Heresy Accusations: Towards a Social Description of
   the Origenist Controversy," forthcoming in *Semeia*.
4. See Methodius's *Treatise on the Resurrection*, as preserved in Epiphanius, *Panarion*
   64:12-62.
5. Especially Epiphanius, who follows Methodius. See also Jon F. Dechow, *Dogma and
   Mysticism in Early Christianity: Epiphanius of Cyprus and the Legacy of Origen* (Macon,
   Ga., 1988); Henri Crouzel, "La Doctrine origénienne du corps ressucité," *Bulletin de
   Littérature Ecclesiastique* 81 (1980): 175-200, 241-266.

question supplied a name for the Eygptian branch of the debate: the Anthropomorphite controversy. According to several fifth-century Christian writers—Socrates, Sozomen, and Palladius, all of whom sided with the alleged Origenists—the simple desert monks were outraged by Theophilus of Alexandria's Festal Letter of 399 that championed God's incorporeality, a position in accord with that of Alexandria's most important theologian, Origen.[6] According to Socrates's account, the monks flocked to Alexandria, rioted, and even threatened to kill Theophilus for expressing such a misguided view. Theophilus, who needed monastic allies in the midst of other battles he was waging (including one to engineer John Chrysostom's downfall), promptly pacified the irate monks by telling them, "In seeing you, I behold the face of God."

Since the notion of God's incorporeality had been backed by appeals to Origen, the monks asked Theophilus to anathematize Origen's books, a request to which Theophilus readily acceded. Theophilus next sent letters to the monastic communites of the desert, instructing their inhabitants to affirm, in agreement with a literal reading of Scripture, that God had bodily parts. Warming to more direct action, Theophilus led a "multitude" to Nitria, armed the Anthropomorphite monks, and routed those who stubbornly persisted in confessing God's incorporeality.[7] The Nitrian monastic communities were thus supposedly purged of Origen's supporters, including the erudite and ascetic Tall Brothers, who according to Socrates were singled out for Theophilus's wrath because they had refused to cooperate in Theophilus's shady management of church finances.[8] The Tall Brothers fled to Palestine and then to Constantinople, where their cause became entwined with that of John Chrysostom.[9] From Socrates, Sozomen, and Palladius we would infer that theology mattered little in these events and that the few theological details mentioned were raised as a "cover" for Theophilus's avaricious and self-serving behavior.

But is it the case that no geniunely theological issues underlay this disturbing and violent episode? I think not: both John Cassian (who claims to have been present when Theophilus's Festal Letter of 399 was received at Scete) and an anonymous Coptic document that records an alleged debate between Theophilus and a monk named Aphou report that a controversy over

---

6. Socrates, *Historia ecclesiastica* 6:7 (*PG* 67:683–688); Sozomen, *Historia ecclesiastica* 8:11–11–19 (*PG* 67:1544–1568); Palladius, *Dialogus de vita S. Joannis Chrysostomi* 6(22)–7(23) (Coleman Norton, pp. 35–38).

7. Socrates, *Historia ecclesiastica* 6:7 (*PG* 67:684–688).

8. Ibid., 6:7 (*PG* 67:685, 688).

9. That Origenism did not disappear from the Egyptian desert with their departure is revealed in fragments of two letters by Theophilus, preserved in Justinian's *Liber adversus Origenem* (*PG* 86:967), one dated from the summer of 400 and the second from late 400 or early 401 on the issue of Origenist monks still present.

the phrase "the image of God"—and its implications for the corporeality or incorporeality of God—was at the center of the disturbances in 399.[10]

According to Cassian, Theophilus's Festal Letter of 399 was directed against the Anthropomorphites. Many of the monks, he reports, became agitated at Theophilus's reference to God's incorporeality, since "in their simplicity" they believed that God had human form: if we were created in "God's image," as Genesis 1 claims, did not God have human shape and characteristics? Cassian adds the revealing detail that three of the four priests serving the churches at Scete opposed Theophilus's anti-Anthropomorphite teaching; only the priest of the congregation to which Cassian was attached, Paphnutius, affirmed the incorporeality of God. Some of the monks, says Cassian, expressed shock at the "novelty" of Theophilus's opinion.[11] Although Cassian probably here represents the anti-Origenists in a negative light, his testimony nonetheless suggests that one aspect of the debate focused on the relation between human embodiment and the nature of the divine.

A second source providing clues about the theological dimensions of the Anthropomorphite debate is an anonymous Coptic document published in 1883 and republished, with a French translation, by Etienne Drioton in 1915 to 1917.[12] The text concerns the life of Aphou, an Egyptian monk from Oxyrhinchus (Pemdjé) in Upper Egypt, who three years after the event described was reputedly raised to the episcopal throne by Theophilus.[13] The document tells of the reception given Theophilus's anti-Anthropomorphite Festal Letter of 399 at Pemdjé. The anonymous author of this text construes the situation differently than does Cassian, stressing that Theophilus recanted his early anti-Anthropomorphite view out of conviction, not political expedience, and that Theophilus's "conversion" was effected by the monk Aphou.

The text reports that it was Aphou's custom to journey from his monastic retreat to the town of Pemdjé once a year to hear the paschal letter from the bishop of Alexandria read aloud to the congregation. When Theophilus's letter of 399 was read, Aphou in distress heeded an angel's summons to undertake a trip to Alexandria to correct the bishop. For three days Aphou stood at Theophilus's door before he gained an audience. Upon being admitted, Aphou told Theophilus his reasons for disagreement and speedily convinced him of his error in imagining that humans had lost God's "image." The repentant Theophilus wrote to "every region" to repudiate his earlier

---

10. Cassian reports that the letters arrived at Epiphany, to announce the dates for Lent and Easter: *Conlationes* 10:2 (*SC* 54:75). Etienne Drioton, "La Discussion d'un moine anthropomorphite Audien avec le patriarche Théophile d'Alexandrie en l'année 399," *Revue de l'Orient Chrétien*, 2d ser., 10 (1915–1917): 92–100, 113–128.
11. John Cassian, *Conlationes* 10:2 (*SC* 54:76); 10:3 (*SC* 54:76).
12. See note 10 above.
13. Drioton, "La Discussion," p. 94.

opinion. Aphou graciously refrained from blaming Theophilus directly: it was rather the Devil's ploy to let the bishop scandalize the faithful so that they would give no heed to the rest of his "holy teaching." By Theophilus's retraction, the anonymous author of the text claims, the Devil was foiled and a praiseworthy example of episcopal humility was provided by Theophilus's admission of error.[14]

Although the historicity of this dialogue is patently dubious, several points of the tale command our interest. For one, the author has shifted the focus *away* from a discussion of whether God does or does not possess a corporeal form. He never replies to Theophilus's ridicule of the gross anthropomorphism of Aphou's supporters.[15] On either account, however, human embodiment in relation to the divine is at issue.

That this intra-Christian struggle over "the image of God" was waged against the background of the attempted demolition of Egyptian paganism—an iconoclastic campaign aimed to eradicate Eygptian image worship ("idolatry") that issued most notably in the destruction of the Serapeum in Alexandria—is probably no accident.[16] A theology of iconoclasm had been conveniently provided by the Origenist ascetic Evagrius Ponticus during this same period, and it is to his anti-iconic theology, with its implications for "bodiliness," that I wish now to turn. No other surviving texts from the period so well illuminate the relationship between concepts of divine incorporeality, human embodiment, and ascetic praxis as do Evagrius's writings.

Among the monks of the Egyptian desert during the 390s, Evagrius Ponticus was the chief expositor of God's utter incorporealty and the eradication of God's "image" in humans. Student in his youth of the Cappadocian Fathers, Evagrius was the friend and confidant of Rufinus of Aquileia and Melania the Elder, who had rescued him for the ascetic life during his sojourn in Jerusalem.[17] Despite his now-recognized importance, Evagrius became the subject of intensive scholarly investigation only in the last forty to fifty years. Although some small part of his writings survives in

14. Ibid.; pp. 95-96; 96-100; 114-115.
15. See the course of the debate in Drioton, "La Discussion," pp. 97-100, 113, 127.
16. For summaries, see H. G. Opitz, "Theophilos von Alexandrien," Pauly-Wissowa, eds., *Real-Encyclopädie der klassischen Altertumswissenschaft* 5A. 2 (1934): 2151; Johannes Geffcken, *The Last Days of Greco-Roman Paganism*, trans. Sabine MacCormack (Oxford, 1978), pp. 170-174.
17. On Evagrius's relation to Gregory of Nazianzen, see Palladius, *Historia Lausiaca* 38:2 (Butler 2:117); Socrates, *Historia ecclesiastica* 4:23 (*PG* 67:516; Evagrius cites a saying of Gregory at 520); Sozomen, *Historia ecclesiastica* 6:30 (*PG* 67:1584). See discussion in Gabriel Bunge, ed., *Evagrios Pontikos, Briefe aus der Wüste* (Trier, 1986), pp. 24-28; Michael W. O'Laughlin, "Origenism in the Desert: Anthropology and Integration in Evagrius Ponticus" (Th.D. diss., Harvard University, 1987), pp. 10-14, 20-28. On the reassignment of "Basil's" *Epistle* 8 to Evagrius, see Robert Melcher's *Der 8. Brief des hl. Basilius, ein Werk des Evagrius Pontikus* (Münster i. W., 1923). Palladius, *Historia Lausiaca* 38 (Butler, 2:119-120).

the original Greek (such as his *Sentences for a Nun*, probably written for Melania the Elder), it is not practical works of guidance that established Evagrius's theological importance but his *Kephalaia Gnostica* (*Gnostic Chapters*).[18] Until the early 1950s the *Kephalaia Gnostica* was known only in a bowdlerized translation that "tamed" Evagrius's ideas to make them seem more orthodox. When Antoine Guillaumont discovered and published a second version of the work, proving that it was closer to the original and more in accord with Evagrian texts such as the so-called *Letter to Melania*, scholars realized that the *Kephalaia Gnostica* was a chief source spurring Origen's condemnation by the Fifth Ecumenical Council in 553.[19]

What aspects of Evagrius's theology illuminate the debate over anthropomorphism? For Evagrius, no concepts drawn from the human sphere and expressed in language can describe the perfection of God. Neither quality nor quantity can define the Divine: it is preferable to admit that God can in no way be comprehended by the human mind than to introduce the possibility of "failure" into the notion of God.[20] As Evagrius phrased it, a defective concept cannot convey to humans the divine perfection.[21] Thus, as might be expected, he and other Origenists developed an allegorical interpretation that "spiritualized" Biblical anthropomorphisms—and "de-historicized" Scripture as a whole.

His emphasis on incorporeality links Evagrius's teaching about God to that regarding the origin and destiny of humans. Just as the original Godhead was "naked" (*gymnos*) and received "clothing" only with the Incarnation, so likewise the minds, before their precosmic "fall," had been "naked"; only when they became involved in the "movement" (Evagrius's word for the

18. Greek text of *Sentences for a Nun* edited by Hugo Gressmann in *TU* 39:4 (1913), pp. 146–151. For the argument that the work was addressed to Melania the Elder, see Joseph Muyldermans, ed., *Evagriana Syriaca. Textes inédits du British Museum et de la Vaticane* (Louvain, 1952), p. 30.
19. The two versions of the Syriac text, with French translations, are printed in *PO* 28:1. For discussion, see Antoine Guillaumont in *Les "Kephalaia Gnostica" d'Evagre le Pontique et l'histoire de L'Origénisme chez les Grecs et chez les Syriens* (Paris, 1962), pp. 120–123. The *Letter to Melania* is preserved in two parts. Only the first part was known to Frankenberg and published by him in his edition of the Syriac translations of Evagrius's writings (*Euagrius Ponticus*. Abhandlungen der königlichen Gesellschaft der Wissenschaften zu Göttingen, philologisch-historische Klasse, n.s. 13, 2 (Berlin, 1912), pp. 612–619. The second part of the *Letter* was published (Syriac text, French translation) by Gösta Vitestam, "Seconde Partie du traité, qui passe sous le nom de 'Le Grand Lettre d'Evagre le Pontique a Mélanie l'Ancienne,' " *Scripta Minora 1963–1964* (Lund, 1964), pp. 3–29. The entire letter in English translation, with commentary, was published by Martin Parmentier, "Evagrius of Pontus' 'Letter to Melania,' " *Bijdragen tijdschrift voor filosofie en theologie* 46 (1985): 2–38. See also Guillaumont, *Les "Kephalaia Gnostica,"* pp. 140–159.
20. Evagrius Ponticus, *Epistula fidei* 3 (*PG* 32:249); compare *Kephalaia Gnostica Supplementum* 19 (Frankenberg, pp. 438–439): "difference" can pertain only to things with bodies; *Kephalaia Gnostica* 1:2; 5:62 (*PO* 28:17, 203): "opposition" comes from qualities, which pertain to the body and to creatures.
21. Evagrius Ponticus, *De octo vitiosis cogitationibus* (*PG* 40:1275).

precosmic fall) did they acquire "fatness" and become attached to bodies.[22] The human mind, Evagrius posits, is essentially the same as the divine mind, and when body and soul are eventually redissolved into mind, minds will flow back into God as rivers to the sea.[23] Humans possessed the "image of God" *only* when they existed incorporeally as minds, never therafter; possession of "the image" is not compatible with human embodiment.[24] Evagrius's understanding of the original incorporeal creation has important implications for his views on the resurrection and on present existence.

Although Evagrius holds that it is blasphemy to speak badly of the body, he nonetheless believes that bodies must be discarded before the *nous* can see the "incorporeals." Thus when he speaks of a "resurrection body," the phrase indicates for him only the first of two transformations after death. To gain once more "the image of the Son," humans must at the end cast off bodies entirely: bodies will ultimately be destroyed, not just transformed.[25] That this aspect of Evagrius's theology was too radical for many Christians is shown by the haste with which it was modified and "softened" within the Syriac tradition and abandoned totally in the Greek and Latin-speaking worlds.[26]

Evagrius's view that the original creation of rational beings was incorporeal found a correlate in an ethical teaching of radically ascetic implication. Since at the creation humans lacked bodies, Evagrius argues, they also lacked the affective traits of *thumos* (anger) and *epithumia* (desire).[27] But when the mind fell, it ceased to be in "the image of God" and voluntarily took on "the image of animals." Now it shares with the animals the movements of the body; in fact, the soul renders the "animal" body even worse by introducing it to pride, vainglory, and avarice. Only one creature has preserved God's true "image," capable of knowing the Father, and this is the incarnate Son, whose divine nature remains one of "naked *nous*."[28] At the end, God will make humans resemble "the image of his Son" (Romans 8:29).[29] The regaining of God's "image" will thus occur only when humans live once more as "naked

22. Evagrius Ponticus, *Epistula fidei* 8 (*PG* 32:261); *Kephalaia Gnostica* 6:20, 85; 1:58; 2:77; 3:66, 68; 6:58, 81 (*PO* 28:225, 253, 45, 91, 125, 241, 251).
23. Evagrius Ponticus, *Epistula ad Melaniam* 4 (Frankenberg, pp. 616–617; Parmentier, p. 12). Ibid., 5; 6 (Frankenberg, pp. 616–617, 618–619; Parmentier, pp. 11–12, 12–13); compare these ideas to those in *Kephalaia Gnostica* 2:17, a sentence that Guillaumont thinks formed the basis for Anathema 14 of the Fifth Ecumenical Council at Constantinople (*PO* 28:67).
24. Evagrius Ponticus, *Epistula ad Melaniam* 9, 4, 6 (Frankenberg, pp. 614–615, 618–619; Parmentier, pp. 16–17, 11, 12).
25. Evagrius Ponticus, *Kephalaia Gnostica* 4:60; 62 (*PO* 28:163); 4:86 (*PO* 28:173); 4:34 (*PO* 28:231); 2:77; 3:66 (*PO* 28:91, 125).
26. For an analysis of the two Syriac versions, see Guillaumont, *Les "Kephalaia Gnostica,"* esp. pp. 24–30; see also pp. 23–32, 166–170, 333–335.
27. Evagrius Ponticus, *Kephalaia Gnostica* 4:85 (*PO* 28:253).
28. Evagrius Ponticus, *Epistula ad Melaniam* 9 (Parmentier, pp. 16–17, based on British Museum Ms. Add. 17192). Ibid., 4 (Frankenberg, pp. 614–615; Parmentier, p. 11). Ibid., 6 (Frankenberg, pp. 618–619; Parmentier, p. 12).
29. Evagrius Ponticus, *Kephalaia Gnostica* 6:34 (*PO* 28:231).

minds," unencumbered by bodies and by passions that cloud the imageless vision of God.

But if the "image of God" no longer remains in embodied humans, what is all *too* present for them, according to Evagrius, is the superabundance of *images* that crowd the human mind. It is these images or "thoughts" (*logismoi*) that arouse our passions and separate humans from God.[30] The *logismoi* can arise from sense experience, from memory, from phantasies, or dreams—and also from demonic temptation: the demons who stimulate the *logismoi* are, significantly, called "idol-makers" by Evagrius.[31] The "images" they suggest must be eradicated in the quest for holiness. The battle against "idols" is thus relocated from the streets of Alexandria to the minds of Christian ascetics: asceticism, in Evagrius's theology, becomes the ultimate iconoclastic device *and* the ultimate aid that helps humans to recover "the image of God."

More than any of his predecessors, Evagrius was responsible for constructing an "internalized" and "mental" understanding of sin through his elaboration of the *logismoi*. Indeed, the medieval notion of the "seven deadly sins" was derived, through Cassian, from Evagrius's teaching on the "eight evil thoughts."[32] Evagrius provides a rationale for the ordering of the "thoughts" that shows their interconnection.[33] From the first three "thoughts" (gluttony, lust, and avarice) stem all the others. Since gluttony leads to lust, the monastic regimen counsels the limitation of food and drink in an effort to curb sexual desire.[34] From avarice (the desire for things) stems anger (presumably piqued when we don't possess them and others do), or pride (when we *do* possess them).[35]

Not only do demons, memory, and dreams all conspire to call up images that cause the monk to lust, covet, or rage; even more disturbing, the demons are able to present "thoughts" as if they were something good and beautiful.[36] Thus the demon of avarice leads the monk to believe that he should

---

30. Evagrius Ponticus, *Scholia in Ecclesiasten* 1:11 (Sch. 3) (Paul Géhin, "Un Nouvel Inédit d'Evagre le Pontique: son Commentaire de l'Ecclésiaste," *Byzantion* 49 [1979]: 197).

31. Evagrius Ponticus, *Peri tōn oktō logismōn* (Ethiopian version) 2 (Spies, pp. 220–221); compare *De octo spiritibus malitiae* 8 (*PG* 79:1153) (comparison of the avaricious man with the "idolmaker").

32. John Cassian, *Conlationes* 5 (*SC* 42:188–217); see also Irénée Hausherr, "L'Origine de la théorie orientale des huit péchés capitaux," *Orientalia Christiana* 30 (1933): 165–166; 167–171.

33. Ibid., p. 171. Compare Evagrius Ponticus, *Skemmata* 41–43 (Muyldermans, "Evagriana: Note Additionelle A," p. 378).

34. Evagrius Ponticus, *De diversis malignis cogitationibus* 1 (*PG* 79:1200); *Antirrheticus* 2:48, 49 (Frankenberg, pp. 490–491); *Practicus* 15 (*SC* 171:536); *De octo spiritibus malitiae* 4 (*PG* 79:1148).

35. Evagrius Ponticus, *De diversis malignis cogitationibus* 1 (*PG* 79:1201).

36. Evagrius Ponticus, *De perfectione* 16 (Muyldermans, "Evagre le Pontique, Les *Capita Cognoscitiva*" [Syriac, p. 102; French, p. 106]).

accumulate goods for the sake of assisting the poor, strangers, and prisoners.[37] The demon of gluttony makes him think that he should eat in order to preserve his health; the demon of vainglory leads him to imagine how blessed it would be to heal the sick (and thus receive the adulation of crowds).[38] The demon of *porneia* tempts the monk to think that marriage and children are "goods" that he might innocently cherish. The demon of vainglory urges him to lead a crowd of brothers and sisters to the monastic life. And worst of all is the demon of pride, who stimulates him to believe that he is the cause of any good he may do: even helping others thus becomes a danger to the monk's salvation.[39]

Against such demonic wiles the monk must arm himself. This he can do in several ways. For one, he should mount a verbal attack, equipping himself with scriptural verses to hurl at the demons when they assault him, after the fashion of Jesus' response to the Tempter.[40] In addition to providing scriptural quotations that will mar the artistry of the demons' illusions, Evagrius advises a strict ascetic discipline to help the monk resist temptation: asceticism becomes the means to break the power of images. Fasting and the limitation of water is essential, and this to the time of death.[41] (Evagrius reports about himself that he ate once a day.)[42] The monk's profession, according to Evagrius, requires that he never take to fullness bread, water, or sleep.[43] Restriction of eating and drinking contributes to the monk's reduced sexual desire and to fewer "evil dreams" while he sleeps.[44] Restriction on food also has another "medico-moral" benefit: by preventing the accumulation of bile it helps the monk to control anger.[45] In addition to the limitation of food and water, toil, solitude, and vigils are also recommended for the quenching

---

37. Evagrius Ponticus, *De diversis malignis cogitationibus* 22 (*PG* 79:1225); *Rerum monachalium rationes* 4 (*PG* 40:1256).
38. Evagrius Ponticus, *Practicus* 7 (*SC* 171:508–510); *Antirrheticus* 1:19, 33, 44, 56, 59 (Frankenberg, pp. 476–477, 478–479, 480–481, 482–483); *Practicus* 13 (*SC* 171:528).
39. Evagrius Ponticus, *Antirrheticus* 2:49 (Frankenberg, pp. 490–491); 7:1 (Frankenberg, p. 530); *Practicus* 14 (*SC* 171:532; *De octo vitiosis cogitationibus* (*PG* 40:1275).
40. Matthew 4:1–11; compare Luke 4:1–13. Evagrius provides scriptural passages with which to ward off each of the eight evil *logismoi* in his *Antirrheticus*.
41. A "scientific" theory accompanies the latter: demons gravitate to water. See *Antirrheticus* 2:22 (Frankenberg, pp. 488–489); *De humilitate* (Muyldermans, *Evagriana Syriaca* [Syriac, p. 112; French, p. 148]).
42. Evagrius Ponticus, *Epistulam ad Melaniam* 7 (Parmentier, p. 14).
43. Evagrius Ponticus, *De jejunio* 8 (Muyldermans, *Evagriana Syriaca* [Syriac, p. 116; French, p. 151]).
44. That one passion leads to another is a central aspect of Evagrius's teaching on the passions: *De diversis malignis cogitationibus* 1 (*PG* 79:1200); *Sententiae ad monachos* 11 (*TU* 39:4, p. 154).
45. Evagrius Ponticus, *De perfectione* 14 (Muyldermans, "Les *Capita cognoscitiva*" [Syriac, p. 105; French, p. 105]).

of desire.[46] Evagrius himself employed a more drastic measure to foil the demon of *porneia*: standing naked in a well on a winter night.[47]

In Evagrius's view the monk should strive for *apatheia* ("passionlessness"), but this goal was not conceived by him as the height of the contemplative life. Indeed, the quest for *apatheia* is practical and surprisingly low on the scale of Evagrian virtues. Nonetheless, all passion must be rooted out before the higher goals of knowledge and contemplation can be achieved.[48] A great achievement is the ability to pray "purely." By "pure prayer" Evagrius means an act of worship—really, an act of contemplation—in which all "thoughts" and concepts are banished from the mind, which becomes "like light" in an intense, imageless contemplation of the Godhead.[49] Antoine Guillaumont has intriguingly suggested that Evagrius's advocacy of "pure prayer," devoid of all mental forms, may have been the original incitement to debate among the monks in Egypt over anthropomorphism and "the image of God" in the 390s.[50]

Thus for Evagrius the Origenist claim that God's utter incorporeality could not be "imaged"—either by human minds or in human natures—was inextricably linked to an ascetic regimen whose aim was to free the mind of all images which, by definition, obscure the vision of God: an iconoclasm directed at mental images is here matched by an ascetic assault on the human body and a literary assault on those who would ascribe "bodiliness" to God. Debates over divine and human corporeality thus underlie the Egyptian wing of the Origenist controversy.

A second set of issues regarding "the body" that surfaced in the Origenist debate is found in the charges against Origenism levelled by Epiphanius of Salamis, Theophilus of Alexandria, and Jerome. As they developed their arguments, both Epiphanius and Theophilus came increasingly to focus on the issue of Origenism's implications for procreation. Jerome provides an instructive contrast to Epiphanius and Theophilus. Not wishing to undercut his *own* ardently ascetic stance by attacking Origenist asceticism, Jerome nonetheless imports to the controversy the notion of a hierarchy of merit based on degrees of renunciation, a notion that he had espoused during the debates over asceticism in the 380s and 390s. Thus even though Jerome never enthused about the goodness of "the body" as did Epiphanius and Theophilus, he nevertheless found the thesis on moral hierarchy that he had crafted during his battles over asceticism useful in combatting the highly egalitarian

46. Evagrius Ponticus, *Practicus* 15 (*SC* 171:536); *Ep.* 55, 3 (Frankenberg, pp. 602–603; Bunge, *Briefe*, p. 270).
47. Palladius, *Historia Lausiaca* 38:11 (Butler 2:121).
48. Evagrius Ponticus, in Cod. Paris. Graec. 913, no. 16 (Muyldermans, "Evagriana: Note Additionelle A," p. 375); *Kephalaia Gnostica* 2:4 (*PO* 28:61, 63); compare *Kephalaia Gnostica* 2:6 (*PO* 28:63).
49. Evagrius Ponticus, *Kephalaia Gnostica* 5:15 (*PO* 28:183).
50. Guillaumont, *Les "Kephalaia Gnostica,"* p. 61.

view of the afterlife porposed by Origenists. To this second link of the Origenist controversy with the ascetic debates I now turn.

Epiphanius of Salamis, best known for his presentation and criticism of various ancient heresies, stands as the first anti-Origenist polemicist in the late fourth-century branch of the war on Origen. In his two early works, the *Ancoratus* and the *Panarion*, written in the mid-370s, Epiphanius *claims* that Trinitarian issues worry him deeply, that "Ariomaniacs" are the worst heretics. Thus it comes as no surprise that he roundly attacks Origen's subordination of the Son to the Father.[51] Despite his claim, Epiphanius is less concerned with Trinitarian issues than he professes.[52] Already in the 370s the major line of his assault pertains to issues of materiality as they manifest themselves in discussions of the body and of allegorical exegesis. For example, Epiphanius faults Origen for not emphasizing the historical reality of the stories of creation and the first sin in Genesis or the physical identity of the resurrection body with present human flesh.[53] Likewise in chapter sixty-four of the *Panarion*, devoted to the errors of Origen, it is issues pertaining to the body that occupy him most fully (although Epiphanius criticizes Origen's subordinationist theology).[54] Here he centers on Origen's view of the fall of souls into bodies, especially on his interpretation of the "tunics of skin" that God gave Adam and Eve in Genesis 3 as "bodies."[55] Epiphanius also attacks Origen's position on the resurrection body, borrowing extensively from Methodius's earlier critique of Origen. Both Methodius and Epiphanius refute Origen's claim that a "corporeal form" (*eidos*) surviving death constitutes a doctrine of "resurrection"; rather, they interpret Origen— somewhat uncharitably—to teach that *nothing* remains of our bodily nature.[56]

Epiphanius's concern for "bodiliness" reaches its height only in 394, the year in which the debate over Origen was heating up in Palestine. Epiphanius himself had fanned the flames by making a not-too-veiled attack upon John of Jerusalem for his alleged Origenism.[57] In a letter of 394 to John Epiphanius raises several of his earlier concerns pertaining to the body: the preexistence of souls and their fall into materiality, the physicality of the

51. Epiphanius, *Ancoratus* 116 (*GCS* 25:144); 63 (*GCS* 25:75–76).
52. Dechow, *Dogma*, pp. 248–251, 265–270.
53. Epiphanius, *Ancoratus* 55, 58, 62 (*GCS* 25:64–65, 67–68, 74–75). Origen's fullest discussion of the "tunics of skins" is in his *Commentary on Genesis*, on verse 3:21 (*PG* 12:101). Epiphanius, *Ancoratus* 87 (*GCS* 25:107–108).
54. Epiphanius, *Panarion* 64, 4, 5 (*GCS* 31²:409–410, 415); compare Origen, *De principiis* 1:1:1, 1:6, 1:8, 2:6 (*GCS* 22:16–17, 20–23, 24–26, 34–37). On Origen's use and understanding of *ktisma*, see Dechow, *Dogma*, pp. 281–284.
55. Epiphanius, *Panarion* 64:4 (*GCS* 31²:411–412). See Dechow, *Dogma*, pp. 297–301. Epiphanius, *Panarion* 64:17, 23 (*PG* 41:1097); text differs from *GCS*.
56. See Crouzel, "Doctrine origénienne," pp. 241–257; followed by Dechow, *Dogma*, pp. 373–384.
57. The letter is preserved in Latin translation by Jerome (*Ep.* 51) (*CSEL* 54:395–412).

resurrection body, and a literal reading of the Genesis creation stories. But to these concerns Epiphanius adds a new charge which is of interest to our argument: Origen's alleged deprecation of the body implies that reproduction is evil. What, Epiphanius asks, would become of God's blessing on Adam, Noah, and their offspring ("Be fruitful, multiply, and fill the earth" [Gen. 1:28; 9:7]) if the soul were shut in the body as in a tomb, as Epiphanius thinks Origen taught? Did God have to wait for angels to sin in heaven before multiplying humans on earth, he scornfully inquires?[58]

Why, we might ask, was Epiphanius now worried about the issue of reproduction in 394 when he did not express such concerns in his earlier attacks, either upon Origen's teaching or upon that of the heretically ascetic Manicheans or Hieracites? Why did he not use the "reproduce and multiply" text against such groups when he wrote the *Panarion*?[59] Given his earlier silence, why in 394 did Eiphanius think that *these* verses were central to the refutation of an Origenist denigration of reproduction?

The answer, I think, lies in the ascetic debates whose fireworks lit up the early 390s. In 393 Jerome had engaged in a heated dispute with Jovinian on questions regarding asceticism. The central scriptural quotations that framed their long literary debate were Genesis 2:24 (that the two shall become "one flesh," ratified by Jesus in Matthew 19:5) and Genesis 1:28 and 9:1 ("reproduce and multiply"). Jovinian had argued that God's blessing not just on Adam and Eve at creation but also on Noah, his wife, his sons, and their wives after the Flood showed that even human sinfulness could not eradicate the goodness of reproduction.[60]

These verses are precisely the ones that Epiphanius notes in his letter to John of Jerusalem.[61] Yet we must ask how probable it is that Epiphanius, in Cyprus, knew about Jerome's literary debate with Jovinian? Unfortunately, all of Jerome's letters written between 387 and 393, the very years in which he might have penned complaints to Epiphanius and other friends about views like Jovinian's, are lost. Hence we have no epistolary evidence for this period. We do know, however, that Epiphanius visited Palestine in 394 and had contact with Jerome's monastery: recall that he had ordained Jerome's brother Paulinianus, who was a monk in Jerome's Bethlehem establishment.[62] That Epiphanius in 394 knew about the debate that had recently raged between Jerome and Jovinian thus seems likely.

The Genesis verses had been central to the controversy between Jerome and Jovinian. Jerome had been hot with anger at Jovinian's insinuation that his ascetic fervor, with its alleged degradation of reproduction, verged on

58. Epiphanius, *Epistula ad Iohannem Episcopum* (Jerome, *Ep.* 51) 4 (*CSEL* 54:402).
59. Epiphanius, *Panarion* 66:56; 67:1; 2; 6 (*GCS* 37²:92, 133–134, 138).
60. Jerome, *Adversus Jovinianum* 1:5 (*PL* 23:225–226).
61. Epiphanius, *Epistula ad Iohannem Episcopum* (Jerome, *Ep.* 51) 4 (*CSEL* 54:402).
62. Ibid., 1 (*CSEL* 54:396–397).

"Manicheanism." He stormed in reply, "I am no Marcionite, Manichean, or Encratite. I know that God's first commandment was 'Be fruitful, multiply, and fill the earth' " —an assertion that he then undercuts by arguing the superiority of virginity to even "honorable marriage." Yet Jerome as well as Jovinian could manipulate Genesis for his own purposes: he points out to his readers that Adam and Eve were virgins in Paradise before the Fall and that marriage entered human life only when they were expelled from Eden.[63] It is likely, I think, that Epiphanius had registered, via Jerome's debate, that the Genesis texts *must* be used as central exegetical strategies for any argument about embodiment and reproduction. Epiphanius's appeal to Genesis stems not from antiquarian interests but from the religious concerns of his own day.

The same pattern of argumentation can be found in the writings of Theophilus of Alexandria against Origenism. These writings—some of which are extant in Jerome's Latin translation and some, preserved fragmentarily in Greek, or in Syriac and Armenian translations—are an especially interesting source because we can see Theophilus's main points of attack shift even in the short period between 400 and 404. We can readily note through a perusal of Theophilus's letters how rapidly the archbishop lost interest in battling Origenism—a point also noted by his contemporaries, who used it to claim that his polemic against Origenism was not entirely sincere.[64]

In letters dating from 400 through 403 Theophilus's charges against Origen are similar to those levelled by Epiphanius: that Origen subordinated the Son to the Father, taught the restoration of the Devil, denied the resurrection of the dead, and affirmed a precosmic fall of souls.[65] Yet even as early as 401, one year after he wrote his first anti-Origenist text now extant, Theophilus had hit upon the implications of Origen's views for a theology of marriage and reproduction, and these he pressed to fault contemporary Origenism.

Theophilus reasons that if bodies could not have existed without souls first sinning in heaven and being cast down, chained to the "penitentiary" (*ergastulum*) of the body, marriage must be condemned. How could marriage be "honorable" and "immaculate" (Hebrews 13:4), Theophilus argues, if the soul becomes enclosed in a body only after it is stained with sin? Hannah, the

---

63. Jerome, *Adversus Jovinianum* 1:3 (*PL* 23:223); 1:16 (*PL* 23:246).
64. Socrates, *Historia ecclesiastica* 6:17 (*PG* 67:716).
65. Theophilus, *Synodica epistula* (Jerome, *Ep.* 92) 2 (*CSEL* 55:149); *Epistula paschalis* (401) (Jerome, *Ep.* 96) 5; 7 (*CSEL* 55:162–163, 164–165). Theophilus, *Synodica epistula* (Jerome, *Ep.* 92) 2 (*CSEL* 55:149); *Epistula paschalis* (401) (Jerome, *Ep.* 96) 8 (*CSEL* 55:165). Theophilus, *Synodica epistula* (Jerome, *Ep.* 92) 2 (*CSEL* 55:149), citing *De oratione* 15; *Epistula paschalis* (401) (Jerome, *Ep.* 96) 13 (*CSEL* 55:172): how is this to conquer the empire of death, Theophilus asks? Theophilus, Fragment 2, *Epistula synodalis prima* (Declerck, "Théophile," pp. 505–506 [Greek]; pp. 506–507 [French]); *Epistula paschalis* (401) (Jerome, *Ep.* 96) 17 (*CSEL* 55:177); *Epistula paschalis* (402) (Jerome, *Ep.* 98) 10, 12 (*CSEL* 55:194–195).

mother of Samuel, would be guilty for desiring a child (1 Sam. 1:10–11) if it were necessary for a soul to leave its beatitude, be weighted down by sin, and fall to earth in order for her to bear her son. When "Moses" foretold that God would multiply the Israelites a thousand times (Deut. 1:10–11), are we to imagine that "crowds of souls in the heavens" were obliged to sin in order for the Israelite race to be established? How could David have said that to see your children's children is a blessing (Psalm 128:5–6) if souls must err in order to increase the family line?[66] To these questions Theophilus thinks Origenism provides no good reply.

Theophilus next develops the argument that Epiphanius had raised in his letter to John of Jerusalem in 394: the "reproduce, multiply, and fill the earth" commandment that God gave to Adam and Eve (Gen. 1:28) would be no *blessing* if souls had to sin and be sent down to earth in order for bodies to be born. Instead, the command would entail a curse, and such a supposition is contradicted by the implication in Genesis that a curse came upon humans only after they sinned in Eden by their own volition. According to Theophilus, God has constituted the nature of the human body directly; it does not originate through the sin of souls. Origen and all "apocryphal Scriptures," Theophilus concludes, are to be rejected by believing Christians.[67]

By the time of his Festal Letter of 404, composed just three years later, the *only* point of Origenist theology that concerns Theophilus is reproduction: there is *no* other topic of Origenist theology that he chooses to debate. Theophilus's argument in 404 proceeds from a consideration of biblical passages. Why would "Paul" have urged young people to marry and procreate (1 Tim. 5:14) if bodies are prisons for "angels" (that is, souls) who fell from heaven? Marriage would be the result of the punishment of souls, not means for the creation of bodies. "Reproduce and multiply" (Gen. 1:28) was meant as a blessing and was reinforced by "Paul" in Hebrews 13:4 ("Marriage is honorable and the nuptial bed without stain"). The purpose of bodily reproduction, according to Theophilus, is to compensate for death by a succession of births. If the souls sinned in Heaven, they certainly did not deserve a blessing but rather a punishment. When the prophet Isaiah (60:22) wrote, "The least shall be in the thousands and the smallest, a great nation," his prediction of an increase of population was meant to signal God's favor.[68]

The discovery (and publication in 1975) of Greek fragments from letters that Theophilus probably wrote from Constantinople in 403 confirms his preoccupation with reproduction as an issue on which Origenists could be

66. Theophilus, *Epistula paschalis* (401) (Jerome, *Ep.* 96) 18 (*CSEL* 55:177–179).
67. Theophilus, *Epistula paschalis* (401) (Jerome, *Ep.* 96), 19 (*CSEL* 55:179); 20 (*CSEL* 55:180).
68. Theophilus, *Epistula paschalis* (404) (Jerome, *Ep.* 100) 12 (*CSEL* 55:225–226).

attacked.[69] In these letters he makes clear that the topic is not one of antiquarian concern for him: the present inhabitants of the Egyptian monasteries, he writes, are being disturbed by Origen's teaching on the incorporeal state in which humans originally existed and their subsequent "fall" into bodies. Once again, Theophilus notes the drastic consequences of such a view for a theology of reproduction. On Origen's thesis why would woman have been created? How could reproduction have occurred if souls had not erred? To the contrary, Genesis teaches us that God "made them male and female, and blessed them, saying, 'Reproduce, multiply, and fill the earth' " (Gen. 1:28). How could these words have conveyed a blessing if the manner of production of bodies involved a fall of sinful souls from heaven?[70] This is, of course, the same argument that Theophilus had mounted in 401, assuming central importance in his letter of 404.[71] The new Greek fragments of Theophilus's letters thus confirm the thesis that his earlier charges of Trinitarian and other errors recede, while contemporary issues about the body gain in importance for his anti-Origenist argument. Theophilus, like Epiphanius before him, moved increasingly to a polemic that centered on issues of the body and reproduction.

What about Jerome? Since he had earlier devoted himself to translating Origen's scriptural commentaries and homilies and to incorporating these teachings into his own writings, Jerome himself was in a dubious position after the attacks upon Origenism became heated. He found, to his surprise and annoyance, that he had to defend *himself* against charges of Origenist-sympathizing—charges that Rufinus was only too happy to press.[72]

It took until 396 for Jerome to register that he, too, was implicated in Origenism: in a letter to Vigilantius dated that same year, Jerome distances himself from four errors of Origen ("I anathematize Origen daily," he informs Vigilantius).[73] But Jerome's subsequent attack on Origen assumes a different coloration than those of Epiphanius and Theophilus, and this difference can be explained by Jerome's differing role in the ascetic debates of the previous two decades.

In the 380s and 390s Jerome had made himself the most vocal champion in the West of the virginal life. So derogatory were his comments on marriage in his book *Against Jovinian* that his Roman friend Pammachius had removed copies of the work from circulation, for the book's antimarital sentiments had shocked Roman Christians.[74] Given these radically ascetic views, now deeply

69. Marcel Richard, "Nouveaux Fragments de Théophile d'Alexandrie," *Nachrichten der Akademie der Wissenschaften in Göttingen* (1975), pp. 2, 58.
70. Theophilus, Fragment 11 (Richard, "Nouveaux Fragments," p. 65).
71. Theophilus, *Epistula paschalis* (401) (Jerome, *Ep.* 96) 18, and *Epistula paschalis* (404) (Jerome, *Ep.* 100) 12 (*CSEL* 55:177–179, 225–226).
72. Especially in his *Apologia contra Hieronymum*; text in *CCL* 20:37–123.
73. Jerome, *Ep.* 61:2 (*CSEL* 54:577).
74. Jerome, *Ep.* 48 (49):2 (*CSEL* 54:347).

implanted in his system of values, it is unlikely that Jerome would construct an argument against Origenism that required him to defend *too* enthusiastically the blessings of marriage or its institution as part of God's original plan for the universe. Rather, he employed a different argument, but one, interestingly enough, that he had elaborated during his campaign against Jovinian a few years earlier. The position he had developed during the debates over asceticism found new expression here.

During the controversy with Jovinian, Jerome had advanced a theory that rewards in heaven would be sharply differentiated, based on one's level of ascetic renunciation. Likewise, there would be grades of punishment in hell. Recall Jovinian's position: all the baptized are of equal merit whether they be virgins, widows, or the married, if they are equal in other respects, and that there is only one reward in heaven for those who keep their baptismal vows. Against Jovinian, Jerome piles up his metaphors of differentiation: of gold, silver, and hay; of grain, stalk, and ears; of hundredfold, sixtyfold, thirtyfold harvests. On Jovinian's premise, complains Jerome, whoremongers would be equal in heaven to virgins, a view Jerome finds shocking *despite* his continued assertion that the church pardons all the penitent, even whoremongers. Pardon, however, does *not* mean that all will have the same recompense. Jerome applies Paul's claim that various "gifts" will have their different "rewards" (see 1 Cor. 7:7, 12:4–11) to the varying ascetic statuses of Christians. Baptism does not erase the difference between virgins and harlots, despite the Christian confession that all become "new men" in baptism. Jovinian's opinion should be faulted, for on it the telling of an ordinary fib would send one to the same "outer darkness" inhabited by those guilty of parricide.[75]

Jovinian's view, that there are only two categories, the saved and the damned, is assessed by Jerome as more akin to the philosophy of the Old Stoics than to that of Christians, and he devotes most of Book Two of the *Adversus Jovinianum* to its refutation. When Jovinian quotes Matthew 25 on the twofold division between sheep and the goats, Jerome reminds him (and his readers) that there is a great difference between one sheep and another. In fact, Jerome takes gradation in the afterlife as a necessary proposition for the defense of God's justice, since, he claims, it would be unfair for God to assign the same reward for unequal merits. The *whole* truth is not taught by the passage on the sheep and the goats, or on that concerning the wise and the foolish virgins. Other biblical references need to be recalled, and Jerome offers suggestions: Jesus' words on the greatest and the least in the Kingdom (Matt. 20:26–27) or on the diverse number of talents that the master gave his

75. Jerome, *Adversus Jovinianum* 1:3 (*PL* 23:224); 1:3 (*PL* 23:223); 1:4 (*PL* 23:225); 1:8 (*PL* 23:231); 1:15 (*PL* 23:245); 1:8 (*PL* 23:232); 1:33 (*PL* 23:267); 2:31 (*PL* 23:342–343).

three servants (Matt. 25:14–30) provide fitting examples of gradations among the ranks of Christians.[76]

Two biblical passages that Jerome leveled against Jovinian are particularly revealing, since they concern the same issue—the hierarchy of merit—that he faced during the Origenist controversy. His interpretation of these passages, *contra* Jovinian, solidified the argument he used soon thereafter to combat the Origenist view that all rational beings will eventually be restored to their primeval unity and goodness. One passage useful to Jerome is the parable of the laborers in the vineyard. Jovinian had noted that all the laborers received the same reward: one penny. No differentiation was made, despite the different lengths of time they had worked. Jerome interprets the parable differently: the one penny means only that the laborers will all arrive at one heaven; the emphasis of the parable lies in their varying calls.[77] Jerome posits here the theme of one afterlife, with gradation within it, the same view he later pressed against the Origenist notion of the *apokatastasis*, the restoration of all things to their primeval unity.

A second passage that Jerome appropriated during his debate with Jovinian recounts Jacob's vision at Bethel in which the angels ascend and descend the ladder. According to Jerome, we are to believe that all the angels on the ladder are saved, are among the "sheep," although they are on higher and lower rungs. Only those angels who have descended completely off the ladder are among the "goats." Does Jovinian imagine that angels who have so descended (the "goats") will receive their inheritance?[78] Jerome's question to Jovinian is striking, because it concerns the exact problem Jerome faced in the Origenist controversy regarding the restoration or the nonrestoration of the Devil. When Jerome, against Jovinian, replied "no," that the descended angels will *not* receive their inheritance, he had formulated the answer he would give eight or nine years later against Origenism.

Jerome's passion to preserve strict hierarchy both on earth and in heaven reappears only a few years after his debate with Jovinian, even before he realized that he was vulnerable to attack as an Origenist. Already by 396, in his *Commentary on Jonah*, Jerome appropriates the views on moral hierarchy based on degrees of ascetic renunciation that he developed in the controversy with Jovinian for his new attack upon Origenism.[79] He focuses on the issue of the restoration of the Devil. He asks, if all "rational creatures" including the Devil are to be raised to the same heavenly dignity, what grounds for distinction will there be between virgins and prostitutes, between

---

76. Ibid., 2:18 (*PL* 23:326–327); 2:21, 33, 35 (*PL* 23:329, 345, 349); 2:18 (*PL* 23:326); 2:23 (*PL* 23:333); 2:25 (*PL* 23:336); 2:33 (*PL* 23:344).
77. Ibid., 2:32 (*PL* 23:344).
78. Ibid., 2:27 (*PL* 23:338); see Genesis 28:12.
79. Text in *CCL* 76.

the mother of Jesus and "the victims of public lust?" "Will Gabriel be like the devil? will the apostles be the same as demons? prophets and false prophets? martyrs and persecutors?" Even if the Origenist proponents were to argue that it will take infinite ages for the final restitution to equality to occur, for them the end is nevertheless eventually the same for all; and if so, Jerome retorts, our actions here and now do not count. A biblical commentary is not the place to argue at length against this "perverse teaching," he claims. Nonetheless, Jerome is enraged by those (John of Jerusalem? Rufinus?) who affirm such beliefs in private but who deny them in public.[80]

Likewise, in works written at the turn of the fifth century Jerome reinforces this point, arguing against the view that virgins and repentant prostitutes will receive the same heavenly reward, or that the Devil will flourish in the same ranks as the Cherubim and the Seraphim.[81] On such grounds it would not even matter if we were pagans or Jews rather than Christians! Moreover, Jerome argues, Origen's notion that new falls may result in souls being reclad with bodies renders dubious the maintenance of proper ranking of men over women and virgins over prostitutes.[82] Instead of Evagrius's vision of the equality of disembodied minds, Jerome favors a hierarchy of bodies.

Thus the issue of hierarchy, forged in the ascetic debates of the 380s and refined in his controversy with Jovinian, resonates throughout Jerome's anti-Origenist polemic. Jerome was still, in the midst of the Origenist debate, fighting a Western controversy over asceticism when he insisted that moral hierarchy based on ascetic renunciation must be preserved and gradations of status in the afterlife upheld. Unlike his allies Epiphanius and Theophilus, who enlisted a pro-reproduction argument against Origenists, ascetic renunciation stands at the center of Jerome's religious concern. As Peter Brown has recently phrased it, the "limitless fluidity of the human person" that Jerome understood to be the center of Origen's thought ran up against beliefs he cherished even more deeply, such as the maintenance of hierarchy both here and hereafter, measured by degrees of bodily renunciation.[83] For Jerome— indeed, for all the disputants—human embodiment remained a problem for theological speculation as well as for Christian praxis.

The ascetic debate, I propose, was not displaced by the Origenist controversy: it was subsumed within it.

80. Jerome, *In Ionam* (*CCL* 76:407–408, on Jonah 3:6–9).
81. Jerome, *Ep.* 84:7 (*CSEL* 55:129).
82. Jerome, *Apologia* 2:12 (*SC* 303:134).
83. Peter Brown, *The Body and Society: Men, Women and Sexual Renunciation in Early Christianity* (New York, 1988), p. 380.

Bijdragen, tijdschrift voor filosofie en theologie 46 (1985) 2-38

EVAGRIUS OF PONTUS' "LETTER TO MELANIA" I

M. PARMENTIER

In what follows below, the so-called "Letter to Melania" by Evagrius of Pontus (=*CPG* 2438) is given in an English translation of its Syriac version, followed by some notes by way of a (by no means exhaustive) commentary.

Three people have been constitutive in the preparation of this translation and commentary of the Letter to Melania: Sister Helen Mary S.L.G. who discovered Evagrius on Bardsey Island and without whose urging the translation would not have been made, Dr. Sebastian Brock without whose help the translation would not have been reliable (any remaining errors are mine) and finally, Prof. Antoine Guillaumont who resuscitated so much of Evagrius' writings and theology for us.

Introduction

Evagrius' life

What we know about Evagrius' life is to be found in chapter 38 of Palladius' *Lausiac History*[1] and in the Church Histories of Socrates[2] and Sozomenus.[3] He was born around 345 in Ibora, a city of Pontus in Asia Minor, his father being a country bishop. St.Basil ordained him a reader and St.Gregory of Nazianzus ordained him a deacon. When the latter became patriarch of Constantinople, Evagrius accompanied him thither and stayed on with his successor Nectarius. Then he fell in love with a married woman and left the City after having been warned in a dream. He then went to Jerusalem where he met Melania "the Roman lady", who had founded a monastery in the Holy City as Palladius tells us in his chapter 46, where he gives her biography. In this monastery also lived "the most noble Rufinus, from Italy, of the city of Aquileia" who translated Origen into Latin. Both Melania and Rufinus initially were friends of St.Jerome who later fell out with them, apparently because of the value they attached to Origen's teachings.

Melania convinced Evagrius to become a monk in 383. According to Palladius, he first lived two years in the monastic settlement on the Mountain of Nitria, then fourteen years in the settlement in the desert of the Cells. He came to know several famous ascetics, and indeed was a great ascetic himself. At the same time,

[1]   Ed. C. Butler, Cambridge 1898, p.116f.; ET W. K. Lowther Clarke, London 1918, p.132f.
[2]   IV,23; ET A. C. Zenos, *NPNF* Second Series Vol. II, p.107f.
[3]   VI,30; ET same vol. p.368f.

he was a great admirer of Origen; his whole theological system has in fact been derived from that of this thinker. In 399, a first Origenist controversy broke out in the Nitrian settlement between the "Anthropomorphists" (a more or less fundamentalist group, the majority of the monks) and the "Tall Brothers" and their followers (an intellectualist group inspired by Origen's system, the minority of the monks). Although Evagrius should have been one of the leaders of the latter group, his name is not mentioned in the context of the controversy, from which we may conclude that he had already died in 399. A century and a half later, at the (Fifth Ecumenical) Council of Constantinople in 553, Origen and his teachings were finally condemned by the whole Church but, as Prof. Guillaumont has shown, the Origenism condemned there was really Origenism in its Evagrian form.[4]

Evagrius' works

Evagrius' influence on later monastic generations has been enormous. His ascetic works inspired professional ascetics of many times and places, the more so because in them the Origenist background of Evagrius' theology is least explicit. This is the reason why a number of his ascetic works have survived in Greek. On top of that, some of them were ascribed to the more orthodox saint Nilus († 430). In the famous eighteenth century compilation of Greek monastic writings called the *Philokalia,* we find two of Evagrius' works under his own name (*CPG* 2441 and 2450) and one under the name of St.Nilus (*CPG* 2452).[5]

First in a list of Evagrius' main works three works must be mentioned which form a kind of trilogy: the *Practicus,* which deals with the "practical life" in the first stage of the monk's ascetic development, the *Gnosticus* which deals with the higher "gnostic" stage and the *Kephalaia Gnostica* which provide the doctrinal background to the state of those addressed in the *Gnosticus.*
The *Practicus* (*CPG* 2430) gives advice for the progressive purification of the "passionable part of the soul", in order to reach impassibility (*apatheia*). A critical edition of the Greek text, a French translation and an extensive commentary have been published by A. and C. Guillaumont.[6] An English translation was made by J. E. Bamberger.[7]

---

4 "Evagre et les anathématismes antiorigénistes des 553", *Studia Patristica* III = *TU* 78, Berlin 1961, p.219-226, and especially in *Les 'Kephalaia Gnostica' d'Evagre le Pontique et l'histoire de l'origénisme chez les Grecs et chez les Syriens, Patristica Sorbonensia* 5, Paris 1962. Cp. also the articles of A. and C. Guillaumont "Evagre le Pontique" in *Dictionnaire de Spiritualité* IV, 1961, col.1731-1744 and "Evagrius Ponticus" in *Reallexicon für Antike und Christentum* VI, 1966, col.1088-1107. For the general background, cp. also D. J. Chitty, *The desert a city,* London ²1977 (see also the Index of Persons on Evagrius and Melania).
5 An ET of all the Evagrian material in the *Philokalia* has appeared in G. E. H. Palmer, Philip Sherrard, Kallistos Ware, *The Philokalia* I, London 1979, p.31-71.
6 *Traité pratique ou le moine, SC* 170 & 171, Paris 1971.
7 *Praktikos and Chapters on Prayer, Cistercian Study Series* vol.4, Washington 1970, p.12-42.

The *Gnosticus* (*CPG* 2431) is a short work which has only been preserved in Syriac, edited with a Greek re-translation by W. Frankenberg,[8] and in Armenian, edited by H. B. Sarghisian.[9] There are a number of Greek fragments, for example in Socrates.[10] Until now no modern translation has been made. The work deals with the "gnostic", that is the man who has reached impassibility, enjoys spiritual contemplation and therefore is able to teach others in his turn.

The *Kephalaia Gnostica* (*CPG* 2432, quoted below as *KG*) or "Gnostic Chapters", form a much longer work which has not been preserved in Greek but in two Syriac translations, the former being much less faithful to the original text than the latter. Both translations were edited and done into French by Prof. Guillaumont, who himself discovered the second, more literal Syriac translation.[11] The tradition of the Syriac Churches only works with the first Syriac translation, which is more like a paraphrase of Evagrius' work made in order to purge it from its many Origenisms – a hardly achievable purpose. This version was widely known in the Syrian world and commented upon by several authors, among whom the Nestorian Babai the Great.[12] This version also served as the basis for an Armenian translation.[13] The *KG* is Evagrius' great doctrinal work. It was written in six "centuries" or collections of one hundred sayings. In fact, each "century" only contains ninety sayings because of Evagrius' fondness of the symbolism of numbers: forty being the number of days in Lent (before Easter!) which symbolize the "second natural contemplation", i.e. the contemplation of material creation; fifty being the number of days between Easter and Pentecost which symbolize the "first natural contemplation", i.e. the contemplation of immaterial creation. In the *KG*, we find much of the Origenist teaching which was summarized in the anathemas of the Council of 553.

Apart from these three works, we must mention:

The *Antirrheticus* (*CPG* 2434). Preserved in a Syriac and an Armenian translation.[14] A Latin translation by Gennadius once existed. The work deals with the eight evil spirits (or vices, the later seven "capital sins") which continually attack the monk. This theme was taken up again in another treatise (*CPG* 2451).

On Prayer (*CPG* 2452), found among the works of St.Nilus. A French translation with an extensive commentary was made by I. Hausherr,[15] an English translation by Bamberger.[16] An earlier English translation by E. Kadloubovsky and G. E. H.

---

[8] *Euagrius Ponticus, AGWG, phil.-hist.Kl.,N.F.* Bd XIII Nr.2, Berlin 1912, p.546-553.
[9] *The Life and writings of the Holy Father Evagrius* (in Armenian), Venice 1907, p.12-22.
[10] III,7; ET p.81 and IV,23; ET p.108.
[11] *Les six centuries des "Kephalaia Gnostica" d'Evagre le Pontique, Patrologia Orientalis* XXVIII,1, Paris 1958.
[12] Edited with a German translation by Frankenberg, *op.cit.* p.48-422.
[13] Edited by Sarghisian, *op.cit.* p.143-207.
[14] Frankenberg, *op.cit.* p.472-544 (with Greek re-translation); Sarghisian *op.cit.* p.217-323.
[15] *Les leçons d'un contemplatif, le traité de l'oraison d'Evrage le Pontique*, Paris 1960.
[16] *op.cit.* p.52-80.

Palmer appeared in a volume with works taken from the Russian (!) version of the *Philokalia*.[17] The work consists of 153 chapters: the number of fish caught by the disciples at Jesus' command (John 21:11).

Commentary on the Psalms (*CPG* 2455), preserved under the names of Origen and Athanasius. In this work, Evagrius tries to lay a scriptural foundation for his doctrine by means of allegorical exegesis. Other Biblical commentaries from his hand have hardly survived (cp. *CPG* 2456-2458).

Letters. Only one letter (in fact more of a sermon) by Evagrius has been preserved in Greek, since it went under the name of St.Basil (*CPG* 2439).[18] This work is important for our knowledge of Evagrius' doctrine of the Trinity. Letters in the proper sense of the word have only been preserved in Syriac and Armenian (*CPG* 2437), they are 62 in number.

The Letter to Melania. One letter by Evagrius is so important, that it is listed separately in the *CPG* (nr.2438). In this letter, we find a veritable synthesis of Evagrius' doctrine. It provides a key to the extremely obscure sayings of the *KG*. In Frankenberg's edition (with Greek re-translation), an incomplete manuscript was used.[19] The latter half of the Letter was published with a French translation by G. Vitestam,[20] after J. Muyldermans[21] had drawn attention to the existence of a second manuscript with a more complete text. This manuscript also enabled Vitestam to correct Frankenberg's text in three places.

In the Armenian tradition, several of Evagrius' letters are addressed to Melania. St.Jerome, who became a fervent opponent of Origenism later in life, tells us that Evagrius wrote to "her whose name bears witness to the blackness of her perfidity", alluding to the meaning of the name Melania.[22] At an earlier stage, he called Melania a "devout lady" and Evagrius a "reverend presbyter".[23] In the letter, Evagrius addresses Melania as if she were a man (translated here by "good Sir"). Hausherr says that in a gnostic context names of women are often masculinised. Yet in the particular instance of the *Letter to Melania* he takes it for a "distraction de copiste".[24] Vitestam points out that the masculine form occurs twice again in the second half of the letter; he believes that the letter was

---

[17] *Early Fathers from the Philokalia*, London 1954, p.129-143. A new ET from the Greek text appeared in G. E. H. Palmer, Philip Sherrard, Kallistos Ware, *op.cit.* p.55-71.
[18] Letter 8: ET in *NPNF*, Second Series, Vol.VIII, p.115f. Cp. also: R. Melcher, *Der 8. Brief des hl. Basilius ein Werk des Evagrius Pontikus, Münsterische Beiträge zur Theologie* 1, Münster 1923.
[19] *op.cit.* p.610-619.
[20] *Seconde partie du traité qui passe sous le nom de "la grande lettre d'Evagre le Pontique à Mélanie l'Ancienne", publiée et traduite d'après le manuscrit du British Museum Add.17192, Scripta Minora Regiae Societatis humaniorum litterarum Lundensis* 1963-1964:3, Lund 1964.
[21] *Evagriana Syriaca, Bibliothèque du Muséon Vol.31*, Louvain 1952, p.78.
[22] Letter 133,3; ET in *NPNF*, Second Series, Vol.VI, p.274.
[23] Letter 4,2; ET p.7. According to Palladius however, Evagrius was a perpetual deacon.
[24] *OCP* 1946, p.290, reprinted in *Etudes de spiritualité orientale, OCA* 183, 1969, p.109. For the "masculinisation" of women cp. the famous last logion of the *Gospel of Thomas*.

in fact addressed to a man originally, and that the later tradition believed Melania to be the addressee as the woman who played such a decisive role in Evagrius' development.[25] Recently, N. Moine suggested that the masculine constructions in the Syriac text should be explained by the masculine form of the name, *Melanius*, used by St.Jerome and Paulinus of Nola.[26] In that case we may perhaps speak of a masculinisation of the name for motives similar to those of the Gnostics?

Evagrius' doctrine

In respect of his spirituality, Evagrius is a real desert father. His practical-ascetic works bear witness to this. Their influence on later monasticism has been very great, but because of his association with Origenism, he is seldom quoted explicitly by later Greek authors. In the Syrian area, where the purged translation of the *KG* was in use, he is mentioned more often, from the *Liber Graduum* onwards, which mentions him in its preface as an authority along with St.Gregory of Nazianzus and St.Basil.[27]

In his philosophical and theological speculations, Evagrius went highly intellectualistic and esoteric ways, starting from Origen. These speculations were foreign to the spirit of most desert solitaries. Barsanuphius witnesses[28] to the confusion which the "gnostic" works of Evagrius caused in the minds of monks in the beginning of the sixth century.[29]

Evagrius' theology seems to be coherent and comprehensive, but he has expressed it mostly in an unsystematic way. This is the reason why the *Letter to Melania* is a great help to get a bird's eye view of his dogmatic thinking. Usually, he writes his more esoteric thoughts in brief, often cryptic sayings: the *KG* are a clear example of this. His preference for obscurity may have been aimed at stimulating his readers to meditate. On the other hand, this may perhaps be called a "gnostic" touch in his personality in the more technical sense of the word. And of course it also served to hide his more disputed opinions, like the one of the preexistence of the souls and the *apokatastasis*, the final atonement of all beings in God.

A rough sketch of Evagrius' metaphysics might look as follows. Originally, there was the Unity, God, who created the pure intellects from himself. This was the "first creation", the creation of the rational, intelligible beings. After this, the intellects fell from "essential knowledge" through their negligence, which started the "movement" downwards. They fell to be souls, and then God created the material beings to give the souls (temporal) homes. This is when the souls were

[25] *op.cit.* p.5 note 4.
[26] Article "Mélanie l'Ancienne", *Dictionnaire de Spiritualité* X, Paris 1980, col.959.
[27] *Patrologia Syriaca* I,3, Paris 1926, col.5, ed. M. Kmosko.
[28] *PG* 86,892f.
[29] Cp. A. Guillaumont, *Les 'Kephalaia Gnostica'*, p.124f.

united with their bodies and became angels, men or demons, depending on the depth of their fall. This was the "second creation", and it was the result of the "first judgement". Although Evagrius sometimes calls this second creation a punishment, the purpose of it all really is to break a way towards the liberation of the fallen souls. For the material, embodied creation is to serve as object of a contemplation which begins to lead the soul back to the state of a "pure mind". This return is to be completed by passing through different stages of contemplation. In this process of salvation by contemplation, Christ plays a very important role. He is the only unfallen intellect, the only being in the universe which remained connected with essential knowledge. He is "the Word" because he has had no part in the "movement". Therefore the second creation could be made through him. It is he also who laid his "wisdom full of distinctions" into this creation, and this is the object sought in the "second natural contemplation", the contemplation of material creation. It is he who was the president of the first judgement and who will preside over all judgements to come. He himself voluntarily adopted a body, alike to that of the fallen rational beings, in order to help them to return to essential knowledge. All rational beings, the demons included, are to become angels. On the "seventh day", Christ will reign over all the rational beings and then, on the "eighth day", his kingdom will have an end, and all rational beings who are "heirs of Christ" will become "coinheritors with him"; bodies, matter and everything to do with it (such as plurality, number, names) will have been annihilated, all things will be reunited in Christ and, like him, be part of essential knowledge and the Unity.

EVAGRIUS OF PONTUS – LETTER TO MELANIA

1. 1 You know, good Sir, that if those who are far apart from each other,
separated by a long distance (something which is apt to happen for many
varied reasons), want to know or to make known to each other, their
respective intentions and secrets (which should not be learnt by everyone,
5 but only by those who have a mind akin to their own), they do this by means
of letters. In this way, though they are far apart, they are near each other;
though being separated, they see and are seen; though remaining silent,
they speak and hear; although they are as it were asleep, they are awake
because their intentions are realised; remaining sick, they are healed; while
10 sitting, they run. Yes, I would even say that although they are dead, they
live. For letters communicate not only the things present, but also the
things past and the things to come. Thus the mutual affection of the senses
becomes apparent, how every one of these shows its power and takes the
place of its comrade. For the hand acts for the tongue, the eye for the ear,
15 writing paper for the soil of the heart which, by the furrows of the lines,
receives the intentions which are sown into it. Many and various benefits,
purposes, arguments and drives can be discovered in them, but this is
neither the time nor the place to discuss them in detail. In all this he who is
able to read, rejoices and so, I would say, does he who cannot read: he can be
20 helped, where necessary, by him who can read. The latter profits by what he
sees, the former by what he hears. Yet the profit of hearing is not as great
and secure as the profit of seeing. You yourself know by experience what
differences there are between the two. And when we take this into account,
we may wonder who is capable of giving appropriate thanks to the Giver of
25 such a great gift – a gift even greater, I think, than most of his gifts in that it
above all demonstrates the power of the wisdom and love of the Giver.
It is clear then, that he who is far apart from his friend can sense that one's
intention through hand, finger, pen, ink, paper and all the other instruments which are at our disposition. On the other hand, he who is near by
30 has no need of any such things; he uses either his mouth, employing speech
and breath which serve both ear and heart, or he uses only his hands and
fingers, which are at the disposition of eye and heart. But he who is far from
his comrade draws true satisfaction from seeing and he who stands close,
from hearing.

2. 35 Now all these things which are done through letters, are a kind of symbol of
the things which in truth are done by those who are far apart from God. For
those who are far from God have made a separation between themselves

and their Creator by their loathsome works. But God, out of his love, has provided creation as a mediator: it is like letters. He did this through his
40 power and wisdom, that is, by the Son and the Spirit, in order that men might come to know and draw closer to, his love for them. And not only do they come to know the love of God the Father through creation, but also his power and his wisdom. Just as someone who reads letters, by their beauty senses the power and ability of the hand and the finger which wrote them
45 together with the intention of the writer, thus he who looks upon creation with understanding, perceives the hand and the finger of its Creator as well as his intention, that is, his love. And if you say to me: How can the hand and finger be equated with power and wisdom, that is to say, with the Son and the Spirit? then listen to the Spirit of God who says: "The right hand of
50 the Lord acts powerfully; the right hand of the Lord has exalted me" [Ps. 118:15f.], and: "Your right hand, Lord, is glorious in power" etc. [Ex. 15:6]. This right hand and this power is the Son. And concerning the Spirit, listen to this: the Son himself said in his Gospel, "if it is by the Spirit of God that I cast out demons..." [Mt. 12:28]; according to another
55 Evangelist he said, "...by the finger of God..." [Lk. 11:20]. So the "finger" and the "wisdom" denote the Spirit of God. Moreover, it is clear that the hand and the finger of God and the power and the wisdom of God are the Son and the Spirit of God, because their whole ministry is exercised through creation, for the sake of those who are far apart from God, some of
60 whom enjoy Him through seeing, and others through hearing.

3. Yet again others, who are particularly receptive because of their purity and their good works, are so close to God that they have no need of those "letters", that is, of creation, to perceive the intention, the power and the wisdom of their Creator; instead, they are ministered to directly by the
65 Word and the Spirit, in other words, by the "hand" and the "finger", without the mediation of created things. Take the case of someone who speaks: his words cannot be heard without the help of his breath; nor can his breath by itself indicate his intention without the help of words. Or in the case of someone giving signs: he cannot point with his finger without
70 using his hand, or point with the hand without the finger; thus the Son of God who is the "word", the "hand" and the "power", cannot do anything without the Spirit who is the "wisdom" and the "finger". For it is written: "By the word of the Lord the heavens were made, and all their host by the breath of his mouth" [Ps. 33:6], and: "The heavens are telling the glory of
75 God and the firmament shows forth the work of his hands" [Ps. 19:1], and: "When they looked upon your heavens, the work of your fingers..." [Ps. 8:3]. Here we have in conjunction both "word" and "spirit" (breath) [Ps. 33:6] and "hand" and "finger", [Ps. 19:1 & 8:3]. There is no need to

ask: Why did you speak of more than one finger, although the Spirit is only
80 one "finger"? For you do not have to accept it on my authority; you can
accept it on the authority of Isaiah, who spoke of the "Spirit of wisdom", the
"Spirit of understanding" and other Spirits [Is. 11:2]. Does he mean to say
that there is more than one Spirit? That would be the wrong conclusion.
Having heard Isaiah, now listen to Paul also who said: "There are many
85 varieties of powers, but the same Spirit who works" [1 Cor. 12:4].
Thus instead of needing ministering creatures who communicate as far as
possible to those who are far off, in the form of signs, the intention, power
and wisdom of their Creator, those who are near by, who are equally created
but who are a pure, rational and intelligible creation, are ministered to by
90 that love, power and wisdom itself. And they themselves give indication of
the power and wisdom of their Creator just as clearly as powerful and
mighty signs. And as the Power and the Wisdom, which are the Son and the
Spirit, are glorious signs in which the love of the Father is recognised, just
so rational beings are signs, as we shall see, by which the power and wisdom
95 of the Father are recognised. The Son and the Spirit are signs of the Father,
who is recognised in them, and rational creatures are signs by which the
Son and the Spirit are recognised, because of the "in our image"
[Gen. 1:26]. And the sensible and corporeal creation is indicative of the
intelligible and incorporeal creation, just as visible things are a symbol of
100 invisible things. We are rational creatures, who have been joined to that
visible creation (the reasons for this we cannot discuss here), and we must
strive to ascend to and perceive the invisible through the visible. But we
ourselves cannot achieve this, as long as we keep failing to recognise the full
meaning of sensible things; for just as the contents of letters remain hidden
105 to those who cannot read, even so he who fails to understand the visible
creation equally fails to perceive the intelligible creation which is hidden in
it, however much he observes it. He, however, who has probed the visible
creation in diligence and purity, knows what it tells about the invisible
creation. Once he has come to perceive this, he shall also have insight in the
110 power and the wisdom of God's steadfastness, and unceasingly proclaim
the intention of his incomprehensible love, which is realised in creation in
power and wisdom.

4.   I can express it simply as follows: just as the body by its actions reveals what
the soul which dwells in it is like, and the soul in its turn by its movements
115 proclaims what the mind, which is its head, is like, thus it is also with the
mind which functions as a body to the Spirit and the Word: as a body, it
reveals what the soul is like which dwells in it; and this soul in its turn
reveals its mind, namely, the Father. And as the mind through the mediation of the soul works in the body, so also the Father through the mediation

120 of his soul works in his body, which is the human mind. Now the body of
the human mind does not know what its mind does, yet the human mind
which is the body of the divine mind, does know what its mind does, has
done and will do, because it is the only one of all the creatures and ranks
which is his true image, which is capable of knowing the Father. For the
125 mind "is being renewed in knowledge after the image of its Creator"
[Col. 3:10]. Therefore if letters, serving those who are far off, can communicate what has happened and what is about to happen, how much more
do the Word and the Spirit who understand everything, communicate this
to the human mind which is their body! Truly, many "doors" full of all kinds
130 of distinctions have presented themselves to me here. But I do not want to
go into detail about them with you now, as I cannot confide them to writing
paper and ink, because of those who may perhaps come across these letters;
also these bold matters are too powerful to be written on paper. Therefore I
cannot say everything. And just as it is clear that there are things which
135 paper and ink cannot convey, thus it may well be that creation, which is
comparable to letters, cannot convey the entire intention of the Writer (I
mean, his nature) to those who are far off, because they are not all his
image. But the Word and the Spirit are direct signs of the Father: they
understand everything and reveal everything, because they are no creatures,
140 but a precise image and a true reflection of the Father's essence. Therefore
every human mind has understanding, because the Word and the Spirit
make everything known to it, as it is itself their true image, and their
likeness is communicated to it – just as he who is near his friend should be
able to know his whole intention through his word and his breath; and
145 where there are things which cannot be made manifest by word and breath,
it is not because the speaker is unable to express them, but because the
listener cannot contain them all. The human mind, because of its divine
mind is capable of everything, but the body does not even know its own
nature; the soul does know the nature of the body, but again not its own. If it
150 did know its own nature, it would no longer be a soul, but a mind. Yet the
mind does only perceive its own nature by means of the Word and the
Spirit, which constitute its soul. Just as the nature of the body is only known
by the soul which dwells in it, and this soul is only known by means of the
body, thus also the Son and the Spirit can only be known by the human
155 mind which is their body. And this soul of the human mind knows that
mind always, even without its human body, because it has the same nature
as its divine mind, that is, the nature of the Father.

5.   And as there will be a time when the human body, soul and mind cease to be
separate, with their own names and their plurality, because the body and
160 the soul will be raised to the rank of mind (this can be concluded from the

text "Let them be one in us, as you and I are one") [John 17 : 22], in the same
way there will be a time when the Father, the Son and the Spirit and their
rational creation which constitutes their body, will cease to be separate,
with their own names and their plurality (this can be concluded from the
165 text "God will be all in all") [1 Cor. 15 : 28]. Yet it must not be thought that
when I said that the rational creation and the Creator will cease to be
separate, with their own names and their plurality, I meant that the
persons and the names of the Father, the Son and the Spirit will cease to
exist. On the contrary, just as the nature of the human mind will be united
170 to the nature of the Father, as it is his body, thus the names 'soul' and 'body'
will be absorbed in the persons of the Son and the Spirit, and remain
continually one nature and three persons of God and his image, as it was
before the Incarnation and as it will be again, also after the Incarnation,
because of the unanimity of wills. It is for this reason, namely the disagree-
175 ment of wills, that the plurality and difference in name of body, soul and
mind exist. But once the plurality and the names which have come upon the
mind as the result of the 'movement', have been removed, then also the
various names by which God is called, will be abolished. For necessarily
arising from the variation among rational beings, due to the effects of his
180 work and the way his providence operates, He is in a derived sense called a
Judge – because of offenders, a Vindicator – because of sinners, a Healer –
because of the sick, Someone who raises the dead – for the dead, Someone
who slays and who repents – because of enmity and sin, and so on. Not that
He does not have all these distinct roles, but those who required their
185 existence are no longer. On the other hand, the names and the persons of
the Son and the Spirit do not pass, because they have no beginning and no
end. A further reason why they will not pass is that they have not received
their names through a transient cause: since He is their cause, they are like
He is; they are not like the rational creation, of which the Father is the cause
190 also, for the latter He created through grace, but the former He caused by
the nature of his essence.

6.   Just now we said that the mind is going to be one in nature, person and
rank. Also there has been a time when, because of its free will, it fell from
this former rank and was called a soul. And having sunk down even further,
195 it was called a body. But in time the body, the soul and the mind, because of
changes of their wills, will become one entity. Because there will be a time
that their wills and their various movements will have passed, the mind
will stand again in its first creation. Now there is one whose nature, person
and name God only knows. And he, as he stands in his nature, is the only
200 one among all the beings whose place and name are unknown. His nature
can be called "naked mind", and he himself is able to say what his nature is.

And do not wonder at my saying that in the unification of the rational beings with God the Father, they will be one nature in three persons, without addition or subtraction. For take the case of the visible sea, which is
205 one in nature, colour and taste: many rivers of different tastes mix into it, but not only does it not get changed into their variations, on the contrary, without difficulty it changes them completely into its own nature, colour and taste; how much more then is this not the case with the intelligible sea, which is infinite and unchangeable, namely God the Father? When minds
210 flow back to Him like torrents into the sea, He changes them all completely into his own nature, colour and taste. They will no longer be many but one, in his unending and inseparable unity, because they are united and joined with Him. And as in the fusion of rivers with the sea no addition in its nature or variation in its colour or taste is to be found, so also in the fusion
215 of minds with the Father no duality of natures or quaternity of persons comes about: as the sea remains one in nature, colour and taste both before and after the rivers mix with it, thus the divine nature is one in three persons of the Father, the Son and the Spirit both after and before the minds mix with it. We observe something similar before the waters of the
220 sea gathered in one place and the dry land became visible: then the rivers were at one with the sea. But after they were separated from it, they became many and differentiated, each varying according to the taste of the land in which they appeared. Just so, before sin had made a separation between the minds and God in the same way that the earth separated the sea and the
225 rivers, they were at one in Him, without distinction. But once their sin was apparent, they were separated from Him and became alienated from Him in taste and colour, in that each of them acquired the flavour of the body with which it was joined. Yet once the earth is taken away from the middle of the sea, the sea and the rivers are one without distinction. Thus also, once
230 sin is blotted out from between the minds and God, they will be one and not many. But you must not conclude from the fact that I said that the rivers were originally in the sea, that the rational beings also were eternally with God in their own nature. For although they are eternally with Him in his wisdom and creative power, their actural creation had a beginning. Still you
235 must not think that they have an end, for they are united with Him who has no beginning and no end.
To all this my mind was drawn, when I wanted to contemplate the great gift of letters, and since their great marvel made me rejoice and aroused me to praise and thanksgiving of their Giver, I also wanted to communicate
240 these things to you, my dear friend, in order that you too will crown with unending praise Him who has fashioned everything praiseworthy. Then let us beseech Him that, just as in his mercy He has deemed us worthy to give praise to Him on account of such little things as letters, He may also

deem us worthy, in his grace, without mediation of any creature, but
245 through the mediation of the Son and the Spirit, to rejoice in his unending
love and to glorify Him for all He created.

7.   Hear then what the cause was for writing these letters to you, good Sir, and
forgive us that we tarried awhile because of them. I am sure you know that
there are people who say that habit is a second nature. It seems to me
250 however, that this proverb is not only unwise, but it also reveals a lack of
education and discernment on the part of those who use it. For, as you as an
educated person know, it is difficult for a camel to fly in the air like an eagle,
or for a fish to thrive on dry land, because these things are unnatural to
them (and many other things which can hardly be realised could be given as
255 examples too), in the same way it is difficult for something to be altered in
its nature. It is different with a habit: as an eagle can easily fly in the air, or
stand on the ground whenever he wants to, or a fish can pass from one river
to another, or from a river to the sea, or from the sea to a river (for this way
of moving about is natural to them), thus it is easy for every action
260 established by habit to be abolished by another habit, for in its nature there
is room both for the one and for the other. What I want to say, is that
matters stand as follows: I have the habit of eating once a day. Now if I
wanted to improve on this habit, I could decide to eat once every other day.
As I said, one habit can abolish another one, because according to nature,
265 what is involved can take one direction or another. It is natural to eat at set
times, supernatural not to eat at all and unnatural to be a constant glutton;
there are all sorts of similar examples which one could quote on this point.
Thus what is above the habit and what is against the habit is not astonishing, because it is all natural. On the other hand, that which is supernatural
270 or unnatural is astonishing. Astonishment about the supernatural brings
praise, but astonishment about the unnatural brings blame.

8.   First of all, we must seek to know how many natural conditions there are,
how many states, combinations and attitudes they have, how many are the
movements of each of them and their opposites. And we must also find out
275 what these movements and their opposites are; which ones of them are
brought into motion naturally from within, in their due time, without any
created cause; which ones of them are enlarged even if it be naturally by
created causes; which ones of them impair their nature when a combination
of warm and dry or warm and moist or moist and cold or of cold and dry
280 elements occurs and one of them has the upper hand, or when all these
elements are combined together proportionally; which ones of them even
if they are brought into motion, may not come into action; which ones of
them do not reach the completion of their action, because they are unstable
in nature; and whether there are some of them which can be eradicated

285 completely from their nature; and whether, if they have been eradicated, others can be implanted in their stead.

Having outlined all this, we will now inquire in detail about natural, supernatural and unnatural actions. I think that before having perceived all the possible distinctions, one cannot occupy oneself with that which is
290 supernatural. I maintain this even if one's course of life is wholly natural, for who can get out of the darkness, or leave the pods [Lk. 15:16] if he cannot find any bread, and so on? But as the blessed Moses told men the story of the visible creation (you know full well the people of whom his audience consisted), thus we also should pray that with the help of God's
295 grace we will be enabled to speak just on the visible body, its combinations, states, attitudes and movements.

This then is the number of the natural conditions of the created beings: as is well known, there are only two, the sensible and the intelligible. He whom, because of his hiddenness and greatness we renounce to approach, can be
300 known (as far as possible, to a certain extent) through the sensible world, just as the soul is known through the body. So let us begin to speak, as far as we are capable, about the nature of the body and its characteristics. You, Sir, as an educated person, know very well that the sensible body has been constituted by the praiseworthy wisdom of God, from four sensible ele-
305 ments. And because it has received its constitution from them and through them, it has also received its life and death, health and sickness through them. Yet this has not happened without the providence of its Creator. It is the same, as we have said, with the movements which conform to those combinations which are found in the body. Now these combinations are the
310 following: warmth and cold, dryness and humidity. Because the body contains these combinations, it cannot live in dryness without humidity or in warmth without cold. So when its combinations are in balance, the body is in health. As a rule, its movements also work in an orderly way. But when one of the combined elements manages to get the upper hand, it upsets the
315 whole order. That is why there is this need for a balance of combinations.

9.   The states of the intelligible body are the same: life and death, health and sickness. So are its attitudes: standing and sitting, walking and lying down, being silent and speaking. And its movements: hunger, sleep, desire, anger, fear, sorrow, hate, laziness, busyness, craftiness, brutality, pride, mournful-
320 ness, sadness, wickedness. The opposites of these movements are: satiety, watchfulness, disgust, calm, courage, joy, love, diligence, serenity, integrity, meekness, humility, gladness, feeling comforted, goodness. Its senses are: sight, hearing, smell, taste, touch. All these and other similar things we may have omitted, we have in common with the animals, because the body has
325 the same animal movements. It is not possible to observe all these move-

ments together in the body; rather, as soon as one of them is brought into
motion in its own time, whether by an internal or by an external cause, it
effectively drives another, opposite, movement out of the body, though this
movement is otherwise potent in it, as it can be observed in its own time.
330 For example, when hunger is present, satiety is far away. The same is the
case with sleep and watchfulness, with sorrow and fear in contrast with joy
and courage, and so on and so forth. But you must know that the opposites
have never disappeared completely. For hunger follows satiety and joy
sorrow. The body does not exist without them, but it does not make use of
335 all of them at the same time. For the body does not always sleep and is not
always awake. It neither feeds all the time, nor does it always remain
without food. It is the same with all the movements and their opposites,
which we have summed up after mentioning the three states (I mean life,
health and sickness) and the six attitudes. Let us take the example of
340 watchfulness and sleep. The movements which are connected with watchfulness and health are not connected with sleep and sickness, even if this
does not concern all of them or any of them completely: we see, that during
sleep, eating, seeing, discernment, anger, sorrow, joy and other similar
movements which exist in waking reality, do cease. But not all the move-
345 ments which cease during sleep, do so during sickness; the degree to which
they cease depends on the measure and seriousness of the illness. On the
other hand, in health and in watchfulness all movements follow on,
although they do not all operate equally strongly. Yet there is one thing
which always operates, whether one is awake, asleep, healthy or sick:
350 breathing. It is present with all the movements of the body, for it is its very
life. And as the breath is present in and with all movements and all
movements occur together with it, thus death is alien to all movements,
because it puts an end to them all.

Since the body is subject to the soul, and the latter is able to act in all respects
355 like God, seeing that it is his image, some of the movements which we have
just described can be ejected from the body even while it is still alive. This is
what certain people also say: if the soul were to be exactly in the likeness of
God as it was created, it would be able to lift the body above all those
movements; but after the soul ceased to be the image of God and voluntarily
360 became the image of animals [Rom. 1:23], it was subjected to all the
movements of the body, which it got in common with beasts and animals,
which are its relatives. Now therefore, because the soul is outside its nature
because of its deeds, it cannot lift the body above its nature, because both
share the same movements. Just as fire cannot extinguish fire nor water dry
365 out water, thus it is in the case of the soul which is in the body because of its
works: not only can it not set the body free from what belongs to it, but it

even confers on the body things which do not belong to it, for pride, vainglory and avarice do not belong to the body.

10.   When the movements of the body occur naturally and in an orderly way,
370 this is something of a sign that the soul is in health. But when the body has no part in these movements which belong to it, this is a sign of perfection. In such a case there is no reason to praise the body, since it does not perform anything marvellous by itself (for that would be above its nature) – but rather the soul. Yet the soul does not really deserve much praise either,
375 since it has not done anything marvellous, seeing that, even if it has elevated the body above its nature, it itself nevertheless remained in its own nature; and what is done naturally is neither praiseworthy nor marvellous. In any case, it is not up to me but to Him who is the Creator of the soul who, knowing what the soul is able to do has said: "When you have done all these
380 things, then say, 'we are useless servants, we have only done what we have been commanded to do'", [Lk. 17:10], and it is obvious that the master does not give his servant any command which he cannot fulfill. Furthermore the soul deserves no praise, because it does not achieve this thanks to itself and from its own present nature, but, just as the body rises above its
385 nature through the health and force of the soul, so too does the soul ascend to its proper nature through the power and the wisdom of God. Something really marvellous is this, that the providence of the Lord of all makes use of all these things in a marvellous way, I mean everything natural, unnatural and supernatural. When a man is found to act unnaturally, this is both a
390 cause of astonishment and of blame. When he acts naturally, there is no reason for either blame or praise. But he cannot act supernaturally; therefore he is neither marvellous nor praiseworthy, the only thing is that he must stay away from blame. However many virtues he performs, he is still only acting according to his nature. For just as the body cannot live without
395 food, so also the soul cannot live without virtues, and just as the food of one day does not suffice to the body for all the rest of its days, so the virtues which are accomplished in one day are not sufficient to keep us alive. Now if this sensible and limited body is constantly in need of suitable nourishment, then how much more does not the soul, which can not be limited by
400 men, continually need the infinite food?
    Now why did I say that virtues are required by the soul in the same way as food by the body? Is it not rather so that virtues are required by the soul in the same way as breath by the body? For the body can exist several days without food, but without breath it cannot last even a single hour. – I did
405 this because I want us not to get weary of cultivating virtuous actions, and not to rely on past ones, while omitting to occupy ourselves with achieving new ones, and holding our previous ones to be sufficient. Also, we should

not require thanks from men or from God for the virtues we have performed or are performing, just as we do not do this in the case of the food
410 which our body takes either: it is unseemly to require thanks from anyone for what we eat. After all, everything we do for our own needs does not make us praiseworthy. For if we do it, it is to our advantage, whereas if we do not do it, we are the losers.

11.   But all that God does, He does naturally, supernaturally and unnaturally. He
415 has not done it for his own sake but for ours, for He had no need of it. Therefore He is worthy of praise for all He did. Still, none of the rational creatures is able to praise Him in an appropriate way. Everything He has done is, as we have said, either natural, unnatural or supernatural; natural and unnatural from his point of view and supernatural from our point of
420 view.
   If a man cannot do anything above his own nature, but performs virtues in accordance with his nature, then how much more will not He who is the supreme head of all good things not do anything which is supernatural to Him? For there are three things which are impossible with God: first, a
425 flaw in his will, second, a flaw in his creative power and third, a flaw in his activity. That means that 1) he does not wish the death of a man [2 Peter 3:9], and 2) that He cannot create another being like Himself, without a beginning, and 3) that He is not capable of sin. There is nothing that could be done, which is supernatural to Him.
430 His very nature is so good, that although we did not exist and He had no need of us, He created us in his image, without any persuasion, and made us heirs of all that is his naturally and essentially. Now what is both unnatural and natural to Him, is that He came down and bore everything which we have earned because we have left our nature, that is, He bore everything
435 which happens to us from conception till death. He however did not allow this punishment to come over Him because of anything He had done which made Him deserve it, but because of his natural loving drive to deliver us from the curse and from all the things which are consequent to it, which we have earned because of our transgressions: He who had not committed a
440 single transgression, took those things upon Himself, and He was able to blot them out for us.

12.   What was unnatural, was that God was born of a woman. But God, because of his love for us, and because his nature is not bound by, or subjected to any law, was born of a woman because He wanted it so, without bringing to
445 nought what He was, in order to deliver from conception and birth us that are subject to the curse and to sin, that He might give us second birth with a birth to which blessing and righteousness belong. For since we have ruined our nature by our free will, we have come down to our present conception

and birth which are subject to the curse. But He, while remaining what He
450 is, in his grace took upon Him, at birth, all the things which follow after
birth until death, things which are not only unnatural to Him but also, I
would say, unnatural to us. For we have fallen into these things because of
the sin we have committed of our own free will. He delivers us from them,
in that He voluntarily, without having sinned, loaded them upon Himself,
455 for we are unable to rise above them by ourselves; because we have
committed this sin we have fallen into them. Not only did He not remain in
them, but He also pulled us out of them, because, as we have said, He had
descended into them out of his love, not as a consequence of sin.

What was supernatural, was that a man was born of a woman without
460 intercourse: the virginity of his mother stayed intact. And what was also
supernatural to men, was that a man died of his own free will and after his
death rose of his own free will, without corruption and the help of others.
Thus God who loves man, became man and was born of his own free will,
without intercourse, and He also died in the way He wanted, and rose again
465 without corruption, according to his will. For "His right hand and his holy
arm saved Him" [Ps. 98:1]; this God who became man, while still being
God. For He is the leaven of the Godhead, who in his goodness has hidden
Himself in the unleavend dough of mankind. And not only did He not lose
his nature, his taste and his power, He even raised the whole dough unto all
470 that is his [cp. 1 Cor. 5:6 & Gal. 5:9]. For leaven that is hidden in unleavened dough, appears itself to be unleavened only for a short time. After
a period however, not only does the dough appear to be leavened, but it
truly is. In the same way our Lord has appeared as a man in our time, in our
world, and in our measure. But in his own time, in his world and in his
475 kingdom, this man does not only appear to be God, but he truly is. And as in
this world there were not two beings, God and man, but one, God for
Himself and man for us; thus in his world too, there are not two beings,
God and man, but one God who for Himself is God and God who is man,
because God has become man. As the one has become man for the other,
480 thus also the other becomes God for the one. For when God became man,
not one of his natural characteristics was lost. On the other hand, the man
does not remain in all his natural characteristics or in a state which is
supernatural to him; he loses that which effectively made him into a man.
That which is natural to man, is that man was created in the image of God;
485 what is supernatural is that we come to be in his likeness, according to the
word "I have come that they may have life and that they may have it in
abundance" [John 10:10], and also: "I was established in my kingdom, and
abundant glory was added to me" [Dan. 4:36]. And in truth when the
prophet foresaw everything that is now happening to us, he was amazed
490 and called Him "wonderful" [Is. 9:6] who was to do all these things out of

his love for rational creatures. And this "wonderful" person is very amazing and praiseworthy. For it is an unspeakable marvel that the nature of rational beings, which because of its createdness, its having a beginning and because of the variability of its will, was alien to the divine nature, which
495 has no beginning, which has made everything and which is unchangeable, should be mingled with the nature of its Creator, and in his grace it will be one in Him in all respects, without end. I tell you, dear Sir, that as the prophet was struck with amazement when he saw all these things and cried "wonderful", thus I am struck by the wondrous aspect in all these things I
500 come across on this path which I have chosen. But I have been prevented from reaching the goal for which I set out, as I am bound in the powerful chain of the love for those things which I have met with in an uncertainable way; I fail to bring to an end what I have begun. Yet it seems to me that this particular beginning has necessarily been made with a view to that particu-
505 lar end, for as the man who wants to stand at the end of all torrents, finds that his journey ends at the sea, thus he who wants to stand at the driving force of any of the creatures, finds that he arrives at the 'wisdom full of distinctions' of Him who has fashioned him. And as the man who stands at the seashore is struck with amazement by its immensity, its taste, its colour,
510 by all that is possesses, by the fact that the rivers, torrents and streams which pour into it become themselves boundless and unlimited, possessing every quality which the sea has, thus also he who observes the making perfect of all intellects, is amazed greatly and marvels because he sees all these various distinct knowledges as they merge into one essential and
515 unique knowledge, and that all those become this one, forever.

13.   But since at present we have given up the first plan, as we have suddenly met within ourselves our own beloved goal, let us see what is in store for you and for me and for all who want it in the great treasury which contains all the stocks of wisdom: this is the breast of Christ to which John lay close
520 during the Supper [cp. John 21 : 20]. John was told who the traitor was; he understood it through the Supper. Thus without the Supper and without the Breast, the traitor was not known. But note that as soon as he became known, he was cut off, and it was peaceful again.

Just as it is unfitting for good land which has been sown in, to produce only
525 as much as it has received, but it should produce thirtyfold, sixtyfold, or a hundredfold, thus also the seed which has been cast into your capable mind should not remain in isolation, but care should be taken that what has been sown into you should increase manifoldly. Then the ploughman will rejoice greatly about this and always entrust you with his seed. Thus the land will
530 be blessed and many poor people will be provided for, with the result that the ploughman, the land and those who are provided for, will send up glory

and praise to the First Ploughman, to whom belongs all seed of blessing in eternity. Amen.

EVAGRIUS OF PONTUS' "LETTER TO MELANIA" II

SUMMARY AND COMMENTS

M. PARMENTIER

Introduction, Nrs.1-6: Letters as means of contact between men symbolize creation as a means of contact between God and man. The natural connection between God and man is the human mind.

1. Communication by letters (l.1-34)

Letters are means of communication between people who are far apart from each other. In letters, all sorts of personal secrets and intentions can be expressed to someone who is far away. He who is able to read letters for himself, has a more direct kind of contact with the senders than he who must have them read to himself. On the other hand, the most direct form of contact can be established when one is near one another. Then there is no need of letters, for one can go and see the other person and speak with him, or communicate even without words. *Parallel in a different context:* Gregory of Nyssa, *Contra Eunomium* II, p.285-286, ET *NPNF* Second Series Vol.V, p.271. *"Good Sir"* (l.1): Cp. Introduction. *Secrets which should not be learnt by everyone* (l.4): Evagrius "has something to hide". His teaching is, he realizes, easily misunderstood and rejected. This is why he refrains from showing the back of his (Origenistic) tongue in his ascetic-prac- tical works, which are addressed to a wider and less intellectual public. Perhaps he alludes to critics who misunderstand him also in *KG* IV,47: "With those who approach obscure matters and want to write on them, the demon of anger fights night and day, who has the habit to blind the thinking and deprive it of spiritual contemplation". *Sight is better than hearing* (l.21-22): In *On Prayer* 150, Evagrius says that "as sight is superior to all the other senses, so prayer is more divine than all the other virtues". Contemplation of God starts with a certain kind of direct perception (cp. Hausherr, *Les leçons* p.181).

2. Letters as a symbol of creation (l.35-60)

Contact by letter is a symbol of the kind of contact with God which those who have separated themselves from Him by their sins, still have. For God has made creation as a means to keep in contact with Him. He did this through his Power and his Wisdom, that is the Son and the Spirit. In this way, men can get to know God through his Power and Wisdom, perceivable in creation. From the beauty of letters it can be concluded that the writer has a powerful hand and an able finger, and one can learn his intention. In the same way, one who contemplates creation with understanding, can sense the hand, the finger and the intention (that is the love) of the Creator in it. That hand and that finger of the Creator are his Power and his Wisdom, the Son and the Spirit. These two work through creation, in order to help those who are separated from God, who can then either see or hear Him.

Letters as a symbol of creation (1.35f.): cp. *KG* III,57: "As those who teach letters to children trace them on tablets, thus also Christ, teaching his wisdom to the rational beings, has traced it in corporeal nature". Compare also IV,1: "God has planted the rational beings for himself; his wisdom, in its turn, has grown in them, by reading all kinds of letters to them". God's wisdom (= the Holy Spirit, see below) leads to God the Father through contemplation of his creation.

Creation as a means of contact with God. The material creation plays an important role in (the beginning of) the mind's return to God. The mind must contemplate creation, for contemplation "is the spiritual knowledge of the things that have been and that will be, it is that which makes the mind ascend to its former rank" (*KG* III,42). "God is said to be in corporeal nature as a master builder in the things he has made and it is said that He is like him as in a statue, if it happens that he makes himself a wooden statue" (*KG* VI,82). The idea is well illustrated by a saying concerning St.Anthony which Evagrius quotes in his *Praktikos* nr.92: "One of the wise men of those days came to the righteous Anthony and said to him: "How can you hold through, father, deprived as you are of the consolation of books?" And he answered: "My book, philosopher, is the nature of things, and it is at hand whenever I want to read the words of God". This contemplation of creation has begun after the Fall; it is the "second natural contemplation": "The second natural contemplation, which was immaterial at the beginning, is revealed in the end by the Creator to the nature of rational beings by means of the material" (*KG* II,20). In *KG* II,61, the "second natural contemplation" is specified: "The contemplation of the incorporeals, which we knew at the beginning without matter, we now know joined together with matter; but the contemplation of the materials we have never seen without matter". Evagrius wants to say that the contemplation of creation as matter is one thing, but that we are really meant to discover the incorporeal, intelligible element which this matter contains. Not only human beings contemplate the world: "The contemplation of this sensible world has not only been given as a nourishment to human beings, but also to other rational natures" (*KG* II,88). It is important to note, that Evagrius considers the ethical element a necessary condition for contemplation: "Virtues show the mind the second natural contemplation, and this one shows the first, and the first in its turn shows the holy Unity" (*KG* III,61). Elsewhere, Evagrius mentions four "transformations" which mark the different stages of contemplation: 1. from malice to virtue; 2. from impassibility (*apatheia*) to the second natural contemplation; 3. from the latter to the knowledge which concerns the rational beings (= the first natural contemplation) and 4. the passing from all things to the knowledge of the Holy Trinity (*KG* II,4). Evagrius is quite confident that an accomplished contemplation of creation will finally lead to God: "The contemplation of all that has been and that will be is such, that the nature which is able to receive it, will also be able to receive the knowledge of the Trinity" (*KG* II,16). Or, as he expresses it elsewhere: "Just as we now approach sensible objects by the senses and in the end, when we shall be purified, we will also know their intelligences, thus also we see the [intelligible] objects first, and the more we shall be purified, the more we shall know the contemplation concerning them, – after which it is possible to know the Holy Trinity completely" (*KG* V,57). There is however a definite difference between the contemplation of creation and that of God, as creation is a means to come to contemplation and God is the goal of all contemplation: "All the times when we consider material things, we come to remember their contemplation. And when we have received that contemplation, we withdraw again from the material things. But this does not happen to us with regard to the Holy Trinity, for this one is the only essential contemplation" (*KG* V,61). Although God is "known through the corporeal and incorporeal nature" (*KG* IV,11), God's own nature is not known: "Everything which exists 'declares the wisdom of God which is full of variations', but there is none of all those beings which gives knowledge about his nature" (*KG* II,21). Evagrius puts it strongly in this saying: "He who sees the Creator behind the harmony of the beings, does not know his nature from it, but knows his wisdom in which He has made all things. And I do not mean his essential wisdom, but that which is seen in the beings, which the knowledgeable people call 'natural contemplation'. And how foolish are they who say they know God's nature!" (*KG* V,51). Similar caution is shown in *On Prayer* 114-116: God the Father and Christ cannot be seen. The Letter to Melania seems to be more daring in this respect (cp. section 4f).

Power and Wisdom, Hand and Finger, Son and Spirit (1.43f.). In Basil's eighth letter, which is by Evagrius, Christ is called "the right hand of God" and the Holy Spirit "the finger of God".[1] R. Melcher remarks[2] that Basil uses many epitheta for the Holy Spirit, but never "finger". We find the images also with Didymus,[3]

---

[1] *PG* 32/265AB, ET p.121.
[2] *op.cit.* p.55f.
[3] *De Spiritu Sancto*, PG 39/1051A,1076C,1077AB (the Son is the hand) and 1051 BC (the Spirit is the finger).

Pseudo-Athanasius[4] and Ambrose.[5] Tertullian[6] makes the important equation of
the finger of God with the power of the Creator. Irenaeus, who sometimes calls
the Son and the Spirit the right and left hand of God, denotes them elsewhere,
like Theophilus of Antioch, as the Word and the Wisdom of God.[7]

3. Direct and indirect contemplation of God (1.61-112)

But there are also specially receptive and pure beings who do good works, who
are so close to God, that they have no need of intermediary "letters", that is, of
creation, to sense the intention, power and wisdom of their Creator. They are in
direct contact with the Son and the Spirit. They are equally created, but they are a
pure, rational and intelligible creation. They show forth, as signs, the power and
the wisdom of the Creator, just as the Power and the Wisdom, the Son and the
Spirit, are themselves glorious signs of the love of the Father. This is because the
rational creation was made in the image of the Son and the Spirit. And just as
rational creatures are signs of the Son and the Spirit, the sensible and corporeal
creation is an indication of that intelligible and incorporeal creation. Human
beings are a mixture of the rational and the sensible creation, and they must
ascend to a wholly rational/intelligible/incorporeal state by making the right use
of the sensible/corporeal creation. Unfortunately, we cannot "read" these "letters" [well enough] and so we cannot grasp their contents: we cannot perceive
the invisible/rational/intelligible/incorporeal creation in the visible/sensible/
corporeal creation. Only he who can do this will have insight in God's power and
wisdom and will proclaim his love, which this power and wisdom realize in
creation.

Receptive and pure beings, who do good works, who are close to God (1.88f.):
We may think here of "the heavenly powers", which Evagrius calls "pure and full
of knowledge", they are bodies of light which "lighten those who approach
them" (*KG* III,5), i.e. the sun, the moon and the stars. They have been appointed
to instruct and help the rational creatures. The angels also have this function.
These are beings who did not fall very far, but remained in the heights, of they are
beings which have returned to a pure state through their contemplation: "It is
characteristic of angels always to feed on the contemplation or the beings, it is
characteristic of human beings not to contemplate always, and it is characteristic
of demons neither to contemplate at certain fixed times, nor at certain other
times" (*KG* III,4). The angelic state is reached through advanced contemplation,

[4] *De Incarnatione et contra Arianos* 19, *PG* 26/1020A (the Spirit is the finger).
[5] *De Spiritu Sancto* III,3, *PL* 16/779D f. (the Son is the hand and the Spirit is the finger of God).
[6] *Adv.Marc.* IV,26, 11, *PL* 2/427A = *CChr* I,p.617.
[7] Cp. G. Kretschmar, *Studien zur frühchristlichen Trinitätstheologie, Beiträge zur historischen Theologie* 21,
Tübingen 1956, p.34 note 8 and p.27f.; also S. Bulgakov, *The Wisdom of God*, London 1937 p.75; and H. B.
Swete, *The Holy Spirit in the Ancient Church*, London 1912, p.8f., 224, 320, 378.

and then the gap between creature and God is narrowed down: "Those who are separated will become inseparable, when they receive the contemplation of the things which have separated them" (*KG* II,67). At the end of section 6, Evagrius admonishes his addressee to pray with him that they may both reach this angelic state of direct contemplation of God, which is the culmination of the constant contemplation of creation which is meant in *KG* III,4. (On the angels and the heavenly bodies, cp. Guillaumont, *Les KG* p.106-107).

Signs (l.92f.): a descending series: Father, Son & Spirit – rational/invisible/intelligible creation – corporeal/visible/sensible creation. The Church Fathers usually interpret Gen. 1:26, "Let us make man in our image" as a statement of the three persons of the Trinity together. Evagrius calls the Son and the Spirit "signs of the Father", his "Power and Wisdom"; the intelligible/rational part of human beings is a sign of the Son and the Spirit, it is in their image. Assuming that we may metaphorically speak of sex differences between the persons of the Trinity, it would be tempting to connect Gen. 1:27, "male and female he created them" with this and suggest that Evagrius implies that men are made in the image of the Son and women in the image of the Spirit. The feminine title "wisdom" (*sophia*) might point into this direction. Cp. G. Kretschmar, *op.cit.* p.21 note 3 and R. Murray, *Symbols of Church and Kingdom,* London 1975, p.142f.

Human beings are a mixture of the rational and the sensible creation (l.100). They must become purely rational/intelligible and shed the sensible element, the body, by finding out what and where the rational element is which the corporeal nature and their own bodies contain: "Whether rational beings are always going to exist or not is a question of the Creator's will, but whether they are going to be mortal or immortal, or whether they are going to be (remain) joined to this or that, this is according to their own will" (*KG* I,63).

We cannot read these letters [well enough] (l.104): human contemplation leaves much to be desired (*KG* III,4, quoted above). "Desirable though the things may be which approach us through the senses, their contemplation is still more desirable than they themselves. But since sense perception does not attain to knowledge because of our weakness, the former is held to be superior to the latter because this has not yet been reached" (*KG* II,10): we prefer material things themselves to the contemplation thereof. This is the reason why we do not progress: only "when the minds have received the contemplation which is relevant to them, the whole corporeal nature will also be lifted up (or: cease, German *aufheben*) and so the contemplation relevant to it will become immaterial" (*KG* II,62).

4. God and man (l.113-157)

To put it simply: the body by its actions reveals what the soul is like, the soul by its movements reveals what the mind, which is its head, is like, the mind, which is

the "body" of the Son and the Spirit, reveals what these are like, just as the human body reveals its human soul. The Son and the Spirit are the "soul" of the Father whom they reveal as their "mind" and "head".
The human mind works in the body through the soul, and likewise the Father works in his "body", the human mind, through his "soul", the Son and the Spirit. The human mind knows what the human body does, but not vice versa. On the contrary, the human mind, the divine "body", *does* know what its "mind", the divine Father, does, has done and will do, because it is his true image unlike any other creature. This knowledge of the Father is mediated by the Son and the Spirit. Evagrius could say more about it, but he dares not, because he fears he might be misunderstood by others who read his words. In the same way, the creation as the "letters" of God can be misunderstood. Those who are far away from the Father and not in his precise image cannot grasp his entire intention, his *nature* (his revealing love, see section 2). The Son and the Spirit however, as the precise image of the Father, know all about Him. Thus the human mind can know all about Him through them, since the human mind is their true image. The body however does not even know its own nature. The soul does know the body's nature, but not its own. Only the mind knows its own nature, by definition, helped as it is by the Son and the Spirit, its "soul" to whom it is a "body". Inversely, the Son and the Spirit are only known in the human sphere through the mind, as a soul is revealed by its body. Yet the Son and the Spirit do not need the human body to know the human mind, for the human mind has the same nature as the Father, the divine "mind" to which it serves as a "body".
In a diagram, this argument might look like this:

MAN

```
┌──────────────────────────────────────────────┐
mixed nature:   sensible    and   intelligible
                corporeal         incorporeal
                visible           invisible
                irrational        rational


                                  Wisdom      Word
body................soul ........ mind ..... Spirit....  Son ........ Father
                                  Finger      Hand

                                  "body"      "soul"                    "mind"

                                  one solely intelligible nature
└──────────────────────────────────────────────────────────┘
                                                                GOD
```

Movements of the soul (1.114): cp. section 8 and 9

The mind is the head of the soul (1.115): cp. *KG* V,45: "The mind is called the "head" of the soul, and the virtues are symbolised by the hair; when it has been deprived of them, the Nazirite will be separated from knowledge and he will be taken away in bonds by his enemies".

The mind functions as a body to the Spirit and the Word (1.116). This thought is expressed in *KG* II,5: "The body of that which is, is the contemplation of the beings, and the soul of that which is, is the knowledge of (the) Unity. He who knows the soul is called the soul of that which is, and those who know the body, are named the body of this soul." Or in other words: the mind who contemplates the creation is the body of the true (intelligible) existence, which he sees reflected in it. The Son and the Spirit are the soul of this existence and they know themselves and the Father (= the Unity) and everything else (cp. 1.138f.). The human mind forms the only human part which knows itself (cp. 1.120f.) and therefore the minds are able to be a body to the intelligible existence, in which knowledge plays such an essential role.

The Son reveals the Father (1.117). Evagrius compares the revealing function of the Word with that of rational nature (note how he distinguishes between the Word and Christ) in *KG* II,22: "Just as the Word makes the nature of the Father known, so also rational nature makes the nature of Christ known".

The human body does not know the human mind (1.120): "Concerning everything which has been constituted out of the four elements, whether it is near or far, it is possible that we assume its likeness. But our mind alone is incomprehensible to us, like God, its maker. For it is impossible for us to understand what is a nature receptive of the holy Trinity, or to understand the Unity, the essential knowledge" (*KG* II,11). The human mind is that which is most important in a human being. It is he who understands its own soul and body, itself and God. The human soul however does not understand the mind above it, only the body below it. It is important to note here that in sections 7-13, the part of the letter edited by Vitestam, the word "mind" disappears from the vocabulary of the Letter altogether. This must be so because Evagrius wants to concentrate on the body-soul fallen humanity there which must be overcome and return to the mind state. In the *KG*, Evagrius also sometimes leaves out the mind perspective and he only speaks about soul and body. Guillaumont, writing before Vitestam,[8] remarks that the *Letter to Melánia* fails to distinguish, unlike the *KG*, between the different modes of origin of the soul and the body respectively: the soul is merely the fallen mind, the body was created especially. It seems to us that the closer relationship between mind and soul explains why the mind perspective disappears in the second half of the Letter. The first half discusses the inherent divinity of the mind; the second half deals with the question just how

---

[8] *Les KG* p.108 note 124; cp. below section 6.

the body can be overcome and the soul can be raised to the state of mind.
Image (l.124): for this term, cp. sections 3,9 and 12.

The mind knows what the Father does (l.124): "Corporeal nature has received 'the wisdom full of distinctions' of Christ, but it cannot receive him. Yet incorporeal nature both shows the wisdom of the Unity and can receive the Unity" (*KG* III,11). "The mind is the seer of the Holy Trinity" (*KG* III,30). On the other hand, "an imperfect mind is one who still needs the contemplation which is known through corporeal nature" (*KG* III,10); it has no direct vision of God.

This section seems summarized in *KG* III,80: "Corporeal and incorporeal nature are knowable, but only incorporeal nature is knowing. God is both knowing and knowable, but He does not know in the manner of incorporeal nature, nor again is He known in the manner of either corporeal or incorporeal nature".

Evagrius could say more (l.130f.). The text says: "many doors full of all kinds of distinctions have presented themselves to me here". Guillaumont, *Les KG* p.121 note 174, wants to correct to "ideas". The same word "doors" occurs once in *KG* V,77: "The intelligible doors are the virtues of the rational and pious soul, which are constituted by the power of God". Judging by other chapters of the *KG* where this is the case, the word "intelligible" here refers to an allegorical interpretation of a Biblical image. We know from *KG* II,4 and II,61 (quoted above in section 2), that virtues, as the first stage of spiritual life, constitute veritable doors to contemplation. Maybe in the Letter to Melania Evagrius also wants to refer to certain "entries" he found to spiritual and mystic knowledge. Babai, who commented on the *KG*, read "the gates of the city", connecting *KG* V,77 with V,74, which speaks of "the intelligible city"; he considers this to be the "city of the living God" of Heb. 12:22.

5. How God will be all in all (l.158-193)

There will be a time when the human body and soul will become mind, without names and plurality. The mind (the rational creation) in its turn, with the Son and the Spirit, will be one with the Father. Yet the Father, the Son and the Spirit will remain three separate persons with one nature. Just as the nature of the human mind will be united to the nature of the Father, as his "body", thus the Son and the Spirit will absorb the names "soul" and "body". But they will not absorb or be absorbed in the "mind", the Father, with whom they are one in nature. The human mind, God's image, will be absorbed in the Godhead. There will be a complete agreement of wills; the present disagreement of wills is the cause of the plurality and difference in name of body, soul and mind. This is the result of the "movement". The various attributes of God will also be abolished, only the Son and the Spirit will continue to be, as they have no beginning and no end; they are uncreated, but the rational beings are created. *There will be a time when body and soul will become mind* (l.159f.): "The knowledge concerning the rational beings will be accompanied by the destruction of the worlds, the dissolution of the body and the abolition of names, while an equality of knowledge conform to an equality of substances remains" (*KG* II,17). "Just as powerful fire possesses its body, thus also a powerful mind will possess the soul, when it will be mingled altogether with the light of the holy Trinity" (*KG* II,29).

Plurality will be abolished (l.164f.): in "Basil's" letter 8 (ET. p.116) Evagrius gives a long statement on the fact that number and quantity belong to creation, not to God. In section 7 (PG 32/260B, ET p.119) he says: "...when God, who is one, is in each, He makes all one; and number is lost in the indwelling of Unity". In a rather obstruse way, Evagrius deals with the same theme in *KG* I,7 and I,8: "When those who are together will have ceased, their number will cease also, and when this has ceased, that which is in us and that in which we must be will be one". And: "When that in which we must be had been separated, it generated that in which we are; and when that in which we are will be mixed, it will cause to cease that which will cease with the number". In *KG* IV,19 he says it in another way: "One is a number of quantity, and quantity is connected with corporeal nature; so the number belongs to the second natural contemplation" And again in *KG* IV,51: "In the second natural contemplation, it is said that necessarily some are superior and others are inferior. But in the Unity, there will be no superiors and inferiors, but all will be gods".[9]

The body will be dissolved (l.158f.): cp. *KG* II,17 above and III,66 and III,68: "Just as the first trumpet made known the generation of the bodies, thus also the last trumpet will make known the destruction of the bodies". And: "Just as the first rest of God made known the diminution of malice and the vanishing of the dense bodies, thus also the second rest will make known the destruction of the bodies, the secondary beings, and the diminution of ignorance". Evagrius does not believe in the resurrection of the body. But the bodies were created to help the mind in its sinful state. The creation was already a blessing at the beginning because it diminished malice and the dense bodies (= the demons): Evagrius cannot be called someone who hates the flesh. The body is a good and helpful organ to ascend back to God. Evagrius writes very sharply against those who hate the flesh: they are people who hate the Creator (*KG* IV 60,62). The body is the house of the soul, the senses are the windows through which the mind looks and sees the sensible things (*KG* IV,68). The body is no prison, it must only be discarded when the soul has become so pure that it can directly contemplate all that is (*KG* IV,70). He who prays to be allowed out of his body while he is still subject to passions, is like a man who is sick and who

---

[9] On the subject of the suppression of number, cp. also Guillaumont, *Les KG,* p.157 note 110.

asks a carpenter to break up his bed (*KG* IV,76). He who leaves the body while being impure, must consider whether he will not find the parent of him he has killed at his door to accuse him (*KG* IV,83)!

Movement (l.177): a key word in Evagrius' cosmology. It describes what went wrong in the beginning, what made the mind separate itself from God. This movement did not originate from God, but from the mind, who made a wrong use of its free will: it turned itself away from God. This movement is the origin of all evil. In order to undo its effects, and bring the mind back to its original state, God created the world to provide the mind with an object of contemplation. "The Unity did not bring itself in motion by itself, but it was brought in motion by the receptivity of the mind which, by its negligence, turned its face away from it and, because it was deprived of it, generated ignorance" (*KG* I,49). The recepetivity of the mind made it vulnerable to sinful negligence. "The first movement of the rational beings is the separation of the mind from the Unity which is in it" (*KG* III,22). "The movement is the cause of malice, and virtue destroys malice, but virtue is the daughter of names and modes, and the cause of those is the movement" (*KG* I,51). We recognize the transition from malice to virtue as the first stage of spiritual life (cp. *KG* II,4). Yet virtue itself is purely a product of the new situation of the universe after the "movement". Virtue and movement are near opposites: "Virtue is that state of the rational soul in which it is set in motion towards evil with difficulty" (*KG* VI,21). Getting away from the "movement" equals being converted: "Conversion is ascending from the movement, from evil and ignorance towards the knowledge of the holy Trinity" (*KG* VI,19). In *KG* VI,20, Evagrius summarizes his ideas of the two creations, with the "movement" in between: "Before the movement, God was good, powerful, wise, Creator of the incorporeal beings, Father of the rational beings and almighty; after the movement He became Creator of the bodies, Judge, Governor, Healer, Shepherd, Teacher, Merciful and Long-suffering and also Door, Way, Lamb, High Priest, with the other names which are used as modes. And He is Father and Prince even before the coming into existence of the incorporeal beings: Father of Christ and Prince of the Holy Spirit".

Before the first creation, Father Son and Spirit were alone together. Then the Father, with the Son and the Spirit, created the rational/intelligible/incorporeal/invisible beings, to which belonged the human minds. Through the "movement", the mind fell and became connected with a soul and, after the second creation, also with a body. That is the situation sketched in the diagram of section 4. Through contemplation of the creation then, the mind must ascend back to God (cp. *KG* II,4). Finally, God and all created beings will be one great unity. This final situation is treated further in the next section.

6. As it was in the beginning and is not now, it shall be again forever (l.192-246).

Once, the mind was one in nature, person and rank with God. But it fell from that rank, through its own free will, and thus it became a soul. Sinking down even further, it became a body. But in the end, body and soul will change their wills and become one with the mind, just as before. At present, there is only one being whose nature, person and name are unknown, since he is a "naked mind": Christ. In being united with God the Father, the rational beings will also be one nature in three persons. Just as into the sea many rivers with their various properties mix, thus God the Father will contain all minds, and these will then be one in nature with Him, yes, they will all be one. The minds will be united with God who is and remains one in nature and three in persons. Before the creation, the waters were one (cp. Gen. 1). After the creation, there were many different rivers. Just so, before sin had separated the minds from God, they were at one with Him. And once their sin had come out, they were separated from Him. But in the end, the earth will be taken out of the sea and the waters will be one again. In the same way, sin will be taken away from the minds and they will be one with God again. The comparison does not only apply completely, since the rivers were only separated from the sea (they were already there), not created, and the rational creation did have a creational beginning.

All these things came to me while I, Evagrius, was contemplating the great gift of letters. Let us therefore praise God and beseech Him to be allowed to rejoice in his love, not through mediation of creation, but only through the Son and the Spirit, and let us glorify Him for all He created.

Once the mind will be one... (l.192). The Letter to Melania seems to be (according to Guillaumont, *Les KG* p.108 note 124) a rather hasty summary of Evagrius' teaching. In this section, he makes no nuance between the fall of the mind to the state of a soul and the fall of the soul which necessitated the special creation of the body: a seemingly rather emanationist and pantheistic thought. The *KG* tell us, that the soul is nothing more (or less) than the fallen mind: "The soul is the mind which, by negligence, has fallen from the Unity and which, because of its carelessness, has descended to the rank of the 'practical life'" (*KG* III,28). But parallel to the next descent, a veritable creation, the creation of the bodies, had to take place: the generation of the bodies does not make known the generation of the rational beings, but the generation of the bodies introduces the nature of the names, and the compositeness of the bodies shows the difference in rank of the rational beings (*KG* II,66). In other words: the fall from the mind to the psychic state is really quite different from the kind of fall which the soul made into the corporeal state.

There is only one... who is a "naked mind" (l.198f.): The mind, which has remained united to the Unity, has no known name, it is a "naked mind". At present, only Christ is in this state, but in the end, all minds will be such (Guillaumont, *Les KG* p.157 note 112). The same idea as here in the Letter occurs in *KG* II,37: "There is one among all beings who has no name and whose place is unknown". The Letter says that the naked mind knows what his (divine) nature is; this we also find in *KG* III,70: "It is proper to a naked mind to say what its nature is, and to this question there is at present no answer, but in the end this question will not even be". A kind of definition of a "naked mind" occurs in *KG* III,6, a definition which however is only applicable to the unfallen naked mind, i.e. Christ: "The naked mind is the mind which, by its own contemplation has remained united to the knowledge of the Trinity". In *KG* III,15 on the contrary, Evagrius speaks of the mind who becomes naked once more: "If, as they say, the perfection of the mind is immaterial knowledge and if only the Trinity is immaterial knowledge, then it is obvious that in perfection nothing will remain of matter. And if this is so, the totally naked mind will become a seer of the Trinity". The difference between the present fallen world and the future harmony is brought out well in *KG* I,65: "In the knowledge of those who are second by their origin, various worlds are constituted and unspeakable combats rage. But in the Unity none of these things happen; there is unspeakable peace and there are only naked minds which satisfy themselves from his insatiability when, according to the word of our Saviour, 'the Father judges no one but has given the whole judgement to Christ' (1 Cor. 6:18)".

One nature in three persons (l.203): the text says that there will be "no duality of natures or quaternity of persons" (l.215); the "Trinity" is not numerically distinguishable, for number is a created category (see section 5). *KG* VI,10,11 and 12 deal with this idea: "The holy Trinity is not like a quaternity, a fivefoldness or a sixfoldness, for these are numerical, forms without substance; but the holy Trinity is essential knowledge". "A numerical trinity is accompanied by a quaternity, but the holy Trinity is not accompanied by a quaternity; so it is not a numerical trinity". And: "A numerical trinity is preceded by a duality, but the holy Trinity is not preceded by a duality; for it is not a numerical trinity". This non-numerical character of the Trinity makes it possible to use the words Unity and Trinity interchangeably. *Not through mediation of creation* (l.244): Evagrius wishes for Melania and himself the kind of direct contemplation, which belongs to the purified minds. This is the monastic ideal of the "angel-like life" (cp. *On Prayer* 113).

The "main argument", Nrs.7-13: The salvation of body and soul through Christ.

7. Habit and nature (l.247-271)

Now I come to what I really want to say, Evagrius says. Some people say that habit is a second nature. This is a foolish proverb, for one cannot get used to things which are not within one's nature. You can change your habits, but not your nature. For example, I myself am in the habit of eating once a day. I could change this habit and eat only once every other day. It is all within my nature: it is natural to eat at set times. But it would be above my nature not to eat at all, and unnatural to keep on eating. Anything outside a habit is not astonishing; anything outside one's nature is. The supernatural is laudable, the unnatural is blameable.

Evagrius now comes to his *cause for writing these letters* (l.247). In the first part, he discussed the origin of man as a naked mind, his fall from that unified state to plurality and matter, and his final destination, which consists in his return to his original state. In the second part, he discusses the ways in which the present state of desolation can be overcome. He discusses the background of the "practical life" which he described so well in several other writings, and also the role of Christ in it. Since the eschatological aspects of the first half of the letter now recede into the background, the mind perspective also is replaced by the soul perspective, for after all the soul is the mind in its fallen state. For the present purpose, Évagrius does not need an anthropological trichotomy; it is sufficient to speak about man as consisting of a body and a soul.

Evagrius *eats once a day* (l.262). Palladius gives us details about his diet: "From the time that I took to the desert, I have not touched lettuce nor any other green vegetable, nor any fruit, nor grapes, nor meat..." Sixteen years he went "without cooked food" before "his flesh felt a need, owing to the weakness of his stomach, to partake of something that had been on the fire; he did not however take bread even now, but having fed on herbs or gruel or pulse for two years, in this regime he died". Chitty[10] tells us that Pachomius had the habit of eating every other day in winter and[11] Poemen also, but "the fathers had learned by experience that it was better to eat a little every day, only very little..."

In this section, Evagrius introduces the distinction *natural-supernatural-unnatural*, which will prove important throughout the rest of the Letter. In the *KG* we do not find this distinction. Twice the word "unnatural" occurs (*KG* III,75 and VI,83).

8. The body as it is (l.272-315)

Let us now enquire about the different natural conditions, their states, combinations, attitudes and movements, especially those of the human body. There are only two natural conditions of the created beings: a sensible one and an intelligible/rational one. The body has been constituted from four sensible elements, giving it its states, and four combinations. The body is only in health when the four combinations are in balance.

[10] *op.cit.* p.9.
[11] *op.cit.* p.69.

Two natural conditions (l.297f.): Intelligible nature was created first, in order to contemplate God. This was the duty of the minds. Because of the movement of the mind, it fell to the rank of a soul. Then God made the second creation, whereby the mind-soul was connected with a body. This was the creation of sensible nature.

States (l.296): Life and death, health and sickness. (cp. section 9).

Combinations (l.309f.): Warmth and cold, dryness and humidity.

Attitudes (l.296): Standing and sitting, walking and lying down, being silent and speaking (cp. section 9).

Movements (l.296): Section 9 mentions 15 of them, with their opposites. The movements are closely connected to the passions in *KG* V,23.

Four sensible elements (l.304f.): Earth, water, fire and air. The higher beings have light bodies (light elements are dominant), the lower beings have heavy bodies (heavy elements are dominant): "It is said that those who possess light bodies dwell on high, and those who have heavy bodies dwell below. And above the former are they who are even lighter than those, and below the latter are they who are even heavier than these" (*KG* II,68). "With the angels there is a predominance of mind and fire, with human beings there is a predominance of desire and earth, and with the demons there is a predominance of passion and air..." (*KG* I,68). "Mind", "desire" and "passion" are the three levels of the human personality, corresponding with "mind", "soul" and "body" (Gk: *nous, epithymia* and *thymos*). Evagrius, who knows the angelic life to be his ideal, has a preference for the element of fire: "Fire alone is distinct from the four elements because of that which lives in it" (*KG* I,30).

9. The body as it could be (l.316-368)

The "intelligible body" has the same states, attitudes, movements and senses as the sensible body. These are now enumerated. Some movements exclude each other. One thing only is always in generation, whatever the body's movement or state: breathing. One thing never occurs as long as the body exists: death, since this is the end of all movements. By the help of the soul, which is the image of God, the body can stop certain movements. But really there is not too much of the image of God left in the soul: it voluntarily became the image of animals, and therefore it became subjected to the movements of the body instead of being able to lift the body above all its movements, as it could before it fell from its original nature. It now even adds certain vices to the body which the body did not have before!

The states of the intelligible body are the same (l.316): The analysis of the sensible body is suddenly interrupted by this cryptic remark, after which the description is continued, now applicable to both bodies. Does Evagrius refer to the fact that the mind is the "body" of the Father? Yet otherwise he does not speak of the mind in these last sections, only about the soul. In the *KG*, we do find metaphorical interpretations of the states etc. of the body, which are applied to the soul, e.g. in I,41: malice is sickness and death to the soul, virtue is life to the soul. Important in Evagrius' theology is the "spiritual sense", which is "the impassibility of the rational soul, which springs from the grace of God" (*KG* I,37). A detailed description of the five spiritual senses of the mind is found in II,35: "The mind also possesses five spiritual senses, with which he senses the matters which are akin to him. Vision shows him the intelligible objects in its bare form, by hearing he receives the "words" concerning them; the smell which is foreign to all falsehood is enjoyed by the breath, and the mouth receives of the taste of those; by means of the sense of touch he is strengthened, taking hold of the precise demonstration of the objects".

The soul is the image of God (l.355): in section 4, the mind was said to be *in* the image of the Son and the Spirit. The soul, which is the mind after the "movement", now really is the image of animals, just like the body. Evagrius šeems to make a distinction also between a "perfect" and an "imperfect" mind (depending on its degree of contemplation, *KG* III,10 and 12) and a "perfect" and an "imperfect" soul (depending on the degree to which it has mastered its "passible power", *KG* III,14 and 16).

10. Body and soul need food and virtues (l.369-413)

When the movements of the body occur regularly, the soul is healthy. But when they do not occur at all, the soul is perfect. Man cannot reach this stage by means of the body, but only through the soul. If the soul raises the body above its movements, this means the soul has returned to its original nature. This return can however only take place through the power and wisdom of God and the virtues of the soul, which are just as important to the soul as food is to the body. Something the body needs even more is breath, but Evagrius does not want to compare virtues to breath, as we do not have to work for breath like we have to work for food. And also, as we do not expect to be rewarded for earning our food, thus we must not expect to be rewarded for accomplishing virtues: they are simply necessary to the soul.

Virtues (l.393f.) are life to the soul (*KG* I,41). Virtue is "that state of the rational soul in which it is set in motion towards evil with difficulty" (*KG* VI, 21). As we have seen, virtues mark the first stage of spiritual life, which is the transition from malice to virtue. Then follows the transition to the second natural contemplation, next the transition to the first natural contemplation, and finally the at-one-ment with the holy Unity (*KG* III,61). Virtues make the body cease to be the image of animals: "Just as they who offer symbolic sacrifices to God, burn the animal movements of the soul by virtues, thus also they who sacrifice to demons, destroy by their vices the natural energies of the soul" (*KG* IV,22). The warning

of St.James 1:22-24 looks like this in Evagrius' words: "The words of the virtues are the mirrors of the virtues, and he who "hears" the words but does not "do" them, sees virtue which is the face of the soul, as in a shadow" (*KG* IV,55).
Food and virtues: The same comparison comes in *On Prayer 101:* "Bread is food for the body and virtue is food for the soul; spiritual prayer is food for the mind". This quotation confirms our impression, that Evagrius only wants to speak of the soul and the body in these sections.

11. God was in Christ, not out of need, but out of love (l.414-441)

Everything God does, He does not do because He needs to, for his own sake, but he does it for us. That makes Him the only being which is worthy of praise, because He had no personal need of doing what He did for us. This praise cannot be given to Him in an adequate way by the rational creation. God does and has done things which are either natural or not natural to Him whereas to us they are supernatural. A man who is virtuous, acts according to his (original) nature; in the same way God does good in a way which is only natural to Him. There are things which are impossible to God because they contradict his nature, but not because they are above his nature. From the goodness of his nature He created us in his image, and made us heirs. In a way both natural and unnatural to Him, He came down and bore our humanity, the humanity which we must bear because we have left our original nature. He did this not because He himself deserved to be punished, but because He loves us and wants to deliver us from our sins. This He could achieve because He is sinless himself.
Things impossible with God (l.424f.): 1) a flaw in his will, i.e. to wish death for one of his creatures instead of life; 2) a flaw in his creative power, i.e. to create a being which could compete with Him – God cannot create his own alternative; 3) a flaw in his activity, i.e. to do wrong, to sin.
He made us heirs (l.431-432): "The heritage of Christ is the knowledge of the Unity; and, if all become coinheritors of Christ, all will know the holy Unity. But it is not possible for them to become coinheritors, if they have not become inheritors first" (*KG* III,72). Through the first creation, the minds began their own existence: they became heirs of all that God has. Through the Fall, the minds lost (most of) the heritage. Ascending back, the mind becomes inheritor again, because of Christ's saving work; this situation is characterized by the fact that the mind knows the "intellects" of all beings after the "first judgement", i.e. it knows all beings which have been joined with a body (*KG* IV,4). Finally, when the mind has returned to the Unity, it enjoys the contemplation of that one together with Christ: it has become coinheritor (*KG* IV,8). Elsewhere, Evagrius connects the "heritage" with the person of the Father: He is inherited by Christ, who, in passing this heritage on, is inherited himself (*KG* IV,78), before his inheritors can become coinheritors with him, through their increase in contemplation. In

another saying, the "heritage" is more specifically connected with the Word, which Evagrius carefully distinguishes from Christ. Christ inherits the Word as a heritage and unites himself with it in this way, the Word however is "free from union" (*KG* IV,9). He calls Christ "a mind which has remained united to the knowledge of the Unity" (*KG* I,77), the only "naked mind" at present (see section 6), who is like a mind to the first (intelligible) nature which is his "soul" and the second (sensible) nature which is his "body". – The Biblical background is in Rom. 8:17 and Gal. 4:7.

12. Christ delivers us from the image into the likeness of God (l.442-515)

What was unnatural, was that God, as an intelligible being, was born as man, who to a large extent is a sensible being. Yet He remained an intelligible being and became partly sensible to make us wholly intelligible again, since that is our proper natural condition. We have become partly sensible through making the wrong decision with our free will. This became a curse to us, for we cannot rid ourselves of its consequences. God as man however could remain true to himself because he had not lapsed into humanity as a result of a degrading use of his free will, but only because of his love for us. In this way he could pull both himself and us out of the fallen condition. What was supernatural about his becoming human, was the virgin birth and his voluntary death and resurrection. Thus God saved himself as man. In becoming man, He did not leave his nature, but restored us to it.

As human beings we are created in the image of God, but we must be brought into his likeness. Our nature now is created, alien to the divine nature, but it will be mingled with it and become completely one with it, while losing its created characteristics, through God's grace. All intellects will be made perfect and all intelligences will merge into the one, essential and unique intelligence.

From image to likeness: Evagrius and his friends fought the concept of the Anthropomorphists, who taught that man *with his body* has been made in the image of God, so that God was thought of as a being looking like man (Guillaumont, *Les KG* p.59-60). Man does not look exactly like God: the image is somewhat hazy, it is no full likeness yet. Cp. section 4, where the mind is called the "true image" of the Word and the Spirit, while at the same time the "likeness" is still in process of being communicated to it. And when the mind has grown into complete likeness with God, it will have lost its body – for that is not even the simple image of God. Cp. Origen, *De Principiis* III,6.

The one, essential and unique knowledge: A very common way of expressing the quality of the Trinity in the *KG*, cp. II,47; III,3; III,12; III,49; IV,77; V,55; V,56; V,81; VI,10; VI,14; VI,16; VI,28; VI,34.

13. Fellowship with Christ brings salvation (l.516-533)

Since we have decided to turn away from God, satisfied as we were with ourselves, we must work from our present, fallen, situation. But we have one great hope: Christ and his wisdom. He can tell us what is wrong with us (= "who the traitor is") when we lay at his breast like John and have fellowship with Him ("the Supper"). Without this close fellowship with Christ, we shall not discover what is wrong with us. But as soon as we do have this close fellowship with him, it is easy to find the contemplation which leads us back to where we belong. Finally, the author of the Letter exhorts his addressee to profit by his teachings and to pass them on. That will cause him, Evagrius, great joy, and stimulate him to write again. And the result of his teaching in Melania and her disciples will be: praise of God.

Summary

Evagrius of Pontus' "Letter to Melania" I & II

The so-called "Letter to Melania" by the fourth century author Evagrius of Pontus, is an important though perhaps rather hasty summary of his Origenist thought system. In the first article, a general introduction to the author's life, his writings and his doctrine, is given. In this, it is important to see Evagrius' place in desert spirituality as well as the role which his writings played in the 6th century condemnation of Origen. Then follows an English translation of the Letter's text, which has been preserved in a Syriac translation only of the original Greek, and which has been edited in two parts by different editors. In the second article, the present writer attempts to summarize and comment upon the contents of the Letter in some detail.

Martin Parmentier was born in 1947 and educated at the Old Catholic Seminary, Amersfoort and at the Universities of Utrecht, Oxford, Geneva (Bossey Institute) and Bonn. His D.Phil. thesis (Oxford 1973) dealt with "St.Gregory of Nyssa's doctrine of the Holy Spirit". At present, he lectures in Early Church History, Patristics and the History of Dogma at the Catholic Faculty of Theology, Amsterdam.
Address: Lieven de Keylaan 49, 1222 LD Hilversum, The Netherlands.

Errata to the English translation of Evagrius of Pontus' "Letter to Melania"
By Martin Parmentier

p.9
line 39 "creation", read: "the creatures"
line 39 "it is", read: "they are"
line 59 "creation", read: "the creatures"
line 69 "giving signs", read: "making signs"
p.10
line 101 "we cannot discuss here", read: "we need not discuss here"
line 104 "meaning", read: "power"
line 105/106 "the visible creation", read: "the visible creatures"
line 107 "he observes it", read: "he observes them (the visible creatures)"
line 107/108 "who has probed the visible creation in diligence and purity", read: "who because of his diligence and purity has been instructed in them (the visible creatures)"
line 111 "in creation", read: "in them"
p.11
line 128 "communicate this", read: "communicate everything"
line 135 "creation, which is", read: "the creatures, which are"
p.14
after line 263, *add*: "If however I acted against my habit, I would eat twice a day."
p.15
line 287 "Having outlined all this, we will now inquire in detail", read: "And if we have understood all this, we now know"
p.18
line 413 "we are the losers", read: "we remain dependent on it"
line 423 "supernatural", read: "unnatural"
p.20
line 520 "was told", read: "came to know"

THE MONASTIC JOURNEY
ACCORDING TO JOHN CASSIAN

Columba Stewart, OSB
(St. John's Abbey,
Collegeville, MN)

John, a miracle in faith and purity. John, I say: that John who truly was like John the Evangelist a disciple of Jesus and an apostle, as it were always reclining upon the Lord's breast and his affection. Remember him, I say. Follow him. Think of his purity, his faith, his doctrine and holiness. Remember him always as your instructor and nurse, on whose lap and in whose embrace you grew up. Remember him who was the common teacher to you and to me, whose pupils and also whose legacy we are. Read his writings. Hold on to his instruction. Embrace his faith and merit. To attain this is great, though difficult; but even to follow is beautiful and sublime.[1]

John Cassian wrote these words about another John, the former bishop of Constantinople and his sometime employer, John Chrysostom. But the words may aptly be applied also to their author. The spiritual theology of John Cassian (ca. 360-after 430) is fundamental to the western monastic tradition.[2] Cassian was a brilliant systematizer and transmitter of eastern monastic teaching for the Latin monasticism he helped to shape. His genius lay in his practical focus; he wrote for beginners, fleshing out the lean schemata of his own teachers. This brief study of Cassian's conception of the monastic journey will trace the emergence of various goals or destinations in the course of Cassian's composition of his monastic works. The intention is to provide both a sense of how he understood the monastic journey, and how his understanding grew in the course of his writing.

The first part of Cassian's monastic spiritual writings consists of a major work in two sections. First are four "books," what we would call "chapters," entitled *On the Institutes of the Cenobites*, followed by eight more chapters entitled *On the Remedies for the Eight Principal Vices*. The whole work is known by the title of the

first section, the *Institutes* (*Inst.*). The *Institutes* were to be comple-
mented by a set of *Conferences* (*Conf.*) which would describe the
teaching of the Egyptian anchorites.[3] Cassian characterizes the
Institutes as devoted to the training of the "outer person" and the
Conferences as concerning the "inner person," one of his many
ways of drawing a distinction between the emphasis on asceticism which he identified with the cenobium and the contemplation characteristic of the solitary life (*Inst.* 2.9; *Conf.* Pref.).

Beginnings: Renunciation

Cassian believes in good beginnings. He often returns to
images which speak of beginning the ascent, laying the proper
foundation, learning the alphabet or syllables, making a good
start.[4] The start of the journey is simply the acts of renunciation
which constitute entry into the monastic state (*Inst.* 4, *Conf.* 3).
These are, in the first place, "external" renunciations: of home and
family, worldly status and wealth and, finally, one's own clothing
as it is stripped off and replaced by the clothing of the monastery.
These are earnests of one's intention to continue the long, slow
work of peeling away the layers of insulation between the self and
God.

The entry rite of monastic clothing evokes the larger task:
touching the monk's very body, the rite marks the passage from
the external renunciations to the bodily and spiritual renunciations which will be the lifelong ascetical program. Thus the
fundamental acts of renunciation draw in closer and closer:
moving from people and things outside the self, to bodily luxury,
and then to the interior possessions of obsessions, false securities,
fears. The agenda for the interior renunciations is presented by
Cassian in the traditional desert form of work on eight principal
vices: gluttony, lust, avarice, anger, sadness, listlessness (*accidie*),
vainglory, pride.[5] These obsessions were to be systematically
unmasked and dealt with according to received modes of treatment. Alongside the therapeutic work of breaking the power of
the obsessions, the monk cultivated virtues, replacing one set of
habits by another.

This process is not undertaken for its own sake, as if simply to
provide the monk something to do. Nor is it undertaken for the

monk's own sake, strictly as a cult of self-development. There is a larger purpose. When Cassian describes the goal of the monastic life, he marshalls an array of phrases and concepts to express the inexpressible "mystic sweet communion" of the integrated human person with God in Jesus Christ. The words succeed and build upon one another in the course of his writings: humility and love; perfect chastity; purity of heart and the kingdom of God; divine contemplation; tranquillity of mind; unceasing prayer and transformation of thoughts; spiritual knowledge and illumination; true patience; the mind united with Christ. Cassian picks up a phrase, explores its scriptural roots, uses it for a while, adds it to the repertoire, and moves on to another one. The different ways of describing the monastic goal do not indicate indecision or confusion on Cassian's part. Rather, the limits of human language are strained as he attempts to articulate what is sublime and ineffable.

The *Institutes* are presented as a survey of received wisdom and traditions. The *Conferences* are attributed to various Egyptian monastic elders in Scetis and the Delta region. The *Institutes* have a readily-discernible coherence of topics, as to a lesser extent does the first set of *Conferences* (1-10), despite their attribution to several elders. But what of the other fourteen *Conferences*? And how to understand the ascription of the *Conferences* to so many different elders? Readers of Cassian have long wondered how accurate his reminiscences of so many colloquies held a good quarter of a century before his writing of the *Conferences* could really be. The elders to whom he attributes the *Conferences* doubtless provided the basic elements of his doctrine, and memory of them and their teaching nourished Cassian's own reflection. The synthesis, however, is Cassian's. By ascribing his *Conferences* to them, he is placing his acknowledgments in his titles rather than in footnotes as a modern writer would. Furthermore, in the service of humility (and perhaps credibility) he does not shirk from inventive use of quotation marks as he places in the mouths of the great elders the monastic teaching which has become his own. Close study of the texts does reveal a coherence which is genuine though not immediately apparent. This coherence is both structural and thematic, evident within sections of the work but also across the whole opus, especially as one tracks the development of his doctrine in his exploration of successive images for the monastic goal.[6]

The *Institutes*: Toward Humility

The most arresting aspect of his teaching in the *Institutes* is the recurring theme of obedience, the characteristic virtue of the cenobite. The fourth book, "On the Institutes of the Renunciants," contains Cassian's famous (and often distressing) discussion of obedience in its explanation of how one becomes a monk and in its many stories of the triumph of heroic obedience over family ties, shame, common sense. The severity of Cassian's teaching on obedience can obscure the real point of this material. Obedience is to be worked at, but is not itself the distinctive mark of cenobitic life. It is a means to the real cenobitic goal, which is humility. Any student of the *Rule of Benedict* will be familiar with the central place this quality plays in Benedict's conception of the cenobitic life. Reading Cassian helps establish why this was so, and one recognizes Benedict's "ladder" of humility (RB 7) in the "signs" of humility in Cassian's *Institutes* (*Inst.* 4.39). These ten signs became the twelve degrees of humility in Chapter 10 of the *Rule of the Master*, which was in turn Benedict's immediate source for his chapter on humility.

For Cassian, somewhat unlike the Master and Benedict, humility is but one way of describing the personal integration which is the cenobite's aim. But the recurrence of the word throughout the books of the *Institutes* suggests its significance as a summary description of monastic virtue. At times Cassian uses *humilitas* to describe the end of a process of development (e.g. *Inst.* 2.3, 12.31); elsewhere, humility is a stage which prepares one for love, chastity, purity, spiritual knowledge, tranquillity (*Inst.* 4.39ff., 6.1, 6.18, 12.32; *Conf.* 14.10, 18.13). However it may be described, humility is not a barren state of static perfection. In the monk who is humble there is no longer any resistance to divine love, nor barriers to spiritual insight: "when humility has been genuinely secured, then at once it leads you on by a still higher step to love which knows no fear" (*Inst.* 4.39). Cassian notes that humility is the indispensable foundation for chastity, for without it, no vice can be mastered (*Inst.* 6.1, 12.23, 12.31f.); until chastity is secured on this foundation, one is incapable of true (that is, spiritual) knowledge (*Inst.* 6.18). By making such a claim, Cassian identifies humility as the basis for both bodily and spiritual transformation. This transformation is always understood to be oriented toward the monk's true vocation of unceasing prayer and contemplation, but these matters he reserves for the *Conferences*.

The *Conferences*: Toward Purity of Heart

At the beginning of the *Conferences*, Cassian makes his clearest statement of the monastic trajectory, and in it he uses the term which is at the center of his monastic theology: purity of heart. *Conference One* is on the goal of the monastic life, and in it Abba Moses makes a distinction between the "end" (*finis*) of the monastic life, which is the Kingdom of God, and its "goal" (*destinatio* or *skopos*), which is purity of heart (*Conf.* 1.4). The phrase of course comes from Matthew 5:8, "Blessed are the ones who are pure of heart, for they shall see God." Cassian actually quotes the biblical text only once in *Conference One* (*Conf.* 1.10), several chapters after the first mention of purity of heart; in the entire corpus of his monastic writings the text is quoted only three times (also *Inst.* 8.20 and *Conf.* 14.9). Nonetheless, the biblical text is the key to understanding Cassian's concept of purity of heart, for in it is the link with contemplation: one who is pure of heart is able to see clearly, and what one desires to see is God. Purity of heart is inseparable from purity of body (see e.g., *Conf.* 12.6, 12.10 and 13, 23.16), and both are linked closely with "spiritual knowledge," which for Cassian is synonymous with divine contemplation (see e.g., *Inst.* 6.8, *Conf.* 1.10, 1.14, 14.9). "Purity" for Cassian also implies "tranquillity," and the terms are used interchangeably, though preference is understandably given to the biblical concept (cf. *Conf.* 9.2, 9.6, 12.10 and 13, 18.13). One who is pure of heart has been established by God in deep peace, and is thereby able to turn complete attention to God. The interplay between purity, tranquillity, and contemplation suggests how one might understand Cassian's concept, and also points toward his source, the monastic teaching of Evagrius of Pontus.

The teaching of Evagrius is complex. He is far more interested in systems than is Cassian, who truncates, simplifies, and repackages the Evagrian schemata. It is clear that Cassian knew Evagrius' writings and not simply his ideas, as he quotes directly from Evagrius' works.[7] It is equally clear that he was aware of the controversial nature of Evagrius' teachings on the perfectibility of the human person. At the heart of Evagrius' conception of the monastic life was *apatheia* "passionlessness," a Stoic term used by early Christian theologians to describe God and applied by Clement of Alexandria and successors also to the human being who has become completely open to divine grace and love. For Evagrius, *apatheia* means integration and stability of emotion and intellect. It is not insensibility or anaesthesia, but mature balance, hard-won by the ascetical work of the practical life of the renunciations described above and finally conferred by God. The state of *apatheia* is neither passive nor aloof; one who has attained *apatheia* is poised for the contemplative tasks of insight into the human heart, entering into the nature of created things, and knowing God. At the time of his death, Evagrius and his teaching had come under strong attack from the non-Hellenistic majority of Egyptian monks, and his teaching was further suspect in the western context of debates over grace and free will. Cassian, as an heir of the Evagrian monastic tradition with its emphasis on ascetical discipline as a means to perfection, was himself at the center of controversy in Gaul. It is understandable, then, that when Cassian hands on Evagrius' teaching, he hits on the brilliant move of dropping the red flag of *apatheia* and adopting the irreproachable banner of a beatitude.

Cassian's link between purity of heart and contemplation is the prime example of his simplification of the Evagrian model. Evagrius divides the monastic journey into three major stages: *praktikē*, or ascetical life; *physikē*, or contemplation of created things as being expressive of God's love; *theologikē*, or contemplation of the Holy Trinity itself.[8] Cassian prefers an alternative model, also found in Evagrius, of *praktikē* and *theōrētikē* (contemplation).[9] In both Evagrian schemata, *apatheia* serves as the link between asceticism and contemplation. When Cassian uses the twofold pattern, he does not show much interest in the distant reaches of Evagrius' *theologikē*, as direct encounter with the Trinity is not part of the earthly monastic life of the monk. All such speculations are gathered into Cassian's "end" of the monastic life, the Kingdom of God, while he devotes virtually all of his attention to his "goal," the purity of heart which in his work merges into other descriptions of monastic perfection, including contemplation. Where Evagrius generally makes more discrete distinctions, Cassian freely compresses, overlays, and adapts. Evagrius crafts an impressive combination of pastoral and speculative elements. Cassian is not interested in speculation: he writes for praxis.

Cassian's pastoral emphasis is evident in the way that he drives home the import of purity of heart through the use of equivalent concepts. He rescues *apatheia* from the realm of speculation and anchors it in the actual practices of monastic life. A comparison of his various descriptions of the monastic trajectories reveals a consistent pattern of preliminary or foundational stages, but a variety of ways of describing the goal. Purity of heart is the global description; the two more focused ones demand their own treatment. They are unceasing prayer and spiritual knowledge.

The Clumination of the Original Set of *Conferences*: Unceasing Prayer

Cassian's ninth and tenth *Conferences*, attributed to Abba Isaac, were intended to complete his presentation of monastic spiritual theology. The fourteen other *Conferences* were composed later in response to further demand. Therefore one must interpret these two *Conferences* in the light of their crowning position in the original plan of Cassian's writings. *Conference Nine* begins with a restatement of the monastic trajectory in words echoing those of *Conference One*, but with a significant shift in terminology: "the entire aim of a monk and perfection of heart tends to continual and unbroken perseverance in prayer, and as far as it is conceded to human frailty, presses forward toward immovable tranquillity of mind and perpetual purity" (*Conf.* 9.2). This is described as the result of "bodily labors as well as contrition of spirit," namely, the *praktikē*. Elsewhere in these two *Conferences*, the state of unceasing prayer is associated with a peaceful condition, a firmly-fixed purpose of the heart, the transformation of thoughts, illumination, knowledge of God and of the divine mysteries, steadfastness of mind (*Conf.* 9.6, 10.10f.).

317

Cassian's teaching on unceasing prayer has become increasingly known in recent years through the centering-prayer movement and the work of Dom John Main. In Cassian's understanding, the basis of unceasing prayer is a single verse of Scripture (he suggests Ps. 69/70:2, "God, come to my assistance; Lord, hasten to help me") which is continually recited on the monk's lips or turned over in the heart (*Conf.* 10.10-11). This simple verse becomes the springboard for the occasional gifts of wordless, inexpressible prayer which Cassian describes as "fiery outbursts" (*Conf.* 9.15,25; 10.11); it is also the safety net which catches the monk's heart and mind as they return to the mundane, verbal and thought-filled state which is the norm even for the perfect monk. The use of a verse of Scripture has a further, sacramental quality which is not always noted in modern discussions of Cassian's teaching. He devotes a significant part of the description of this practice in *Conference Ten* to his conviction that the "poverty" of clinging to one verse simplifies and stabilizes the mind and heart so that they can approach the wealth of Scripture with a focus they would otherwise lack. He invokes another beatitude, "Blessed are the ones who are poor in spirit, for theirs is the kingdom of heaven" (Mt. 5:3), echoing the assertion in *Conference One* that the monk's "end" is the Kingdom (*Conf.* 10.11; cf. 1.4). The text chosen for continual repetition, then, becomes an aperture through which one regards the whole of Scripture. Encompassing in a few words the message of the entire Bible, the formula is both a beachhead for further exploration and a basecamp to which one returns for shelter and security.

Cassian's linking of prayer to Scripture, which is both starting point and resting place of unceasing prayer, invites the question of how Scripture might be related to "contemplation." Indeed, when he decided to prepare a second set of *Conferences* (11-17), the centerpiece was his teaching "spiritual knowledge," which for him meant the interpretation of Scripture.

Conference Fourteen: Scripture and Contemplation

Conference Fourteen recapitulates Cassian's borrowed Evagrian schema by constantly emphasizing the basic progression from *praktikē* to *theōrētikē*, from ascetical discipline with its focus on self-exploration and healing to a stance of contemplation with the cleansed heart now fixed on God (*Conf.* 14.2-3, 14.9, 14.10, 14.16). Practically speaking, this contemplation is anchored in the Word of God, the monk's daily companion. Cassian rescues "contemplation" from abstraction or daydreaming by giving it an "object" one can recognize. Cassian understands the Bible in the patristic sense of inspiration to be a genuine self-revelation of God, and not simply human reflection on God's interaction with individual and society. But Scripture is not simply uni-directional communication, from God to the human person. The Bible also provides the most elemental way for the monk to respond to God. Like an icon, the Bible is a window through which we contemplate God. But even more profoundly, as we contemplate, we show ourselves to the One whom we regard. Contemplation for Cassian is not static: it is dynamic, revealing, communicative. It is love.

As love, then, contemplation deepens as it comes to fullness. So too, one's encounter with God in the scriptural text. Thus Cassian returns to Origen's explanation of the deepening levels of understanding the Bible as one moves from letter to spirit, from history and description to intent and spiritual signification (*Conf.* 14.8). If modern biblical studies are often devoted to discerning the biblical author's intention as distinct from later interpretations, Origen, Cassian and their heirs are intent on discerning *God's* intention within the text. They were perfectly comfortable with critical study of the text, sensitive to *Sitz im Leben* and the rest, but they had their eyes trained on a farther horizon. God called them close in the Word, and like Moses contemplating the burning bush or the disciples gazing upon their transfigured Lord, they were invited to see more than curious events or paranormal phenomena. The divine Word, the creating and sustaining Logos, was inscribed in the Word of Scripture as he was incarnate in human flesh. As Jesus attracts followers by his humanity, but then draws them into the mystery of his divine life, so the biblical text provides ease of access through the historical and the literal and then permits entry into the deeper realities of the text. These are generally three: what the text signifies morally to us, what it means allegorically in terms of God's salvific will, and finally what it means theologically in its prefigurement of the truth to be known fully only in heaven (*Conf.* 14.8). Not every text may carry such depth of meaning, but the Bible as a whole certainly does. It is in those most profound of spiritual meanings that the monk is able to have a real apprehension of the mysteries of heaven.

Just as humility or purity of heart or unceasing prayer develop through processes of transformation, so too the monk's heart and mind are reshaped through the deepening encounter with Scripture. One moves beyond simple recognition of experience to an assimilation so profound that one grasps the meaning of the text even before the words themselves have registered (*Conf.* 10.11). Identification with the text thus moves from a cognitive to an intuitive level. The mind itself, writes Cassian, becomes "an ark of testimony," with the two testaments enshrined in the memory through reading and continual meditation or rumination of the biblical texts (*Conf.* 14.10).

This process comes not simply through diligent study. Nor is philological aptitude any guarantee of insight into the spiritual knowledge which indwells the biblical text. Cassian insists that this deep reading is not the preserve of the scholar, and warns against the arrogant presumption of teaching what one knows by intellect alone (*Conf.* 14.9). In the *Institutes* he cautions the monk against relying on commentaries for spiritual insight: the time and effort spent learning what others say about the Bible would be better spent working on what impairs one's own ability to read the scriptural text. This impairment is not mental, but moral (*Inst.* 5.34). *Conference Fourteen* explores in depth the relationship between *praktikē* and *theōrētikē*, and gradually one realizes that these are not phases of monastic life which succeed one another. They are inseparable. The monk who has reached the freedom of contemplation still needs ascetical discipline. However, discipline itself becomes free in the monk's joyful recognition of its purpose. As Benedict will write, the experienced monk now runs the path of God's commandments with a heart expanded by the inexpressible delight of love (RB Prol. 49).

Summary

The monastic journey as described by John Cassian, then, consists of four principal stages: renunciation (beginning), ascetical discipline (means), stability in purity of heart (goal), life in the Kingdom of God (end). While the journey is *progressive*, these "stages" must not be understood as *successive*. The monk does not leave one stage by entering another: the movement is cumulative and dynamic as one returns again and again to the fundamental aspects of the life even as one grows, consolidates, and matures. the monk is never finished with the ascetical disciplines of the monastic life; one never stops praying and meditating Scripture. What one does on the first day of monastic life, one is still doing on the last. But, in Cassian's understanding, that prayer and meditation become more and more transparent to the divine light, preparing the monk for the full brilliance of God's Kingdom.

NOTES

[1]John Cassian, *On the Incarnation of the Lord, against Nestorius*, 7.31.

[2]See the overviews by M. Olphe-Galliard, "Cassien (Jean)," *Dictionnaire de Spiritualité* 2.214-276 and B. McGinn, *The Foundations of Mysticism* (New York, 1991), 218-227. I am at work on a study of Cassian's monastic spiritual theology.

[3]The standard edition of Cassian's works is that of M. Petschenig in CSEL 17 (*Inst.*, Vienna, 1888) and CSEL 13 (*Conf.*, Vienna, 1886); the basic Latin text with French translation can be found in *Sources Chrétiennes* 109 (*Inst.*, ed. J.-C. Guy, Paris, 1965) and 42, 54, 64 (*Conf.*, ed. E. Pichery, Paris, 1955-59). The closest we have to a complete English translation is that of E.C.S. Gibson in the Library of Nicene and Post-Nicene Fathers, Second Series, 11 (rpt Grand Rapids, 1982). Portions of some of *Conf.* have been translated by C. Luibheid in the Classics of Western Spirituality Series (New York, 1985). A complete translation has been promised by Cistercian Publications.

[4]See *Inst.* 4.2,7,9,23,32-43; 5.12; 6.1, 18; 7.1,14,15-16,19; 12.26,32; and *Conf.* 4.21; 5.8; 7.3; 9.2; 10.8,10; 14.2,9.

[5]See *Inst.* 5-12 and *Conf.* 5 for Cassian's major discussions of the eight vices. His source is Evagrius, whose teaching is conveniently summarized in the *Praktikos*, chs. 6-39. The standard edition is that of A. and C. Guillaumont in *Sources Chrétiennes* 170-171 (Paris, 1971); Enlgish translation by J.E. Bamberger, Cistercian Studies 4 (rpt Kalamazoo, 1981).

[6]See for example by own brief explorations in "John Cassian on Unceasing Prayer," *Monastic Studies* 15 (1984), 159-177 and "Scripture and Contemplation in the Monastic Spiritual Theology of John Cassian," *Studia Patristica XXV: Proceedings of the Eleventh International Conference on Patristic Studies, 1991* (Leuven, forthcoming), 457-461.

[7]The major studies are: S. Marsili, *Giovanni Cassiano ed Evagrio Pontico. Dottrina sulla carità e contemplazione*, Studia Anselmiana 5 (Rome, 1936) and

H.-O. Weber, *Die Stellung des Johannes Cassianus zur ausserpachomianischen Mönchstradition. Eine Quellenuntersuchung,* Beiträge zur Geschichte des alten Mönchtums und des Benediktinerordens 24 (Münster, 1961).

[8]Readable summaries may be found in A. Louth, *The Origins of the Christian Mystical Tradition* (Oxford, 1981), 100-113 and McGinn, *Foundations of Mysticism,* 144-157.

[9]See Cassian's explanation in *Conf.* 14.2 and 16.

Acknowledgments

Gallagher, Eugene V. "Conversion and Salvation in the Apocryphal Acts of the Apostles." *The Second Century* 8 (1991): 13–29. Reprinted with the permission of Johns Hopkins University Press.

van den Hoek, Annewies. "The 'Catechetical' School of Early Christian Alexandria and Its Philonic Heritage." *Harvard Theological Review* 90 (1997): 59–87. Copyright 1997 by the President and Fellows of Harvard College. Reprinted by permission.

Bammel, C.P. "Justification by Faith in Augustine and Origen." *Journal of Ecclesiastical History* 47 (1996): 223–35. Reprinted with the permission of Cambridge University Press.

Jeanes, Gordon. "Baptism Portrayed as Martyrdom in the Early Church." *Studia Liturgica* 23 (1993): 158–76. Reprinted with the permission of Liturgical Ecumenical Center Trust.

Burns, J. Patout. "On Rebaptism: Social Organization in the Third Century Church." *Journal of Early Christian Studies* 1 (1993): 367–403. Reprinted with the permission of Johns Hopkins University Press.

Sivan, Hagith. "Ulfila's Own Conversion." *Harvard Theological Review* 89 (1996): 373–86. Copyright 1996 by the President and Fellows of Harvard College. Reprinted by permission.

Brock, Sebastian. "The Prayer of the Heart in Syriac Tradition." *Sobornost* 4 (1982): 131–42.

Hill, Robert C. "The Spirituality of Chrysostom's *Commentary on the Psalms.*" *Journal of Early Christian Studies* 5 (1997): 569–79. Reprinted with the permission of Johns Hopkins University Press.

Burns, Paul. "Augustine's Distinctive Use of the Psalms in the Confessions: The Role of Music and Recitation." *Augustinian Studies* 24 (1993): 133–46. Reprinted with the permission of *Augustinian Studies.*

McGuckin, John Anthony. "Martyr Devotion in the Alexandrian School: Origen to Athanasius." *Studies in Church History* 30 (1993): 35–45. Reprinted with the permission of the Ecclesiastical History Society.

Markus, R.A. "How on Earth Could Places Become Holy? Origins of the Christian Idea of Holy Places." *Journal of Early Christian Studies* 2 (1994): 257–71.

Reprinted with the permission of Johns Hopkins University Press.

Zinn, Grover A., Jr. "Exegesis and Spirituality in the Writings of Gregory the Great." In *Gregory the Great: A Symposium*, edited by John C. Cavadini (Notre Dame: University of Notre Dame Press, 1995): 168–80. Reprinted with the permission of the University of Notre Dame Press.

Goehring, James E. "The Origins of Monasticism." In *Eusebius, Christiantiy, and Judaism*, edited by Harold W. Attridge and Gohei Hata (Detroit: Wayne State University Press, 1992): 235–55. Reprinted with the permission of Yamamoto Shoten Publishing House.

Goehring, James E. "Withdrawing from the Desert: Pachomius and the Development of Village Monasticism in Upper Egypt." *Harvard Theological Review* 89 (1996): 267–85. Copyright 1996 by the President and Fellows of Harvard College. Reprinted by permission.

Clark, Elizabeth A. "New Perspectives on the Origenist Controversy: Human Embodiment and Ascetic Strategies." *Church History* 59 (1990): 145–62. Reprinted with permission from *Church History*.

Parmentier, M. "Evagrius of Pontus' 'Letter to Melania' I." *Bijdragen* 46 (1985): 2–38. Reprinted with the permission of *Bijdragen* and the author.

Stewart, Columba. "The Monastic Journey According to John Cassian." *Word and Spirit* 15 (1993): 29–40. Reprinted with the permission of St. Bede's Publications.